VIDEO VERSIONS

VIDEO VERSIONS

Film Adaptations of Plays on Video

Edited by Thomas L. Erskine
and James M. Welsh

With John C. Tibbetts and Tony Williams

GREENWOOD PRESS
Westport, Connecticut • London

Library of Congress Cataloging-in-Publication Data

Video versions : film adaptations of plays on video / edited by Thomas L. Erskine and
  James M. Welsh ; with John C. Tibbetts and Tony Williams.
       p. cm.
    Includes bibliographical references and index.
    ISBN 0–313–30185–9 (alk. paper)
    1. Film adaptations—Catalogs. 2. Drama—Film and video adaptations—Catalogs.
I. Erskine, Thomas L. II. Welsh, James Michael. III. Tibbetts,
John C. IV. Williams, Tony.
PN1997.85.V53   2000
791.43'6—dc21   99–36428

British Library Cataloguing in Publication Data is available.

Library of Congress Catalog Card Number: 99–36428
ISBN: 0–313–30185–9

First published in 2000

Greenwood Press, 88 Post Road West, Westport, CT 06881
An imprint of Greenwood Publishing Group, Inc.
www.greenwood.com

Printed in the United States of America

The paper used in this book complies with the
Permanent Paper Standard issued by the National
Information Standards Organization (Z39.48–1984).

10 9 8 7 6 5 4 3 2 1

CONTENTS

INTRODUCTION: DRAMA INTO FILM

This book is especially for people who love theatre and would prefer the immediate experience of the "real thing," who would rather see plays mounted onstage than theatre transformed into another medium. But few Americans have the opportunity to see professional theatre onstage, beyond those who live in or near cosmopolitan urban centers where theatre still thrives and is honored—for example, New York, Washington, D.C., Chicago, and Los Angeles. Hollywood performs a service for the rest of us by providing a secondhand representation, the nearest thing to the real thing. Purists unwilling to compromise for an inferior medium can gratify their theatrical appetites only by becoming pilgrims, traveling to London to worship at the time-honored shrines of theatrical England, for example, from the National Theatre complex and the restored Globe on the South Bank, to the Royal Court on Sloane Square, to Covent Garden and Leicester Square. We understand that the theatrical experience is unique and that some of the best plays are simply unfilmable. Cinema cannot replicate the effect of John Dexter's staging of Peter Shaffer's *Equus*; or Stephen Daldry's revival of J. B. Priestley's *An Inspector Calls*; or Willy Russell's *Blood Brothers* at the Phoenix; or Caryl Churchill's *Serious Money*, with its abusive chorus; or Dennis Potter's *The Chosen One* at the Barbican; or David Hare's *Pravda* at the National Theatre. In short, theatre is one medium, and film quite another. The two are not entirely interchangeable.

Although the Swedish director Ingmar Bergman once claimed that theatre had nothing to do with film, that claim is surely an overstatement. Plays are, after all, written in dialogue that is intended to be spoken and performed, and cinema is a performance medium. On the other hand, film should not be simply photographed theatre. Such approaches were taken in the early days of cinema when great moments of drama were captured on film in an attempt to appropriate the "prestige" of the legitimate stage. But as cinema developed from the turn of the century, this approach, which did not take full advantage of film's unique processes and effects, was dismissed because of its obvious limitations. Clearly, the circumstances of performance are different. Onstage the action is limited to a given space, viewed by the spectator from a fixed position and distance. Acting, voice, and gesture, will necessarily be exaggerated to compensate for that distance.

In cinema, on the other hand, the camera is able to bridge that distance, bringing the viewer closer to the action and the actors, embracing a "reality" that is simulated. Gone are the constraints of the stage, since the camera is able to transport the viewer into apparently "real" settings. The acting no longer needs to be exaggerated and is more subdued and "natural." The action is performed and captured in short sequences. Because the action is organized differently, actors do not have to dominate the playing space for extended periods of time. Film acting requires less training, therefore, than acting onstage. Some film directors even prefer to work with nonprofessional "actors" and have achieved good results, but professional training for actors can also be an advantage.

Some basic distinctions have been offered by Peter R. Gerdes in a special issue of *The Australian Journal of Screen Theory* (No. 7, 1980), and a recapitulation of these may be useful here. Theatre involves unrepeatable performances: because "each performance is unique, there is no 'finished product.' " Filmed performances are repeatable, however, because "[f]ilm is a finished product; it can only be 'shown,' not performed" (12–13). Onstage the actor is the "creator," whereas on film the actor is the "created." Theatre is an actor's medium: "The art of the stage is an art of the actor." Film, however, is a director's medium: "The art of the screen is an art of the image," as orchestrated by the director who "is responsible for the script and its representation," whereas onstage "the representation serves the play." Theatre requires trained specialists: "On stage the actor is always present with the whole of his personality," whereas on film "the physical presence of the actor may be indicated by showing parts of his body only" (14–15). For example, in Joshua Logan's film of the William Inge play *Picnic*, the action reaches an emotional climax at a Labor Day picnic dance in Kansas. The scene, remarkable for its sensuality and suggestiveness, involves Kim Novak and William Holden, who was not a gifted dancer; however, his lack of skill is disguised by close camera work that shows only parts of their entwined dancing bodies.

Finally, Gerdes contends that "the drama text is an independent art work to be read or performed," whereas "the film script is not an independent art work and cannot be read or 'performed'; it is a preparatory element for a future art work," nothing more (11). However, the original film scripts of Ingmar Berman and others have been published and can be read and studied and in that respect may be considered coequal to play scripts.

Such a script as *Persona*, however, could not be performed onstage, particularly the fusion sequence in which the camera merges and blends the faces of Liv Ullmann and Bibi Andersson, an effect impossible to achieve onstage.

Tony Richardson, who worked both onstage and on-screen, wrote: "The director in the cinema is a real creative force, while in the theatre he's just an interpreter of the text." According to Richardson, his frequent collaborator, the playwright John Osborne, regarded "a script once finished as the script of a play, with the director being responsible for staging the author's vision in the most effective way he can. But in movies the director's is the final sensibility. Every choice, every decision, has to be filtered through him and he converts them all into images the way a writer converts his experience into words" (159). In his later career, Richardson preferred to work in cinema, but he also continued to direct onstage, and several of his films derived from the plays of John Osborne, Shelagh Delaney, Edward Albee, and William Shakespeare. The latter, as will be seen, poses distinctive problems for the film director to resolve.

"Something touching the Lord Hamlet" (Ophelia, *Hamlet* I.iii)

Plays were written as performance vehicles, and one could argue that they cannot be fully realized or completely understood until they have been properly performed onstage. Yet they are also read and studied as independent works of literature. Students commonly spend whole semesters reading the plays of Shakespeare, for example, to appreciate dramatic poetry of the highest order without necessarily giving much attention to how such a play as *Hamlet* or *King Lear* might be performed onstage. To stage a play is also to interpret it, however, as Tony Richardson noted, for the director will have to make many critical decisions about how the characters should be played, how to enact and frame the action, and what subjects and themes to emphasize.

In the case of *Hamlet*, for example, how should the prince be represented? As the conventional, melancholy Dane consumed by his grief and sadness, disappointed by his mother's behavior, disgusted by her "o'erhasty marriage" to his uncle Claudius, both horrified and debilitated by the information brought to him by a ghost that claims to be his dead father's spirit, and uncertain about how to avenge his father's murder? There are no fixed answers here. The character of Hamlet is multidimensional, so each generation is free to invent its own Hamlet. The oedipal Hamlet played by Laurence Olivier in 1948, for example, is far different from the impudent Hamlet played by Nicol Williamson in the 1969 Tony Richardson version or the brutally misogynist Hamlet of Kenneth Branagh in 1996. All of these interpretations have validity, and not one of them is necessarily "right" or "wrong."

But these decisions necessarily influence how the supporting characters are played. How should his mother, Gertrude, be represented? As a potential co-conspirator aware of what Claudius has done or as an innocent, but frail, loving, mother who is simply too free with her affection? Claudius himself is the villain of the piece, but he is also a scheming and devious politician, smart enough to be a worthy opponent of Hamlet, a dangerous foe who will stop at nothing to consolidate his rule and to marginalize any threat that Hamlet might pose.

The play is very long by modern standards, and the text will often be cut and reduced for the sake of convenience in stage productions. To cut the text and abridge it require compromise. What scenes or lines may be considered expendable? What will be lost if, for example, Young Fortinbras is removed from the end of act V? If the role of Horatio is diminished, can the viewer fully grasp the theme of friendship that was so meticulously developed by Shakespeare? Who would presume to tamper with the unity, balance, and harmony of Shakespeare's design?

Purists respectful of Shakespeare's integrity will strenuously object to such tampering. Theatrical people will be more tolerant, perhaps, realizing that reasonable compromises will have to be made out of pragmatic considerations, if the running time has to be kept under three hours plus, for this play is simply too long for contemporary audiences. Few productions onstage will therefore achieve a full realization of the play, offering little more than a fragmented interpretation that, if the director is clever enough, will make sense.

As already noted, cinema is also a performance medium, and a director mounting a filmed production of Shakespeare will be faced with the same dilemma when faced with *Hamlet* or *Lear*, though shorter plays, such as *Macbeth* or *Romeo and Juliet*, may be easier to render in full. But the challenge of mounting a longer and more complicated text such as *Hamlet* will be made even more difficult, since the text will have to be "translated" and simplified for a mass audience less capable than an experienced, educated theatre audience of following the verbal density of Shakespeare. Hollywood will attempt to popularize Shakespeare by casting star talent in the lead roles as a hedge to protect the studio's investment, since cinema productions are obscenely expensive to finance.

Thus, Franco Zeffirelli's *Hamlet* (1990) hedged its bet by casting the tremendously popular Mel Gibson, an action star, as the meditative Prince and Glenn Close as Gertrude. Helena Bonham Carter, an actress with some screen exposure, was well cast as Ophelia. The rest of the cast was made up of British actors with stage credentials, most notably, Ian Holm as Polonius, Paul Scofield as the Ghost, Alan Bates as Claudius, and Stephen Dillane, who would later play Hamlet himself on the London stage, playing Horatio for Zeffirelli.

It is difficult to fault the casting of Zeffirelli's *Hamlet*, but in other respects the film was a failure. Franco Zeffirelli's career was launched by his brilliant staging of operas. He had directed a wonderfully atmospheric film adaptation of *Romeo and Juliet* (1968) that was operatic, overwrought, and overdone but tremendously popular and well regarded, even though it had simplified the text, removing the house of pestilence complication for Friar John, Romeo's visit to the Apothecary, and the blocking presence of Paris at the Capulet crypt. The emotional treatment was appropriate for this play, but simplifying the text of *Hamlet* was not so easily done.

At the expense of completely removing act I, scene 1, Zeffirelli began his film with a flashback to the dead King's funeral, stealing lines from I.ii to cover the action. This is followed by a badly abridged rendering of the court scene (I.ii), the better part of which is represented not in public at court, as in Shakespeare, which gave the King's words the full authority of a royal proclamation, but in a domestic setting in the King and Queen's quarters, which diminishes the importance of what is said by changing the context in which Claudius' criticisms of Hamlet are voiced. Whole scenes that should follow, moreover, are removed. Hamlet's advice to Ophelia, "Get thee to a nunnery," for example, is absurdly inserted into the "Mouse-trap" scene where Hamlet has instructed the traveling players to perform a modified play, *The Murder of Gonzago*, which is intended to test the King's guilty conscience and the verity of what the Ghost has told Hamlet about the circumstances of his murder. Alan Bates plays a weak Claudius, who seems no match for Hamlet's scheming. Horatio is so diminished that he seems to be merely a casual acquaintance rather than the very emblem of friendship and loyalty.

Shakespeare develops Hamlet's psychological state of mind carefully through the four major soliloquies that trace his emotional progression from suicidal melancholy, to horrified revulsion and righteous rage and, finally, to resolution in the fourth and final soliloquy, which is missing from the Zeffirelli film. However, compensations are to be found in the film's medieval setting, impressively photographed by David Watkin, and in the duel scene in act V, which, though operatic, extended, and overdone, brings the play to an effective emotional conclusion. Nonetheless, the idea of the play has been severely stunted. In this instance, Shakespeare was more un-done than done.

Hamlet was better served by the low-budget adaptation filmed by Tony Richardson at the Round House Theatre in London in 1969, starring Nicol Williamson as Hamlet and Anthony Hopkins as Claudius. This film, done essentially as modified filmed theatre, is not especially "cinematic" but strikingly contrasts Nicol Williamson's remarkable, inventive, and energetic interpretation of the Prince with the earlier lethargic, moping Hamlet of Olivier that had become the pedantic standard. Richardson cut about half the text cleverly and judiciously, pruning lines carefully to shorten the di-alogue in such a way that the play seems more complete than it is. This is an actor's *Hamlet* that works especially well on the television screen because of the camera technique that favors close-ups and medium shots and places the emphasis squarely on the text, which is to say, on Shakespeare.

The most complete and, arguably, the most impressive rendering of *Hamlet* on film, however, was the adaptation directed by Kenneth Branagh in 1996, which ran to just over four hours and was graced by an amazing international cast led by Branagh himself as Hamlet and Derek Jacobi as the most malicious Claudius ever realized on film. Though purists might question the peculiarities of the casting—Robin Williams as a not-so-young Osric, for example, or Billy Crystal as the First Gravedigger, or Gerard Depardieu as Reynaldo, sent by Polonius to his native Paris to spy on Laertes—they could not complain about the film's fidelity to the text, which is exactly as Shakespeare wrote and rewrote it.

More important, however, is Branagh's audacious use of situation and setting. Branagh moves the film forward in time to the nineteenth century, which at first seems a little odd but ultimately makes sense. Hamlet's great "To be, or not to be" soliloquy is ingeniously staged in the mirrored hall at Blenheim Palace, with Claudius and Polonius eavesdropping behind a two-way mirror. Hamlet delivers his lines not only to himself—his mirrored image—but directly to his adversary, so that Jacobi knows exactly what is on Hamlet's mind. The supernatural spectacle of the Ghost is extended to metaphysical dimensions. When Brian Blessed's Ghost appears, the ground trembles and quakes. The spectacle of the duel scene is even more exaggerated and overdone than Zeffirelli's: Laertes takes a fall off a balcony and breaks his back after having been poisoned by his own treachery, and Hamlet throws his sword like a javelin the length of the great hall to puncture Claudius, then swinging the length of the hall on a chandelier, as Fortinbras and his army crash into the palace to restore order. The cinema has the wherewithal to deliver amazing spectacles; the problem is that such an indulgence in spectacle can divert attention away from the poetry. A Shakespeare film with no spectacular potential, such as the one by Tony Richardson, may, therefore, in its very simplicity have an advantage over the spectacular treatments of Zeffirelli and Branagh, at least in the case of *Hamlet*. A different case, perhaps, needs to be made for *Henry V*, since in that play the spectacle of the Battle of Agincourt is the main action of the play, and, as Olivier and Branagh both demonstrated in their film adaptations, it is a battle spectacle more adaptable to the screen than to the stage.

Fidelity: A "Tiresome" Consideration?

In both his *Hamlet* and his *Henry V* (1989), Kenneth Branagh displayed a particular genius for adapting Shakespeare to the screen in a way that "fidelity" to the source was not an impediment. Besides demonstrating superior skills as a filmmaker, Branagh is capable of being true to both the spirit and the letter of the text. To anyone who knows, has studied, and appreciates literature, this should be an obvious and important consideration. But to show enthusiasm for such considerations is not, alas, the fashion these days. Dudley Andrew, addressing a cinema studies orthodoxy that he helped to create, dismisses considerations of textual fidelity as merely "tiresome" when he asserts that "the truth of adaptation is the reproduction in cinema of something essential about an original text" (100). But how can a film adaptation be coherently evaluated by those who respect literature without reference or regard for the text that is being treated? Andrew prefers the "more fashionable" approach of semiotics, less fashionable now than it was when he pontificated on it so absurdly in his *Concepts in Film Theory* in 1984. Then he utilized a "vocabulary" (i.e., jargon appropriated from French critics and linguists) that truly gave meaning to the word "tiresome" but that was used by academic philistines intent upon demonstrating their superior intelligence by parlaying a "language" that would be nearly incomprehensible to more reasonable people.

Andrew would ask, How does adaptation serve the cinema? More responsible literary and dramatic critics might turn that question around by asking, How does film adaptation serve literature? Clearly, some plays are more easily adapted to cinema than others, and some are so unique as to be virtually unfilmable. The more theatrical and abstract the design of a play, the less likely it is to be adapted successfully. Peter Shaffer's *Equus*, for example, is abstract and symbolic. The six horses blinded by the psychotic Alan Strang were originally represented by actors onstage. Of course, Sidney Lumet's film adaptation used real horses because film is a literal medium, and mass audiences would have scoffed to see actors in these horsey roles. What worked as an astonishing novelty onstage would have seemed simply too weird on film, so Lumet's approach was to literalize the play; but a spectacle that shows real horses being blinded with a metal spike (in the play) or a sickle (in the film) is neither abstract nor elegant but merely repulsive. Changing the spectacle in this way also changes the play and its impact on the audience. To examine such changes is not necessarily "tiresome" but enables one to better understand what may be at the heart of the theatrical experience. Onstage, the symbolic spectacle is astonishing, but that symbolic experience cannot be replicated by realistic staging.

Lumet's *Equus* was certainly true to the letter of the text at the risk of verbally overloading the film by anchoring it to the extended, disturbed monologues of Dr. Dysart (effectively delivered by Richard Burton), but it was not true to the "spirit"—which is to say, the *magic*—of the play. Without that magic the play is not exactly pointless (e.g., it still effectively addresses the concerns of Burton's wretchedly unhappy and burned out psychiatrist who laments his own inability to experience "passion" in a way that comes naturally to his patient), but it inherits the verbal density of the text while rejecting the novelty of the performance text. Even so, watching this failed film may help the viewer to unlock the secrets of the play by paying close attention to what the film lacks and the way it emphasizes the ordinary at the expense of the extraordinary. Dr. Dysart himself is exonerated of any hints of homosexual attraction to his patient in the film, which instead suggests an established heterosexual relationship between Dysart and Hesther Salomon, the magistrate who first brings Alan to Dysart, asserting, "The boy's in pain" and needs professional help. The thematic concerns of the play—a doctor's professional obligation to treat and "cure" his patient and his reluctance to do so; the issue of madness, shared, transformed, and transfigured; and symbolic impotence and displaced passion—are faithfully represented, though less ambiguous. The magic is gone, and the passion is differently imagined.

The book you are holding in your hands expresses enthusiasms and passions shared by its editors and contributors toward the variety of attempts to translate stage plays into film. We do not apologize for this. Passion is often lacking in much of the film criticism one reads. It all too studiously avoids the enthusiasm ordinary people may experience by reading a novel, watching a play, or viewing a film, but, surprisingly, almost no one has deigned to challenge the cinema studies establishment or call their critical bluff. One exception is Kevin Brownlow, whose enthusiasm for the work of Abel Gance launched his career as filmmaker, historian, archivist, and television producer. In Brownlow's documentary, *The Charm of Dynamite*, Gance remarks, "Enthusiasm is essential in the cinema. It must be communicated to people like a flame. The cinema is a flame in the shadows fed by enthusiasm. It can dispel them. This is why enthusiasm is everything to me." Sharing that sense of enthusiasm in his own way, Brownlow has been more productive than whole legions of film theorists. His *Unknown Chaplin* television series, for example, built upon "lost" footage Brownlow discovered in Lady Chaplin's vaults, revealed more about Chaplin's working habits and the development of his comic genius than any of the books published on the subject.

The Recycling of Drama: Stage to Screen and Screen to Stage

Commercial cinema demands new material or exploitable material that can be reshaped in the interest of profits. What has succeeded in one medium might be transformable to another; what has succeeded in the medium of film could be reworked and updated profitably. Each adaptation may build upon the one preceding it. Consider, for example, the classic Ernst Lubitsch comedy *The Shop Around the Corner* (1940), adapted by Samson Raphelson for Lubitsch from an original Miklos Laszlo play entitled *Parfumerie*. In 1949 the film was remade as a Judy Garland musical directed by Robert Z. Leonard under a new title, *In the Good Old Sum-*

mertime, which held to the play's core concept involving pen pals falling in love. The "concept" (in the Hollywood parlance) was then transformed into the Broadway musical *She Loves Me*, only to be revived again years later, in 1998, by director Nora Ephron and her sister Delia, and upgraded to e-mail technology in *You've Got Mail*, which not only recycled Laszlo and Lubitsch but also the romantic pairing of Tom Hanks and Meg Ryan from Nora Ephron's earlier hit, *Sleepless in Seattle* (1993).

This is a two-way street, however, and the process has also worked in reverse order. Consider, for example, *The Little Shop of Horrors*, which began as a cheap and cheesy Roger Corman B-movie shot in two days in 1960. This "black" comedy was then transformed into a campy stage musical on Broadway and in London's West End at the Comedy Theatre on Panton Street and finally was recycled back into cinema as the musical directed by Frank Oz in 1986. A film that made the transition from stage to screen to stage was *La Cage aux Folles* (1978), which began as a French stage farce involving a gay couple. Edouard Molinaro's 1978 film adaptation appeared just as the door of the closet began to swing open in a new era of sophisticated tolerance about what was awkwardly called "alternative lifestyles" and was so popular that it generated two movie sequels in 1980 and 1985. The Broadway musical won Tony awards for best musical, book, direction, costumes, and star, George Hearn. It was even more popular onstage in London than in New York. After the film was transformed into the successful stage musical during the 1980s, it was then reworked again in the 1990s as an American remake called *The Birdcage*, starring Robin Williams and Nathan Lane.

Movies are often accused of artistic plagiarism, which could more kindly be called creative cross-fertilization, borrowing liberally from other sources. But a similar kind of borrowing sometimes takes place in drama. In 1967, for example, Tom Stoppard constructed a whole play out of a slice of *Hamlet* by telling the story of Hamlet from the cockeyed and uninformed perspective of Rosencrantz and Guildernstern, Hamlet's false friends brought to Elsinore by Claudius to spy on Hamlet. Stoppard then made his first foray into film directing by adapting *Rosencrantz and Guildenstern Are Dead* to the screen in 1990, featuring the acting talents of Tim Roth, Gary Oldman, and Richard Dreyfuss. Playwriting "is slow and painstaking, and you keep more in view all the time," Stoppard explained in 1998. "But you can manipulate the bits in a screenplay and you don't need a week to sit down and worry about it. Sometimes they're shooting it the next day. You're involved with something that's not in love with its own mystery. It's pragmatic" (Span C1). Stoppard made these comments after having appropriated bits and pieces of *Romeo and Juliet* for the film *Shakespeare in Love* (1998), directed by John Madden from a screenplay started by Marc Norman and completed by Stoppard. Stoppard imagined Shakespeare as a young, untried playwright who was a blocked writer facing a deadline, hacking out a potboiler called "Romeo and Ethel" that was ultimately to become, well, something else and something better.

Screenwriting is more spontaneous, perhaps. "Film is drama at its most impatient, 'What happens next?' the perpetual nag," according to the British playwright Alan Bennett, who transformed his play *The Madness of George III* into *The Madness of King George*, having to change the title to protect uninformed American viewers from thinking that the film was a sequel. "One can never *hang about*, thinks the writer, petulantly. There's a bit more leeway on stage, depending on the kind of story one's telling, and more still on television, where the viewers are so close to the characters as not to mind whether they dawdle a bit. But with film, meandering is out of the question; it has to be brisk" (ix).

Art "Encased by Technology"

"The movies stand between the past and the future, between human history and human extinction," the playwright David Mamet wrote. "They come into being at the beginning of the last stage of the Industrial Revolution, which is to say at the beginning of the End of the World" (161). "As a sometime movie director, I have had the experience of standing, encased by technology, between those two worlds of the past and the future, of dealing with the most ancient art of Drama in a medium requiring the assistance and compliance of several hundred people, of being, in effect, a pilot" (162). Motion pictures "draw on existing arts and combine them into a legitimate new art. They are made to be shown in a theater so that members of the audience can commune with *each other*. To order the dreams of the populace so that the populace en masse, acting as 'the audience,' can celebrate itself, is the art of the movies" (163–164). Thus, for Mamet, "The movies are a momentary and beautiful aberration of a technological society in the last stages of decay" (164). By contrast, the theatre requires "no technology whatever" and simply involves telling stories "in a formulized manner."

Movies are both communal and technological and the most appropriate form of artistic expression in the twentieth century. In contrast to Mamet's melancholy fixation on contemporary decadence and his disillusionment late in the century is the excitement the French director Abel Gance had seventy years earlier: "I've always tried to use this magical instrument, this absolutely magical instrument," the cinema, Gance remarked to Steven Kramer in 1973 at the age of eighty-four, stressing the magical and tribal potential of the cinema. "As Novalis said, 'An image is an incantation: a certain spirit is called; a certain spirit appears.' But the spirit *must* be called! The spirit is found *between* the images" (qtd. in Kramer 165). "For me," Gance continued, "a spectator who maintains his critical sense is not a true spectator. I wanted the audience to come out of the theater amazed victims, completely won over, emerging from paradise to find, alas, the hell of the street. *That* is the cinema!" (167). That is exactly what the cinema can do better than drama, to transport the audience completely into another world. "There will always be people to do *normal* dramas," Gance said, but it is "more difficult to make Epics." Gance believed, to his dying day, in a new divinity in gestation: "God is not an accomplished thing, but something eternal which recreates itself, which dies and does not die, which transfigures itself in different ways, according to generations, continents, and time. That transcendental aspect is fundamental" (170). But to tap into that transcendental sense requires men of vision inventive enough to adapt the technology to their goals.

A Selective Approach

We have sought a balance between old and new, between originals and remakes, because the newer "versions" will be more familiar to our younger readers. Knowing we could not include everything, we had to compromise mightily, while still attempting to offer a reasonable sampling. Therefore, our approach has been necessarily selective rather than comprehensive. Because of space limitations, we could not include all the film adaptations of plays that have either been written in English or translated into English. We have omitted film adaptations of plays that are not readily available in print or that have little literary or social relevance. We have included as many "classics" as we could. Shakespeare, Shaw, O'Neill, Williams, Inge, Pinter, and Mamet, all of whom are included, are widely taught, and instructors frequently use films to supplement the reading of their dramatic texts. We have included plays and films that deal with contemporary social issues, such as disabilities (*Johnny Belinda*), euthanasia (*Whose Life Is It, Anyway?*), prejudice (*A Soldier's Story*), and alternative lifestyles (*Bent*).

We did omit film adaptations that were, at the time we worked on the book, not available on video. In fact, the availability of both plays and videos is capricious in today's marketplace, which is why we have not included specific distributors for each entry, but supplied a list of them later in this chapter. For the most part, we omitted filmed stage plays, such as the British Broadcasting Corporation's Shakespeare series, because there are so many other film adaptations of Shakespeare, and because interested readers can consult books by Herbert Coursen, Kenneth Rothwell, and other scholars. In some cases we have included filmed stage plays: Ibsen's popular play *Ghosts*, for example, is unavailable except as a literal adaptation, but we think readers may enjoy seeing how that play might be performed. Similarly, *The Beggar's Opera* is also an exception, simply because there are so few film adaptations of eighteenth-century drama. Some films made for television have also been included. The Charlton Heston television version of *A Man for All Seasons*, for example, is, of course, eclipsed by the Fred Zinnemann, Oscar-winning feature film, but the Heston version is included here because it is far closer to Robert Bolt's original text.

We have excluded teleplays—there are simply too many of them—except for the case of Paddy Chayefsky, who was an important playwright and screenwriter. We also had difficulty resolving the question of musicals. Some musicals, such as Madonna's *Evita* and Fosse's *Cabaret*, we decided to include because of their popular success and their political relevance. So, in general, though represented, the genre has not been fully covered, due to space limitations. We had similar problems with remakes, updates, and spin-offs. We decided to include *Meet Joe Black*, the updated remake of *Death Takes a Holiday*, because it presents the issue of death and a life well lived in a more contemporary perspective; the 1999 version of *The Out-of-Towners* was included because of its star power and the way it suggests that Simon's story has not exactly become dated. On the other hand, we decided to omit teen remakes, such as *Cruel Intentions* and *Ten Things I Hate about You*, because they were designed to appeal to a teenage audience rather than to adults and because the films do not deal seriously with their sources.

Concerning Selections and Availability

Although this book is not comprehensive, we have attempted to cover a number of adaptations of plays that are most likely to be used in classrooms by teachers and students as those plays are studied. Whenever possible, we have listed the ratings for the films included, but not all foreign films are rated, and readers should understand that the Motion Picture Association of America (MPAA) rating system was revised several times since it was originally designed to protect younger viewers. The entries are intended as starting points for further discussion; other potentially helpful sources are listed for all entries. Most of the titles included here should be available from video rental operations such as the nationwide Blockbuster chain. Major commercial sources for classroom rentals or individual purchases are Facets Multimedia, 1517 West Fullerton Avenue, Chicago, Illinois 60614, telephone 1–800–331–6197; Home Vision Cinema, 4411 North Ravenswood Avenue, 3rd Floor, Chicago, Illinois 60640–5802, telephone 1–800–826–3456; Viewfinders, Inc. Uncommon Video, P.O. Box 1665, Evanston, Illinois 60204–1665, telephone 1–800–342–3342; Swank Motion Pictures, Inc., 201 South Jefferson Avenue, St. Louis, Missouri 63103–2579, telephone 1–800–876–5577. Such companies should be especially helpful in locating "obscure" or foreign titles outside the American mainstream.

Works Cited

Andrew, Dudley. *Concepts in Film Theory.* New York: Oxford University Press, 1984.

Bennett, Alan. *The Madness of King George.* New York: Random House, 1995.

Gerdes, Peter R. "Film and/or Theatre: Some Introductory Comments." *The Australian Journal of Screen Theory* No. 7 (1980): 1–17.

Kramer, Steven Philip, and James M. Welsh. *Abel Gance.* Boston: Twayne, 1978.

Mamet, David. *Some Freaks.* New York: Viking, 1989.

Richardson, Tony. *The Long-Distance Runner: An Autobiography.* New York: William Morrow, 1993.

Span, Paula. "Living on Bard Time." *The Washington Post* (26 December 1998): C1, C8.

THE FILMS

ABOUT LAST NIGHT . . .

See SEXUAL PERVERSITY IN CHICAGO

AGNES OF GOD (1979)
John Pielmeier

Agnes of God (1985)

Directed by Norman Jewison

Adapted by John Pielmeier

Cast: Meg Tilly (Sister Agnes), Anne Bancroft (Mother Superior), Jane Fonda (Dr. Livingston)

Length: 98 minutes

Rated: PG-13

The play, written in two acts, was first staged at the Eugene O'Neill Playwrights Conference in 1979 and first produced professionally at the Actors Theatre of Louisville in 1980. The Broadway production at the Music Box Theatre in 1982 featured Elizabeth Ashley as Dr. Livingston, Geraldine

Page as the Mother Superior, and Amanda Plummer as Agnes. Sister Agnes, a novitiate nun at a convent in Quebec, turns up pregnant but claims not to have had any contact with men. How she was impregnated is the mystery to be solved, and since the disturbed nun has murdered her baby, a court-appointed psychiatrist, Dr. Martha Livingston (Jane Fonda), is the expert brought in to investigate the case. Mother Superior Mirian Ruth (Anne Bancroft) believes that Agnes has been "touched by God" in some mysterious way that science cannot explain and wants to protect Agnes. The worldly Dr. Livingston does not believe in miracles, however, and wants merely to heal the nun's shattered mind. Under therapy Agnes is forced to relive the disturbing experience so that the truth can be revealed. The play's design resembles Peter Shaffer's *Equus*, which it seems to imitate. The play's concept, like Agnes' conception, turns out to be less than immaculate, and the play is faithfully followed by the film, but the performances by Anne Bancroft as the Mother Superior and Jane Fonda as the more cynical, apostate, chain-smoking Dr. Livingston are quite good in this boilerplate imitation, despite its metaphysical trickery. The film, which the playwright himself adapted to the screen, opens and extends the action but faithfully follows the play. Although sometimes too frazzled, Fonda is still effective. *(J. M. W.)*

Resources: Angela Bonavoglia, *"Agnes of God,"* Cineaste 14.3 (1986): 41–42; James M. Welsh, "Dream Doctors as Healers in Drama and Film," *Literature & Medicine* 6 (1987): 117–127.

AH, WILDERNESS! (1933)
Eugene O'Neill

Ah, Wilderness (1935)

Directed by Clarence Brown

Adapted by Albert Hackett and Frances Goodrich

Cast: Wallace Beery (Sid Davis), Aline MacMahon (Lily Davis), Lionel Barrymore (Nat Miller), Eric Linden (Richard Miller), Cecilia Parker (Muriel McComber), Spring Byington (Essie Miller), Mickey Rooney (Tommy Miller), Charley Grapewin (Mr. McComber), Frank Albertson (Arthur Miller), Edward Nugent (Wint Selby), Bonita Granville (Mildred Miller), Helen Flint (Belle)

Length: 101 minutes

Eugene O'Neill's *Ah, Wilderness!*, his only comedy, was first produced at the Nixon Theatre in Pittsburgh in 1933. A nostalgic look at a childhood he never had, the play concerns the coming-of-age of Richard Miller, an intellectual, left-leaning high school senior whose reading (Oscar Wilde, Carlyle, Shaw) worries his mother and infuriates Mr. McComber, who believes Richard has corrupted his daughter, Muriel. After he receives Muriel's "Dear Richard" letter, Richard initially plays the role of injured lover; but he later accompanies Wint, a college friend of his brother Arthur, to a bar, where he gets intoxicated and chats with a woman of dubious reputation. When he arrives home drunk, the Miller family are concerned, and he is contrite. All ends well when he and Muriel meet at the beach, discuss his behavior, and kiss and make up. There is a subplot involving Sid Davis, a newspaperman whose drinking has caused Lily Miller (Davis in the original), Richard's aunt, to reject his marriage proposal. By the end of the play, not only are they reconciled, but Richard and his father, who have discussed Richard's bar behavior, come to an understanding. The last lines of this play about love come from Mr. and Mrs. Miller, who admit the joys of spring (youth) but also believe "winter" is wonderful "if you're together." Scriptwriters Hackett and Goodrich retained, for the most part, the setting of the play, which takes place, except for the beach and bar scenes, at the Miller home in Connecticut during the July 4th holiday in 1906. They do add a prologue, which defines the naive egotism, pretentious posturing, and idealistic intensity of Richard (Eric Linden). He is shown practicing his commencement address in an empty classroom, enlightening Muriel (Cecilia Parker) about the liberal changes he plans to make in his speech, and then, as the climax to a graduation ceremony full of comic recitations, delivering his speech. However, Mr. Miller (Lionel Barrymore), who had seen Richard's additions, manages to stop him before he gets to the socialistic changes. There are a few other changes caused by the censors: in the bar scene Belle, the "tart" (Helen Flint), does not mention either the five dollars for sex or even the "upstairs," where the sex would occur. In the film the Lily/Sid subplot is retained, but Sid has a larger role, probably because he was played by the popular Wallace Beery. Sid goes to Waterbury to get a newspaper job, gets fired, and reenters town on a beer wagon. In the film Muriel does not write a second, conciliatory letter to Richard; after she throws pebbles at his bedroom window, he comes out to talk with her, and they resolve their differences. The film concludes with the father-son talk about sex, a conversation that brings the two together, and with the "winter/spring" dialogue of the play. *(T. L. E.)*

Resources: Lionel Barrymore, *We Barrymores* (New York: Appleton-Century-Crofts, 1951); Allen Estrin, *Capra, Cukor, Brown* (South Brunswick, NJ: A. S. Barnes, 1980).

Summer Holiday (1948)

Directed by Rouben Mamoulian

Adapted by Frances Goodrich and Albert Hackett

Cast: Mickey Rooney (Richard Miller), Gloria DeHaven (Muriel McComber),

Walter Huston (Nat Miller), Frank Morgan (Uncle Sid), Butch Jenkins (Tommy Miller), Marilyn Maxwell (Belle), Agnes Moorehead (Cousin Lily), Selena Royle (Mrs. Miller)
Length: 92 minutes

Ah, Wilderness!, the 1930s play upon which the musical *Summer Holiday* is based, stands out in the O'Neill canon not only for being a comedy but also for depicting the past as a source of nostalgia, rather than of psychic turmoil. It would seem paradoxical for MGM ever to have filmed one of the playwright's works, so committed was MGM head, Louis B. Mayer, to the verities of small-town Americanism. However, the attention in *Ah, Wilderness!* to, in O'Neill's words, "an exact evocation of a dead past," appealed to the studio not once but twice. The play itself was filmed in 1935 by Clarence Brown. The addition of songs by Harry Warren and Ralph Blaine in the 1948 adaptation works effectively. In fact, *Summer Holiday* is underrated and unnecessarily overlooked, perhaps because the incorporation of song and dance in some senses does not call attention to itself. Several of the songs are delivered in rhythmic, rhymed speech rather than sung, particularly the opening introduction of the main characters, "It's Our Home Town." Furthermore, the dance numbers, choreographed by Charles Walters (who would later direct *Easter Parade* [1948], *Summer Stock* [1950], and *Lili* [1953]), are unassuming, more matter-of-fact episodes of collective movement than the bravado expositions of technique typical of MGM and the Arthur Freed musical unit. These and other elements of the film can, perhaps, be partly attributed to director Rouben Mamoulian, whom David Thomson has characterized as "like one of his movies, a garland of pretty blooms held together without obvious support." Mamoulian was prone to displays of technical prowess, showmanship for its own sake, but that tendency is subdued in *Summer Holiday*. Aside from the rich color of the cinematography and the incorporation during the graduation sequence of familiar visual iconography from Grant Wood and Thomas Hart Benton, the narrative focuses upon the graduation and social maturation of Richard Miller, whom Mickey Rooney plays with an ebullience that comes just near to going over the top, were it not for the very excessive emotions of the character. O'Neill's sympathetic evocation of the artist as a young man takes to the musical form with vigor and bears reexamination as both an adaptation and a film musical. *(D. S.)*

Resources: Tom Milne, *Mamoulian* (London: Thames and Hudson, 1969); David Thomson, *A Biographical Dictionary of Film*, 3d ed. (New York: Knopf, 1994).

ALFIE (1963)
Bill Naughton

Alfie (1966)

Directed by Lewis Gilbert

Adapted by Bill Naughton

Cast: Michael Caine (Alfie), Millicent Martin (Siddie), Julia Foster (Gilda), Graham Stark (Humphrey), Alfie Bass (Harry Clamacraft), Vivien Merchant (Lily Clamacraft), Sydney Taffer (Frank), Shelley Winters (Ruby), Jane Asher (Annie)

Length: 113 minutes

Rated: PG

Three years after his play was produced in 1963, Bill Naughton adapted it to film. The play concerns the sexual misadventures of a swinging Londoner who finally gets his just deserts. In the course of the play Alfie refuses to commit himself to Gilda and their son Malcolm, steals hitchhiking Annie from Lofty, another sexual predator, and then throws her out, seduces Lily, the wife of his hospital roommate, and then fails to see her through the abortion he arranges, and has a relationship with Ruby. A firm believer in looking out for himself, he has a series of jolts that shake his colossal ego: Annie refuses to return to him; he sees the aborted baby and thinks he hears it crying; and he finds Lofty in Ruby's apartment when he visits her. At the end of the play, however, he encounters Siddie, the married woman he was having sex with at the beginning of the play; he "is his old cheery self again" when he and she walk offstage. For the most part, in the film Naughton retains the basic plot and the dialogue from his play. The film audience sees events that Alfie only describes in the play: his sex with the dry-cleaning manager, his seduction of Lily at the park, and his conversation with his employer about "fiddling" (stealing). Naughton also retains Alfie's direct addresses to the audience, an old dramatic device but one relatively new to film. Although the plot is basically the same, the film-makers seem intent on deepening Alfie's villainy and punishing him for it. In the play Lily asks him to leave when she has the abortion, and he gladly does; in the film she wants him to stay, but he will not. He is punished for his behavior by seeing Malcolm's baptism and Gilda's happiness with Humphrey, her husband; by having Ruby, who is sleeping with a rock musician, tell him that he isn't as young as her current love; and by having Siddie reject his advances at the end of the film, much as he rejected her at the start of the film. The film, like the play, begins and ends with Alfie and Siddie; but Naughton adds a stray dog to their encounters. At the very end of the film a rejected Alfie goes off with the dog. Like the immensely popular play, the film was a hit with audiences; but it also was a critical success, garnering several Academy Award nominations and winning the Golden Globe award for best foreign film. *(T. L. E.)*

Resources: Michael Caine, *Acting in Film: An Actor's Take on Movie Making* (New York: Applause, 1997); Shelley Winters, *Shelley: Also Known as Shirley* (New York: Morrow, 1980).

AMADEUS (1979)
Peter Shaffer

Amadeus (1984)

Directed by Miloš Forman

Adapted by Peter Shaffer

Cast: F. Murray Abraham (Salieri), Tom Hulce (Mozart), Elizabeth Berridge (Constanze), Simon Callow (Emanuel Schikaneder), Roy Dotrice (Leopold Mozart), Jeffrey Jones (Emperor Joseph II), Charles Kay (Count Orsini-Rosenberg), Jonathan Moore (Baron Van Swieten), Patrick Hines (Kappel-meister Bonno), Herman Meckler (Priest), Christine Ebersole (Katerina Cavalieri)

Length: 158 minutes

Rated: PG

The central conflict of this play, which premiered at Britain's National Theatre in 1979, is between composer Antonio Salieri and his more gifted contemporary Wolfgang Amadeus Mozart. The two acts are set in 1823 in an insane asylum where Salieri's extended monologues take the audience back thirty-two years to the period 1781–1791, when Mozart was brought to the Imperial Court of Joseph II in Vienna, where Salieri was court composer. Insanely jealous of Mozart, Salieri conspires to spoil the younger composer's prospects. Finally, he even takes the blame for Mozart's death due to poverty, kidney failure, and alcoholism, willing to settle for notoriety, since fame has passed him by. The challenge of adapting this play to cinema was to transform its essential theatrical design in such a way that Mozart's musical genius would become more central and obvious. Shaffer revised the play to make Salieri clearly "the wicked center of the action," for the screen version that starred F. Murray Abraham as Salieri and Tom

Hulce as an astonishingly vulgar Mozart. The film is not a biography but a dramatic meditation on the nature of evil and the corrosive effects of vanity and jealousy. A major change in the screenplay is the newly invented character of a young priest who visits Salieri in order to hear his confession after an attempted suicide. The film reverses this incident from the play (in which Salieri cuts his throat at the end) in order to set up the confessional framework at the opening, so the story can be told in voice-over to the priest, rather than through Salieri's theatrical monologues. Another added character is the maid Salieri hires to spy on Mozart. Other theatrical devices, such as the "Venticelli" chorus, are excised from the film. Also missing are Salieri's seductions of the "songbird" Katherina Cavaleri and of Mozart's wife, Constanze (Elizabeth Berridge), who, in the play, was willing to prostitute herself to advance her husband's career. In the film Salieri does not rant about poisoning Mozart; instead, he kills Mozart by overworking the composer on his deathbed to complete a commissioned Requiem Mass. Shaffer also dispenses with Baron Van Swieten's anger over Mozart's betrayal of the Masonic brotherhood's secret rituals. The film ends with Mozart's burial in a pauper's grave as the Requiem is sung. Though Van Swieten attends the funeral, there is no hint in the film that he paid for it. Finally, the film brings Mozart's father, Leopold, into the action in order to explain the "Messenger of Death" who spooks Mozart into the overworked frenzy that brings about his death. The film amplifies Salieri's hatred and jealousy effectively, making perfectly clear why he belongs in a mental institution. Arguably, the play is both clarified and improved by the film. *(J. M. W.)*

Resources: David Ansen, "A Genius despite Himself," *Newsweek* (24 September 1984): 85; Miloš Forman and Jan Novak, *Turnaround: A Memoir* (New York: Villard Books, 1994); Michiko Kukutani, "How 'Amadeus' was Translated from Play to Film," *New York Times* (16 September 1984): Sec. II, 1, 20.

AMERICAN BUFFALO (1975)
David Mamet

American Buffalo (1997)

Directed by Michael Corrente

Adapted by David Mamet

Cast: Dustin Hoffman (Teach), Dennis Franz (Donny), Sean Nelson (Bobby)

Length: 88 minutes

Rated: R

Described as a cross between film noir, Maxim Gorky, and Samuel Beckett, David Mamet's 1975 play is a chamber piece about three dingy characters in a Pawtucket, Rhode Island, junk shop who are planning a heist. Donny, the owner of the shop, wants to rob the man who he thinks conned him into selling a valuable buffalo nickel. He enlists the assistance of his friend, Teach, a small-time criminal in the grip of a potentially violent paranoia, and Bobby, a black kid who looks up to him. But nothing comes of the plan; instead, Teach assaults Bobby and trashes the shop. In a fit of remorse in which Teach bewails the meaninglessness of everything, he and Donny take Bob to the hospital. As critic Andy Pawelczak notes, these men represent American enterprise "writ small"; they are metaphors "for everything that's gone wrong with our mercantile civilization" (67). Filmmaker Michael Corrente faced the challenge of making a movie from a play where there is no decisive action, just talk—and lots of it. Rather than just locking the camera down on the dialogue, Corrente tries to "open out" the exchanges. While they converse, the men are constantly roaming around the shop, handling objects, exiting and then entering again, sitting in the car outside, walking up and down the streets, and so on. These incessant bits of business—the film was actually shot in Pawtucket, Rhode Island—ultimately distract the weary viewer from the intensity of the words. Mamet's demystification of the American Dream—symbolized here by the metaphor of the vanishing American buffalo (and cleverly confirmed by the device of the buffalo nickel)—is thus reduced to a series of tedious rants from three unprepossessing lowlifes. The sole dramatic edge comes from Dustin Hoffman, who invests the scruffy Teach with his patented, ratlike energy and bristle. Otherwise, the film transforms the already maddeningly enigmatic play—as commentator David Savran says, Mamet's characters can never fully account for what they do—into a confusing babble. *(J. C. T.)*

Resources: Andy Pawelczak, *"American Buffalo," Films in Review* 48, 1, 2 (January–February 1997): 67; David Savran, *In Their Own Words: Contemporary American Playwrights* (New York: Theater Communications Group, 1988).

ANASTASIA (1954)
Marcelle Maurette, adapted by Guy Bolton

Anastasia (1956)

Directed by Anatole Litvak
Adapted by Arthur Laurents
Cast: Ingrid Bergman (Anastasia), Yul Brynner (Bounine), Helen Hayes (Em-

press), Akim Tamiroff (Chernov), Felix Aylmer (Russian Chamberlain), Ivan Desny (Prince Paul), Sacha Pitoeff (Petrovin)

Length: 105 minutes

Guy Bolton's English adaptation of Marcelle Maurette's play was staged at the Lyceum Theatre in New York in 1954. Prince Bounine's house on the outskirts of Berlin is the only set in the play. Bounine and coconspirators Petrovin and Chernov have been financed by Russian émigrés to find Anastasia, the one member of Nicholas II's family rumored to have escaped execution by the communists. Bounine believes he has a convincing candidate in Anna Broun, who disappeared after he discovered her at a hospital in Dausdorf. He finds her ready to commit suicide by drowning and brings her to his home, where the conspirators decide that her eyes and wounds may enable them to convince Drivinitz, head of the financing committee, that she is authentic. Thanks to some coaching, which involves memorizing anecdotes, names, events, and so on, she persuades Drivinitz, Prince Paul, and some of the czar's old retainers that she is genuine, but the real test involves the Empress, the "Old Ikon," who has been disappointed by several impostors. Despite the intervention of Michael Serensky, a doctor at the Dausdorf hospital who believes she is a fraud, Bounine and his friends succeed when Anna convinces the Empress by coughing when she is nervous and calling the Empress by a pet name. (Anna also suddenly speaks Russian, which she had been unable to do.) In the last act, Bounine's somewhat tacky living room is furnished with a rented throne and converted to an audience room for Russian nobility. If Bounine's scheme works, Anna will be named heir to the millions of rubles the czar deposited in foreign banks, and Bounine and his backers will get a percentage of the funds. After a discussion with the Empress and a disappointing answer from Paul, who wants to marry her but cannot understand why she is willing to give away her fortune, Anna leaves the reception to find "life, her real life." Bounine, according to the Empress, has been defeated by "royal tradition." The film opens up the play, showing us Bounine (Yul Brynner) finding Anastasia (Ingrid Bergman) by the canal, shooting her in Copenhagen at an interview (the dramatic highlight of the film) with the Empress (Helen Hayes), and moving the royal reception from Bounine's home to Copenhagen, where it takes place in a huge, opulent palace. The major change in the film adaptation concerns the developing, but unacknowledged, love between Anna and Bounine, who becomes a Pygmalion figure who falls in love with his "creation." When she leaves the reception after being advised by the Empress to follow her heart, Anna goes with Bounine, thereby providing a romantic happy ending to the film. Hayes as the Empress is wonderful, and Bergman's first performance before an American audience in eight years won her an Oscar and returned her to stardom in the United States. *(T. L. E.)*

Resources: Helen Hayes, *My Life in Three Acts* (San Diego: Harcourt Brace Jovanovich, 1990); Laurence J. Quirk, *The Complete Films of Ingrid Bergman* (New York: Carol Comunications, 1988).

ANDROCLES AND THE LION (1912)
George Bernard Shaw

Androcles and the Lion (1952)

Directed by Chester Erskine

Adapted by Chester Erskine and Ken Englund

Cast: Jean Simmons (Lavinia), Alan Young (Androcles), Victor Mature (Captain), Maurice Evans (Caesar), Robert Newton (Ferrovius)

Length: 98 minutes

First staged in 1912, *Androcles and the Lion* concerns a Christian who pulls a thorn from the paw of a lion only to encounter the lion again at the Coliseum in Rome. Before the second meeting, the Romans have rounded up a group of Christians who persist in singing "Onward Christian Soldiers" as they march to Rome. One converted Christian named Ferrovius does backslide, loses his temper, and kills several gladiators, causing Caesar to free all the other Christians, except for Androcles, who he says must be sacrificed to a lion to appease the bloodthirsty crowd. Tommy, the lion, recognizes Androcles, and the two waltz together in the arena. Caesar, who can no longer doubt the truth of Christianity, must conquer his fear of the lion so that he can save face by saying he tamed it. In addition to this plot, Shaw provides a subplot involving Lavinia, who will not renounce her faith, despite the entreaties of the Roman captain who has fallen in love with her. At the end of the play Androcles and Tommy leave together, Ferrovius joins Caesar's Pretorian Guard, and Lavinia agrees to let her captain come to visit her and argue about religion. The film adaptation locates the action in A.D. 161 in Rome, where, as a security measure, the authorities decide to arrest Christians in Syracuse, where Androcles lives. As he flees the Roman soldiers, Androcles encounters the lion. Aside from some additional scenes (e.g., Ferrovius demonstrates his strength by lifting a carriage off a Roman soldier), action in the film follows the play quite closely with the exception of the Lavinia-captain subplot, which assumes more importance in the film, probably because of the star status of Simmons and Mature. *(T. L. E.)*

Resources: Bernard F. Dukore, ed., *Bernard Shaw on Cinema* (Carbondale: Southern Illinois Press, 1997); Valerie Pascal, *The Disciple and His Devil* (New York: McGraw-Hill, 1970).

ANNA CHRISTIE (1921)
Eugene O'Neill

Anna Christie (1930)

Directed by Clarence Brown

Adapted by Frances Marion

Cast: Greta Garbo (Anna Christie), Charles Bickford (Matt Burke), Marie Dressler (Marthy Owen)

Length: 90 minutes

"Men, I hate 'em—all of 'em," says the whore, Anna Christie. O'Neill's 1921 play tells of her regeneration under the influence of the sea and the love of a man. After years as a prostitute, Anna reunites with her father, Christopher Christopherson, the grizzled captain of a coal barge. Life on the coastal waters of Massachusetts brings her a sense of rebirth, and she falls in love with Matt Burke, a roistering Irishman whom she has saved from a shipwreck. But when she turns down Matt's proposal of marriage and confesses to her illicit past, both men reject her. In the play's final act, she reconciles with Matt and agrees to his demand that she pledge to him an oath of loyalty and purity. O'Neill's play was chosen by MGM studios for Greta Garbo's talking debut. (MGM had already made a silent version in 1923 starring Blanche Sweet.) George F. Marion recreated his stage role as Christopherson, Charles Bickford took on the part of Matt, and Marie Dressler played Old Marthy Owen, Christopherson's seedy mistress. Despite favorable critical and popular acceptance, the picture suffered from the stagy, proscenium-bound nature of so many theatrical films of the day. Director Brown and scenarist Marion chose to retain most of the substance and flavor of O'Neill's text, at the expense of achieving a more "cinematic" film. For example, Anna's soliloquies about her past were retained without benefit of flashbacks or the inclusion of a visualized prologue (which would become a standard practice in theatrical films within the next few years). Medium shots, static camera placements, and studio soundstage sets predominated, although a few added scenes opened up the play a bit, including exterior shots of the barge docking at the Provincetown port and Anna and Matt's outing at the Coney Island amusement park. Today the film is regarded as a relic of the early talking picture era, whose main claim to fame is Garbo's first screen utterance: "Gimme a whisky—ginger ale on the side. And don't be stingy, baby." At the same time a German-language version utilizing the same cast and sets was directed by Jacques Feyder. It is purportedly less stagy than the Clarence Brown picture, and, because censorial restrictions were not as severe in Europe, Anna's past history as a prostitute is more frankly depicted. *(J. C. T.)*

Resources: Barrett H. Clark, *Eugene O'Neill: The Man and His Plays* (New York: Dover, 1947); John C. Tibbetts, *The American Theatrical Film* (Bowling Green, OH: Bowling Green State University Press, 1985).

ANNE OF A THOUSAND DAYS (1948)
Maxwell Anderson, adapted by Richard Sokolove

Anne of a Thousand Days (1969)

Directed by Charles Jarrott

Adapted by Bridget Boland and John Hale, from Sokolove's adaptation of Anderson's verse play

Cast: Richard Burton (King Henry VIII), Genevieve Bujold (Anne Boleyn), Irene Papas (Queen Katherine), Anthony Quayle (Wolsey), John Colicos (Cromwell), Michael Hordern (Thomas Boleyn), Katherine Blake (Elizabeth Boleyn), Peter Jeffrey (Norfolk), William Squire (Thomas More), Terence Wilton (Lord Percy), Lesley Paterson (Jane Seymour)

Length: 145 minutes

Rated: PG

Anderson's play, a verse drama, appeared in New York at the Shubert Theatre in 1948 and was adapted to film in 1969, after Henry VIII's life and times had been screened in such successes as *The Lion in Winter* (1968) and *A Man for All Seasons* (1966). The play, which is full of long monologues and epilogues and prologues for each of the three acts, begins as Anne Boleyn, Henry's second wife, awaits her fate. The play, in flashback, recounts her experiences from Henry's first visit to her, her determination not to meet her sister Mary's fate, pregnant and abandoned by Henry, Henry's final capitulation to her demand that she be made queen, Wolsey's unsuccessful efforts to secure Henry's divorce from Katherine of Aragon, and opportunistic Cromwell's scheme to have Henry break with the Vatican, secure church property, and marry Anne. When her first child is a girl, the future Queen Elizabeth, and her second child, a boy, is stillborn, Henry turns his attentions to Jane Seymour; but to marry Jane, Henry must have

Anne agree to a divorce, which would make Elizabeth illegitimate. When she refuses, Cromwell frames Anne for adultery by torturing Smeaton and getting him to testify against her. Almost against his will, for his final speech, which is haunted by Anne's face, reveals that it is not over between them, Henry signs Anne's death warrant. The film adaptation makes drastic cuts in the long speeches and dispenses with the prologues and epilogues, but it does begin with Henry (Richard Burton) reluctantly signing Anne's death warrant and then proceeds, as did the play, with a flashback. Although the plot in the film follows the source, the film humanizes Wolsey (Anthony Quayle) and stresses the battle between him and Anne (Genevieve Bujold), who manages to turn Henry against him and to secure Hampton Court, his possession, for herself. Anne, who states that "power is as exciting as love," is herself a skilled politician. Katherine (Irene Papas), who does not appear in the play, declares to Henry, "I will not betray our daughter" by granting him a divorce; this decision parallels Anne's similar refusal later in the play. After their marriage and Anne's failure to provide Henry with a son, Henry turns to Jane Seymour (Lesley Paterson) at court; and Anne, as Katherine did at the beginning of the film, leaves Henry in disgust. These two parallels make the plot tighter, but they also suggest that "what goes around comes around" and that Henry's actions are futile. The film also devotes more time to the efforts of Cromwell (John Colicos) to frame Anne and to the trial itself. At the end of the film Anne is at the execution site, and Henry is hunting outside London. When he learns of Anne's death, he and his party (the same group that appeared at the start of the film) head for Jane Seymour's home. After this scene the film ironically cuts to the young Elizabeth (Katharine Blake) posing before a mirror and pretending to be the Queen of England. The sets are lavish, the acting superb—Burton won an Oscar nomination for his role. This is an example of an adaptation transcending its sources by tightening the plot, gleaning the best dialogue, deepening the characters, and suggesting the futility of Henry's quest to have a male heir. (T. L. E.)

Resources: Hollis Alpert, *Burton* (New York: Putnam, 1986); Melvyn Bragg, *Richard Burton: A Life* (Boston: Little, Brown, 1988).

AS YOU LIKE IT (1599)
William Shakespeare

As You Like It (1936)

Directed by Paul Czinner

Adapted by Robert J. Cullen and Carl Mayer; treatment suggested by James M. Barrie

Cast: Henry Ainley (Duke), Felix Aylmer (Frederick), Gavin Gordon (Amiens), Leon Quartermaine (Jaques), Austin Trevor (Le Beau), Lionel Braham (Charles), John Laurie (Oliver), Laurence Olivier (Orlando), Fisher White, (Adam), George More Marriott (Dennis), Mackenzie Ward (Touchstone), Aubrey Mather (Corin), Henry Ainley (Silvius), Peter Bull (William), Elisabeth Bergner (Rosalind), Sophie Stewart (Celia), Joan White (Phoebe), Dorice Fordred (Audrey).

Length: 97 minutes

All paths lead to the Forest of Arden in this romantic comedy. Orlando, cheated of his inheritance by his older brother Oliver, wins a wrestling match against the champion Charles at the court of Duke Frederick, whose usurped brother has retreated into the forest, where he holds court. Rosalind, the banished duke's daughter, witnesses the match, and she and Orlando fall in love. Rosalind goes into exile disguised as a boy (Ganymede), seeking her father, along with her friend Celia, daughter of Duke Frederick, and the jester, Touchstone. Orlando has also retreated to the forest with his faithful servant Adam and becomes a member of the banished Duke's court, where he encounters the melancholy Jaques, and Ganymede, whom he does not immediately recognize as his beloved Rosalind. Oliver goes to the forest in search of Orlando, is reconciled with his brother, and falls in love with Celia. Finally, Duke Frederick goes into the forest to capture his brother but has a religious conversion and decides to become a hermit and restore the dukedom to his brother. Several sets of lovers are united at the conclusion of this green comedy.

Even though Laurence Olivier played Orlando, Paul Czinner's film is stiff and artificial and overly theatrical. It is terribly dated and dull. Elisabeth Bergner wanted to play Rosalind and, as Czinner's wife, managed to get the role, despite a husky voice and a foreign accent that seems out of place. As Celia, Sophie Stewart carries her part much better. Novelist-reviewer Graham Greene objected to Henry Ainley's Duke (whose "false fruity enunciation carries us back to the Edwardian stage") and Leon Quartermaine's Jaques, whose melancholy is less than stinging because the comedy has been sanitized. In his *Spectator* review (11 September 1936), Greene ridiculed Quartermaine's "rather banal recital" of the famous "Seven Ages of Man" speech, though John Marks, writing for *Sight and Sound*, thought the delivery was "magnificent" (Manvell 31). Lionel Braham, moreover, is too corpulent to be very threatening as Charles, the wrestler. Greene criticized the director for being "too respectful towards stage tradition" and unimaginative in his technique: "all the camera can offer is more space: more elaborate palace sets and a real wood with room for real animals." The play does not need to be as silly as it seems in this production, which cuts nearly 50 percent of the text. Shakespeare was not well served. *(J. M. W.)*

Resources: Roger Manvell, *Shakespeare and the Film* (New York: Praeger, 1971); Peter Morris, *Shakespeare on Film* (Ottawa: Canadian National Film Board, 1971).

AVANTI! (1968)
Samuel Taylor

Avanti! (1972)

Directed by Billy Wilder

Adapted by Billy Wilder and I.A.L. Diamond

Cast: Jack Lemmon (Wendell Armbruster III), Juliet Mills (Pamela Piggott), Clive Revill (Carlucci)

Length: 144 minutes

Rated: R

Samuel Taylor's 1968 play was far from successful—it lasted only twenty-one performances—but Billy Wilder was attracted by its plot and its author, for he had adapted Taylor's earlier and better-known work, *Sabrina Fair*, as *Sabrina* in 1954. Originally, *Avanti!* was a stage romance in which Wendell Armbruster III, an American businessman, arrives on the island of Ischia to claim the body of his dead father. There, he encounters an Englishwoman, Pamela Piggott, only to discover that her mother was killed along with his father, for they were lovers who had met clandestinely each year on the island for quite some time. In Taylor's play, Armbruster finds a soul mate in Ms. Piggott right from the start. Wilder complicates the encounter by making Armbruster nauseatingly brusque and Ms. Piggott an unusual romantic lead: a plump boutique clerk. The two, however, are clearly fated to be lovers and to replicate, the film's ending implies, the relationship shared by their parents. Entranced by the leisurely atmosphere of Ischia, Armbruster loses his emotional armor and, in a memorable scene (the sole such occasion in Wilder's work), reluctantly but gamely joins Ms. Piggott in skinny-dipping at dawn in the Mediterranean Sea. As much a narrative of the collision of cultures as the complications between the sexes, *Avanti!* is one of Wilder's most underrated films. In this film, Wilder, who often cynically portrays the relationship between the sexes, instead incorporates an unusually gentle romance between middle-aged protagonists. At the same time, the film is a narrative triggered by, and consumed with, human mortality. The comedy is leavened by a graceful assessment of death, as in the scene where the couple identify their parents' bodies. Wilder is not a director prone to visual flourishes, but the tentative northern light that illuminates the mortuary illustrates the unique and rewarding combination of sensibilities that makes *Avanti!* a captivating narrative and a rich addition to Wilder's career. The film was a financial and critical flop at the time of its release, indicative of the director's allegedly declining abilities. While it cannot be considered an overly faithful adaptation of Taylor's material, it nonetheless constitutes an undervalued element in Wilder's long and diverse film career. *(D. S.)*

Resources: Bernard Dick, *Billy Wilder* (Boston: Twayne, 1980); Kevin Lally, *Wilder Times: The Life of Billy Wilder* (New York: Henry Holt, 1996); Steve Seidman, *The Film Career of Billy Wilder* (Pleasantville, NY: Redgrave, 1977).

BABY DOLL (1956)

See THE LONG STAY CUT SHORT/OR/THE UNSATISFACTORY SUPPER and 27 WAGONS FULL OF COTTON

THE BACHELOR PARTY (1953)
Paddy Chayefsky

The Bachelor Party (1957)

Directed by Delbert Mann

Adapted by Paddy Chayefsky

Cast: Don Murray (Charlie Samson), E. G. Marshall (Walter), Jack Warden (Eddie), Philip Abbott (Arnold), Larry Blyden (Kenneth), Patricia Smith (Helen Samson), Carolyn Jones (the Existentialist), Nancy Marchand (Julie)

Length: 105 minutes

Chayefsky's teleplay, which takes place in low-income housing in Jersey City, New Jersey, begins with Helen's telling Charlie that she is pregnant. Because money is scarce, Charlie is unenthused. On the subway to work he talks with coworker Kenneth about "missing something." That evening they go to Greenwich Village with office bachelor Eddie; Arnold, who needs reassurance about marrying his bride-to-be; and Walter, a bookkeeper with health problems. The evening is punctuated with Arnold's doubts, Walter's fears, Charlie's wish that he had not quit college, and Eddie's determination to pick up a woman. As a result of one of Eddie's offhand comments, Arnold calls off his wedding; and while Eddie is left with a sorry-looking tramp, Charlie takes Arnold to his girlfriend's place, where he tells Arnold that marriage is a "job." Charlie then returns home to his wife and his own marriage. In adapting his play to film, Chayefsky deepened Charlie's educational commitment (he attends evening classes), thereby making his reservations about Helen's pregnancy more understandable. He also presents Charlie as ready to quit both night school and his marriage. Ken's advice keeps Charlie from sleeping with "the Existentialist," played by Carolyn Jones, who was nominated for an Oscar for her performance. Instead, Charlie takes Arnold home, repeats Ken's advice, and tells him that "life is nothing if you don't love somebody." When he returns to Helen, Charlie and she exchange "I love you"s, making literal what was implied in the play. Like *Marty* (1955), which featured the same writer, the same director, and the same producers, *Bachelor Party* focuses on the everyday lives of everyday people caught in everyday crises. *(T. L. E.)*

Resources: John M. Clum, *Paddy Chayefsky* (Boston: Twayne, 1976); Shawn Considine, *Mad as Hell: The Life and Work of Paddy Chayefsky* (New York: Random House, 1994).

THE BAD SEED (1954)
Maxwell Anderson

The Bad Seed (1956)

Directed by Mervyn LeRoy

Adapted by John Lee Mahin based on the play by Maxwell Anderson and the novel by William March

Cast: Nancy Kelly (Christine Penmark), Patty McCormack (Rhoda Penmark), Henry Jones (LeRoy), Eileen Heckert (Mrs. Daigle), Evelyn Varden (Monica Breedlove), Paul Fix (Richard Bravo)

Length: 129 minutes

The Bad Seed first appeared at New York's 46th Street Theater on 8 December 1954, with Nancy Kelly and Patty McCormack in the leading roles. The film version retained them, along with the play's other successful performers such as Henry Jones, Eileen Heckert, and Evelyn Varden. Set in the small-town southern apartment of Colonel and Mrs. Penmark, *The Bad Seed*'s action occurs over a period of several days in June. While Colonel Penmark is away in Washington, Christine Penmark comes to the realization that her perfectly behaved eight-year-old daughter Rhoda is an unscrupulous, cold-blooded killer lacking any moral sense who has murdered at least three people. Learning that she is the surviving daughter of a serial murderess whose genetic "bad seed" has skipped a generation, Christine decides to give her daughter a lethal overdose of sleeping pills and shoot herself. The play ironically ends with the revelation that Rhoda has survived. Both play and film version were popular since they emerged in a time of increased juvenile delinquency and increased affluence. Cold War and McCarthyite discourses avoided "liberal," environmentally based theories and turned to scapegoating devices such as the formerly discredited theories involving heredity. Like *Rebel without a Cause* (1955), the film also scapegoats motherhood, past and present. Realizing she is the daughter of a female serial killer, Christine blames herself for the problem—"It isn't what she's done. It's what I've done!"—even though both play and film make clear that there is little she could have done about it anyway. The film version also eliminates humorous references to psychoanalysis, incest, and cancer and provides a morally approved "happy ending" when Christine recovers from her suicide, and a divinely sent lightning bolt incinerates the "evil" child at the climax when she searches for the medal she stole from a classmate she murdered. Like the stage production, the film ends with a "curtain call" in which Nancy Kelly playfully spanks young Patty— "And as for you young lady!"—emphasizing parental control and disavowing all the reactionary genetic theories advanced in the film. *(T. W.)*

Resources: Roy S. Simmonds, Cathy Ames, and Rhoda Penmark, "Two Child Monsters," *Mississippi Quarterly* 39.2 (1986): 91–101; Tony Williams, *Hearths of Darkness: The Family in the American Horror Film* (Cranbury, NJ: Fairleigh Dickinson University Press, 1996).

THE BALLAD OF THE SAD CAFE (1963)
Edward Albee, from Carson McCullers' novella

The Ballad of the Sad Cafe (1991)

Directed by Simon Callow

Adapted by Michael Hirst

Cast: Vanessa Redgrave (Miss Amelia), Keith Carradine (Marvin Macy), Cork

Hubbert (Cousin Lymon), Rod Steiger (Reverend Willin), Austin Pendleton (Lawyer Taylor), Beth Dixon (Mary Hale), Lanny Flaherty (Merlie Ryan), Mert Hatfield (Stumpy McPhail), Anne Pitoniak (Mrs. McPhail), Frederick Johnson (Jeff), Laurie Raymond (Sadie Ricketts), Joe Stephens (Henry Ford Crimp), Keith Wommack (Tom Rainey), Kevin Wommack (George Rainey), Laura Burns (Molly Kelly)

Length: 100 minutes

Rated: PG-13

Hirst's screenplay drew from both McCullers' novella and Albee's dramatic adaptation, which appeared in New York in 1963. In the play, which has only one set, Miss Amelia's house/café, Miss Amelia uses lawsuits and moonshine liquor to rule the sleepy southern town. The Narrator, who acts as a kind of chorus or stage manager, describes the current state of the dilapidated house and the "terrible, dim face" that looks out the upstairs window. The flashback to eight years ago that follows details how the café came into being and how it died. A "brokeback" (hunch back) who claims to be Miss Amelia's cousin enters town and is taken in and pampered by her. At his instigation she transforms the first floor of her house into a café, which prospers for four years until the reappearance of Marvin Macy, the husband whom Miss Amelia rejected and who has just been released from jail. Cousin Lymon, the "brokeback," is fascinated by Marvin and switches his allegiance from Miss Amelia to him after he learns about the ten-day marriage. Lymon moves Marvin into Miss Amelia's house, and she knows that she and Marvin will have to fight it out. On Groundhog Day the fistfight occurs, and Miss Amelia is winning until Lymon aids Marvin, who savagely beats her and leaves town with Lymon. Miss Amelia retreats to her upstairs room and never leaves it. As the Narrator explains, the story is about love (Amelia for Lymon, Lymon for Marvin, and Marvin for Amelia), and "No good will come of it." When Callow read Albee's play, he found it "too talkative" and cut the dialogue, as well as eliminated the Narrator. To open up the play, Hirst added scenes of Lymon (Cork Hubbert) and Miss Amelia (Vanessa Redgrave) hunting and traveling to her still, and to provide a frame for the film, he added a shot of the chain gang mentioned in the play—that shot begins and ends the play. (One addition, Lymon's stumbling upon a Ku Klux Klan [KKK] rally, seems to have no relevance to the film.) In the play Miss Amelia had set a trap for Marvin (Keith Carradine) in the woods; in the film she attempts, in an effective sequence, to poison his dinner. The play stresses Marvin's love for Miss Amelia and his moral reformation before he proposes to her; the film slights that material, focusing instead on the love Miss Amelia develops for Lymon, who, she says, is all she has. As a result of adding outside scenes (Lymon and Marvin destroy her still) and elaborating on the development of the café, the nuances in the relationships of the characters are lost; and the viewer's only clue, since the Narrator has been omitted, that the film is about love comes from an added scene involving Reverend Willin (Rod Steiger), who tells his congregation that love is a "lonely, solitary thing" and that "the lover craves the love, even if it causes pain." The film must rely on words to do what it visually fails to convey, the "strange fairy-story" McCullers claims she wrote. In the play and the novella the characters are real, and they are metaphorical, mythological beings; in the film they are just real characters. *(T. L. E.)*

Resources: David Denby, *"The Ballad of the Sad Cafe," New York* (27 May 1991): 62; Tom Milne, *"The Ballad of the Sad Cafe," Monthly Film Bulletin* (April 1991): 99.

BAREFOOT IN THE PARK (1963)
Neil Simon

Barefoot in the Park (1967)

Directed by Gene Saks

Adapted by Neil Simon

Cast: Robert Redford (Paul Bratter), Jane Fonda (Corie Bratter), Mildred Natwick (Ethel Banks), Charles Boyer (Victor Velasco)

Length: 109 minutes

Neil Simon's stage play about newlyweds in love or, more accurately, lust, was a big hit on Broadway in the 1960s and continues to be a favorite of community and summer stock theatre seasons. The film version is quite faithful to the play due, in part, to a number of transfers from the original stage version to the screen in both the cast and production staff, including Simon as screenwriter and Gene Saks as director. This light comedy tells the tale of Paul (Redford, reprising his original stage role), a stuffed-shirt lawyer who has recently married Corie (Fonda), a worshiper of life and love and anything unusual. The play opens just after the honeymoon, six glorious nights at the Plaza Hotel in New York. In the opening scenes of the movie, viewers are actually invited to the honeymoon and treated to some great location shots of New York, including wonderful interior shots of the Plaza. Some rather dated jokes about Paul and Corie's appetite for constant sex prove to be a problem later on in the story (the happy couple has nothing in common *other* than sex). When Paul finally goes to work after the honeymoon, we get a real picture of how differently these two crazy lovebirds choose to behave in public. Paul likes to be proper, and Corie likes to have fun. We never doubt their love for a second, but we are set up from the beginning for disaster. Corie arrives at her new apartment, an unusual studio flat on the sixth floor of a building with some very strange neighbors (i.e., for the 1960s). Once the honeymoon is over, and the marriage begins, we are in for a series of all-too-familiar episodes between bride and groom as they work through the difficulties of learning how to live with each other. After all, a marriage cannot be only about good sex. The beginning scenes in both the movie and play are slow-going. Simon seems to need this time to set up all his running "jokes" for eventual payoff at various places later in the play. Slow-going, that is, until the arrival of Corie's mother, Ethel (the brilliant Mildred Natwick, also reprising her Broadway role). Natwick's continual battle with the six flights of stairs leading to Paul and Corie's flat is priceless. She has a knack for Simon's comic one-liners ("I thought I'd died and gone to heaven, but I had to climb the stairs") and manages to deliver his awkward "serious" lines about love and marriage with ease and unpretentious wisdom. Corie and Paul's story is an all-too-familiar tale of what happens during the period of adjustment after the honeymoon. The story seems very dated by our standards. Nonetheless, Simon's dialogue rings true, even for later decades. Redford and Fonda are on sure ground as actors, and their characters become more complex when their marital spat leads to talk of divorce. In the end, both need to compromise to make the marriage work. It's a familiar tale told with spirit and humor; Redford's drunk scene helps to make the film worth sitting through. Of special interest are Johnny Mercer's lyrics for the title song. *(J. S.)*

Resource: Edyth M. McGovern, *Neil Simon: A Critical Study* (New York: Frederick Ungar, 1978).

THE BEGGAR'S OPERA (1727)
John Gay

The Beggar's Opera (1983)

Directed and adapted by Jonathan Miller

Cast: Stratford Johns (Peachum), Peter Bayliss (Lockit), Roger Daltrey (Macheath), Carol Hall (Polly Peachum), Rosemary Ashe (Lucy Lockit)

Length: 135 minutes

The Begger's Opera, Gay's popular 1727 masterpiece, has been literally adapted by Jonathan Miller, whose video recreates through crowded sets and period costumes the sense of London lowlife preserved in Hogarth's engravings. The plot concerns Macheath, a highwayman addicted to women who secretly marries Polly Peachum, much to the dismay of her parents. When Peachum, a lawyer and fence for stolen goods, determines to "peach" (inform on) Macheath to get a reward, Polly warns Macheath, who leaves her, only to be betrayed by his old lover, Jenny Diver. In prison he is visited by Lucy Lockit, daughter of the jailer who is in league with Peachum; he convinces the pregnant Lucy he is not married but will marry her. She helps him escape, but his inability to avoid gambling and women causes him to be recaptured. Because they can both profit by Macheath's hanging, Lockit and Peachum take him to the gallows. Macheath is accompanied by Polly and Lucy but also by four more "wives" with children. Macheath, however, is not hanged but receives a "reprieve" by the beggar whose opera is being staged. (In an "introduction" at the start of the play, the beggar and an actor discuss the "opera" that is to be presented.) The beggar's last comments reveal the satiric edge Gay intended: "It is difficult to determine whether (in the fashionable vices) the fine gentlemen imitate the gentlemen of the road, or the gentlemen of the road the fine gentlemen." Just as Peachum uses his gang for his own ends, so the government through Walpole, first minister, exploited the people. As the play concludes, a free Macheath chooses Polly, and there are dancing and merriment. The video adaptation follows the opera to the letter (dialogue, songs, and sets) until the end. The beggar and actor make their appearance, and the beggar/author acquiesces to the actor's demand for a reprieve to conform to the current fashion. As their dialogue occurs in the foreground, the audience sees Macheath on the gallows. As word of the reprieve is passed through the crowd, the actor waves in recognition to the hangman, and Macheath goes off the scaffolding. Macheath's "hanging," which ironically is apparently caused by a misinterpreted gesture, halts the action, which is stopped in a freeze-frame. There is no reunion between Macheath and Polly. *(T. L. E.)*

Resources: Jonathan Miller, *Subsequent Performances* (New York: Viking, 1986); Yvonne Noble, ed., *Twentieth-Century Interpretations of "The Beggar's Opera": A Collection of Critical Essays* (Englewood Cliffs, NJ: Prentice-Hall, 1975); Michael Romain, *A Profile of Jonathan Miller* (New York: Cambridge University Press, 1992).

See also THE THREEPENNY OPERA

BELL, BOOK, AND CANDLE (1950)
John Van Druten

Bell, Book, and Candle (1958)

Directed by Richard Quine

Adapted by Daniel Taradash

Cast: James Stewart (Shepherd Henderson), Kim Novak (Gillian Holroyd), Jack Lemmon (Nicky Holroyd), Ernie Kovacs (Sidney Redlitch), Hermione Gingold (Mrs. De Pass), Elsa Lanchester (Queenie), Janice Rule (Merle Kittridge)

Length: 106 minutes

Bell, Book, and Candle, which was first presented in New York in 1950, is set entirely in Gillian's Murray Hill apartment in New York. When Shepherd enters her apartment to complain about her Aunt Queenie's behavior (she has somehow entered his apartment), he does not realize that Gillian, Queenie, and Nicky, her brother, are witches. Gillian, who is attracted to Shepherd and who learns that he is slated to marry Merle, a college enemy of hers, puts a spell on Shepherd, who falls in love with her and cancels the wedding. Shepherd proposes to her, and Gillian accepts, despite misgivings about giving up her life as a witch. When she discovers that Nicky intends to help Redlitch, a witchcraft author, write a book about witches in New York City, she uses her cat, Pyewacket, her "familiar," to prevent its publication. Gillian tries unsuccessfully to convince Shepherd that she's a witch, but Shepherd believes her only when an angry Nicky corroborates her story. After a $5,000 "cure" by Mrs. De Pass, another witch, Shepherd returns to Gillian's apartment to say good-bye, but when Gillian finds that Pyewacket has left, she knows she has lost her powers. When Shepherd sees her blush and cry, impossible acts for a witch, he realizes that she really loves him, and they embrace. While the film adaptation retains most of the dialogue from the play, it does take the action outside so that the audience sees Shepherd's office, Manhattan venues, Mrs. De Pass' "haunted" house, and the Zodiac Club, where witches convene. In fact, the film adds a meeting between Shepherd and Merle, who does not appear in the play, with Gillian's family. That meeting, which establishes Merle as a vicious snob, compensates for the film's omission of Merle's vindictive letter to Shepherd's partner. In the play when Shepherd discovers the letter, he rejects Merle; in the film he simply loses interest in her. The only other changes involve additions to the roles played by Lemmon, Kovacs, Gingold, and Lanchester, all accomplished comics. *(T. L. E.)*

Resources: Gordon Gow, *Hollywood in the Fifties* (New York: A. S. Barnes, 1971); Larry Kleno, *Kim Novak on Camera* (San Diego: Barnes, 1980); Don Widener, *Lemmon: A Biography* (New York: Macmillan, 1975).

BENT (1980)
Martin Sherman

Bent (1997)

Directed by Sean Mathias

Adapted by Martin Sherman

Cast: Clive Owen (Max), Lothaire Bluteau (Horst), Brian Webber (Rudy), Ian McKellen (Uncle Freddie), Jude Law (Stormtrooper), Mick Jagger (Greta)

Length: 104 minutes

Rated: NC-17

The original play was mainly a two-hander, involving two homosexuals, Max and Horst, falling in love at the Dachau prison camp during World War II. The first act is set in decadent Berlin in 1934, evoking that city's gay atmosphere before the Nazis began their campaign of antihomosexual repression and terror. Max (Clive Owen) picks up a German soldier at a nightclub owned by Greta (Mick Jagger), a drag queen, and then takes the soldier to the home he shares with his partner, Rudy (Brian Webber). The next day the Gestapo comes and kills the soldier, but Max and Rudy escape. Eventually, they are captured and sent by train to Dachau. During this train journey to the concentration camp, Max meets Horst (Lothaire Bluteau), who later becomes his work partner. They fall in love and manage to stay sane by reciting erotic dialogues privately, while being watched by their captors. Sherman rewrote the play for the screen during a monthlong rehearsal-workshop with the film's cast. One challenge was to integrate the concentration camp setting of act 2 with the Berlin setting of act 1. "Most plays are claustrophobic," Sherman noted, "and that's why they are so hard to turn into film." In act 2 Max and Horst are given the pointless task of moving piles of rocks, symbolic action onstage that had to be transformed into realistic action located outdoors around an abandoned power station in Glasgow, where the film was shot. Above all, Sherman did not want to approach the drama merely as filmed theatre, because, he explained, "if it's done really well with impeccable actors, it can look like a definitive production of the play, and then why would anyone want to do the play on the stage again?" The adaptation was experimental in the collaborative and extensive rehearsal approach Sherman took with the film's cast. Director Sean Mathias had revived the play in London with Ian McKellen for the National Theatre in 1990. (*J. M. W.*)

Resources: Alexandra Bandon, "Thinking Past the Barriers to Making a Movie of 'Bent,' " *New York Times* (30 November 1997): Sec. II, 17–18; Stephen Holden, "Sent from Gay Berlin to Labor at Dachau," *New York Times* (29 November 1997): B5.

BETRAYAL (1978)
Harold Pinter

Betrayal (1983)

Directed by David Jones

Adapted by Harold Pinter

Cast: Ben Kingsley (Robert), Patricia Hodge (Emma), Jeremy Irons (Jerry)

Length: 95 minutes

Rated: R

The play, first directed by Peter Hall for London's National Theatre in 1978, begins in 1977, when two adulterous lovers, Jerry, a writer, and Emma, married to Jerry's publisher, Robert, meet two years after their affair has ended. Throughout the following scenes, the action moves backward in time, tracing the history of their affair to 1968, when drunken Jerry first flirted with Emma while a party was going on at Emma and Robert's house. The design of the play is innovative and complex, but the direction by David Jones is straightforward, although the film follows the play's chronological reversals, starting in the present and moving back into the past. Even though the film follows the text quite closely, Pinter adds two scenes, one with Robert and Jerry on the telephone, when Robert invites Jerry to lunch on the day Jerry is to meet Emma, and another in which Jerry and Emma examine the flat they rent for their romantic assignations. Robert is far more subtle than Jerry, and it is no wonder that Emma eventually tires of her lover after their betrayal has pretty well wrecked her marriage. British director David Jones had worked for thirteen years with the Royal Shakespeare Company before turning to film. Pinter had worked with Jones before and took an active interest in the film production, visiting the sets and examining the rushes while the film was made.

The film, which was reshaped by the playwright, is about as authoritative as any adaptation could be, besides being splendidly acted. This is a worthy adaptation. *(J. M. W.)*

Resource: John Russell Brown, *A Short Guide to Modern British Drama* (London: Heinemann, 1982).

THE BIG KNIFE (1949)
Clifford Odets

The Big Knife (1955)

Directed by Robert Aldrich

Adapted by James Poe

Cast: Jack Palance (Charlie Castle), Ida Lupino (Marian Castle), Wendell Corey (Smiley), Jean Hagen (Connie Bliss), Rod Steiger (Stanley Hoff), Everett Sloane (Nat Danziger)

Length: 111 minutes

The Big Knife, directed by Lee Strasberg, first appeared at New York's National Theatre on 24 February 1949, with John Garfield in the role of Charlie Castle. Obviously based on unfortunate, real-life experiences in the Hollywood studio system, the play was finally adapted in 1955 as an independent Aldrich production. Its attack on the Hollywood machine made it too controversial for any major Hollywood studio to produce. After Burt Lancaster turned down the role of Charlie, the part finally went to Jack Palance. Aldrich and Poe followed Odets' play closely but modified several controversial elements. As in the play, Charlie Castle has had a financially successful, but artistically frustrating, screen career and wishes to avoid another studio long-term contract and return to New York. However, the studio uses his guilt over a hit-and-run accident involving the death of a child to force him to sign a fourteen-year contract. When his marriage suffers under the strain, Charlie begins drinking. The film omits any reference to Marion's late abortion following Charlie's signing a new contract. Charlie's caustic speech about postwar America is absent from the film since it would have been politically incorrect for Cold War America. Furthermore, the screenplay omits Bel Air racism against Charlie's Negro maid, Lucille, when a local store refuses to supply her with the correct-size uniform. The film opens with shots of Bel Air accompanied by Richard Boone's voice-over commentary leading to a helicopter shot of Charlie training like a boxer—an obvious reference to John Garfield in *Body and*

Soul, a reference later reinforced by the boxing movie clip Charlie shows his guests. Like future Aldrich heroes, Charlie has a problem with "survival." Boone tells us, "Charlie sold out his dreams. His problem is he can't forget them." Although the play is claustrophobically set in Charlie's home, Aldrich opens up the action by using outside locations, both to avoid a stifling theatrical interpretation as well as to emphasize implications of Charlie's material and spiritual entrapment until the very end of the film. *(T. W.)*

Resources: Edwin T. Arnold and Eugene L. Miller, *The Films and Career of Robert Aldrich* (Knoxville: University of Tennessee Press, 1986); Albert Wertheim, "Hollywood's Moral Landscape: Clifford Odets' *The Big Knife,*" *American Drama* 7.1 (1997): 67–81.

BILOXI BLUES (1984)
Neil Simon

Biloxi Blues (1988)

Directed by Mike Nichols

Adapted by Neil Simon

Cast: Matthew Broderick (Eugene Morris Jerome), Christopher Walken (Sgt. Merwin J. Toomey), Penelope Ann Miller (Daisy Hannigan), Matt Mulhern (Joseph Wykowski), Park Overall (Rowena), Corey Parker (Arnold Epstein), Markus Flanagan (Roy Selridge), Casey Siemaszko (Don Carney)

Length: 105 minutes

Rated: PG-13

Biloxi Blues was first presented on 8 December 1984 at the Ahmanson Theatre, Los Angeles, and on 28 March 1985 at the Neil Simon Theatre, New York City. The production was directed by Gene Saks. In 1985 *Biloxi Blues* won Tony Awards in all three of the categories for which it was nominated: Neil Simon (Best Play); Gene Saks (Director); Barry Miller (Actor, Featured Role–Play). The 1988 film version, having such a distinguished pedigree, was directed by Mike Nichols and brought many of the original Broadway cast onto the big screen, including Matthew Broderick, Matt Mulhern, and Penelope Ann Miller. In spite of his Tony Award, Barry Miller's role of Arnold Epstein was given to Corey Parker for the film, and Alan Ruck, whose career got a jump start by leaving the Broadway production of *Biloxi Blues* to film *Ferris Bueller's Day Off* with Matthew Broderick, was passed over for the film version in favor of Casey Siemaszko.

Biloxi Blues is part two of Neil Simon's comedic autobiographical trilogy, which also includes *Brighton Beach Memoirs* and *Broadway Bound*. Simon's play explores the experiences of his alter ego Eugene as he battles his way through the rigors of army basic training during World War II in Biloxi, Mississippi. Reading the play version of *Biloxi Blues* can't help but make one laugh out loud as Eugene experiences everything from the oppressive heat of Biloxi, Mississippi, to the discovery that sexual intercourse might actually consist of more than seventeen different positions. In anticipation of someday becoming a recognized author, Eugene makes a practice of religiously keeping a journal of his experiences, which allows author Neil Simon to have Eugene interact both with the other characters on stage as well as with the theatrical audience. On the first page of the script, Simon instructs us: "(All set pieces are representational, stylized and free-flowing. We have a lot of territory to cover here . . .)." Indeed, he does. *Biloxi Blues* is a two-act play in fourteen scenes, and the representational style was a huge help in not handicapping the transfer to film. Anything we "imagined" seeing in the play onstage became visually depicted on film. Mike Nichols does a marvelous job of keeping the Simon play flowing. Dialogue that Neil Simon added to the film version, which resonates so clearly with veterans, is in Eugene's speech at the end of the film as he is riding back home on the train: "As I look back now, a lot of years later, I realize my time in the Army was the happiest time of my life. God knows not because I liked the Army, and there sure was nothing to like about a war. I liked it for the most selfish reason of all. Because I was young. We all were. . . . I didn't really like most of those guys then, but today I love every damn one of them. Life is weird, you know." *(J. D.)*

Resources: Neil Simon, *Biloxi Blues* (New York: Random House, 1984); Neil Simon, *Rewrites, a Memoir* (New York: Simon and Schuster, 1996).

THE BIRTHDAY PARTY (1958)
Harold Pinter

The Birthday Party (1968)

Directed by William Friedkin

Adapted by Harold Pinter

Cast: Robert Shaw (Stanley Webber), Sydney Tafler (Nat Goldberg), Patrick

Magee (McCann), Dandy Nichols (Meg Boles), Moultrie Kelsall (Peter Boles), Helen Fraser (Lulu)

Length: 124 minutes

Rated: M

When this comedy of menace and mystification opened at the Lyric Theatre, Hammersmith, the London *Sunday Times* reviewer Henry Hobson was quoted by Ronald Hayman as believing that Harold Pinter "possesses the most original, disturbing, and arresting talent in theatrical London." Critic Ronald Hayman considered the play's "moments of terror and violence . . . the best Pinter has contrived" and its structure "the most impressive he's yet achieved." Pianist Stanley Webber lives at a boardinghouse operated by old-age pensioner Peter Boles and his wife, Meg, who takes a maternal interest in Stanley. When two strangers, Goldberg and McCann, arrive, Stanley appears to be threatened; perhaps they intend to murder him, since Goldberg speaks ambiguously of "doing the job." They organize a birthday party for Stanley, attended by Lulu, a flirtatious neighbor, and a night of drunken revelry follows, which results in a complete breakdown for Stanley. The next day the strangers leave with Stanley, presumably taking him to a doctor. Pinter's adaptation removes the motive for Stanley's retreat to the boardinghouse and any explanation about his earlier associations with the strangers, as well as Stanley's sexual interest in Lulu, which makes the film more puzzling than the play. Stanley seems to be a victim persecuted by Goldberg and McCann, harboring a sense of guilt. This comedy of menace is transformed into what one critic called "a brooding essay in pure paranoia." No context is given, and no background is given for McCann and Goldberg, an Irishman and a Jew, both of them outsiders and possibly homosexual lovers. The film attempts to maintain the claustrophobic stage setting, only slightly expanding the confines of Pinter's one-room set. *(J. M. W.)*

Resources: William Friedkin, *AFI Dialogue on Film* 3.4 (February 1974); Ronald Hayman, *Harold Pinter* (New York: Frederick Ungar, 1973); Nat Segaloff, *Hurricane Billy: The Stormy Life and Films of William Friedkin* (New York: William Morrow, 1990).

BLOOD WEDDING
(BODAS DE SANGRE) (1933)
Federico Garcia Lorca

Bodas de Sangre (1981)

Directed by Carlos Saura

Adapted by Alfredo Manas

Cast: Antonio Gades (Leonardo), Cristina Hoyos (the bride), Juan Antonio Jimeniz (the groom), Pilar Cardenas (the mother)

Length: 71 minutes

Blood Wedding (1933) belongs to the late period of the Spanish playwright Garcia Lorca. Like *Yerma* (1934) and *The House of Bernarda Alba* (1936), it abandons the partisan politics of his early works and concentrates on the collision between erotic passion and societal constraints. Told in three acts (seven scenes), *Blood Wedding* combines stylized diction and poetry with a fantasy world of the supernatural and the surreal. The human and the symbolic move side by side. It begins on the eve of an arranged wedding in the Andalusian countryside between a young man and a woman who was formerly betrothed to another, Leonardo, whose family had murdered the groom's father and brother. The marriage ceremony is interrupted when the bride bolts with Leonardo. The groom and his friends leap onto their horses and pursue them through the forest. Surreal elements dominate the chase sequence in act 3, scene 1, with symbolic characters appearing who represent the light of the moon and the darkness of death. The knife fight that leaves both men dead transpires offstage before the beginning of act 3, scene 2. The anguished bride returns to the slain groom's mother and offers to end her life with the same knife that killed her son. Although Lorca's play was an instant international success, he had little time to enjoy his celebrity. His life was cut tragically short when he was executed in August 1936 by a fascist firing squad. With the assistance of Antonio Gades, Spain's leading dancer-choreographer and former director of the National Ballet of Spain, Carlos Saura filmed a pantomime flamenco ballet version of the Lorca play. This was a bold move, considering the play is so verbally rich in poetic dialogue and songs. Yet Gades' superb choreography, complemented by Teo Escamilla's virtuoso camera work, conveys the essential spirit, if not the literal text, of the play. The film begins with Gades' dance troupe arriving at a studio, where they prepare for a dress rehearsal. While the dancers apply their makeup and don their costumes, their interior voices provide monologues about their past experiences as performers. Out on the dance floor, after Gades leads the assembled troupe through a few practice steps, the ballet proper begins. The action is conveyed entirely through dance pantomime; the only words heard are the song texts performed by offstage singers to the accompaniment of two flamenco guitars. There are no scenery and no props, just the bare stage with three illuminated windows arranged symmetrically across the back wall. Scene divisions are eschewed, and there is only a brief respite midway while the ensemble and the musicians pause for a group photograph. The highlight of the performance is the knife fight (which occurs offstage in the original play) between the groom and his rival. The entire scene is choreographed—*not* photographed—in slow motion as the two men warily circle each other and finally lunge toward each other in their fatal thrusts, falling to the ground in a maddeningly slow descent. The image of the wedding photograph reappears over the concluding credits. Saura and Gades have achieved in dance form what Lorca intended: "a musical orchestration of changing rhythms, folk songs, and lamentations . . . in which there is no concern with psychological motivation but with pagan forces in a primitive pageant of revolt, vengeance, and death" (Lewis 240). *(J. C. T.)*

Resources: Mildred Adams, *Garcia Lorca: Playwright and Poet* (New York: George Braziller, 1977); Allan Lewis, *The Contemporary Theatre: The Significant Playwrights of Our Time* (New York: Crown, 1971).

BOEING BOEING (1960)
Marc Camoletti

Boeing Boeing (1965)

Directed by John Rich

Adapted by Edward Anhalt

Cast: Tony Curtis (Bernard Lawrence), Jerry Lewis (Robert Reed), Thelma Ritter (Bertha), Suzanna Leigh (Vicky), Dany Saval (Jacqueline), Christiane Schmidtmer (Lisa)

Length: 102 minutes

Boeing Boeing was first produced on 10 December 1960 at the Theatre du la Comedié-Caumartin and later appeared in London and Broadway in translation. The original three-act play was set in Bernard's Paris apartment, while the film version opened out the setting to include scenes at Orly Airport, the newspaper offices of Bernard and Robert, and a restaurant and taxi scenes. In the original play, Bernard has an idyllic romantic relationship with three airline hostesses from America, Germany, and France whose flight schedules allow him to conduct his affairs. However, the introduction of new flight schedules due to high-speed airliners, such as the Boeing Boeing, disrupts his carefully planned romantic schedule, leading to a farcical situation where Bernard, his college friend Robert, and worldly-wise maid, Bertha, attempt to prevent the three women's meeting each other in his apartment. The film version changes the nationalities of Bernard, Robert, and Bertha to American, resulting in the casting of Curtis, Lewis, and Ritter, with Ritter's reprising her Stella performance from *Rear Window*. American hostess, Janet, now becomes British hostess, Vicky. The film ends with Bernard and Robert's fleeing the apartment and discovering a female taxi driver whose living situation with two other female workers parallels Bernard's former Edenic world before the introduction of high-speed planes. Jerry Lewis delivers a surprisingly subdued comic performance by complementing Tony Curtis' frustrated romantic lead. He never resorts to the well-known excessive persona of his other comedy films. Furthermore, as Bernard explains to Robert, his plan fits into the romantic ideology espoused by Hollywood cinema since he can enjoy the benefits of romance without being encumbered by its eventual marital conclusion. But despite the heroic attempts by the three major performers to reproduce the Gallic farce tradition that made the original play a success, John Rich's pedestrian direction traps the humor in a television sit-com style. Rich moved into directing in the 1960s after his involvement with *The Dick Van Dyke Show*. But his pedestrian manner of feature film direction soon resulted in his speedy return to television. *(T. W.)*

Resources: Marc Camoletti, "Boeing Boeing," *L'Avant Scene du Theatre* 240 (1961): 1–37; James L. Neibur and Ted Okuda, *The Jerry Lewis Films: An Analytical Filmography of the Innovative Comic* (Jefferson, NC: McFarland, 1994).

BOPHA! (1986)
Percy Mtwa

Bopha! (1993)

Directed by Morgan Freeman

Adapted by Brian Bird and John Wierick

Cast: Danny Glover (Micah Mangena), Malcolm McDowell (DeVilliers), Alfre Woodard (Rosie Mangena), Marius Weyers (Van Tonder), Maynard Eziashi (Zweli Mangena), Malick Bowens (Pule Rampa)

Length: 120 minutes
Rated: PG

Mtwa's *Bopha!*, which means both arrest and detention in Zulu, takes place in Moroka Township, South Africa, in 1980. The three main characters are Njandini, a black policeman; Naledi, the policeman's brother; and Zwelakhe, the policeman's son—the actors who play these roles also play, by donning mustaches and hats of different colors, the roles of twelve other minor characters. Njandini, who, in the course of training black police recruits, declares that the derogatory term "pig" is an acronym for pride, intelligence, and guts, wants his son to join the police force, but his son joins a student rebellion about Afrikaans being the only official language. Njandini's brother, who joins the police only as an alternative to a jail sentence, also rebels against the discriminatory laws; he arrests a white man. Because of harsh, repressive measures by the Security Forces, the student rebellion turns into bloody riots, and Njandini's wife is injured by gunfire. When he finally realizes that his job has made him an enemy of his people, Njandini resigns his post and joins his brother and son in a ceremonial song. The film adaptation significantly alters the play. The multiple-role playing is discarded, characters' names are changed, the character of the uncle is omitted, the action is taken outside to capture the African landscape, the Security Forces are demonized, and the upbeat ending is changed. In the film, the confrontation between Micah (Danny Glover) and his son, Zweli (Maynard Eziashi), is given more context; and the effects of Micah's actions on the family are demonstrated, particularly in terms of how Rosie (Alfre Woodard), Micah's wife, is treated by the community. In fact, the film generally provides more motivation and complexity to the characters: for example, Van Tonder (Marius Weyers), the sympathetic, liberal white commanding officer, initially opposes the harsh measures of DeVilliers (Malcolm McDowell) but reluctantly relents when confronted with threats to career and family. The most significant departure from the text of the play occurs at the end of the film when Micah and Rosie travel to an outdoor rally where Zweli addresses the crowd. As his son speaks, Micah is stabbed and killed by blacks who see him as the enemy. On the beautiful African horizon a convoy of police vehicles head for the rally and another bloody confrontation. *(T. L. E.)*

Resources: Michael Medved, "Bopha!" *New York Post* (24 September 1993): 40; Kenneth Tynan, "Bopha!" *Los Angeles Times* (24 September 1993): Calendar, 16.

BORN YESTERDAY (1946)
Garson Kanin

Born Yesterday (1950)

Directed by George Cukor

Adapted by Albert Mannheimer, and Garson Kanin [uncredited]

Cast: Judy Holliday (Billie Dawn), Broderick Crawford (Harry Brock), William Holden (Paul Verrall), Howard St. John (Jim Devery)

Length: 102 minutes

After Judy Holliday made her mark on Broadway in Garson Kanin's play *Born Yesterday*, George Cukor, who was to direct the film version, invited her to recreate her performance in the film. As Billie Dawn, Holliday gave an Oscar-winning performance in which she rendered an archetypal portrait of a beautiful, but dumb, blond. An ex-chorine, Billie is the mistress of a wealthy junk dealer, Harry Brock (Broderick Crawford), who is determined to buy his way into Washington politics. Harry engages Paul Verrall (William Holden) to give the scantily educated Billie an elementary course in political science, so that she will not embarrass him when he is entertaining the politicians he hopes to bribe. Proving that she was not "born yesterday" after all, Billie learns enough from Paul to know that what Harry is doing is vile, and she threatens to expose his plans unless he abandons them. The first draft of the screenplay for the film was done by Albert Mannheimer, who presumably worked on the assumption that a screenwriter is not exercising his own creativity unless he makes significant alterations in the work that he is adapting for the screen. Cukor confided that he took one good look at this version of the screenplay and turned it down flat, since the screenwriter had jettisoned excellent material from Kanin's play. He then asked Garson Kanin to take a hand in fashioning the script. Kanin, who received no screen credit for composing the final shooting script for the movie, did more than simply restore some of the material that Mannheimer had excised from the play. Taking his cue from references in the original dialogue to the Jefferson Memorial and other Washington landmarks that Billie mentions visiting, he opened out the play for the screen by constructing a number of scenes that were filmed on location at these very sites. Billie's tour of the city's monuments enables her to discover America's meaningful past and hence to reject Harry's attempts to manipulate government officials as a perversion of the democratic principles on which America was founded. Throughout the movie Judy

Holliday demonstrates her ability to make us laugh at Billie's dim-witted remarks, at the very same time she is stirring our compassion for Billie's vulnerable stupidity. In one scene the apelike Harry becomes so exasperated with Billie that he strikes her savagely across the face. As she whimpers and cries softly, we realize just how deeply the actress has made us care for Billie. Cukor admired Holliday's knack for touching a moviegoer's heart as well as their funny bone: "It is a rare quality, possessed by only the truly great comediennes," he noted. "And Judy had it to a superlative degree." *(G. D. P.)*

Resources: Emmanuel Levy, *George Cukor, Master of Elegance: Hollywood's Legendary Director and His Stars* (New York: Morrow, 1994); Patrick McGilligan, *George Cukor: A Double Life* (New York: St. Martin's Press, 1997).

Born Yesterday (1993)

Directed by Luis Mandoki

Adapted by Douglas McGrath

Cast: Melanie Griffith (Billie Dawn), John Goodman (Harry Brock), Don Johnson (Paul Verrall), Edward Herrmann (Ed Devery)

Length: 102 minutes

Rated: PG

Luis Mandoki's *Born Yesterday* is more of a remake of George Cukor's adaptation (1950) than an adaptation of Garson Kanin's play about a former chorus girl who is transformed, to her corrupt boyfriend's detriment, into a caring, intelligent woman by a newspaper correspondent. (See previous entry for a plot summary of the Kanin play.) Like Cukor's adaptation, Mandoki's opens up the play by adding outside settings. Instead of photographing Washington landmarks, however, which would relate to Billy's developing knowledge of history and politics, he adds sequences at a health facility and nightclub (both settings seem designed to demonstrate the physical fitness of the overweight Harry), one at a public radio station where Billie reveals her lack of knowledge, and two party scenes where Billie impresses Washington society by relying on Paul's eight one-liner answers and by memorizing, to the tune of "The Twelve Days of Christmas," the amendments to the Constitution. The last two scenes and the "Teach Me Tonight" recording on the soundtrack reflect Paul's role as Pygmalion, the sculptor who molds the perfect woman. Despite some updating in the dialogue ("Eastern bloc," which Billie thinks is a city block) and some deft comic touches, Mandoki's adaptation is more ominous than Cukor's. As Harry Brock, John Goodman is too physically intimidating and too violent (especially when he assaults Billie) to explain Billie's staying with him. The role of Ed Devery, the once-promising young lawyer who has been "dead" for the twelve years he's been in Harry's employ, is also expanded, stressing the debilitating effect Washington has on people; and instead of Kanin's one corrupt senator, Mandoki supplies several, also emphasizing Washington corruption. *(T. L. E.)*

Resources: Vincent Canby, *"Born Yesterday," New York Times* (26 April 1993): C17; Leonard Klady, *"Born Yesterday," Variety* (29 March 1993): 82.

THE BOYS IN THE BAND (1968)
Mart Crowley

The Boys in the Band (1970)

Directed by William Friedkin

Adapted by Mart Crowley

Cast: Kenneth Nelson (Michael), Frederick Combs (Donald), Cliff Gorman (Emory), Keith Prentice (Larry), Laurence Luckinbill (Hank), Reuben Greene (Bernard), Leonard Frey (Harold), Peter White (Alan), Robert La Tourneaux (Cowboy)

Length: 119 minutes

Rated: R

Mart Crowley's comedy of gay manners opened in New York during the spring of 1968 and closed early in September more than two years later at its Theatre Four venue. The play, featuring eight explicitly homosexual characters, proved revolutionary in offering mainstream audiences an up-close and personal view of alternative lifestyles at the end of the volatile 1960s. That it ended its run a year after the Stonewall Riots of 1969, which heralded the social and sexual revolution of gay liberation and subsequent identity politics, makes this play something of a watershed between two cultural eras.

The plot is simple. Alan (Peter White), a presumably straight former Georgetown University roommate, visits Michael (Kenneth Nelson) unexpectedly while the latter is hosting a birthday party for Harold (Leonard Frey), who describes himself as "an ugly, pock-marked Jew fairy." All the celebrants are homosexual men. Emory (Cliff Gorman), the most effeminate of the men, for example, presents Harold with a male hustler, a "midnight cowboy" (Robert La Tourneaux), as his gift for the evening. In the course of the night those attending participate in an affairs-of-the-heart game wherein each player must telephone the one person he truly believes he has loved. This pursuit results in numerous emotional, humorous, and theatrical revelations from the past. Despite Michael's belief that Alan is a closeted gay man and will call another male of their acquaintance, his out-of-town visitor calls his wife to declare his love for her. Michael has no one to call. As Harold explains, Michael is a homosexual and does not want to be. This theme of self-hatred has presented problems in dealing with Crowley's play over the years, yet it is understandable in the context of social oppression and hostility of the time period. In retrospect, Crowley's play may too often seem to affirm rather than challenge the straight world's stereotypical judgment of gay men; nevertheless, in giving "heterosexual eavesdropping," as Stanley Kauffmann termed it, on gay representation, the play presented strength, sympathy, and credibility.

The film version included just below the title in its advertising: ". . . is not a musical." William Friedkin's rather gaudy direction might suggest otherwise, as does the syncopated rendition of Cole Porter's "Anything Goes," which accompanies the opening sequence, which consists of a series of brief shots of the "boys" activities prior to their appearance at the party. Here Friedkin exhibits iconic clues to establish gay identity such as showing Michael, a bit too well attired, shopping and Emory walking a poodle. This last action is perhaps inspired by Michael's comment in Crowley's playscript: "If one is of the masculine gender, a poodle is the insignia of one's deviation."

The film version largely preserves the interior setting of the stage version. Memorable performances like Leonard Frey's Harold and Cliff Gorman's Emory endure in a more permanent form than theatre permits. The AIDS epidemic devastated this cast in subsequent years with the loss of five of the original nine actors. The movie remains subtle and persuasive in ways that might not have been recognized at the time of its first release. *(E. T. J)*

Resources: Richard Dyer, ed., *Gays and Film* (London: BFI, 1977); Stanley Kauffmann, Review of "The Boys in the Band," *New Republic* (18 April 1970): 20, 28–29.

BRIEF ENCOUNTER

See STILL LIFE

BRIGHTON BEACH MEMOIRS (1982)
Neil Simon

Brighton Beach Memoirs (1986)

Directed by Gene Saks

Adapted by Neil Simon

Cast: Blythe Danner (Kate Jerome), Bob Dishy (Jack Jerome), Brian Drillinger (Stanley Jerome), Judith Ivey (Blanche Jerome), Jonathan Silverman (Eugene Jerome), Lisa Waltz (Nora Jerome), Stacey Glick (Laurie Jerome), Fyvush Finkel (Mr. Greenblatt), Steven Hill (Mr. Stroheim), Alan Weeks (Andrew)

Length: 110 minutes

Rated: PG-13

Brighton Beach Memoirs was first performed on 10 December 1982 at the Abmanson Theatre, Los Angeles, and then at New York's Alvin Theatre. All performances were directed by Gene Saks and featured Matthew Broderick as Eugene and Joyce Van Patten as Blanche. The original play's sets involved the porch exterior and the interior of the Jerome house. Drawing upon memories of his early life, Simon used the real-life bickering between two families living under one roof as the basis of a play, "partly because the small war that was being played out in the small bungalow was a microcosm of the harrowing great war that was then engulfing the world." But Simon regarded it as one of his lesser works and scarcely mentions it in his autobiography. Both play and film operate as an exercise in family nostalgia little different from Woody Allen's film *Radio Days*. Gene Saks opens out the original play in several ways by having Eugene vary his theatrical, direct-to-audience address by using occasional cinematic voiceovers, depicting Brighton Beach's lower-middle-class ethnic environment by including street scenes outside the house, Stanley's work environment, the Brighton Beach station where Jack arrives exhausted from a day's work and where Stanley leaves to join the army. The film also includes other characters unseen in the play such as Mr. Murphy and his mother, Stanley's German boss Mr. Stroheim, and his unfortunate black worker Andrew, whom Stanley supports. It also includes a poignant scene not in the play where Mrs. Murphy directly informs Blanche about her son's involvement in a drunken driving accident, which ruins the intended evening date and possible future romance. The Murphys intend to move upstate so that the son can attend a rehabilitation clinic. As was his practice in adapting other works such as *California Suite*, Simon adds additional dialogue for scenes not in the original play. The adaptation is generally faithful to the play's mood, but an overemphatic and intrusive musical score often mars the film and ruins scenes where the dialogue is often sufficiently well written to stand on its own feet. *(T. W.)*

Resources: Nina Darnton, "Jonathan Silverman and Neil Simon: A Not-So-Odd Couple," *New York Times* (28 December 1986): 9, 19; Neil Simon, *Rewrites: A Memoir* (New York: Simon and Schuster, 1996).

THE BROWNING VERSION (1948)
Terence Rattigan

The Browning Version (1994)

Directed by Mike Figgis

Adapted by Ronald Harwood

Cast: Albert Finney (Andrew Crocker-Harris), Greta Scacchi (Laura Crocker-Harris), Matthew Modine (Frank Hunter), Ben Silverstone (John Taplow)

Length: 97 minutes

Rated: R

Cloistered buildings, hallowed halls, a game of cricket, and the retirement of a prep school master constitute the background of Terence Rattigan's gently moving 1948 drama of wintry discontents. Andrew Crocker-Harris is facing several crises: a heart condition is forcing his retirement as master of the Lower Fifth, where he is feared and hated by his pupils; his wife, Millie, is having an affair with a younger master; and his pension is in jeopardy. The one ray of light in this miserable existence is the respect and affection of one of his pupils, John Taplow, who gives Crocker-Harris a copy of Robert Browning's version of *Agamemnon* (hence, the play's title). Newly inspired, Crocker-Harris defies the authorities and refuses to defer to a younger colleague when it comes time to deliver his leaving speech. Two film adaptations have been made. Anthony Asquith directed a 1951 film version, adapted by Rattigan himself and starring Michael Redgrave as Crocker-Harris. The Mike Figgis/Ronald Harwood version updates the play to the 1990s and casts Albert Finney as Crocker-Harris. Although photographed on location amid the lush colors of the Dorset County countryside, the film remains true to the rather bleak tone of the play. Finney's flint-hard face and chunky body have the texture and substance of the stone-and-ivy walls. His best scenes occur when he reads Aeschuylus' *Agamemnon* to his students. Then, as the lurid tale unfolds of Clytemnestra's infidelity to her husband and her subsequent cold-blooded murder of him (a tale with more than a few parallels with his own troubled marriage), he shakes off his inertia and comes alive. *That* is the Crocker-Harris to whom young Taplow pays tribute when he presents him with Browning's translation. "From a distance God looks down kindly upon such a gentle man," reads the boy's inscription in the book. No matter that Mrs. Crocker-Harris (here renamed "Laura")—glacially portrayed by Greta Scacchi—tries to spoil the moment. It remains a benediction that graces the rest of the movie, a tiny blaze from which we (and Crocker-Harris) can warm our cold hands. To the movie's credit, it remains true to Rattigan's insistence that none of these characters are entirely likable. Unfortunately, a jarring note (as it were) comes from Mark Isham's music score, which tends to underscore dramatic moments with a sledgehammer emphasis, marring the otherwise restrained quality of the performances. *(J. C. T.)*

Resources: Geoffrey Wansell, *Terence Rattigan* (New York: St. Martin's Press, 1991); Bertram A. Young, *The Rattigan Version: Terence Rattigan and the Theatre of Character* (New York: Atheneum, 1986).

BUFFALO BILL AND THE INDIANS, OR, SITTING BULL'S HISTORY LESSON

See INDIANS

BUS STOP (1955)
William Inge

Bus Stop (1956)

Directed by Joshua Logan

Adapted by George Axelrod

Cast: Don Murray (Bo), Marilyn Monroe (Cherie), Arthur O'Connell (Virgil), Betty Field (Grace), Robert Bray (Carl), Hope Lange (Elma)

Length: 94 minutes

Inge's *Bus Stop*, which had its origin in his earlier *People in the Wind*, was radically altered when it was translated to film. In the play there is just one setting, a street-corner restaurant in a town thirty miles west of Kansas

City, Missouri. Because of a blizzard farther west, the bus stops at a restaurant at 1:00 A.M. and the play ends at about 6:00 A.M the same day. In those five hours Inge uses his cast to explore the nature of love. Bo Decker, a naive, boisterous, young ranch owner, is abducting Cherie, a dancer at the Blue Dragon night club in Kansas City. Dr. Gerald Lyman, a drunken college professor and three-time marital loser, pursues Elma, a young high school student/waitress. Carl, the bus driver, gets together with Grace, a lonely "grass widow"/waitress. By the end of the three-act play Bo, who has met and been "familiar with" Cherie in Kansas City, has learned to temper his enthusiasm with gallantry and sensitivity, partly because Will, the sheriff, has beaten him in a fistfight. When the bus leaves, Cherie, touched by his changed character, goes with him. Lyman, who has suffered a breakdown during his *Romeo and Juliet* scene in the impromptu "floor show," abandons his plans to seduce Elma. The most touching "love' is exhibited by Virgil Blessing, Bo's mentor and guide, who stays behind while Bo and Cherie head for Montana. The film begins in Montana, when Bo and Virgil are preparing for the rodeo in Phoenix. On their way by bus, they stop at Grace's diner. In Phoenix, Bo wins four events and $4,000 and meets Cherie, a self-proclaimed chanteuse and drink hustler, and decides that she is the "angel" he seeks. Attracted to Bo but unwilling to give up her Hollywood career plans, symbolized by a straight line on a map from the Ozarks to the West Coast, Cherie is unwilling to make a detour to Montana. Bo packs her on the Montana bus, which stops again at Grace's diner—the rest of the film encompasses all three acts of Inge's play. There are some significant omissions, partly because so much of the film takes place in Phoenix. Lyman is deleted, and with him the attempted seduction of Elma. Will, the sheriff, is omitted, and the function of softening up Bo is transferred to Carl, the driver. As a result, the film retains its focus on the Cherie-Bo relationship. The changes, including the rodeo scenes and Cherie's performance, make the film more visually entertaining and less claustrophobic than the play. (*T. L. E.*)

Resources: Michael Conway, *The Films of Marilyn Monroe* (New York: Citadel, 1964); Joshua Logan, *Josh: My Up and Down, In and Out Life* (New York: Delacorte Press, 1976).

BUTLEY (1971)
Simon Gray

Butley (1973)

Directed by Harold Pinter
Adapted by Simon Gray

Cast: Alan Bates (Ben Butley), Jessica Tandy (Edna Shaft), Richard O'Callaghan (Joey Keyston), Susan Engel (Anne Butley), Michael Byrne (Reg Nuttall), Georgina Hale (Miss Heasman), Simon Rouse (Gardner)

Length: 130 minutes

In 1971 Harold Pinter agreed to direct Simon Gray's play in the West End. Their successful collaboration led to the production of this film as one of the eight plays adapted for the screen for the first and only season of Ely Landau's American Film Theatre. It was Pinter's first (and only) film as director, and yet reviewers like Jay Cocks described it as "a quite superior directorial debut" (*Time*, 29 April 1974). Pinter has acknowledged his debt to Joseph Losey for the closeness of their collaboration on *The Servant*, *Accident*, and *The Go-Between*. It also helped that Gerry Fisher, who had served as director of photography on the latter two works, was hired for *Butley*, as was art director Carmen Dillon. Pinter had relished being part of the filmmaking process in his work with Losey, so he treated Simon Gray accordingly in the shooting of this film: "After each take the first person I looked at was, on the whole, not the cameraman or the operator or the continuity girl or the sound mixer, but Simon Gray" (*Cinebill*, 8). The film opens up Ben Butley's world a little from the play. In a compelling opening sequence, we see the self-destructive environment in which he exists: a lack of shaving cream and an old razor blade result in a cut chin and blood stanched with a ragged piece of paper. However, the impulse to provide a realistic context for Butley's situation does not lead Pinter and Gray to undermine the intensity and spareness of the work. It remains sharply focused on the claustrophobic reality of Butley's office as it reflects his self-destructive behavior. Alan Bates, recreating stage triumphs in the West End and on Broadway, brilliantly interprets the unraveling of this academic, whose caustic wit has become an autonomic protection against self-knowledge. Simon Gray simply loved the film. In the program issued at the British premiere, he was quoted as saying that "Harold's film is more faithful to the original text than the play, because with a film one can control what an audience sees. Whereas on the stage certain nuances might escape an audience, in the film one can highlight them as subtly or definitely as the director may wish." (*W. L. H.*)

Resources: *American Film Theatre Cinebill* 1.7 (January 1974): 1–28; Michael Billington, *The Life and Work of Harold Pinter* (London: Faber and Faber, 1996).

CABARET (1966)
Joe Masterhoff (based on the stage play *I Am a Camera* by John Van Druten and the writings of Christopher Isherwood)

Cabaret (1972)

Directed by Bob Fosse

Adapted by Jay Presson Allen

Cast: Liza Minnelli (Sally Bowles), Michael York (Brian Roberts), Helmut Griem (Maximilian von Heune), Joel Grey (Master of Ceremonies), Fritz Wepper (Fritz Wendel), Maria Berenson (Natalia Landauer), Elisabeth Neumann-Viertel (Fraulein Schneider), Sigrid Von Richthofen (Fraulein Maur), Gerd Vesperman (Bobby)

Length: 124 minutes

Rated: PG

Masterhoff's *Cabaret*, based on Van Druten's *I Am a Camera*, itself an adaptation of Isherwood's Berlin stories, appeared in New York in 1966. The play, set in Berlin in 1929–1930, depicts the growing power of the Nazi movement and its impact on the lives of Berliners and expatriates;

but, because of the stage mirrors, which allow the audience to see itself, the play implicates audiences in the plot. After a welcome to the cabaret, the Kit Kat Klub, the play shifts to Clifford Bradshaw, an American writer en route by train to Berlin, and Ernst Ludwig, a smuggler who becomes Clifford's friend. Clifford moves into one of Frau Schneider's rooms and is joined by Sally Bowles, a singer at the Kit Kat Klub. When Sally becomes pregnant, Clifford agrees to a smuggling run to raise some money for baby expenses. Meanwhile, the romance between Frau Schneider and Herr Schultz, her Jewish tenant, culminates in an engagement party, which is ruined by Ernst's arrival with a swastika armband. Because of Nazi harassment, Frau Schneider breaks her engagement, and Sally, who wants to stay in Berlin, has an abortion. Disillusioned, Clifford leaves Berlin by train. As this plot proceeds, Masterhoff intersperses scenes from the Kit Kat Klub, where the musical numbers become more ominous and anti-Semitic. (One number has the emcee comparing a gorilla to a Jew, and another one, "Tomorrow Belongs to Me," becomes more threatening each time it is performed.) At the end of the play Clifford is joined expressionistically on the train by the emcee and the girl orchestra and the characters from the first scene: "German uniforms and swastika armbands are apparent." Fosse's film adaptation is less a musical than a drama in which only two characters, Sally (Liza Minnelli) and the emcee (Joel Grey), have singing roles; and their songs are performed onstage. The only other song is by a young, blonde German youth whose "Tomorrow Belongs to Me," performed at an outdoor café, becomes increasingly frightening as the audience joins him in what becomes a nationalistic foreshadowing of Nazi dominance. The film drops the Schneider-Schultz subplot, substituting a romance between wealthy Jewish Natalia Landauer (Marisa Berenson) and Fritz Wepper (Fritz Wendel), a "closet" Jew; and they are subjected to Nazi abuse. Clifford becomes Brian Roberts (Michael York), a writer who must confront his bisexuality (the film thereby alludes to Isherwood's sexual preferences) after he and Sally are both seduced by Maximilian von Heune (Helmut Griem). The Nazi theme is intensified, particularly at the Kit Kat Klub, where patrons and performers (the dancers goose-step) become increasingly Nazi; and the sexuality and sexual ambiguity of the performers and performances (Fosse's trademark erotic choreography) are exaggerated. The acting is superb, and Joel Grey won an Oscar for Best Supporting Actor. Although the play was a critical success, the film surpasses it in quality. (*T. L. E.*)

Resources: Martin Gottfried, *All His Jazz: The Life and Death of Bob Fosse* (New York: Bantam Books, 1990); Kevin Boyd Grubb, *Razzle Dazzle: The Life and Work of Bob Fosse* (New York: St. Martin's Press, 1989).

See also I AM A CAMERA

CAESAR AND CLEOPATRA (1906)
George Bernard Shaw

Caesar and Cleopatra (1945)

Directed and produced by Gabriel Pascal

Adapted by George Bernard Shaw

Cast: Claude Rains (Caesar), Vivien Leigh (Cleopatra), Cecil Parker (Britannus)

Length: 135 minutes

Shaw's *Caesar and Cleopatra* had its American debut in New York in 1906. Set primarily in Alexandria, Egypt, the play concerns Caesar's meeting with Cleopatra in 48 B.C. and the following five months, culminating in Caesar's leaving Egypt. The play has both a prologue and an alternative to the prologue, both of which serve as exposition and political commentary. Caesar meets Cleopatra, who is presented as a precocious child, at the Sphinx, and she uses Caesar to depose her brother, Ptolemy. Subsequent events include political infighting, Cleopatra's being enclosed in a carpet, fighting between the Egyptians and Roman soldiers, the burning of the library at Alexandria, Caesar's swimming escape from the lighthouse, a table-rapping seance, and Caesar's promising to send Mark Antony to Cleopatra. While the play, which is subtitled "A History," deals with Egypt, it also includes many pointed barbs about modern life. A nationalistic Egyptian shouts, "Egypt for the Egyptians!"—surely, a typical conservative slogan—and Caesar is busy at one point "settling the Jewish question." Throughout the play Shaw undermines solemnity: Britannus, Caesar's nationalistic Englishman, is concerned about Caesar's postswim appearance, and Caesar almost forgets Cleopatra when he leaves. While Shaw seems bent on suggesting analogies between ancient and modern civilization, Pascal goes to great pains to present a historically accurate film adaptation through costuming and spectacular sets. Shaw's cinematic additions essentially show events that occur offstage in the play and provide smooth transitions between the play's acts and scenes. Little was cut from the play aside from some satire directed at Britannus, and the complex political and military situation was simplified. Because of the lavish sets and costumes, the play was the most expensive film made in Great Britain at the time; and because Shaw and Pascal retained so much of the theatrical dialogue, the film was a critical and financial disaster. It is, according to Donald P. Costello, "the least cinematic of all three Shaw-Pascal film adaptations." (*T. L. E.*)

Resources: Donald P. Costello, *The Serpent's Eye: Shaw and the Cinema* (Notre Dame, IN: University of Notre Dame Press, 1965); Valerie Pascal, *The Disciple and His Devil* (New York: McGraw-Hill, 1970).

CALIFORNIA SUITE (1976)
Neil Simon

California Suite (1978)

Directed by Herbert Ross

Adapted by Neil Simon

Cast: Jane Fonda (Hannah Warren), Alan Alda (Bill Warren), Michael Caine (Sidney Cochran), Maggie Smith (Diana Barrie), Walter Matthau (Marvin Michaels), Elaine May (Millie Michaels), Richard Pryor (Dr. Chauncey Gump), Bill Cosby (Dr. Willis Panama), James Coburn (cameo)

Length: 102 minutes

Rated: PG

Performed in Los Angeles and New York from April to June 1976 and directed by Gene Saks, *California Suite* represented Simon's return to the form he utilized successfully in *Plaza Suite*, namely, a series of one-act plays dealing with the serious and comedic aspects of marital and family life. The original four plays occurred in the same suite in successive order. The film version links all four stories together in a chronological manner by beginning with Sidney and Diana's arrival by plane at Los Angeles, the Chicago couple's problem with a hired automobile, the Warrens' battle over their daughter, Jenny, leading to the departure of the main characters some twenty-four hours later with Jenny Warren bidding farewell to her mother at the airport and ironically presenting her with a copy of a guide to the homes of Hollywood movie stars. Bill and Hannah first meet at the hotel suite, then go outside to a restaurant, swim at a beach, and argue over custody at Bill's house before returning to the hotel. Unlike earlier film versions of Simon's plays, Herbert Ross attempts to "open up up" the stage version in more cinematically plausible ways, rather than just using outside locations as mere fillers between acts. Simon also adds some new funny lines not in the original play. Prior to Bill's arrival at her suite, Hannah looks at the high cost of hotel whiskey and inquires whether she could rent the liquor instead. She also receives a phone call from her Washington lover, Bob, and describes the Beverly Hills environment as akin to "Paradise with a lobotomy." Unlike the original play, the "Visitors from Chicago" are now black rather than white, middle-class. But the combination of Pryor and Cosby does not succeed, and the farcical elements in the original act appear forced. However, the best performances in the film are by Jane Fonda as the "Visitor from New York," Michael Caine and Maggie Smith as the "Visitors from London," and Walter Matthau and Elaine May as the "Visitors from Philadelphia," who all capture the bittersweet tones contained in Simon's original two-act play. *(T. W.)*

Resources: Robert K. Johnson, *Neil Simon* (Boston: Twayne, 1983); Edythe M. McGovern, *Not-So-Simple Neil Simon: A Critical Study* (Van Nuys, CA: Perivale Press, 1978).

THE CARETAKER (1960)
Harold Pinter

The Guest (1963)

Directed by Clive Donner

Adapted by Harold Pinter

Cast: Alan Bates (Mick), Donald Pleasance (Davies), Robert Shaw (Aston)

Length: 105 minutes

Pinter overcame the failure of his play *The Birthday Party* with *The Caretaker*, a three-act play first performed in London in 1960. The play concerns two brothers, Mick and Aston, and a tramp, Davies. The action is set in an old, run-down house in London, which Mick has bought for his older brother Aston. At the play's start, only one room in the house is habitable. The mentally deficient, but well-meaning, Aston enters with the tramp, Davies, whom he has saved from a fight at a café. Davies is racist and xenophobic, constantly complaining about blacks, Greeks, and Poles. Aston treats the man kindly, allowing him to stay at the house and eventually offering him a position there as caretaker. Later, when Aston is out, Mick also mentions the possibility of a job. Davies attempts to take advantage of the situation by playing the brothers against one another. Despite a growing tension between Aston and Davies, Aston reveals to the tramp that he used to hallucinate. His mother committed him to an institution and, against Aston's wishes, approved electric shock treatments for her son. Rather than acting sympathetically, Davies uses the knowledge against Aston in conversation with Mick. The younger brother rejects Davies, as does Aston, and the play closes with Davies' realizing he must leave. Critics were impressed by Pinter's new play. Martin Esslin quotes especially strong reviews from Kenneth Tynan and Noël Coward, who praised its "impeccable" acting and direction, noting that it was "written with an original and unmistakable sense of theatre." When *The Caretaker* opened in New York in 1961, Robert Shaw replaced Peter Woodthorpe as Aston. In December 1962, filming of the play began in a run-down house. The New York cast reprised their roles. Pinter straightforwardly adapted his play, and Clive Donner directed. The £30,000 budget was raised by a group of show business notables, including Noël Coward, Richard Burton, Elizabeth Taylor, Peter Sellers, Peter Hall, and Leslie Caron. The film premiered at the Berlin Film Festival in 1963 and won a special jury prize. In November the film opened in New York, retitled *The Guest. (B. D. H.)*

Resource: Martin Esslin, *Pinter: A Study of His Plays* (New York: W. W. Norton, 1976).

CASABLANCA

See EVERYBODY COMES TO RICK'S

CAT ON A HOT TIN ROOF (1955)
Tennessee Williams

Cat on a Hot Tin Roof (1958)

Directed by Richard Brooks

Adapted by Richard Brooks and James Poe

Cast: Elizabeth Taylor (Maggie), Paul Newman (Brick), Burl Ives (Big Daddy), Jack Carson (Gooper)

Length: 108 minutes

Elia Kazan's direction of *Cat on a Hot Tin Roof*, which opened on Broadway on 25 March 1955, brought Tennessee Williams his second Pulitzer Prize. When the play was to be adapted to the screen, film director Richard Brooks wanted to be faithful to Williams' play, but the homosexuality in the play posed censorship problems. Skipper, Brick's close friend, is in love with him; but when Brick rejects that love, Skipper, who has unsuccessfully tried to prove his manhood with Maggie, commits suicide. Unable to shoulder any responsibility for Skipper's death, Brick blames Maggie and withdraws from her. Without sex, Maggie and Brick will not have children, and Big Daddy's estate will go to Gooper, Brick's brother, who has sired "no-neck monsters." Brooks' film suggests that Brick's emotional immaturity rather than his fear of his own latent homosexuality keeps him away from Maggie. In the film Brick's suppressed sexual desire is suggested by his burying his face in Maggie's slip and by phallically brandishing his crutches. At the end of the film, after Maggie claims she is pregnant, Brick supports her lie and shows that he is ready to sleep with her. This upbeat ending is at odds with that of the play, which portrays only a tentative reconciliation between the two. Besides altering the ending, Brooks tones down the bawdy language, softens the religious satire, cuts quite a bit of dialogue, and takes the action outside Big Daddy's house. Brooks films a drunken Brick attempting the hurdles in an empty stadium. Brick hears the roar of the crowd, but after he breaks his leg, he hears nothing. This scene explains Brick's physical problem and also illustrates the difficulty of determining the truth. Williams' play focuses on the lies that people tell each other and themselves: the family's lies about Big Daddy's cancer and Brick's lies about the causes of his sexual problem and his alcoholism. In another scene, which begins in the basement, Brick and Big Daddy make each other confront the truth. That honest confrontation, which is juxtaposed to the upstairs lies of Gooper's family, proceeds symbolically outside into the open. Brooks' changes proved popular at the box office, even though the critical response was less enthusiastic. Williams commented that his play was "jazzed up, hoked up a bit" in the film. *(T. L. E.)*

Resources: Gene Phillips, *The Films of Tennessee Williams* (East Brunswick, NJ: Associated University Presses, 1980); Maurice Yacowar, *Tennessee Williams and Film* (New York: Frederick Ungar, 1977).

CHAPTER TWO (1977)
Neil Simon

Chapter Two (1979)

Directed by Robert Moore

Adapted by Neil Simon

Cast: James Caan (George Schneider), Marsha Mason (Jennie MacLaine), Joseph Bologna (Leo Schneider), Valerie Harper (Faye Medwick), Alan Fudge (Lee Michaels), Judy Farrell (Gwen Michaels)

Length: 124 minutes

Rated: PG

Neil Simon has stated that this autobiographical play was painful to write because it concerned his grief over the death of his first wife, Joan, and his later decision to marry Marsha Mason, who plays the role of Jennie in the film adaptation. Severely depressed after his wife, Barbara's, death, writer George Schneider (James Caan) has just returned to New York after a stay in Europe. Meanwhile, Jennie Malone (Marsha Mason) has also returned from a trip with her friend, Faye Medwick (Valerie Harper). Jennie has been married for six years to a professional football player and is ready to start a new "chapter" in her life. Faye and her "old flame," Leo Schneider (Joseph Bologna), George's brother, want to get George and Jennie together in order to "make them happy." Although both are reluctant, they get together by scene 6 of the play. Romance develops, and by act 2 they are thinking about marriage, which ensues but not without complications. George is called to Los Angeles for a movie contract but quickly returns to New York after becoming "unstuck" in Los Angeles, in order to "embrace his happiness." Despite the play's focus on George's grief and bereavement, the play is still packed with Simon's comic dialogue. Although the play was originally directed by Herbert Ross, the film was directed by Robert Moore, whose handling of the dramatic scenes seems mechanical and pedestrian. James Caan does a serviceable job of portraying George Schneider but not a very convincing one in representing George as a blocked writer. Marsha Mason turns in the best performance in the film, though the role must have been awkward for her, since it must have struck awfully close to home; but there is not, unfortunately, a consistent emotional context here that embraces both performers. (*J. M. W.*)

Resources: Gary Arnold, "Chapter and Vice," *Washington Post* (5 March 1980): B1, B11; Edythe M. McGovern, *Neil Simon: A Critical Study* (New York: Frederick Ungar, 1979).

CHILDREN OF A LESSER GOD (1980)
Mark Medoff

Children of a Lesser God (1986)

Directed by Randa Haines

Adapted by Mark Medoff and Hesper Anderson

Cast: William Hurt (James), Marlee Matlin (Sarah), Piper Laurie (Mrs. Norman), Philip Bosco (Dr. Curtis Franklin)

Length: 110 minutes

Rated: R

Medoff's Tony Award–winning play does not appear to have cinematic possibilities. It takes place in James' mind, and characters step forth from his memory to play their parts on a stage with only benches and a blackboard as props. In the play, James comes to teach at a school for the deaf, meets Sarah, falls in love with her, and marries her; but before the end of the play the couple have to overcome Sarah's memories of adolescent sexual exploitation, James' desire to be her mentor, and problems in communication. When the play was adapted, Haines added realistic interior and exterior scenes, which changed the perspective on the action; the film is not a memory but a third-person view of real events. Other than the nude scenes in the swimming pool, some of which seem designed to suggest thought or memory, the film is rooted in physical reality. There are also significant changes in the plot and the characters. Orin, who was omitted from the film, is a deaf person who lip-reads and speaks, a dorm counselor who is James' rival for Sarah's affection and who initiates a lawsuit against the school for their employment practices. The film also eliminates the lawsuit and lawyer Edna Klein, who has a large role in the play, and further omits the rivalry for Sarah's love. Lydia, a deaf student, also is love with James; but that subplot is also deleted. Instead, the film focuses almost exclusively on the obstacles that threaten the relationship of James and Sarah. Sarah, who has been emotionally damaged in adolescent sexual encounters and by her mother's rejection of her, fears commitment. James, who wants to "help" her, discovers that he really wants to control her, to teach her to speak so she can live in his world. When Sarah confronts him about his Pygmalion-like behavior, he is defensive but comes to understand that he has underestimated the problems Dr. Curtis Franklin has brought to his attention. The struggle is resolved when he understands that she wants to be an "I" rather than a "we." When that occurs, the full meaning of "connect," which they have discussed, becomes clear: they are "joined" as equals. The other focus of the film is on James' work, in and out of class, with his students; and his success, which feeds his ego, causes his problems with Sarah. (Marlee Matlin won an Oscar for her role as Sarah.) *(T. L. E.)*

Resource: Rudolf Euben, *Mark Medoff* (Boise: Boise State University Press, 1995).

THE CHILDREN'S HOUR (1934)
Lillian Hellman

The Children's Hour (1961)

Directed by William Wyler
Adapted by John Michael Hayes, Lillian Hellman

Cast: Audrey Hepburn (Karen Wright), Shirley MacLaine (Martha Dobie), James Garner (Dr. Joe Cardin), Miriam Hopkins (Mrs. Lily Mortar), Fay Bainter (Amelia Tilford), Karen Balkin (Mary Tilford)

Length: 107 minutes

These Three (1936)

Directed by William Wyler

Adapted by Lillian Hellman

Cast: Miriam Hopkins (Martha Dobie), Merle Oberon (Karen Wright), Joel McCrea (Dr. Joe Cardin), Catherine Doucet (Mrs. Lily Mortar), Alma Kruger (Amelia Tilford), Bonita Granville (Mary Tilford)

Length: 93 minutes

In 1933 Dashiell Hammett read a book titled *Bad Companions* about interesting British court cases. The chapter "Closed Doors, or the Great Drumsheugh Case" caught his eye. The chapter concerned the case of two headmistresses of a Scottish girl's school accused by a student of having a lesbian relationship. The ensuing scandal forced the school's closing, and the two accused women filed suit for libel. Hammett mentioned the story to Lillian Hellman as a possibility for her first play. Hellman liked the idea and used it as the basis for *The Children's Hour*. Mary, chastised for lying, creates the story of the lesbian relationship and tells her grandmother, Amelia Tilford. Amelia withdraws Mary from the school and spreads the rumor to the other parents. Her nephew Joe, who is also Karen's fiancé, defends the two women with no success, and the school shuts down. In the aftermath of the failed lawsuit, Karen breaks up with Joe, and Martha realizes she does indeed love Karen. This realization drives Martha to suicide. The play ends with Amelia's discovery and admission that Mary's story was a lie. The play premiered in November 1934 to rave reviews and box office success. The controversial subject matter did create censorship problems in London, Boston, and Chicago. In addition, the Pulitzer Prize committee is widely believed to have overlooked the play for consideration because of the lesbian theme. Samuel Goldwyn bought the play from Hellman for $50,000, despite the knowledge that the Hays Office would not allow the play's title or plot to be used in a film. Hellman convinced the independent producer that the destructive power of a lie, rather than the lesbian issue, was the play's true theme. She proved this by successfully reworking the story for the big screen. Instead of charging Martha and Karen with an "unnatural" relationship, Mary accuses Martha of having an affair with Joe. The new angle increased the story's depth by adding an element of mistrust and doubt to Martha and Karen's relationship. Goldwyn lured Wyler into a three-year contract by offering him the chance to direct *The*

Children's Hour. The film, retitled *These Three* to satisfy censors, was a critical success and drew glowing reviews from such illustrious critics as Graham Greene.

Despite the film's success, Wyler regretted that he could not shoot the original story. In 1960, after the Production Code had been dismantled, Wyler decided to remake *The Children's Hour*. He asked Hellman to once again adapt her play, but previous commitments limited her involvement. Despite the cast of Audrey Hepburn, Shirley MacLaine, and James Garner, the film was a failure. John Michael Hayes' adaptation was too literal and Wyler's direction too restrained. The result was a dated film that never fully tackled its subject. Wyler and Hellman both regretted the result. *(B. D. H.)*

Resources: Jan Herman, *A Talent for Trouble: The Life of Hollywood's Most Acclaimed Director, William Wyler* (New York: G. P. Putnam's Sons, 1995); Axel Madsen, *William Wyler* (New York: Thomas Y. Crowell, 1973); William Wright, *Lillian Hellman, the Image, the Woman* (New York: Simon and Schuster, 1986).

CHIMES AT MIDNIGHT (FALSTAFF)

See HENRY IV, PARTS I & II, HENRY V, RICHARD II, and THE MERRY WIVES OF WINDSOR

CLASH BY NIGHT (1941)
Clifford Odets

Clash by Night (1952)

Directed by Fritz Lang

Adapted by Alfred Hayes

Cast: Barbara Stanwyck (Mae), Paul Douglas (Jerry), Robert Ryan (Earl), Marilyn Monroe (Peggy), J. Carrol Naish (Uncle Vince), Keith Andes (Joe Doyle), Silvio Minciotti (Papa)

Length: 105 minutes

Odets' *Clash by Night*, which opened in New York in 1941, is a grim tragedy set in Staten Island, New York, in 1941. The love triangle (Odets called it his "trio play") consists of Jerry, a simple day laborer; Mae, his wife, who "dreams of eagles"; and Earl, a movie projectionist who presumably has what Jerry lacks. At Jerry's insistence Earl moves in with Jerry and Mae and soon is sleeping with Mae. The trusting Jerry finally discovers their relationship and, encouraged by his malevolent, alcoholic Uncle Vince, goes to the projection booth at the movie theatre and strangles Earl. At the end of the play, Mae climbs the steps to the booth—the audience can only guess her fate. In contrast to the Jerry-Mae mismatch is the relationship of Joe Doyle, a nondrinking, responsible young man and Odets' spokesman, and Peggy, his willing-to-wait girlfriend; their marriage is imminent at the end of the play. When Lang adapted Odets' play, he lessened the economic plight of the characters and virtually eliminated the effect of the summer heat, which caused tension between Jerry and Mae. Jerry becomes captain of a fishing boat, so Mae's desire to escape life on the "installment plan" by leaving with the more affluent Earl is eliminated. Lang also lengthened the time in the play, which took place in August. The film begins with Mae's return to the fishing village and her meeting with Jerry. Even though she warns him that she is not right for him (there is no warning in the play), he marries her, and they have a child. When he discovers Mae's infidelity, Jerry goes to the projection booth but cannot kill Earl. He takes the baby to his boat; and, after realizing what she has done, Mae dismisses Earl and joins Jerry at the boat, where he says, "You gotta trust." This saccharine ending totally distorts what critics have called Odets' most "despairing" play. In the film Jerry is not an economic loser; Mae is not a woman without a conscience; and Earl is not a sleazy, despondent man who needs someone to love him. On the other hand, Joe Doyle (now Mae's brother) and Peggy are radically altered. Perhaps because Marilyn Monroe played her, Peggy is more flamboyant and sexy and even proposes a drunken toast at Jerry and Mae's wedding. Joe, who espouses Odets' ideas about human relationships, becomes in the film a violent, chauvinistic physical force devoid of ideas. Although Lang captures the seedy quality of the fishing village, his plot reversal and character changes seriously undermine Odets' messages. *(T. L. E.)*

Resources: Robert A. Armour, *Fritz Lang* (Boston: Twayne, 1977); Paul M. Jensen, *The Cinema of Fritz Lang* (New York: A. S. Barnes, 1969); Frederick W. Ott, *The Films of Fritz Lang* (Secaucus, NJ: Citadel Press, 1979).

COCOANUTS (1925)
George S. Kaufman and Morrie Ryskind;
music and lyrics by Irving Berlin

Cocoanuts (1929)

Directed by Robert Florey and Joseph Santley
Adapted by George S. Kaufman and Morrie Ryskind

Cast: Groucho Marx (Henry Schlemmer) supported by the rest of the Marx Brothers (Harpo, Chico, Zeppo), Margaret Dumont (Mrs. Potter)

Length: 96 minutes

The action of the Kaufman-Ryskind-Berlin Broadway hit is set in Florida during a real estate boom. Henry W. Schlemmer (Groucho) is in charge of the Hotel de Cocoanut, whose only paying guest is the wealthy and haughty Mrs. Potter (Margaret Dumont). Naturally, she is the target of fortune hunters, including Schlemmer himself. Among the songs by Irving Berlin were "A Little Bungalow," "We Should Care," and "Monkey Doodle Doo." Against this broad outline, the Marx Brothers' improvised antics continually altered and reconfigured the production as it moved from its Boston tryout to the New York premiere on 8 December 1925 at the Lyric Theatre. As David Ewen reports in his book on the American musical theatre, "[A]ny resemblance of dialogue and plot to the original concept of the authors is purely coincidental" (93). Paramount was attracted to the verbal pyrotechnics of the brothers and chose *Cocoanuts* for its first musical-comedy film talkie. During the four-week shoot in the autumn of 1929 at the Astoria Studios in Queens, the brothers found themselves doing double duty—performing *Cocoanuts* at Astoria before the cameras by day and playing their newest show, *Animal Crackers*, on Broadway by night. Stage director Joseph Santley collaborated with film director Robert Florey to produce what historians Paul D. Zimmerman and Burt Goldblatt have described as "the best record we have of [the Marxes'] vaudeville style," a record of the brothers "at the height of their stage art rather than [at] their film beginnings" (19). Joining the brothers from the original cast was Margaret Dumont, who would remain with them as their perennial foil in the years to come. Two of the original songs were retained ("Florida by the Sea" and "Monkey Doodle Doo"); and Berlin contributed a new song, "When My Dreams Come True," as the movie's recurring theme. Rarely do the results seem anything but a canned stage performance: played out against painted flats and shallow-depth playing spaces, interminable monologues alternate with static tableaux and an occasional song and/or dance number. Yet, just as they had done onstage, the brothers unleash such furious energy that they triumph over the otherwise mediocre material. It is worth noting that one dance number introduces a uniquely cinematic device: cameraman George Folsey shot the sequence looking *straight down* from the rafters. "It is this brief moment," says historian Miles Kreuger in *The Complete Book of the American Musical Theater*, "that marks the emancipation of the screen musical from its theatrical roots; for the first time the camera offered the moviegoer a new perspective on a theatrical event." It would soon be imitated and brought to perfection by a newcomer on the scene—Busby Berkeley. *(J. C. T.)*

Resources: David Ewen, *The Complete Book of the American Musical Theater* (New York: Holt, Rinehart, and Winston, 1970); John C. Tibbetts, *The American Theatrical Film* (Bowling Green, OH: Popular Press, 1985); Paul D. Zimmerman and Burt Goldblatt, *The Marx Brothers at the Movies* (New York: Putnam's, 1968).

COME BACK, LITTLE SHEBA (1949)
William Inge

Come Back, Little Sheba (1952)

Directed by Daniel Mann

Adapted by Ketti Frings

Cast: Shirley Booth (Lola Delaney), Burt Lancaster (Doc Delaney), Terry Moore (Marie)

Length: 99 minutes

William Inge's 1949 two-act drama was his first Broadway success and the first of his plays to reach the screen. Doc Delaney is a failed physician struggling with alcoholism and a dysfunctional marriage to his fat and smothering wife, Lola. When Lola encourages their attractive lodger, Marie, to entertain her lover in her room, the sexually frustrated Doc hits the bottle and, in a fit of violence, smashes up the apartment and tries to kill Lola. He "dries out" in a hospital and, upon returning home, reconciles with Lola. She, in turn, realizes that her daydreaming (including laments over her lost baby and her long-lost puppy, Sheba) has jeopardized the relationship. Doc and Lola prepare to get on with their marriage. When producer Hal Wallis decided to make a screen adaptation with Shirley Booth repeating her stage role as Lola, Paramount executives were appalled. "Prepared to accept glamorous men and women in melodramas of the seamy side of life, they were shocked at the thought of making a picture with beaten, unkempt, depressing people," Wallis told Robert Windeler. Perhaps that's why young Burt Lancaster, fresh from his triumph in the swashbuckling *The Crimson Pirate*, was signed on to replace the stage's Sidney Blackmer and portray the sixtyish Doc. It was Lancaster's idea to transform the weakling Doc into a strong man debilitated by his wife over a period of years. Lancaster padded out his trim physique with a shapeless sweater, wore baggy trousers to make him appear wide at the hips, and adopted a stoop in his posture. Shirley Booth won the Best Actress Oscar for 1952. *(J. C. T.)*

Resources: Ralph F. Voss, *A Life of William Inge: The Strains of Triumph* (Lawrence: University of Kansas Press, 1989); Robert Windeler, *Burt Lancaster* (New York: St. Martin's Press, 1984).

COME BACK TO THE 5 & DIME, JIMMY DEAN, JIMMY DEAN (1976)
Ed Graczyk

Come Back to the 5 & Dime, Jimmy Dean, Jimmy Dean (1982)

Directed by Robert Altman

Adapted by Ed Graczyk

Cast: Sudie Bond (Juanita), Cher (Sissy), Sandy Dennis (Mona), Mark Patton (Joe), Kathy Bates (Stella May), Marta Heflin (Edna Louise), Karen Black (Joanne)

Length: 109 minutes

Rated: PG

Come Back to the 5 & Dime, Jimmy Dean, Jimmy Dean was first produced by Players Theatre of Columbus, Ohio, in September 1976 and was directed by Ed Graczyk. The Broadway production opened on 18 February 1982 and was directed by Robert Altman. Altman then brought his entire Broadway cast to the big screen in a compelling film version that is a good example of how to bring a stage play to film and keep the integrity of the play intact without the necessary Hollywood pressure to open it up to free it from the confines of the stage. Altman is no stranger to bringing stage plays to the screen and followed up *Jimmy Dean* with *Streamers* (1983), *Fool for Love* (1985), *Beyond Therapy* (1987), and *The Caine Mutiny Court-Martial* (1988). *Jimmy Dean* takes place in a Five-and-Dime store in McCarthy, a small town in west Texas, and the action of the film bounces back and forth between 1955 and 1975. The story revolves around the lives of the "Disciples of James Dean," a group of women who have formed a James Dean fan club and are about to celebrate the twentieth anniversary reunion of their group. Their organization came into existence after James Dean arrived in the vicinity of their Texas community to work in the film *Giant*. The play shows how the lives of ordinary individuals can be altered for life by even the slimmest exposure to celebrity. The distance of twenty years can be both cruel and kind when it comes to serving one's memory, and these women are certainly no different from anyone else when it comes to keeping and cherishing secrets from the past, even if those secrets turn out to be quite ugly. The advantage Altman has in using the medium of film for this play is his ability to layer images from the past on top of, and into, images of the present. This gives us a nice feel for how none of us can escape the images of our former selves. As the film reaches its climax, the image of a passing thunderstorm is used as an analogy for the mental storm just experienced by the six women. Like Woody Allen, Robert Altman is a filmmaker of such caliber as to be able to bring together performers of exceptional ability. Having three Academy Award winners— Sandy Dennis, Cher, and Kathy Bates—in this film makes it worth the effort to seek it out, if for no other reason than to watch Cher's hysterical impersonation of Sandy Dennis' mannerisms. *(J. D.)*

Resources: Ed Graczyk, *Come Back to the 5 & Dime, Jimmy Dean, Jimmy Dean* (New York: Samuel French, 1976, 1982); Alan Karp, *The Films of Robert Altman* (Metuchen, NJ: Scarecrow Press, 1981).

CONDUCT UNBECOMING (1970)
Barry England

Conduct Unbecoming (1975)

Directed by Michael Anderson

Adapted by Robert Enders

Cast: Michael York (2d Lt. Arthur Drake), Richard Attenborough (Major Lionel Roach), Trevor Howard (Col. Benjamin Strang), Stacy Keach (Capt. Robert Harper), Christopher Plummer (Maj. Alastair Wimbourne), Susannah York (Mrs. Marjorie Scarlett), James Faulkner (2d Lt. Edward Millington), James Donald (Regimental Doctor), Persis Khambatta (Mrs. Bandanai)

Length: 107 minutes

Rated: PG

England's play, set in India in the late 1800s, appeared in New York City in 1970. Millington, a junior officer intent on failing at this assignment and being returned to England, is charged with assaulting Mrs. Hasseltine, a sexy widow. He is defended by Drake, another officer, who is equally intent on doing his duty and preserving his honor. Drake's spirited defense of Millington jeopardizes his own military career since the regiment fully expects Millington's conviction in the Subaltern's Court-Martial, a secret trial akin to a "kangaroo court." By insisting on calling Mrs. Hasseltine as a witness and calling her a liar and by questioning the doctor about details of the assault, Drake angers Captain Harper, who presides over the court. When Major Roach's testimony undermines Mrs. Hasseltine's, and when Drake proves that Mrs. Bandanai was also attacked in a similar way, one similar to the regiment's pig-sticking ceremony, Major Roach changes his mind since Millington was not in India at the time of the earlier attack. Convinced that another officer committed the assault, Drake suspects that the culprit is Major Scarlett; but he is dead, and his hero's tunic is on display in the officers' mess. Mrs. Hasseltine retracts her testimony but refuses to identify her attacker. As she leaves the court, she describes all the officers as the same; she calls them stupid, cruel men who treat pigs and women as objects. Colonel Strang, whose faith in his men is destroyed, accepts responsibility; but it is Major Wimbourne who ties up the loose ends. He meets Major Roach, who has worn Major Scarlett's tunic when he attacks women, shoots the mannequin wearing Scarlett's tunic, forces Major Roach to admit his guilt, and leaves Roach a gun, with which he commits suicide. The action in the film adaptation occurs mostly in the officers' mess, where the trial is conducted, but there also are exterior scenes showing the regiment on the parade ground and in the field—the latter scenes, which show Roach's discovery of Scarlett's mutilated body, help explain how Roach came to be "possessed" by Scarlett. To tighten the plot, Mrs. Hasseltine becomes Mrs. Scarlett in the film; and her anguished testimony, delivered while crawling on the floor, helps free Millington. In fact, the film stresses the pig-sticking ceremony, which is graphically depicted; and Mrs. Scarlett's bloody dress is displayed in the court. One added scene seems motivated by a desire for suspense: Wimbourne seems the culprit when he emerges from the shadows after a secret conversation with Mrs. Scarlett about the case. Of course, Wimbourne has only been trying to protect Major Roach and the traditions of the regiment; and only when Major Roach emerges from the shadows in the officers' mess does the audience know who "Scarlett" really is. *(T. L. E.)*

Resources: Vivienne Knight, *Trevor Howard: A Gentleman and a Player: The Authorized Biography* (New York: Beaufort Books, 1987); Michael Munn, *Trevor Howard: The Man and His Films* (Chelsea, MI: Scarborough House, 1990); Michael York, *Accidentally on Purpose: An Autobiography* (New York: Simon and Schuster, 1991).

THE CONNECTION (1959)
Jack Gelber

The Connection (1962)

Directed by Shirley Clarke
Adapted by Jack Gelber

Cast: William Redfield (Jim Dunn), Warren Finnerty (Leach), Carl Lee (Cowboy), Roscoe Lee Browne (J. J. Burden)

Length: 110 minutes

When it opened off-Broadway in July 1959, Jack Gelber's *The Connection* became a theatrical cause célèbre. Directed by Judith Malina for the Living Theatre, Gelber's unflinching probe into the netherworld of self-centered junkies was scorned by the New York dailies as an apologia for drug use. Despite the broadsides, *The Connection* won a staunch following that resulted in a two-year run. For adventurous theatregoers, there were multiple attractions. First, Gelber's play was a production of the Living Theatre, at the time America's most influential experimental theatre troupe. Second, it upped the naturalistic ante of Tennessee Williams and William Inge by suggesting a slice of life stripped of theatrical artifice. Third, it dealt forthrightly with the then largely taboo subject of heroin addiction. Fourth, it spotlighted a quartet of jazzmen who provided a half-hour's worth of bebop for each of the play's two acts. Finally, Gelber's interracial casting, in contrast to prevailing social and theatrical attitudes, suggested that skin color was of little consequence. The prizewinning production was hailed by critic Kenneth Tynan in the *New Yorker* and in his Introduction to the published text as the "most exciting new play that off-Broadway has produced since the war." In her faithful adaptation of Gelber's screenplay, noted experimental filmmaker Shirley Clarke made few changes except for the substitution of a film-within-a-film for a play-within-a-play structure. Instead of opening up the play, Clarke confined her camera to a claustrophobic loft where a group of addicts awaits the arrival of Cowboy, their drug-dealing connection. To help pay for the heroin, the junkies agree to let documentary filmmaker Jim Dunn and his cameraman J. J. Burden film them for a fee. As they kill time, they reveal themselves through small talk and half-baked philosophical quips. Interludes of spirited jazz are played by pianist Freddie Redd, alto saxophonist Jackie McLean, bassist Michael Mattos, and drummer Larry Ritchie. When Cowboy arrives, the men file one by one into the bathroom for their brief moments of injected ecstasy. Dunn also shoots up so that he'll have a deeper appreciation of his film's subject. At the end, Dunn deems his experiment a failure. Reviews were mixed. Dwight Macdonald praised its depiction of junkies as individuals, while Stanley Kauffmann found it a flawed exercise in naturalism. As a low-budget, independent film, *The Connection* received only limited distribution. Because it used "shit" as a junkie synonym for heroin, its New York opening was delayed by censors until successfully litigated. The film, then, never had a chance to win even an art house following. Today, while having historical value as a glimpse into the late-1950s worlds of drugs and experimental theatre, *The Connection* is as dated as the argot of its hipster-junkies. *(C. M. B.)*

Resources: Jack Gelber, *The Connection* (New York: Grove Press, 1960), which also contains Kenneth Tynan's insightful "Introduction"; Stanley Kauffmann, *A World on Film* (New York: Harper and Row, 1966); Dwight Macdonald, *On Movies* (Englewood Cliffs, NJ: Prentice-Hall, 1969).

COQUETTE (1927)
George Abbott and Ann Preston Bridgers

Coquette (1929)

Directed by Sam Taylor

Adapted by John Grey and Sam Taylor

Cast: Mary Pickford (Norma Besant), John Mack Brown (Michael Jeffrey), John St. Polis (Dr. Besant)

Length: 75 minutes

Jed Harris' production of George Abbott's *Coquette* was the big hit of the early 1927 Broadway season, premiering on 8 November and running for 253 performances. The title character, Norma Besant, is a beautiful, flirtatious, and conniving daughter of a gallant of the Old South, Dr. John Besant. One of her admirers is young Michael Jeffrey, who, because of his relative poverty and lack of social connections, is discouraged by Dr. Besant. When Jeffrey persists in his attentions, Besant shoots him dead. At Besant's subsequent murder trial, Norma conceals the fact that she is pregnant with Jeffrey's child. Rather than allow this revelation to come out in court, thus weakening her father's defense case and staining her own honor, she commits suicide. Mary Pickford, in searching for a vehicle for her first talking picture, was attracted by the dramatic implications of the tragic Norma (played onstage by Helen Hayes), a chaste, yet coquettish, southern belle trapped between the restrictions of her social code and her own sexual awakening. However, the limitations imposed upon filmmakers by the censorial Hays Office required major changes in the screenplay. The world's "imperfections" might be the stuff of good drama, historian Greg Black notes, but the Hollywood censors "saw no reason why films should not show simple and direct solutions to complex moral, political, economic, and philosophical issues" (41–42). Thus, scenarists Sam Taylor and John Grey sidestepped Norma's pregnancy, keeping her character essentially chaste and restricting her encounters with Jeffrey (John Mack Brown) to a few tepid kisses. It is not Norma who commits suicide at the conclusion of the courtroom scene, but her father (John St. Polis). Although suicide was generally forbidden by movie censors, Dr. Besant's self-destruction could be construed as an act of expiation for murdering Jeffrey. The film's production values strongly reflect the stage-confined nature of the original play, as well as the restrictions imposed upon filmmakers by the new sound technology. Entire scenes from the play transfer virtually intact, and the blocking of the action is limited to shallow-depth interior sets (designed by William Cameron Menzies). Entrances and exits use the right and left sides of the frame as if they were the wings of a stage. Cinematographer Karl Struss shot the courtroom scenes in a flat light with six cameras running simultaneously, minimizing the cutting. Moreover, John Mack Brown's performance as Jeffrey (originally played onstage by Elliott Cabot) is all too typical of the stiffness associated with actors unaccustomed to the microphone. While Pickford's performance is hardly any better—marred by a thin voice and an insistently declamatory style—it did earn her a Best Actor Oscar. *Coquette* grossed over $1.3 million domestically, establishing it as one of her most successful pictures. *(J. C. T.)*

Resources: Gregory Black, *Hollywood Censored* (Cambridge, UK: Cambridge University Press, 1994); Scott Eyman, *Mary Pickford: America's Sweetheart* (New York: Donald I. Fine, 1990); John Tibbetts, "*Coquette*: Mary Pickford Finds a Voice," *Films in Review* 48. 1, 2 (January/February 1997): 61–66.

THE CORN IS GREEN (1940)
Emlyn Williams

The Corn Is Green (1945)

Directed by Irving Rapper

Adapted by Casey Robinson and Frank Cavett

Cast: Bette Davis (Miss Moffat), Nigel Bruce (the Squire), Rosalind Ivan (Mrs. Watly), John Dall (Morgan Evans), Joan Lorring (Bessie Watly)

Length: 114 minutes

Emlyn Williams' *The Corn Is Green* enjoyed a run of 236 performances on Broadway during 1940–1941 and after a national tour returned to Broadway for a two-week revival in 1942. The play, which featured Ethyl Barrymore as Miss Moffat, was subsequently transformed into a quite faithful film adaptation in 1945. Miss Moffat, an educated spinster, moves to Glensarno, Wales, with her housekeeper, Mrs. Watly, and Mrs. Watly's daughter, Bessie. When she discovers that illiteracy is widespread, she establishes a school for the children; but the boys begin work at the nearby mine at the age of twelve. She pays their parents what the boys would earn at the mine, but the local squire conspires to prevent her from finding a school building. Using her home as a school, she, Mr. Jones, and Miss Ronberry teach the youngsters and older people in the community. When she discovers Morgan Evans' writing ability, she determines to get him a scholarship at Oxford University; but she has depleted her own financial resources. Temporarily abandoning her independence and feminist views, she is able to con the squire into helping her, a defenseless woman, and bringing some honor to himself by sponsoring Morgan. Morgan, however, begins to resent acting like her puppet (she has offered intellectual, but not emotional, support) and encounters some teasing from his friends about his newly acquired skills at spoken English. When Bessie Watly attempts to seduce him, she succeeds; but he returns to Miss Moffat's classroom. He passes the scholarship exam, succeeds in the subsequent interview at Oxford, and returns in triumph to Glensarno. During this time Bessie, impregnated by Morgan, has a baby and returns to Glensarno the same day Morgan arrives. To save Morgan's future, Miss Moffat promises to adopt the baby, freeing Bessie to marry a new admirer. The film adaptation closely parallels the play. In fact, four of the film actors appeared in the original play. For the most part, Rapper restricts the action to Miss Moffat's schoolroom, the only set in the play, and to the surrounding area. It is where the battle over literacy is conducted and where Miss Moffat and Morgan, who is a bit rebellious, come to terms with each other as equals. There are two important outside scenes. In one, the audience sees Bessie seduce Morgan, and in the other, Miss Moffat drives to town to inquire about renting a building for a schoolhouse. While she is there, Rapper photographs Morgan's being taunted by his "friends" and thrown out of the bar because he speaks English rather than Welsh. The emphasis in this scene on language compensates, in part, for the lack of spoken Welsh in the film; the play contains several pages of Welsh dialogue, which Rapper wisely omitted from the film. Other than minor changes, the film dialogue is taken directly from the play. *(T. L. E.)*

Resources: Richard Findlater, *Emlyn Williams* (London: Rockliff, 1956); Gene Ringold, *Bette Davis: Her Films and Career* (Secaucus, NJ: Citadel Press, 1985).

THE COUNTRY GIRL (1950)
Clifford Odets

The Country Girl (1954)

Directed and adapted by George Seaton

Cast: Bing Crosby (Frank Elgin), Grace Kelly (Georgie Elgin), William Holden (Bernie Dodd), Anthony Ross (Phil Cook), Gene Reynolds (Larry)

Length: 104 minutes

Odets' *The Country Girl*, one of his most successful plays, was produced in New York in 1950 and adapted to film in 1954. The play concerns Bernie's efforts to get an excellent performance from Frank, a former star who is now an alcoholic with no self-esteem. Despite the opposition of Cook, the producer, who has a substantial investment in the play and prefers a safer actor without Frank's potential, Bernie gives the lead to Frank, and the play goes to Boston for rehearsals and some road performances. Bernie, who is recovering from a failed marriage, does not like domineering women, and he blames Frank's weakness on Georgie, Frank's long-suffering, but loyal, wife. When he learns that Frank has lied about Georgie's drinking, suicidal efforts, and arson, Bernie apologizes to Georgie, to whom he is now attracted. With the help of Bernie and Georgie, Frank is a success when the play opens in New York. Despite her own love for Bernie, the loyal Georgie stays with the regenerated Frank. Seaton's adaptation makes an interesting change; with Bing Crosby playing Frank, the show is changed from a drama to a musical. As a result, the film uses Crosby's singing talent; and one of his songs about "learning" relates directly to Frank's confession about his drinking and the return of his self-esteem. In addition, Frank's role is that of a man who must earn the trust of his community, much like Frank, who struggles to gain the respect of the theatre company. The screenplay also contains a flashback prompted by Frank's hearing one of his recordings; that flashback takes him back to the recording studio and his son's death (to accommodate a photographer on the street he lets go of his son's hand, and the boy is hit by a car). That memory recurs throughout the film: Frank poses by a "Wanted for Murder" poster with his picture on it and relives the past; at the bar when he gets drunk, his look in the mirror recalls the event; and at the cocktail party at the end of the film the song is played again but this time without incident. His refusal to respond negatively to the song demonstrates his assumption of responsibility and his recognition that he has used his son's death to legitimatize his drinking. The film also stresses the love triangle. In the film Frank recognizes the mutual attraction of Georgie and Bernie and directly addresses the problem. Georgie's conflicting desires are superbly demonstrated by Grace Kelly, who won an Academy Award for her performance. Seaton's screenplay, which, while adding some outside sequences, focused primarily on the battleground of the theatrical world, also received an Oscar. *(T. L. E.)*

Resources: Robert Bookbinder, *The Films of Bing Crosby* (Secaucus, NJ: Citadel, 1977); Gabriel Miller, *Clifford Odets* (New York: Ungar, 1989).

CRAIG'S WIFE (1925)
George Kelly

Craig's Wife (1936)

Directed by Dorothy Arzner

Adapted by Mary McCall, Jr.

Cast: Rosalind Russell (Harriet Craig), John Boles (Walter Craig), Billie Burke (Mrs. Frazier), Jane Darwell (Mrs. Harold), Thomas Mitchell (Fergus Passworthy), Alma Kruger (Miss Austen)

Length: 75 minutes

George Kelly's Pulitzer Prize–winning play *Craig's Wife* opened at New York's Morosco Theatre on 12 October 1925 and was revived at New York's Playhouse on 12 February 1947. Both versions were directed by the author, who admired Ibsen. Though barely familiar with Ibsen when he wrote *Craig's Wife*, Kelly later realized that he had written *A Doll's House* in reverse by dramatizing the liberation of a husband from a selfish, domineering wife. The three-act play is set in Mrs. Craig's living room between 5:30 P.M. and 9:00 A.M. the following morning. It is a character study of a parasitic, castrating female who venerates her home more than her husband. Eventually, Walter Craig divests himself of his romantic illusions and leaves his wife. The play ends with her in sole possession of her home but alone, "her eyes wide and despairing." Three film versions resulted: a silent film version with Irene Rich and Warner Baxter (1928), a radically revised version of Kelly's play adapted to Joan Crawford's star persona as *Harriet Craig* (1950), and the 1936 version, which has received the most critical attention. While not altering the basic structure of Kelly's play, feminist director Dorothy Arzner subtly emphasizes the motivations behind Mrs. Craig's behavior, implicit in the original text, as well as adding certain cinematic features that undermine Kelly's patriarchal attitudes. As a young girl, Harriet saw her mother deprived of husband and home by an overbearing rival who seduced her father. Furthermore, although Harriet's conduct is basically inexcusable, her monstrous nature is the result of a woman trapped within a restrictive, patriarchal society dominated by monogamy and possessiveness. Arzner opens up Kelly's play by adding scenes depicting Walter's friends Brinkmeyer and Fergus, who are also affected by marital misery: Brinkmeyer takes his father, who is clearly overjoyed at his temporary freedom away from his wife, out for a night on the town; Fergus Passworthy appears as a neurotically dependent male who later murders his wife in a fit of possessive jealousy. When Harriet talks to her niece, Ethel, her dialogue unconsciously echoes later feminist warnings against the dangers of romantic love and the necessity for female economic security, which undermines the original play's total condemnation of its heroine. Finally, the film's closing images linger ambiguously on the supposed punitive isolation of Harriet Craig, reinforced by the caption, "People who live for themselves are usually left to themselves." Arzner suggests that Harriet Craig has gained not only the equivalent of Virginia Woolf's *A Room of One's Own*, but a female-dominated home of her own free of male control. *(T. W.)*

Resources: Foster Hirsch, *George Kelly* (Boston: Twayne, 1974); Judith Mayne, *Directed by Dorothy Arzner* (Bloomington: Indiana University Press, 1994).

CRIMES OF THE HEART (1978)
Beth Henley

Crimes of the Heart (1986)

Directed by Bruce Beresford

Adapted by Beth Henley

Cast: Diane Keaton (Lenny Macgrath), Jessica Lange (Meg Macgrath), Sissy Spacek (Babe Botrelle), David Carpenter (Barnette Lloyd), Sam Shepard (Doc Porter), Tess Harper (Chick Boyle), Hurd Hatfield (Old Granddaddy), Beeson Carroll (Zachary Botrelle), Gregory Travis (Willie Jay)

Length: 105 minutes

Rated: PG-13

Beth Henley's Pulitzer Prize–winning play enjoyed popular favor and considerable critical prestige, also winning the New York Drama Critics Circle Award in the early 1980s. It made its way to Broadway after being named cowinner of the Great American Play Contest, sponsored by the Actors Theatre of Louisville, then to off-Broadway at the Manhattan Theatre Club, and finally to a long Broadway run and subsequent film version. Bruce Beresford's movie merits praise for the performances of its three principal actresses, who deliver Henley's lyrical looniness of the Macgrath sisters with grace, conviction, and, surprisingly, great plausibility. Indeed, Diane Keaton, Sissy Spacek, and Jessica Lange embody these characters about as well as any they have ever done in notable careers.

The immediate crisis that reunites the sisters in Hazlehurst, Mississippi, is the arrest of Babe (Sissy Spacek), who has shot her husband because "she doesn't like his looks." In truth, Zachary Botrelle has learned of his wife's affair with a fifteen-year-old man of color. In the film version, unlike the stage play, these two characters appear in brief vignettes to clarify plot elements. Likewise, the movie adds Old Grandaddy (Hurd Hatfield) in flashback sequences and in two hospital scenes, the latter after he has suffered a stroke, which we assume will result in his death. Henley finds macabre humor in mortality in this work with the reported demise of the sisters' mother, who hanged herself along with the family cat years before. The movie shows a tabloid photograph from that past event—"Woman and Cat in Double Suicide"—with shrouded bodies, one of human proportions and the other more appropriately feline in its dimensions. Babe attempts suicide by less than efficient means in the course of the drama; she is saved, but Meg suggests that "we've just got to learn how to get through these real bad days here. I mean it's getting to be a thing in our family." As David Ansen wrote, "Henley's comedy is unusually attuned to the thin line separating grave matters and giggles." What rescues the content from absurdity are the inherent decency and innocence of the characters themselves. Onstage the disasters and coincidences sometimes seemed a bit too gothic and exaggerated to the point of incredibility, however amusing. Beresford's film with its balance of interior and exterior sequences and a more leisurely unfolding of events is less strained. Pauline Kael captured this quality when she suggested that Henley offers "a comedy about wacked-out normality"—a more apt description for the film version than for the play. The sisters in a nearly Chekhovian finale close the heart-embossed album that the movie uses as its frame with a belated birthday cake for the eldest sibling, the lovelorn Lenny (Diane Keaton), who finally has the promise of a beau. Keaton, as Kael noted, is especially adept "at playing a sense of injustice for laughs." This unconventional and often touching comedy continues to please primarily because of the ensemble performances of three distinguished actresses in material worthy of their talents. *(E. T. J.)*

Resources: David Ansen, "When Dittsyness Was in Flower," *Newsweek* (22 December 1986): 75; Pauline Kael, "Families," *New Yorker* (15 December 1986): 81–87.

THE CRIMINAL CODE (1929)
Martin Flavin

The Criminal Code (1931)
Directed by Howard Hawks
Adapted by Fred Niblo, Jr. and Seton I. Miller

Cast: Walter Huston (Martin Brady), Phillips Holmes (Robert Graham), Constance Cummings (Mary Brady), Boris Karloff (Ned Galloway)

Length: 96 minutes

The Criminal Code premiered at New York's National Theater on 2 October 1929 and ran for 174 performances. In the prologue, politically ambitious district attorney Martin Brady convicts Robert Graham on a charge of second-degree murder, although he could easily have pleaded mitigating circumstances if he were the defense lawyer. After six years in prison, Graham's mental deterioration advances to dangerous levels, until Brady (now the prison warden) appoints him as his daughter's chauffeur, and they become romantically involved. However, after a failed prison break, the convicts seek revenge on an informer, and Graham becomes accused of a murder actually committed by Ned Galloway. Faithful to the criminal code of never informing, he is put in solitary confinement while Brady indirectly attempts to make him talk and give him parole. But Galloway sneaks a knife into Graham's cell and kills brutal Captain Gleason with it. The play ends with the romance between Mary Brady and Graham over and the latter facing life imprisonment for murder. Although Hawks broadened the adaptation cinematically, *The Criminal Code* has not received much critical attention. The film's prologue does not take place in Brady's office as in the play but uses the mobile camera to introduce the nightclub scene of Graham's accidental killing. When the convicts create a diversion, enabling Galloway to kill the informer, Hawks uses montage to build tension. Galloway's killing of the informer behind a closed door is a fine example of how Hawks cinematically knows how to tell a story. However, such creative instances are few, and the film rarely transcends its theatrical origins. Hawks claimed that he changed the ending so that Galloway clears Graham and kills the sadistic Gleason before being shot himself. Mary and Graham can now live happily ever after. Film performances are generally perfunctory, with the exception of Boris Karloff as Galloway. As a paroled convict sentenced to twelve years for drinking one glass of beer, he nurtures his vengeance against Gleason for informing against him. Karloff's performance is a masterpiece of cinematic menace. He had played the role of Galloway for seven months in the West Coast production of the play. His acting combines the silent threat characteristic of his role in *Frankenstein* (1931) with the best qualities of understated, early sound acting, which contrast favorably with Walter Huston's overbearing performance. Columbia later remade the film in two unsatisfactory versions as *Penitentiary* (1938) and *Convicted* (1950). *(T. W.)*

Resources: Martin Flavin, *The Criminal Code* (New York: Horace Liveright, 1929); James Robert Parish, *Prison Pictures from Hollywood* (Jefferson, NC: McFarland, 1991).

CROSSING DELANCEY (1985)
Susan Sandler

Crossing Delancey (1988)

Directed by Joan Micklin Silver

Adapted by Susan Sandler

Cast: Amy Irving (Izzy), Peter Riegert (Sam Posner), Reizl Bozyk (Bubbie Kantor), Jeroen Krabbé (Anton Maes), Sylvia Miles (Hannah Mandelbaum)

Length: 97 minutes

Rated: PG

Crossing Delancey, which opened at the Jewish Repertory Theatre in New York in 1985, has only three sets: Bubbie's kitchen, the bookstore, and the bench. In the play Bubbie, Izzy's grandmother, enlists the services of Hannah, a matchmaker, to find a husband for Izzy. Izzy, however, fantasizes about Tyler, a well-known writer who frequents the bookstore where she works. When she meets Sam, the "pickle man," who owns his own business, she is not impressed; but he alters her perspective by giving her a new hat. (He has told her a story about a friend who changed his life after he replaced his lost hat—it blew off his head at Delancey Street—with a new one.) She stands up Sam when Tyler makes some overtures, which consist of his attempt to find a new secretary/sex object to replace one who has just left him. Disgusted with her naïveté, she returns to Bubbie's apartment, where Sam is waiting. Izzy and Sam, with a little help from Bubbie, discover each other. When she adapted her play to film, Sandler not only added many characters and New York settings but also complicated the plot. The scenes at the steam bath, the circumcision ceremony, the workout at the health club, the poetry reading, and Izzy's apartment (when her causal married lover appears) all seem designed to show that Izzie, who doesn't belong in her Bubbie's world, has a lifestyle rather than a life. In contrast, the audience sees Sam, a philosopher/poet, playing handball in the neighborhood where his business is. Sandler not only provides a panoramic view of the tawdry, phony world Izzy inhabits but also adds a twist to the plot by having Izzy set up one of her girlfriends with Sam. The Tyler of the play becomes Anton Maes, a Dutch-born, Americanized writer; and the scene featuring Anton and Sam helps demonstrate the former's snobbery and the latter's class. Silver, whose earlier *Hester Street* also featured a Jewish woman in New York, provides a Jewish version of *Moonstruck* (1988), another film about a post-thirties woman who finds happiness in love rather than fantasized passion. *(T. L. E.)*

Resources: Sarah Blacher Cohen, *From Hester Street to Hollywood: The Jewish-American Stage and Screen* (Bloomington: Indiana University Press, 1983); Richard Lippe, "Joan Micklin Silver," in *International Dictionary of Films and Filmmakers,* ed. Nicholas Thomas, vol. 2 (London: St. James Press, 1991): 778–779.

THE CRUCIBLE (1953)
Arthur Miller

The Crucible (1996)

Directed by Nicholas Hytner

Adapted by Arthur Miller

Cast: Daniel Day-Lewis (John Proctor), Joan Allen (Elizabeth Proctor), Winona Ryder (Abigail), Paul Scofield (Judge Danforth), Bruce Davison (Rev. Parris), Rob Campbell (Rev. Hale), Jeffrey Jones (Thomas Putnam), Karron Graves (Mary Warren), Charlayne Woodard (Tituba), Elizabeth Lawrence (Rebecca Nurse), Peter Vaughan (Thomas Putnam)

Length: 123 minutes

Rated: PG-13

The play, set in 1692 in Salem, Massachusetts, involves witch-hunting in Puritan America and has been widely recognized as an allegory concerning the political hysteria in America during the McCarthy era. The trouble begins after Abigail Williams, a sexually active servant, seduces John Proctor and is consequently dismissed by Mrs. Proctor. The headstrong Abigail leads a group of weak-minded girls into the forest one night, where they attempt to concoct love charms, but their cavorting is discovered by the Reverend Parris, who concludes that they are in league with the Devil. Experts are called in to investigate, the Reverend Hale and Judge Danforth, who interrogate and intimidate the girls, asking them to name other local Puritans they saw keeping company with the Devil. Those who are identified are brought in and required to repent and confess or be hanged. Due to Abigail's spite, Elizabeth Proctor is named, but John is not interested in leaving his wife for Abigail, whom he attempts to expose. He stands on principle and pays with his life. In his Introduction to the screenplay, Miller notes that the play has outlived Senator McCarthy and has assumed a more general significance in the way it speaks to contemporary problems, such as "the bigotry of religious fundamentalism" and "communities torn apart by accusations of child abuse," so the film may be seen as a sort of updating of the play. Terrence Rafferty complained that the film was "overwrought" in the way it demonizes "teen-age female sexuality" and "hatred of youth." The film extends the action of the play and opens differently, with Parris' discovering the girls in the forest. The casting is particularly fine, especially Paul Scofield's Judge Danforth, as well as Daniel Day-Lewis and Joan Allen as the wronged Proctors, but Winona Ryder is simply brilliant as the deceitful and evil Abigail Williams. *(J. M. W.)*

Resources: Arthur Miller, *The Crucible Screenplay* (New York: Penguin, 1996); Terrence Rafferty, "Playing with Fire," *The New Yorker* (2 December 1996): 116–120; Paula Span, "Miller's Dialogue with the World," *Washington Post* (15 December 1996): G1, G6; Matt Wolf, "No Thorns in Hytner's Hollywood," *Times* (London) (21 January 1997): 34.

CYRANO DE BERGERAC (1897)
Edmond Rostand

Cyrano de Bergerac (1950)

Directed by Michael Gordon

Adapted by Carl Foreman and Brian Hooker

Cast: José Ferrer (Cyrano), Mala Powers (Roxanne), William Prince (Christian)

Length: 112 minutes

Edmond Rostand's five-act comedy opened in Paris in 1897. Cyrano de Bergerac not only excels at fencing, philosophizing, and rhyming verse but also boasts an extraordinarily large nose. Thus, despite his poetic inventiveness and ardently romantic nature, he is reluctant to declare his love for the beautiful Roxanne. Besides, she loves the handsome Baron Christian de Neuvillette. Unselfishly, Cyrano assists the inarticulate Christian in wooing Roxanne; and he promises Roxanne to protect Christian while on the battlefield. When Christian is killed, the heartbroken Roxanne retires to a convent, where the faithful Cyrano visits her until his death fifteen years later. Only then does she discover, too late, who her real lover has been. Apart from the swashbuckling sword fights, the real glory of the play was in its poetically charged language, which critic Max Beerbohm described as "gusts of rhetoric," lines "loaded and encrusted with elaborate phrases and curious conceits." Appearing as Cyrano in the original stage production was the legendary French actor Coquelin, who became instantly identified with the role. He first brought Cyrano to film, with a synchronized-sound short film of one of the dueling scenes. Subsequently, both Alexander Korda and Orson Welles, successively, considered, then discarded, plans to make a full-length film version. Finally, Stanley Kramer obtained the rights and completed his own version in 1950. Screenwriter Carl Foreman made extensive cuts in Brian Hooker's English translation of the play, which lasted more than three hours onstage. In Spot's book on Kramer, Foreman recalled that "I found it necessary to perform major surgery on the beginnings of each of the five acts, for in every instance Rostand had paused to recapitulate and set the stage anew. Surgery and suture were necessary, we felt, for space, tempo, and cinematic movement." Actor José Ferrer reprised his Broadway role, and his enormous nose was exaggerated even further by the use of cinematographer Franz Planer's new wide-angle "Garusto lens," which kept both the nose, in the foreground, and Cyrano's antagonists, in the background, in perfect focus. The action is paced zestfully, particularly in the first half of the film, wherein Ferrer's duel with an overbearing nobleman (while composing a poem on the spot) and his tussle with a gaggle of villains are dazzlingly choreographed in the best swashbuckling manner. The sets by Rudolph Sternad—the theatre, Roxanne's garden, the pastry shop, the streets, and the plains of Arras—strike a perfect equipoise between cinematic naturalism and theatrical stylization. Composer Dimitri Tiomkin's musical score nicely preserves the flavor of seventeenth-century French balladry. Best of all is Ferrer, who won a Best Actor Oscar and whose rich, bass voice and athletic agility are quite up to the role's special demands. "Around and through Rostand's arch romanticism," declares historian Donald Spoto, "[Ferrer] creates a deeply human soul who in fact lives in a decaying and grotesque society that seems to have concentrated all its cruelties into his dreadful deformity."*(J. C. T.)*

Resources: Max Beerbohm, *Around Theatres* (Westport, CT: Greenwood Press, 1978); Donald Spoto, *Stanley Kramer: Filmmaker* (New York: G. P. Putnam's Sons, 1978).

Cyrano de Bergerac (1990)

Directed by Jean-Paul Rappeneau

Adapted by Rappeneau and Jean-Claude Carriere from an English translation by Anthony Burgess

Cast: Gerard Depardieu (Cyrano), Anne Brochet (Roxanne), Vincent Perez (Christian de Neuvillette)

Length: 135 minutes

Rated: PG

Edmond Rostand's 1897 tragicomedy receives its most sumptuous treatment to date in this elegantly appointed historical conception. From the opening scenes in a Paris theatre, where Cyrano (Depardieu) denounces a piece of phony stage histrionics, to the duel with the Vicomte de Valvert (when Cyrano declaims couplets between thrusts and parries), to the brooding, moonlit balcony scenes, to the breathless pursuit of Cyrano by 100 men, to the penultimate battle scenes, this *Cyrano* is an excitingly cinematic conception that seldom betrays its theatrical origins. Depardieu won a Cannes Best Actor award in 1990; indeed, his is the first Cyrano whose schnozzola needed only minimal enhancement. The film is equally effective when language, not action, demands our attention. For example, the pastry cook-poet Ragueneau steals some of the best moments when he supervises his assistant cooks with a philosophical line or two and when he wraps his rolls and buns in papers ripped out of his poetry books. Cyrano, after refusing to work as a paid poet, broods by a window, alone, in a static shot—soliloquizing about the choices he makes, to look at the moon, to be alone . . . Indeed, the moon itself is omnipresent; it flies ahead of Cyrano as he strides purposefully along the city's walls to Roxanne's wedding; and it hovers like a benediction above the convent walls at the end as the dying Cyrano announces his intention to travel there at last. The famous balcony scene is splendidly staged and edited: Cyrano stands below, hidden in shadows, while his puppet, the lover Christian de Neuvillette (Vincent Perez) declaims the words to the rapt Roxanne (Anne Brochet). A restless camera circles and surrounds the scene, while the editing slices up the action with the deftness of Cyrano's sword. Alas, after all this, the climactic sequence is too stage-bound: it takes Cyrano entirely too long to die—suffering from an attack by an assassin, he slumps, revives, slumps again, revives again, and so on—and it takes the silly Roxanne much too long to realize he was the author of the precious love letters she presumed to have been penned by Christian. More judicious cutting of Rostand's text would have hurried more expeditiously this otherwise enchanting cinematic conception to its close. *(J. C. T.)*

Resources: Max Beerbohm, *Around Theatres* (Westport, CT: Greenwood Press, 1987); Denson Howe, "Cyrano de Bergerac," *Washington Post Weekend* (21 December 1990): 41.

Roxanne (1987)

Directed by Fred Schepisi
Adapted by Steve Martin
Cast: Steve Martin (C. D. Bales/Cyrano), Daryl Hannah (Roxanne)
Length: 107 minutes
Rated: PG

Steve Martin adapted and starred in this update of Rostand's 1897 classic French romantic tragedy *Cyrano de Bergerac*. The familiar story is full of wonderful paradoxes. It is about the world's ugliest man falling in love with the loveliest woman. This man, moreover, wields his eloquent love lyrics not on his own behalf but secretly in the service of another swain, who is as handsome as he is dull. Martin's version updates the seventeenth-century action in Paris to a modern-day small town in the Northwest. His Cyrano is "C. D. Bales," a fireman who sings love lyrics to Roxanne Kowalski (Daryl Hannah) as he jogs, dances, and twirls his way to work. While he can scarcely gain her attention at first, he can negotiate the balconies, railings, and rooftops of her house with effortless ease. His is not just the poetry of words; it is the poetry of motion. He dispatches his enemies—those who ridicule his nose—not with a sword but with a tennis racket. We knew all along that behind Steve Martin's foolish pratfalls and humor lay the grace of a dancer. Appropriately, his current love, Roxanne, is an astronomer. She perches high on her rooftop, a crown of stars above her. She's looking for a comet, but she finds Cyrano instead. Rostand notwithstanding, happy endings are permitted here. When the two lovers finally embrace at the end, the sought-for comet slides by, but now it is unnoticed. *(J. C. T.)*

Resources: Ron Base and David Haslam, *The Movies of the Eighties* (New York: Portland House, 1990); Max Beerbohm, *Around Theatres* (Westport, CT: Greenwood Press, 1978); Hal Hinson, "Roxanne," *Washington Post* (19 June 1987): D1, D7.

DA (1973)
Hugh Leonard

Da (1988)

Directed by Matt Clark

Adapted by Hugh Leonard

Cast: Martin Sheen (Charlie), Barnard Hughes (Da), William Hickey (Drumm), Karl Hayden (Young Charlie), Doreen Hepburn (Mother), Hugh O'Conor (Boy Charlie), Jill Doyle ("Yellow Peril")

Length: 102 minutes

Rated PG

Da, which first appeared in Dublin in 1973 and in New York in 1978, is an autobiographical play by Hugh Leonard, who also wrote the screenplay for the film adaptation. The principal set is the kitchen of the family home in Dalkey, Ireland, and the time is May 1968, though Leonard notes that other sets and times evolve as "remembered" by Charlie, a playwright living in New York. In fact, the play takes place in Charlie's head as he visits the family home after his father's death. In his reverie, he attempts to resolve his ambivalent feelings about his father (Da) through a series of events that portray his father as ineffective, retiring, and yet loving. Among his memories are his father's humiliation at the hands of his employers, who provide him with a trifling gift and paltry pension; his own attempted seduction of the "Yellow Peril," a tempting target humanized by his father, who interrupts the tryst with some information about the young woman; his mother's story about her true love, Ernie Moore, and his father's jealous response; his employment with Mr. Drumm, his surrogate father, whom he snubs; his departure for Belgium to marry; and his unsuccessful efforts to get his father to move to New York with him. Near the end of the play, Drumm reappears and tells Charlie that his Da has left him the thirty pairs of spectacles melded together by a fire (a "gift" from his "Quality" employers) and some money, the money Charlie had been sending him over the years. When he leaves the family home, Charlie asks his Da to leave him alone, but his Da says he will keep up with him, surely a sign that Charlie will not be able to get his Da out of his mind. For the film adaptation Leonard added an opening sequence in New York, where Charlie apprehensively waits for opening night of his most recent play. After receiving a phone call about his father's death, he and his wife fly to Ireland and attend the funeral and wake, and then she leaves him to go through his father's belongings, all of which evoke memories. Leonard retained most of the play but added one sequence involving Da's unsuccessful effort to drown Blackie, a dog addicted to attacking nuns and priests. After Charlie jumps in to save the dog, Da follows, saving both of them. When the three return home, Charlie's mother, who had insisted on Blackie's demise, is ecstatic about their return. The added scene underscores the affection between Charlie and his adoptive parents. At the end of the film Leonard includes Charlie's return home to New York, his preparations for opening night, and his sight/memory of his Da, who, in taking him to task, demonstrates that he now will stay with Charlie in New York. *(T. L. E.)*

Resources: Vincent Canby, *"Da," New York Times* (29 April 1988): C 10; Rita Kempley, *"Da," Washington Post* (17 September 1988): C 9.

DANGEROUS LIAISONS

See LES LIAISONS DANGEREUSES

DAYS OF WINE AND ROSES (1973)
J. P. Miller

Days of Wine and Roses (1962)

Directed by Blake Edwards
Adapted by J. P. Miller

Cast: Jack Lemmon (Joe), Lee Remick (Kirsten), Charles Bickford (Arnesen, Kirsten's father), Jack Klugman (Jim Hungerford)
Length: 117 minutes

J. P. Miller's *Days of Wine and Roses* began as a live television play on *Playhouse 90* (1958) and was adapted by Miller to the stage in 1973, well after Edwards' updating of the television play. The stage play is essentially identical to the television play, which served as the source for the Edwards' film. The television play begins at an Alcoholics Anonymous (AA) meeting, where Joe admits his alcoholism and describes his life in flashback. At a party for his client, he meets Kirsten, secretary to his boss, and they begin drinking together. They soon marry, but the birth of their child ends Kirsten's drinking until Joe insists on a drinking partner. Eventually, Joe loses his job, then other jobs as the drinking continues, and they are reduced to selling Kirsten's literary collection and drinking vanilla extract. After drying out for a while at Kirsten's father's nursery, they get drunk, and Joe is hospitalized for alcoholism. With the aid of Jim Hungerford, an AA member, Joe sobers up, but Kirsten reverts to drink; and when Joe finds her at a motel, she entices him to drink again. At the end of the television play a sober Joe rejects Kirsten, who cannot give up alcohol. Miller's screenplay omits the flashbacks and begins with Joe's meeting a nondrinking Kirsten at a cocktail party on a yacht. The basic plot of the television play is retained, but there are some changes, such as a location switch from Long Island to California. Other changes involve opening up the play to include sequences in Houston and a scene in which a drunken Joe steals a bottle from a liquor store and is humiliated by the store owner. In the film Joe is shown as more insecure and immature (he buries his head in Kirsten's lap, he assumes the fetal position when he drinks, and he holds a liquor bottle as a baby holds a bottle). More introspective, he gazes at himself in store windows and mirrors; and when he must force Kirsten to look in the mirror, she is shown as unwilling to confront herself. Although he achieves sobriety, Joe pays a heavy price for his drinking. Early in the film he says that his pimping duties for parties make him "feel like a eunuch in a harem," and his "striptease" at the nursery leads to drunkenness, not sex. When he tries to bring Kirsten back from the motel, she challenges his manhood; and his delirium tremens hallucination features a "green man with shears," perhaps a symbol of Kirsten's father but also indicative of an emasculation threat. At the end of the play Joe assumes the maternal role and is alone. As in most of Edwards' films, there is no positive heterosexual coupling; here Blake stresses the "wine," not the "roses," and depicts the demise of a married couple. *(T. L. E.)*

Resources: Peter Lehman and William Luhr, *Blake Edwards* (Athens: Ohio University Press, 1981); Dick Stelzer, *The Star Treatment* (Indianapolis: Bobbs, Merrill, 1977).

DEAD END (1936)
Sidney Kingsley

Dead End (1937)

Directed by William Wyler

Adapted by Lillian Hellman

Cast: Joel McCrea (Dave Connell), Humphrey Bogart (Baby Face Martin), Sylvia Sidney (Drina), Billy Halop (Tommy), the Dead End Kids

Length: 93 minutes

In 1937 director William Wyler (*The Little Foxes*) filmed *Dead End*, Sidney Kingsley's social protest drama about juvenile delinquents, from a screenplay by playwright Lillian Hellman. The film proper begins with a panoramic shot of the New York skyline, after which it pans to the waterfront below. Finally, the camera zooms in on the film's elaborate principal setting; as in the play, it is a tenement on a slum street that comes to a dead end at the waterfront. This tenement is where the members of the juvenile gang live. Moreover, the tenement is located on a dead-end street, which symbolizes how the boys have already reached a dead end; that is, they have no prospects for a promising future. A former inhabitant of the riverfront slum, Baby Face Martin (Humphrey Bogart), comes back for a nostalgic visit to his old stomping grounds. He is now a major figure in the New York underworld, and the members of the youth gang idolize him. Martin's sole satisfaction while he is back in the old neighborhood is to bask in the adulation of Tommy's gang of tough kids on the block, who admire him for making good in the rackets uptown. The plot thickens when Mr. Griswald accuses Tommy of beating up his boy; Tommy stabs Griswald's hand with a knife and makes his getaway. Drina, who constitutes the only family he has, is distraught when she learns that her kid brother is being pursued by the police at Mr. Griswald's behest. Dave Connell (Joel McCrea), Drina's boyfriend, has a confrontation with Martin in an alley shortly afterward. Dave warns the mobster to stay away from the neighborhood kids because he is a bad influence on them. The pair get into a scuffle; Martin then pulls a gun on Dave and retreats down the alley. Dave, in turn, grabs another gun and pursues Martin up a fire escape; Dave fires upward at Martin, who falls into the alley below and soon dies. The image of Martin's ignominious fall from the top of the fire escape to the ground below symbolizes that he has been knocked off the pedestal on which Tommy and the other boys placed him. As the film draws to a close, Dave assures Drina that he will bail Tommy out of jail with the reward money that is his due for bringing down Baby Face Martin, who had a price on his head. He thereby saves Tommy from going to reform school—in contrast to the play, where Tommy's future remains in doubt. Lillian Hellman, who wrote the script, was praised by most reviewers of the film for producing a taut screenplay that retained much of the play's unvarnished realism. Moreover, the young actors who played the delinquents were billed as the Dead End Kids in the films they made together immediately after *Dead End*, to cash in on the movie's huge success. *(G. D. P.)*

Resources: Jan Herman, *A Talent for Trouble: The Life of Hollywood's Most Acclaimed Director, William Wyler* (New York: Da Capo, 1997); Marilyn Yoquinto, *Pump 'Em Full of Lead: Gangsters on Film* (New York: Simon and Schuster, 1998).

DEATH OF A SALESMAN (1949)
Arthur Miller

Death of a Salesman (1986)

Directed by Volker Schlondorff

Cast: Dustin Hoffman (Willy Loman), Kate Reid (Linda), John Malkovich (Biff), Stephen Lang (Happy), Charles Durning (Charley)

Length: 135 minutes

This adaptation of Miller's classic American play features Dustin Hoffman as Willy Loman, the hapless and tormented salesman whose life, professionally and personally, has deteriorated to such an extent that he is suicidal. Willy has come to inhabit a netherworld, caught between past and present, reality and fantasy, sanity and insanity. His long-suffering wife, Linda (Kate Reid), loves and admires Willy but can do nothing finally to save him from himself, especially since Willy tends to ignore her and his younger son, Happy (Stephen Lang), in favor of his first son, Biff (John Malkovich). At the age of thirty-four, Biff has yet to "find himself" and has just returned to New York from an unsuccessful foray in the West. Biff, a high school football star whose glory days have passed, resents Willy for having had an affair while on the road as a salesman. Indeed, Biff's discovery of the affair during his senior year of high school causes him to relinquish his dream of playing football at the University of Virginia, and Willy is not entirely wrong when shortly before his suicide he tells Biff: "Spite, spite is the word of your undoing!" The film version under the direction of Volker Schlondorff adheres closely to the original text; in fact, some might find Willy's flashbacks better suited to film than to the stage. The sets for the film are more realistic than those for the play, without diminishing the original in any way. The film departs from the play by opening with Willy's getting into a car crash, which relates to his early unsuccessful suicide attempt of driving his car into a river and anticipates the later deliberate car crash that ends his life. Miller declared that *Death of a Salesman* was intended to portray "the tragedy of the common man," and while only arguably successful in that attempt, Miller did provide one of the most compelling of American plays and one that readily makes the transition from drama to film. *(G. H.)*

Resources: Alice Griffen, *Understanding Arthur Miller* (Columbia: South Carolina University Press, 1996); Arthur Miller, *Timebends: A Life* (New York: Grove Press, 1987).

DEATH TAKES A HOLIDAY (1929)
Alberto Casella, rewritten for the American stage by Walter Ferris

---

Death Takes a Holiday (1934)

Directed by Mitchell Leisen

Adapted by Maxwell Anderson, Gladys Lehman, and Walter Ferris

Cast: Guy Standing (Duke Lambert), Katherine Alexander (Alda), Fredric March (Prince Sirki), Evelyn Venable (Grazia), Kent Taylor (Corrado), Gail Patrick (Rhoda), G. P. Huntley, Jr. (Eric)

Length: 79 minutes

Death Takes a Holiday, which made its New York debut in 1929 and was adapted to film in 1934, has only one set, the Great Hall in the Duke's castle. When the play opens, the Duke and his guests are discussing the passing shadow that plagued their drive home and are wondering why there were no fatalities. Later in the evening the "Shadow" appears to the Duke and identifies himself as Death, who is taking a three-day holiday to find out why people fear him and to discover the meaning of human love. He says he will assume the identity of Prince Sirki and warns the Duke not to reveal his true identity. Prince Sirki captivates Alda, Rhoda, and Grazia, fiancée to Corrado, the Duke's son; but he angers not only Corrado but also Eric, who is attracted by Alda's "restlessness and hunger." Both Rhoda and Alda make advances to the Prince, who asks them to look at the Lamp of Illusion and then deep into his eyes. Both recoil at what they see. Grazia, who has been hesitant to marry Corrado and seems almost removed from the real world, returns the last night of the Prince's holiday. When he discovers that the Prince wants Grazia to go with him, the Duke informs his guests about the Prince's identity and tells the Prince he must reveal himself to Grazia. He does, and Grazia responds that she already knows him and will go with him. The Prince says, "Then there *is* a love which casts out fear, and I have found it." At twelve midnight there is complete darkness. The film adaptation is quite literal, except for three added scenes, one of the speeding cars and the passing shadow, another of the Prince winning at the gaming tables, and one of Grazia at prayer in the chapel, separated from the party. The last addition serves to illustrate Grazia's spirituality. On the other hand, there are some omissions, the Lamp of Illusion and Major Whitread, who is hardly essential to the plot. At the end of the film Grazia and the Prince disappear after his speech about love being greater than illusion. *(T. L. E.)*

Resources: David Chierichetti, *Hollywood Director: The Career of Mitchell Leisen* (New York: Curtis Books, 1973); Lawrence J. Quirk, *The Films of Fredric March* (New York: Citadel, 1971).

Meet Joe Black (1998)

Directed by Martin Brest

Adapted by Ron Osborn, Jeff Reno, Kevin Wade, and Bo Goldman

Cast: Brad Pitt (Joe Black), Anthony Hopkins (William Parrish), Claire Forlani (Susan Parrish), Jake Weber (Drew), Marcia Gay Harden (Allison), Jeffrey Tambor (Quince), David S. Howard (Eddie Sloane)

Length: 170 minutes

Rated: PG-13

In this updated and overlong adaptation, twice removed from its source, *Death Takes a Holiday*, media tycoon William Parrish (Anthony Hopkins) awakes in the middle of the night with chest pains, and a voice enters his mind repeating the word "yes." That voice continues to follow him the next day, when Parrish then meets Death himself in the person of Joe Black (Brad Pitt). Curiosity, rather than any kind of emotional attachment to the human world, has led Death to his decision to "take" the body of a man who recently died in order to see for himself what life on earth is like. By chance Parrish's daughter Susan (Claire Forlani) had recently met that man in a coffee shop before his death and felt a strong attraction to him. Although Death intends to take Parrish into the afterlife, first he wants to see a bit of the world, to experience it firsthand and discover what it is like to be human. Death wants Parrish to be his companion and guide, and Parrish, desperate to prolong his life by whatever means possible, agrees. Joe accompanies Parrish everywhere, even to work, and falls in love with Susan, who does not realize that the man she had met has changed. As Parrish's time is running out, he finally begins to understand those things in life that are so important to him, things he had previously taken for granted, such as his relationship with his daughters and the loyalty of his son-in-law, Quince (Jeffrey Tambor). Meanwhile, Joe experiences the love of other human beings, both physically, through sexual contact, and emotionally. The film was inspired by the 1920s play *Death Takes a Holiday* but even more by the 1934 film adaptation, scripted by Maxwell Anderson, Gladys Lehman, and Walter Ferris and directed by Mitchell Leisen, starring Fredric March and Evelyn Venable. Fascinated by the earlier film, Brest worked on the script for over ten years, concluding that Joe Black should be played not as an angel of death but as "a sort of blank slate that seemed like death." James Sterngold described the film as a cinematic essay that might have been called "The Education of Death." The length of this loosely based and updated adaptation was a major drawback. The original Mitchell Leisen film came in at 79 minutes, and Brest would have done better to follow that example. *(J. M. W.)*

Resources: Owen Glieberman, "Reaper Madness," *Entertainment Weekly* No. 459 (20 November 1998): 89–92; James Sterngold, "At the Movies: Death and Life," *New York Times* (14 August 1998): B9.

DEATHTRAP (1978)
Ira Levin

Deathtrap (1982)

Directed by Sidney Lumet

Adapted by Jay Presson Allen

Cast: Michael Caine (Sidney Bruhl), Christopher Reeve (Clifford Anderson), Dyan Cannon (Myra Bruhl)

Length: 116 minutes

Rated: PG

Sidney Bruhl is in need of a hit play. The successful playwright is experiencing a dry spell, compounded by the failure of his last mystery. To add insult to injury, one of his seminar students, Clifford Anderson, has sent him a brilliant play entitled *Deathtrap*, one so perfect that Bruhl comments:

"A gifted director couldn't even hurt it." Bruhl jokes with Myra, his nervous, affected wife, about killing Anderson and claiming credit for the play, but is he joking? Sidney concocts a plot to kill Anderson and claim *Death-trap* as his own to redeem his name and become the toast of Broadway once again. Soon Clifford arrives as Sidney's guest, reluctantly drawn into this desperate game. It is soon apparent, however, that things are not as they seem. Plot twists abound in Lumet's version of Levin's wildly successful mystery. Two more characters, Helga Ten Dorp, a psychic with a new, best-selling book, and Porter Milgrim, Bruhl's attorney, are introduced, and the whodunit continues until the film's conclusion caps an intensifying number of twists and turns. The script is both a send-up of, and homage to, the murder mystery play, with most of Levin's references to the genre and his own play left intact in the film script. When Sidney comments on his protégé's script ("A thriller in two acts. One set. Five characters. A juicy murder in Act One, unexpected developments in Act Two. Sound construction, good dialogue, laughs in the right places. Highly commercial") he is commenting on both the genre's requirements and his play's structure all at once. Many such clever lines are interspersed throughout the film in order to acknowledge obvious staples of the genre and toy with the viewer's expectations of them. Unfortunately, the film's editing degenerates toward the end, creating some unnecessary confusion. However, all performances are strong, including Reeve, heretofore known only as Superman to most moviegoers, and Caine, who palpably relates the writer's frustration to the audience. Many critics compared this film unfavorably to *Sleuth*, Caine's 1972 murder mystery, which this film most resembles in plot and setting, but *Deathtrap* stands as a faithful adaptation of one of Broadway's most popular plays. *(J. A.)*

Resources: Jay Boyer, *Sidney Lumet* (New York: Twayne, 1993); Frank R. Cunningham, *Sidney Lumet: Film and Literary Vision* (Lexington: University of Kentucky Press 1991).

A DELICATE BALANCE (1966)
Edward Albee

A Delicate Balance (1973)

Directed by Tony Richardson

Adapted by Edward Albee

Cast: Katharine Hepburn (Agnes), Paul Scofield (Tobias), Kate Reid (Clair), Joseph Cotten (Harry), Betsy Blair (Edna), Lee Remick (Julia)

Length: 132 minutes

Although matriarch Agnes (Katherine Hepburn) is dominant, her marriage to Tobias (Paul Scofield) has achieved a "delicate balance" between love and hate that is challenged when they are joined by another couple, Harry and Edna (Joseph Cotten and Betsy Blair), who move in with them. This becomes an awkward complication when their daughter Julia (Lee Remick) returns home after a failed marriage and finds Harry and Edna in her room. Their marriage is also challenged by the presence of Clair (Kate Reid), Agnes' sister, who drinks excessively to alleviate her desire for Tobias. Agnes and Tobias are also haunted by the memory of a young son who died. Agnes asserts that "there is a balance to be maintained," to offset the "terror" of life. There is a need to provide a sanctuary by offering love and compassion. Richardson's film is faithful to its source but perhaps as faithful to its weaknesses as to its strengths. Richardson later remembered finding "the play itself, the more we worked on it, unsatisfying in its emotional underpinnings." The text of the play was dismissed as pompous, windy, and arch. The characters are diminished by dialogue that seems whiny and petty. As Richardson later noted, "The moral dilemmas at the core seem small in comparison with the intricacy of the trappings." Unfortunately, Richardson decided to shoot the film as a recorded play rather than a cinematic event, going against his usual penchant for location shooting. The cast was praised, especially Hepburn and Reid, as was David Watkin's cinematography, which suggested the harsh, naked truth of the characters. But by the time the film was made, the play seemed outdated and pointless to many. *(J. M. W.)*

Resources: Vincent Canby, " 'A Delicate Balance,' " *New York Times* (22 April 1996): C11; Tony Richardson, *The Long-Distance Runner: A Memoir* (New York: William Morrow, 1993); James M. Welsh and John C. Tibbetts, eds., *The Cinema of Tony Richardson* (Albany: State University of New York Press, 1999).

DESIRE UNDER THE ELMS (1924)
Eugene O'Neill

Desire under the Elms (1958)

Directed by Delbert Mann

Adapted by Irwin Shaw

Cast: Sophia Loren (Anna Cabot), Anthony Perkins (Eben Cabot), Burl Ives (Ephraim Cabot), Frank Overton (Simeon Cabot), Pernell Roberts (Peter Cabot)

Length: 111 minutes

O'Neill's play, which opened in New York in 1924, has been controversial because of its themes of incest and infanticide. It was banned in Boston and not performed in England until 1940. The play, set in the Cabot farmhouse in spring 1850, concerns the relationship between Ephraim Cabot, fond of quoting from the Old Testament; his son Eben, who hates his father for stealing the farm from his mother and working her into an early grave; and Abbie Putnam, an attractive young woman who becomes Ephraim's third wife to get his farm. As the play opens, Eben and his two older brothers discuss their father's two-month absence. When he learns his father has remarried, Eben uses his father's hidden money to buy out his brothers' rights to an inheritance, and they leave for California when their father arrives. Despite an initial antagonism, Eben and Abbie are attracted to each other, and when Abbie becomes pregnant, Eben, not Ephraim, is the father. At a party where he celebrates "his" son's birth, Ephraim tells Eben that the farm will be Abbie's. Infuriated at what he sees as Abbie's betrayal, he tells her he wishes the baby had never been born. To prove her love for Eben, Abbie smothers their baby; when a repentant Eben returns to her and learns what she has done, he goes to the sheriff but returns to share the guilt with her. When the play was adapted to film, O'Neill's stress on New England Puritanism and his use of ancient Greek drama, especially the oedipal story, were omitted; and what was a modern Greek tragedy becomes a domestic drama involving Eben (Anthony Perkins) and Anna Cabot (Sophia Loren, playing the Abbie of the play). In the film Anna is twenty, not thirty-five, and an immigrant whose disgust with Ephraim (Burl Ives) is apparent to all except him. Because the film focuses on the Eben-Anna sexual relationship, Eben's likeness to his father and his complex relationship with him are slighted. The film, however, adds material not in the play, notably, the return from California of Eben's brothers, Simeon (Frank Overton) and Peter (Pernell Roberts), who have struck gold in California and returned with wives who resemble saloon girls and who are insulted by Ephraim at the party given for "his" son. One of the wives discovers that the child is Eben's, but in the film everyone at the party seems to know who the father is. In fact, the most effective sequence in the film comprises the juxtaposition of the guests' knowing looks and comments and the frenzied, manic dancing of Ephraim, who is intent on demonstrating his manhood. O'Neill scholars were appalled by how much was lost and how little was gained in the film adaptation. *(T. L. E.)*

Resources: Tony Crawley, *The Films of Sophia Loren* (Secaucus, NJ: Citadel Press, 1976); John Orlandello, *O'Neill on Film* (Rutherford, NJ: Fairleigh Dickinson University Press, 1982).

THE DEVIL'S DISCIPLE (1897)
George Bernard Shaw

The Devil's Disciple (1959)

Directed by Guy Hamilton

Adapted by Roland Kibbee and John Dighton

Cast: Burt Lancaster (Anthony Anderson), Kirk Douglas (Dick Dudgeon), Laurence Olivier (Gen. Burgoyne), Janette Scott (Judith Anderson), Eva Le Gallienne (Mrs. Dudgeon), Harry Andrews (Maj. Swindon), Neil McCallum (Christopher Dudgeon), Jenny Jones (Essie)

Length: 82 minutes

Because Shaw never liked his *The Devil's Disciple*, it was performed just once, for copyright purposes, in London in 1897 and was not seen again until it was later staged in New York. The play, which takes place in Websterbridge, New Hampshire, in 1777, concerns the conflict between the British and the rebellious colonists. The play begins with the news that the British have hanged two Dudgeon brothers as rebels, and the Dudgeon family gathers for the reading of the will, which leaves most of the property to Dick Dudgeon, a godless, dissolute man despised by the rest of the family. Anthony Anderson, the Protestant minister who consoles the vengeful Mrs. Dudgeon, learns that the British intend to hang another rebel and, thinking that Dick is the intended victim, warns him. The British, however, have targeted Anderson and come to his house to arrest him. Dick is at the Anderson house with Judith, who hides her attraction to him by verbally attacking him; Dick is mistaken for Anderson and arrested. He does not reveal his true identity and is taken to jail and joined by Judith, who confesses her love for him. After Dick is tried and convicted, Judith tells General Burgoyne that Dick is not her husband; but the sentence stands. At the gallows Dick is saved by Anderson, who arrives with a safe-conduct pass and demands that Dick be freed. Anderson has found his true calling as a soldier and offers to exchange occupations with Dick, who promises Judith that he will not tell Anderson about her infatuation. While the film retains many of Shaw's anti-British quips, mostly given to Dick and Burgoyne, there are some alterations to the plot. Through animated sequences, the film provides a historical context; and the film uses outside scenes to show how the Americans' guerrilla tactics frustrate the British, to explain why Anderson is the intended victim (he buried Dick's father's body), and to show Anderson's development from minister to soldier as he becomes progressively involved in the battle and finally ignites the British ammunition dump. Another addition occurs at the end of the film, when Anderson reclaims his wife by riding after her and sweeping her up into his arms. That ending serves to preserve the sanctity of marriage for film audiences. *(T. L. E.)*

Resource: Bernard F. Dukore, ed., *Bernard Shaw on Cinema* (Carbondale: Southern Illinois University Press, 1997); Foster Hirsch, *Laurence Olivier* (Boston: Twayne, 1979).

DIAL M FOR MURDER (1952)
Frederick Knott

Dial M for Murder (1954)

Directed by Alfred Hitchcock

Adapted by Frederick Knott

Cast: Ray Milland (Tony Wendice), Grace Kelly (Margot Wendice), Robert Cummings (Mark Halliday), John Williams (Inspector Hubbard), Anthony Dawson (Captain Lesgate)

Length: 105 minutes

Dial M for Murder first appeared at the Plymouth Theatre, New York, on 29 October 1952, with Maurice Evans in the role of Tony Wendice. John Williams and Anthony Dawson repeated their stage roles in the film version. Frederick Knott adapted it for Hitchcock in 1954, and the film version was shot in 3-D by Robert Burks during thirty-six days. *Dial M for Murder* has usually appeared in a conventional flat version due to its release when the 3-D boom came to an end.

The theatrical version takes place entirely in the living room of the Wendice apartment in London over a period of several months. Although the conventionally shot version attempts to break away from its theatrical origins by showing several outside scenes and the Wendice bedroom and using cinematic techniques such as close-ups, low-angle shots, and a striking, high-angle view when Tony acts like a theatrical director rehearsing Lesgate for his new role as designated murderer, the 3-D version is much more innovative. As with his other experiments in *Rope* and *Rear Window*, Hitchcock creatively employs this short-lived technology. Tony Wendice engages in a power game with his chosen victims and dominates them through most of the film. Hitchcock uses the spatial dimensions of 3-D technology to depict his actors either in the foreground or in the background according to the relative gains they make in the plot. Tony Wendice prominently occupies the major 3-D space for the majority of the film. When Inspector Hubbard takes over the dominating role in the final act, Hitchcock emphasizes his position spatially while decreasing that of Tony Wendice. However, the most striking 3-D shot occurs when Lesgate attempts to murder Margot. When she falls on Tony's desk, her hand reaches out to the audience as if begging for help. She then grasps the scissors lying on the desk and stabs Lesgate. Before she does so, the scissors appear over the heads of the audience, thus implicating them in Margot's violent act, an act she will be blamed for by the forces of the law. Both Inspector Hubbard and Wendice place an important apartment key into the face of the audience as if making a theatrical gesture via the new technology. Hitchcock used 3-D to emphasize the theatrical aspects. He never shows Margot's trial but films her against a screen background with voice-overs on the soundtrack. This background has color lights revolving around her, which become more reddish and dark before the judge sentences her to death. As in *Rope* and *Rear Window*, Hitchcock still uses his expressionist heritage by adding color to it. *(T. W.)*

Resources: William Rothman, *Hitchcock: The Murderous Gaze* (Cambridge: Harvard University Press, 1982); François Truffaut, *Hitchcock* (London: Panther, 1969).

A Perfect Murder (1998)

Directed by Andrew Davis

Adapted by Patrick Smith Kelly

Cast: Michael Douglas (Steven Taylor), Gwyneth Paltrow (Emily Bradford Taylor), Viggo Mortensen (David Shaw), David Suchet (Detective Mohamed Karaman)

Length: 108 minutes

Rated: R

New York financial tycoon Steven Taylor (Michael Douglas) becomes insanely jealous when he discovers his heiress wife Emily (Gwyneth Paltrow) is romantically involved with a struggling artist, David Shaw (Viggo Mortensen). The presumably enraged husband offers the lover $400,000 to murder his wife, a form of blackmail, since the husband has also discovered the artist has a criminal past as a con man who has taken advantage of women. Although jealousy is apparently the husband's prime motive, Emily's well-endowed trust fund must also be a motive behind this carefully plotted "perfect murder." The remake was "inspired" by Frederick Knott's play *Dial M for Murder*, adapted to the screen by Alfred Hitchcock in 1954, but the new suspense thriller was loosely adapted—updated and expanded—with alterations made to the plot and characters. Screenwriter Kelly relocated the action from London in the 1950s to New York City in the 1990s, a world he believed he knew. Reviewer David Ansen found the artist's dilemma of being blackmailed to kill the woman he loves interesting but not fully developed: "In the Hitchcock film the hired killer and the lover were two different characters" (70). The redefined characters are relatively shallow because the remake exhibits little curiosity about them. Ansen praised the film for casting Constance Towers, from an older Hollywood tradition, as Emily's patrician mother and for its sense of interior design, which situates the remake, in his opinion, "closer to Architectural Digest than Alfred Hitchcock." The twisted and suspenseful conclusion does work, however, in its own way. *(J. M. W.)*

Resource: David Ansen, "Dial R for Remake," *Newsweek* (15 July 1998): 70.

DINNER AT EIGHT (1932)
George S. Kaufman and Edna Ferber

Dinner at Eight (1933)

Directed by George Cukor

Adapted by Herman J. Mankiewicz and Frances Marion with additional dialogue by Donald Ogden Stewart

Cast: John Barrymore (Larry Renault), Wallace Beery (Mr. Packard), Jean Harlow (Mrs. Packard), Lionel Barrymore (Mr. Jordan)

Length: 113 minutes

The prolific George S. Kaufman may have joked that satire is what closes on Saturday night, but this curt dismissal should not dissuade one from acknowledging the continuous presence of a critical consciousness in his theatrical work. *Dinner at Eight*, written in 1932 in collaboration with the novelist Edna Ferber, takes as its sphere the world of cosmopolitan socialites but does not take them lightly. Kaufman and Ferber treat with a cocked eyebrow the machinations that ensue when a flighty and oblivious upperclass hostess, Mrs. Millicent Jordan (played onstage and onscreen by Billie Burke), gives a lavish dinner party for Lord and Lady Ferncliffe. Her guests are, as a group, vain, obsessed with privilege, and driven by the need to maintain appearances, even at the risk of their lives. The nouveau riche capitalist Dan Packard (Wallace Beery) can't ignore the fact that his chic mistress (Jean Harlow) cheats behind his back; the shipping magnate and husband of Mrs. Jordan (Lionel Barrymore) is in ill health and even worse financial shape; and the once-illustrious Broadway actor Larry Renault (John Barrymore) is on his way to eventual suicide because of the loss of his looks and legend. Typical of Kaufman, the bons mots betray a hollow bonhomie, which would seem to be in collision with the gloss and grandeur one associates with either MGM, the releasing company, or David Selznick, the producer of the film, let alone the work of director George Cukor. None of them were prone to seek out material with even this veneer of relevance and certainly were not driven to criticize, however mildly, the nation's ruling class. Cukor in particular does make short shrift of the play's astringency, but the energy of the performances and the lavishness of the production make *Dinner at Eight* an enjoyable film, while not a critique of social mores. The depression may have been just outside the theatre doors when the film was released, yet despite the satiric thrust of the material, in the end the rich are confirmed as being, in F. Scott Fitzgerald's words, "not like you or me." *(D. S.)*

Resources: Gary Carey, *Cukor and Co.: The Films of George Cukor and His Collaborators* (New York: Museum of Modern Art, 1971); Patrick McGilligan, *A Double Life: George Cukor* (New York: St. Martin's Press, 1991); Gene D. Phillips, *George Cukor* (Boston: Twayne, 1982).

THE DOCK BRIEF (1957)
John Clifford Mortimer

Trial and Error (1961)

Directed by James Hill

Adapted by Pierre Rouve

Cast: Peter Sellers (Morganhall), Richard Attenborough (Fowle), Beryl Reid (Mrs. Fowle), David Lodge (Boarder)

Length: 78 minutes

This legal satire, adapted by Pierre Rouve from John Mortimer's first play, *The Dock Brief*, concerns the bumbling efforts of a barrister, Mr. Morganhall (Peter Sellers), to represent the pathetically henpecked and extremely timid owner of a birdseed shop, Mr. Fowle (Richard Attenborough). Fowle is accused of murdering his loud, boisterous, fun-loving wife (Beryl Reid), whom the poor man attempts to ignore but whose practical jokes get on his nerves after a boarder (David Lodge) is asked to leave because this exuberant jokester, whose fun-loving nature matches the wife's, has made a pass at her. The boarder's presence gave the husband some respite from his wife's folly, but after the boarder leaves, the man snaps. Ultimately, the accused is released because of his barrister's incompetence. The play operates like a two-hander, a play involving only two characters, the barrister and his client, but the film effectively uses flashbacks to tell the story of the accused. Best known for his television series *Rumpole of the Bailey*, John Mortimer, who was associate producer for the film, began his writing career as dramatist by drawing upon his experiences as a barrister. Mortimer believed that comedy is "the only thing worth writing in this despairing age, provided the comedy is truly on the side of the lonely, the neglected, the unsuccessful, and plays its part in the war against established rules and against the imposing of an arbitrary code of behavior upon individual and unpredictable human beings" (Hayman 50). Therefore, *The Dock Brief*, first performed as a radio play in 1957 before being performed onstage, dramatizes the plight of a lonely and pathetic criminal attempting to communicate with his barrister, who wins the case despite his incompetence (or because of it) in defending his client. *(J. M. W.)*

Resources: Ronald Hayman, *British Theatre since 1955: A Reassessment* (Oxford: Oxford University Press, 1979); David Pickering, *Dictionary of Theatre* (London: Sphere Books, 1988).

DOCTOR FAUSTUS (1589)
Christopher Marlowe

Doctor Faustus (1967)

Directed by Richard Burton and Nevill Coghill

Adapted by Nevill Coghill

Cast: Richard Burton (Doctor Faustus), Elizabeth Taylor (Helen of Troy), Andreas Teuber (Mephistopheles), Ian Marter (Emperor), Elizabeth O'Donovan (Empress)

Length: 93 minutes

In 1966 Richard Burton returned to Oxford to take part in a stage production of Christopher Marlowe's *The Tragicall History of Doctor Faustus* under the direction of the Merton Professor of English, Nevill Coghill, who had been his tutor during a six-month course at Exeter College in 1944. Accompanied by Elizabeth Taylor, who took on the nonspeaking part of Helen of Troy, he played the role of Doctor Faustus for the Oxford University Dramatic Society. Funds were raised for the University Theatre, but the play received poor reviews, perhaps because Burton failed to learn his lines. Nevertheless, as the couple proceeded to Italy to make *The Taming of the Shrew*, they decided to finance a film version of the play to be shot in Rome in 1967. Burton directed, in tandem with his former mentor, Coghill. Forty-eight undergraduates from the Oxford University Dramatic Society were employed at union minimum wages. The resulting film was a disaster of epic proportions. To say that the film was savaged by critics is an understatement. Renata Adler in the *New York Times* wrote of "an awfulness that bends the mind" (7 February 1968). The adaptation purports to be faithful to the original blank verse tragedy, but, in fact, it involves considerable excisions from the text. Moreover, Coghill arbitrarily added lines from other Marlowe works such as *Tamburlaine* and *The Jew of Malta*. Visually, the film is full of tiresomely heavy-handed and literal interpretations of the text; skulls and skeletons, pearls and gold coins abound. Worst of all, however, and the cause of fatally unintended comic effect are the multiple silent appearances of a heavily made-up Taylor as the décolleté embodiment of Faustian lust: "Was this the face that launched a thousand ships/And burnt the topless towers of Ilium?" Nevertheless, the film has a certain fascination, for, despite itself, it serves as an ironic index of Burton's life. Indeed, he told friends that "*Faustus* is the one play that I don't have to do any work on . . . I am Faustus" (Junor 116). The work may be replete with cinematic clichés, but it also affirms Burton's considerable capacity for the resonant articulation of blank verse. Moreover, it provides a telling parable for a man who sacrificed artistic integrity in favor of the worldly rewards of celebrity. *(W. L. H.)*

Resources: "Dr. Faustus," *Films and Filming* 13.4 (January 1967): 53–55; Penny Junor, *Burton: The Man behind the Myth* (New York: St. Martin's Press, 1985).

A DOLL'S HOUSE (1897)
Henrik Ibsen

A Doll's House (1973)

Directed by Patrick Garland

Screenplay by Christopher Hampton

Cast: Claire Bloom (Nora), Anthony Hopkins (Torvald Helmer), Ralph Richardson (Dr. Rank), Denholm Elliott (Krogstad), Anna Massey (Kristine Linde)

Length: 96 minutes

Rated: G

Ibsen's 1897 play about a woman who leaves her husband and children when she discovers her ideas about marriage are only illusions was appropriate to a time (1973) when the women's movement was at its peak. Claire Bloom had recently played Nora on the New York and London stage, and a film adaptation was inevitable (Jane Fonda played Nora in a competing film adaptation—see next entry). Bloom's husband, Hillard Elkins, produced the film with Bloom as Nora. Christopher Hampton, who had staged his own version of Ibsen's play, wrote the screen play, which is extremely faithful to Ibsen's text. Garland's film retains the one-day action of Ibsen's play and restricts the setting to interiors; but the camera does move from room to room and even adds a Christmas ball scene when Nora dances the tarantella. The most striking shot in that scene is when the camera moves to an extreme close-up of a whirling Nora, thereby suggesting the emotional chaos she is experiencing. Garland also uses the camera to reflect the shifting relationship between the patronizing Torvald and the submissive, but manipulative, Nora. Early shots include both characters within the frame; shots after Torvald's discovery of Nora's forgery include only the speaker, denying a relationship between them. The strength of Garland's adaptation is in the acting. Hopkins' Torvald is not aloof and emotionally distant: he is physically affectionate and warm with Nora and with his children. As a result, when he strikes Nora after he discovers her forged note and realizes that he is in the blackmailing Krogstad's power, most audiences are shocked. Showing the darker side of a passionate, possessive love mirrors the contemporary "stalking" behavior. Bloom's Nora is also effective. Behaving like a squirrel, acting like a pouting child, Nora embodies the woman-child who has never left the dollhouse. When she realizes that her husband is not the protector she thought he would be, her behavior changes, her steps slow, and her speech becomes steady rather than breathless. This physical transformation mirrors the inner transformation she has experienced. *(T. L. E.)*

Resources: Claire Bloom, *Leaving a Doll's House: A Memoir* (Boston: Little, Brown, 1996); Claire Bloom, *Limelight and After: The Education of an Actress* (New York: Harper and Row, 1982); Quentin Falk, *Anthony Hopkins: The Authorized Biography* (New York: Interlink Books, 1993).

A Doll's House (1973)

Directed and adapted by Joseph Losey

Cast: Jane Fonda (Nora), David Warner (Torvald Helmer), Trevor Howard (Dr. Rank), Delphine Seyrig (Kristine Linde), Edward Fox (Krogstad)

Length: 99 minutes

Rated: G

In his adaptation of Ibsen's controversial play (1897) about marriage, Losey adds an introductory sequence that simplifies Ibsen's complicated plot.

To save Torvald's life, Nora forges her father's signature to borrow money from Krogstad, who exposes her crime when her husband fires him from his bank job. When he learns of her actions, Torvald angrily charges her with ruining his career. When Kristine, who had earlier rejected Krogstad and married a rich man in order to support her family, persuades Krogstad to return the incriminating note, Torvald magnanimously forgives Nora; but she, having discovered that he is not the man she believed him to be, leaves him and her children to develop herself as a person. Ibsen's play takes place in one room, thereby suggesting Nora's imprisonment, but Losey takes the opening sequence outside to a frozen pond where Nora and Kristine skate and then enter a restaurant, where Krogstad accuses Kristine of marrying for money, not love. This action takes place eight years in the past and explains the anger Krogstad exhibits at the beginning of Ibsen's play, which occurs in just one day. Losey thereby loosens both time and space limitations, and the several scenes that are shot outside make his adaptation a film rather than a photographed play. Other cinematic touches include the juxtaposition of scenes at the Christmas party, where a fearful Nora dances the tarantella and then goes downstairs to kiss her children good-bye, with the scene at Krogstad's, where Krogstad leaves Kristine to care for his upset children. This scene and other outdoor scenes with his sledding children humanize Krogstad. Losey approached Fonda about playing Nora, but she and he disagreed about how to film the play. As a feminist, Fonda wanted to retain and even strengthen the play's position on marriage and women; but Losey, who was concerned with the large amount of dialogue, which was appropriate to drama but not to film, opted to cut much of the discussion at the end of the play. This decision and the addition of outside scenes might reduce the sense of Nora's entrapment, but Losey has maintained that Nora's imprisonment is psychological, not physical or spatial. Although it was a low-budget endeavor designed for television (first aired in the United States on ABC), Losey's *A Doll House* is a most cinematic movie. *(T. L. E.)*

Resources: Michel Ciment, *Conversations with Losey* (London: Methuen, 1985); Foster Hirsch, *Joseph Losey* (Boston: Twayne, 1980).

DON'T DRINK THE WATER (1966)
Woody Allen

Don't Drink the Water (1994)

Directed and adapted by Woody Allen

Cast: Woody Allen (Walter Hollander), Julie Kavner (Mrs. Hollander), Mayim Bialik (Susan Hollander), Michael J. Fox (Axel Magee), Josef Sommer (Ambassador Magee), Dom DeLuise (Father Drobney), Austin Pendleton (Chef Oscar), Ed Herlihy (Narrator)

Length: 100 minutes

This slapstick farce, a Cold War comedy about a family from New Jersey held captive in an Iron Curtain country, was Allen's first play produced on Broadway, where it ran successfully for over a year. Walter Hollander (Woody Allen), a "creative caterer" from Newark, New Jersey, has taken his family behind the Iron Curtain on vacation, but they are somehow mistaken for spies. They seek refuge at the American Embassy and find themselves under the protection of young Axel Magee (Michael J. Fox), an incompetent idiot left in charge in the absence of his father, the ambassador, recalled to Washington for consideration for a cabinet posting. Also at the embassy is a dissident priest, Father Drobney (Dom DeLuise), who moonlights as a magician and has been an exile in residence there for six years. Allen scripted and directed this adaptation for ABC television, but it is far better than the feature film directed by Howard Morris and made without Allen's involvement in 1969 that starred a badly miscast Jackie Gleason as Walter, with Estelle Parsons as his wife. Gleason's bombastic style bulldozed the rhythm of Allen's lines, written for Allen's own stand-up comic style, and by the time this adaptation was made, Allen had aged gracefully into the role. No one would know the material better than Allen himself. *(J. M. W.)*

Resources: Ken Tucker, "The Woodman Cometh," *Entertainment Weekly* (16 December 1994): 52–54; Maurice Yacowar, *Loser Take All: The Comic Art of Woody Allen* (New York: Frederick Ungar, 1979).

DRACULA (1924)
Hamilton Deane and John Balderston

Dracula (1931)

Directed by Tod Browning
Adapted by Garrett Fort

Cast: Bela Lugosi (Dracula), Helen Chandler (Mina), Dwight Frye (Renfield), Edward Van Sloane (Dr. Van Helsing)

Length: 75 minutes

The 1931 Universal horror film classic starring Bela Lugosi as Dracula was not based on the Bram Stoker novel but on a dramatization by Hamilton Deane and John Balderston. Stoker himself had presented a play version, *Dracula, or the Un-Dead*, in collaboration with actor Henry Irving in 1897, within days of the book's first publication. Historian Donald Glut claims the five-act, four-hour play demonstrated little dramatic creativity—"it was hardly more than a dramatic reading of the book" (78). More successful was the adaptation by Deane and Balderston, written in 1923 with the blessing of Stoker's widow and premiered in Derby, England, in June 1924. In simplifying the novel's complex narrative, Deane jettisoned Jonathan Harker's visit to Castle Dracula in Transylvania and the nightmarish pursuit of Dracula back to Transylvania and confined the story to three London settings—Harker's house, Mrs. Harker's boudoir, and Carfax Abbey. Deane created the Count we know so well today, a clean-shaven, regal figure in full evening dress who affects a courtly air and romantic demeanor (Deane himself portrayed the character of Van Helsing). Despite critical cavils, the play was a smash, and it attracted the attention of American producer Horace Liveright. After receiving a "modernized" polish by writer John L. Balderston—the three acts were now set in the library of Dr. Seward's sanatorium, in Lucy's boudoir, and in Seward's secret vault—it opened at New York's Fulton Theatre in October 1927. Appearing as Dracula was a Hungarian newcomer named Bela Lugosi (Bela Blasko), whose appearance epitomized the image fabricated by Deane. When Universal put *Dracula* into production in 1931, screenwriter Garrett Fort decided to model it after the play version rather than the novel. Accordingly, several of the play's cast members were retained—Lugosi in the eponymous role, Dwight Frye as Renfield, and Edward Van Sloane as Professor Van Helsing. The bulk of the film, with the exception of a marvelously atmospheric opening that depicts Harker's visit to Castle Dracula, is tediously stage-bound, with Karl Freund's camera occupying the place of a theatre patron seated third-row center. Most of the action transpires offscreen (even Dracula's fatal impalement by Van Helsing occurs offscreen), the acting is stilted and stagy, and none of Dracula's transformations into bats and animals are depicted. As in the play, the climactic action transpires in a London crypt rather than back at Castle Dracula. Audiences loved it, and the film's success—it was Universal's top grosser of 1931—imparted new life into Deane's play. Indeed, Deane realized a lifelong ambition when he himself appeared as Dracula in 1939. The play is still being presented in amateur and professional versions around the world, including a successful

1977 version featuring Edward Gorey–designed stage settings and Frank Langella in the title role. *(J. C. T.)*

Resources: Donald R. Glut, *The Dracula Book* (Metuchen, NJ: Scarecrow Press, 1975); Leonard Wolf, *Dracula: The Connoisseur's Guide* (New York: Broadway Books, 1997).

THE DRESSER (1980)
Ronald Harwood

The Dresser (1983)

Directed by Peter Yates

Adapted by Ronald Harwood and Peter Yates

Cast: Albert Finney (Sir), Tom Courtenay (Norman), Zena Walker (Her Ladyship), Eileen Atkins (Madge), Cathryn Harrison (Irene), Lockwood West (Geoffrey Thornton), Edward Fox (Oxenby)

Length: 118 minutes

Rated: PG

Set during the German blitz of World War II, the play follows the fortunes of a troupe of actors struggling to perform Shakespeare in the British countryside, but it is mainly about the relationship between a famous Shakespearean actor (Albert Finney) and his loyal servant and "dresser," Norman (Tom Countenay). The actor is on his last legs, barely able to pull himself together for a performance of *King Lear* without Norman's coaxing and encouragement. The challenge in the second act is to prepare the actor to perform as King Lear, Shakespeare's most challenging character. It proves to be the performance of a lifetime, and after the curtain comes down, the actor dies, leaving Norman disconsolate. The play has only two settings. The film extends the action outside the theatre to show one of the actor's bouts with dementia in the wrecked setting of a bombed-out town. The troupe's manager (Eileen Atkins) wants to cancel the performance, but Norman convinces her that he can get the old man in shape to perform, even though the actor is inclined to scramble together lines from several plays and cannot even remember Lear's opening lines. But once the performance begins, the actor is in his element and manages to give an unforgettable performance, partly because the state of the actor's mind is nearly as disturbed as that of Lear in the play. The play was inspired by the memory of Sir Donald Wolfit, for whom Harwood once worked. The film is graced by outstanding performances from Albert Finney and Tom

Courtenay, both of whom were nominated for Academy Awards. The play is splendidly adapted. *(J. M. W.)*

Resources: David Ansen, "Fools of Fortune," *Newsweek* (5 December 1983): 125; Michael Billington, "All the Stage Is a Movie," *New York Times* (26 June 1983): II, 17; Vincent Canby, "Ronald Harwood's 'Dresser,' " *New York Times* (6 December 1983): C19.

DRIVING MISS DAISY (1987)
Alfred Uhry

Driving Miss Daisy (1990)

Directed by Bruce Beresford

Adapted by Alfred Uhry

Cast: Morgan Freeman (Hoke Colburn), Jessica Tandy (Daisy Werthan), Dan Aykroyd (Boolie Werthan), Patti LuPone (Florine Werthan), Esther Rolle (Idella), Joann Havrilla (Miss McClatchey), William Hall, Jr. (Oscar), Alvin M. Sugarman (Dr. Weil)

Length: 99 minutes

Rated: PG

Alfred Uhry's Pulitzer Prize–winning play, set in Atlanta during the years 1948 to 1973, has only three characters: Daisy Werthan, a widow, seventy-two years old when the play begins, her son Boolie (age forty), and Hoke Coleburn, sixty years old when Boolie first hires him to be Miss Daisy's chauffeur. Daisy is Jewish, and Hoke is African American, both of them outsiders in the American South, but as society changes in the South, so does their relationship. At first Daisy, whose pride is wounded when her son arranges a chauffeur for her, treats Hoke like a servant, but over the years a friendship develops, as Daisy begins to understand what the two of them have in common. The text is extended in the play; this is not simply a matter of padding but is intended to give the play a wider social and visual context. The film takes the viewer to Boolie's factory, for example, to introduce Hoke, who is resourceful enough to repair an elevator that is not working; this convinces Boolie that Hoke would make a good and loyal companion for his aging mother. The film also takes the viewer to Boolie's home, giving his wife, Florine, a higher definition. Idella, the maid (Esther Rolle), extends Miss Daisy's understanding of African Americans as well, as Miss Daisy is "driven" to a new understanding of herself, her station, and the New South. She achieves a new understanding of her pride, a new appreciation for Idella and Hoke, who is himself the very emblem of kindness and tolerance as Daisy becomes older and realizes how much she depends on him. Although the play is extended, the original playwright was called upon to reshape his work into an excellent screen adaptation. *(J. M. W.)*

Resources: Helen Vann and Jane Caputi, "*Driving Miss Daisy*: A New 'Song of the South,' " *Journal of Popular Film & Television* 18.2 (1990): 80–82; J. M. Welsh, "*Driving Miss Daisy*," *Films in Review* 41.4 (1990): 231.

EASY VIRTUE (1925)
Noël Coward

Easy Virtue (1927)

Directed by Alfred Hitchcock

Adapted by Eliot Stannard

Cast: Isabel Jeans (Larita Filton), Franklin Dyall (Filton), Eric Bransby Williams (Claude), Ian Hunter (Charles Burleigh), Robin Irvine (John Whittaker), Violet Farebrother (Mrs. Whittaker)

Length: 73 minutes

Noël Coward's original, three-act play takes place entirely in the country house hall of a wealthy English upper-middle-class family. *Easy Virtue* represents Coward's subversive contribution to the drawing-room dramatic plays that dominated the English stage from the 1880s to the beginning of World War I and dealt with the psychological and social problems of the upper classes. Coward takes Pinero's *The Second Mrs. Tanquery* as his model. Although both plays deal with the theme of the fallen woman victimized by a hypocritical society, his heroine does not perish as an atonement for her "guilty past." Instead, Larita Filton realizes her mistake in marrying a weaker, younger man and lives to walk away from a repressive British social system and return to France. Alfred Hitchcock opens up the play by beginning the film with a caption that characterizes Larita as one of the many unjustly socially proscribed "guilty women" who fascinated him throughout his career: "Virtue has its own reward, they say, but easy virtue is society's reward for a slanderous reputation." The opening sequence depicts Larita in a divorce court, where she is victimized by a male society. A judge gazes at her but needs a monocle to focus his vision. This is one of several cinematic references Hitchcock makes to the blurred and unjust nature of a patriarchal voyeurism damning his heroine. Hitchcock includes scenes that act as preludes to the actual play. The audience sees Larita victimized by a brutal husband and let down by her devoted artist admirer, Claude, who anticipates the later role of John Whittaker. Neither Filton nor Claude appears in the play. But Hitchcock casts Coward's original houseguest, Charles Burleigh, as the prosecuting lawyer Larita later meets at her in-laws' country house. She goes to recover in Cannes, but John accidentally hits a tennis ball at her eye. This leads to both becoming acquainted and getting married. Ironically, Larita will later find her new husband socially castrated by a hypocritical social system represented by his mother. The director's monstrous mother figure is not only confined to his American films. When John proposes to Larita on the phone, a telephone operator voyeuristically "listens in" to the conversation. When Larita's past life is exposed, she leaves the Whittaker home, as in the play. But Hitchcock concludes the film with Larita outside the divorce court positioned like a victim before a firing squad of cameras saying, "Shoot, there's nothing left to kill." Although both Coward and Hitchcock equally condemn a hypocritical British class system, the director's vision is more pessimistic than the playwright's. *(T. W.)*

Resources: Stephen Cole, *Noël Coward: A Bio-Bibliography* (Westport, CT: Greenwood Press, 1993); Maurice Yacowar, *Hitchcock's Silent Films* (Hamden, CT: Archon Books, 1977).

EDUCATING RITA (1980)
Willy Russell

Educating Rita (1983)

Directed by Lewis Gilbert

Adapted by Willy Russell

Cast: Julie Walters (Rita/Susan White), Michael Caine (Frank Bryant), Maureen Lipman (Trish), Michael Williams (Brian), Jeananne Crowley (Julia),

Malcolm Douglas (Denny), Godfrey Quigley (Rita's Father), Darbina Molloy (Elaine), Pat Daly (Bursar), Philip Hurdwood (Tiger)

Length: 110 minutes

Rated: PG-13

The Royal Shakespeare production of *Educating Rita* was voted Best Comedy of 1980, and by 1983, the year it was adapted to cinema, it was rated the fourth most popular play on the British stage. The play is a two-hander (just two actors) involving only the relationship between Rita, a twenty-six-year-old hairdresser from Liverpool, and her Open University tutor, Frank, a burned-out alcoholic who discovers that Rita is smart enough to succeed in college but is reluctant to change her because he is charmed by her working-class common sense. His reservations are overpowered by her raw ambition, however, and her education eventually spirals beyond his immediate control. As Rita, whose real name is Susan White, becomes more educated, she also becomes alienated from her husband, who eventually leaves her, and from her family. But she is tough and determined. She develops the self-confidence to succeed on her own and takes control of her life, to the extent that she no longer needs Frank, once he has taught her how to think for herself. The setting of the play is much extended in order to show Rita at home and at work as well as in Frank's office and to offer an effective contrast between working-class Liverpool and the university setting. Julie Walters, who introduced the role on the London stage, is brilliant in her ability to show Rita's transformation, as her language is improved, and her appearance, her wardrobe, and her hairstyle change gradually to reflect her change in station and class. Michael Caine is equally capable of portraying her infatuated tutor, whose own life shows promise of being reformed as a result of his relationship with Rita. He learns as much from her as she learns from him, and at the end of the play he is ready to pursue a new life in Australia. The play ends with Rita's giving Frank a haircut; the film ends with an emotional leave-taking at the airport, leading one to think that Rita just might eventually accompany him. *(J. M. W.)*

Resources: Sheila Johnston, "*Educating Rita,*" *Monthly Film Bulletin* 50 (May 1983): 130; Marcia Magill, "*Educating Rita,*" *Films in Review* 34.9 (November 1983): 569; Willy Russell, "Educating the Author," in *Educating Rita,* ed. Richard Adams (Harlow, Essex: Longman Study Texts, 1985).

EDWARD II (1592)
Christopher Marlowe

Edward II (1992)

Directed by Derek Jarman

Adapted by Derek Jarman, Ken Butler, Steve Clark-Hall, Stephen McBride, and Antony Root

Cast: Steven Waddington (Edward), Andrew Tiernan (Gaveston), Tilda Swinton (Queen Isabella), Nigel Terry (Mortimer), John Lynch (Spencer), Annie Lennox (singer)

Length: 90 minutes

Rated: R

Derek Jarman's unrepentantly political and stylized version of what is widely regarded to be Marlowe's greatest artistic achievement is at times more social commentary than adaptation. Jarman's film work (which includes a version of Shakespeare's *The Tempest*) deals openly with gay themes, and his interpretation of *Edward II* presents the king as a tragic hero, a victim of repression and sexual intolerance whose passion for the "basely born" Gaveston leads to his overthrow and murder. In fact, Jarman's attempt to draw parallels between Elizabethan and twentieth-century views of power, sexuality, and homophobia effectively underscores the radical political nature of Marlowe's original work. Critics have long located the tragedy of Edward's death within his failure to maintain the strict class hierarchies of the social order. By emphasizing the allegorical nature of the play's sexual conflicts, Jarman largely overlooks such historical class criticisms. In their place, however, he effectively represents Marlowe's vision of "the possibility of sexuality and sexual difference as a separate category" (Goldberg), a separation most clearly manifested by Jarman's portrayal of the distinction between heterosexual and homosexual relationships within the film. Queen Isabella and Mortimer, the leader of the rebellion, are presented as consummate role-players, maneuvering each other into position as usurpers of royal power (as well as into bed), with Edward's sexuality providing the scapegoat for their machinations. Mortimer's sadomasochistic proclivities and Isabella's awakening Tory-ish absolutism, counterposed by the increasingly militaristic dress and sadistic play habits of her son, the future Edward III, brilliantly satirize the English aristocracy and its legacy of oppression. By contrast, the union between Edward and Gaveston—and later, Spenser—underscores the mutuality,

honesty, and openness integral to the film's gay relationships. Jarman depicts Edward as a self-reflective and sympathetic figure who develops from
a hedonist into an outspoken political and sexual activist (the events of the
play's fifth act frame the film's action and, more importantly, testify to
the development of Edward's sexual-political awareness). Yet much of the
film's effectiveness lies in Jarman's refusal to canonize the love between
Edward and Gaveston, which is at times both reckless and vindictive. Although clearly a revisionist interpretation, Jarman's often unsettlingly explicit film conveys the radical spirit of Marlowe's original play in its
unstinting refusal to be bound by conventions—generic, sexual, or stylistic.
(R. R.)

Resource: Jonathan Goldberg, *Sodometries* (Stanford, CA: Stanford University
Press, 1992).

THE ELEPHANT MAN (1979)
Bernard Pomerance

The Elephant Man (1980)

Directed by David Lynch

Adapted by Christopher DeVore, Eric Bergren, and David Lynch

Cast: Anthony Hopkins (Treves), John Hurt (Merrick), Anne Bancroft (Mrs.
Kendall), John Gielgud (Gomm), Wendy Hiller (head nurse)

Length: 125 minutes

Rated: PG

The film is not exactly an adaptation of the award-winning play by Bernard
Pomerance, whose *The Elephant Man* (1979) won every major drama
award of the year, including three Tonys, the New York Drama Critics
Circle Award, and several Obies. In fact, the studio denied that the play
had influenced the film, evidence to the contrary. In his introductory note,
the playwright argues against "any attempt to reproduce his [Merrick's]
appearance and his speech naturalistically" as "distracting" from the play,
which tells the story of John Merrick, a grotesquely deformed Englishman,
and his relationship with Dr. Frederick Treves. Much of the dramatic tension in the play rests on collapsing boundaries: between Treves, the benevolent physician whose career benefits from exhibiting Merrick, and the
brutal, animalistic exhibitor from whom the doctor rescues Merrick; between those who cause their own deformities through corsets (a subject
upon which Treves has written a pamphlet) and Merrick's natural condi-

tion; and between the avaricious carnival hacks and the penurious hospital board, concerned that Merrick's residence not be an expense. A central metaphor in the play is a model cathedral that Merrick is building from found materials, a suggestion of man's reach for the spiritual and striving toward beauty unseen. David Lynch's film draws on the same source materials, including Sir Frederick Treves' *The Elephant Man and Other Reminiscences* (1923) and Ashley Montague's *The Elephant Man: A Study in Human Dignity* (1973), and has the same main characters, but his treatment of the material is completely different. Lynch evokes the sights and sounds of 1880s London and builds interest in Merrick's grotesque appearance by concealing it early in the film through shadows and a cloth garb with only an eyehole. Lynch, too, is interested in boundaries, but different ones: between animal and human, between beauty and grotesque, between theatre (and, by extension, film) and "reality." Whereas Pomerance groups Merrick with other so-called freaks, like the pinheads, Lynch emphasizes the contrast between his frightening, bestial appearance and his tender, artistic nature. In both play and film, Merrick dies by sleeping stretched out, rather than upright, with his large head supported. But in the play, this decision is made by the pinheads, who call themselves the "Queens of the Cosmos," while the film gives Merrick the power to decide to sleep like a "normal" man, after a long-anticipated trip to the theatre. *(K. R. H.)*

Resources: Kenneth Kaleta, *David Lynch* (New York: Twayne, 1993); Martha Nochimson, *The Passion of David Lynch: Wild at Heart in Hollywood* (Austin: University of Texas Press, 1997).

THE EMPEROR JONES (1920)
Eugene O'Neill

The Emperor Jones (1933)

Directed by Dudley Murphy

Adapted by DuBose Heyward

Cast: Paul Robeson (Brutus Jones), Dudley Digges (Smithers)

Length: 72 minutes

Heavily influenced by German expressionist techniques, Eugene O'Neill's 1920 play is structured in a series of episodes, flashbacks, and dream visions chronicling the adventures of Brutus Jones, an African American Pullman car attendant who killed a man in a dice game, served time on a prison chain gang, and escaped to a small West Indian island, where he assumed the mantle of "Emperor." Because he has plundered the island, a native uprising forces him to escape to the rain forest. He loses his way, encountering several phantoms and memories from his racial heritage and his past before being shot and killed by four silver bullets. A steadily accelerating crescendo of drumbeats underpins the final sequences. The 1933 screen adaptation was an attempt by two white men—independent filmmaker Dudley Murphy (who three years before had directed two important African-American two-reelers, *St. Louis Blues* and *Black and Tan Fantasy*) and DuBose Heyward, author of *Porgy* (the basis for Gershwin's later *Porgy and Bess*)—to make a feature film about the black experience that would appeal to major American distributors and exhibitors. Paul Robeson, who had appeared as Jones in a 1925 revival of the play and who was riding a wave of success with his "Joe" in the London production of *Show Boat*, was signed on. With O'Neill's blessing, Murphy and Heyward fashioned a prologue depicting Brutus' back story as a railway porter and chain-gang victim, adding, for good measure, scenes of life in jazzy Harlem. The "haunts" that afflict Jones during his jungle flight are provided courtesy of simple effects superimpositions. The score, by black composer J. Rosamond Johnson, represented four categories of musical motifs—African, Gullah, Harlem jazz, and, finally, voodoo. The film's reception, reports Thomas Cripps in *Slow Fade to Black*, was generally favorable: "It was an impressive debut of blacks into independently produced and financed feature films outside the confines of Hollywood and crafted with finer stuff than that of the race movies" (217). *(J. C. T.)*

Resources: Thomas Cripps, *Slow Fade to Black* (New York: Oxford University Press, 1977); John Lahr, "Eugene O'Neill," in *Automatic Vaudeville* (New York: Alfred A. Knopf, 1984), 63–88; Mardi Valgemae, *Accelerated Grimace: Expressionism in the American Drama of the 1920s* (Carbondale: Southern Illinois University Press, 1972).

ENTERTAINING MR. SLOANE (1964)
Joe Orton

Entertaining Mr. Sloane (1970)

Directed by Douglas Hickox

Adapted by Clive Exton

Cast: Beryl Reid (Kath), Harry Andrews (Ed), Peter McEnery (Sloane), Alan Webb (Kemp)

Length: 95 minutes

Entertaining Mr. Sloane first appeared at London's New Arts Theatre in 1964 before moving to Wyndham's Theatre. Orton's first play, dedicated to his lover, Kenneth Halliwell, who later murdered him, was recognized by *Sunday Times* critic Alan Brien and Sir Terence Rattigan as one of the most exciting plays to have appeared in London over the past thirty years; it was also attacked by theatrical Establishment figures. The play is an amoral black comedy by a writer sometimes described as the Oscar Wilde of Britain's welfare state. It deals with the manipulative activities of a bisexual, murderous hero who manipulates a middle-aged nymphomaniac and her homosexual brother until his killing of their father leads to a climatic ménage à trois in which he will service both until his usefulness ends. John Lahr described Orton in his introduction to the 1973 Methuen edition as "the first playwright to dramatize the psychopathic style of the '60s— that restless, ruthless, single-minded pursuit of satisfaction—transformed by drugs and rock music into myth." Unfortunately, the cinematic version of the play vulgarizes Orton's original by not subordinating mise-en-scène and acting devices to complement, rather than overwhelm, the keen theatrical dialogue. As in the play, Peter McEnery's Mr. Sloane is a sly manipulator of two self-deceiving people. But Beryl Reid and Harry Andrews tend to stereotype their roles, falling short of the nuanced performances of Sheila Hancock and Edward Woodward in a late 1960s British independent television production. In her opening scene, Beryl Reed wears a ridiculous see-through dress, while Ed wears classy clothes and a leather hat gratuitously marking him as an archetypal British "poof." This costuming conflicts with the original Orton dialogue, rather than contributing to the characters' already grotesque absurdity. The film also changes the location of Kath's house from the middle of a rubbish dump to near a graveyard. This changes Orton's concept from people living off the scraps of life to the British ideological fascination with a culture dominated by the dead hand of past tradition. It thus moves Orton's play away from its superb exemplification as a collage of contemporary popular culture and more toward the typical type of "naughty" British comedy. Playwright Clive Exton adds new scenes to the film: the opening graveyard sequence where Kath first discovers Mr. Sloane sunbathing on a tombstone and a swimming pool where Ed admonishes Sloane about the dangerous attractiveness of the female sex. Director Hickox also features an irrelevant montage sequence involving Sloane, Kath, and Kemp, merely to provide a redundant opportunity for Georgie Fame's musical number based on the film's title. *(T. W.)*

Resources: Maurice Charney, *Joe Orton* (London: Macmillan, 1984); John Lahr, "Introduction," *Entertaining Mr. Sloane* (London: Eyre Methuen, 1973); Susan Rusinko, *Joe Orton* (New York: Twayne, 1995).

EQUUS (1973)
Peter Shaffer

Equus (1977)

Directed by Sidney Lumet

Adapted by Peter Shaffer

Cast: Richard Burton (Dr. Martin Dysart), Peter Firth (Alan Strang), Eileen Adkins (Hesther Saloman), Joan Plowright (Dora Strang), Colin Blakely (Frank Strang), Harry Andrews (Harry Dalton), Jenny Agutter (Jill Mason), John Wyman (Horseman on beach), Kate Reid (Margaret Dysart)

Length: 137 minutes

Rated: R

Although the design of the play is highly abstract and complex, the plot is fairly simple. Magistrate Hesther Saloman persuades overworked psychiatrist Martin Dysart to take under his care a disturbed adolescent, Alan Strang, who has blinded six horses with a metal spike. The play explains the mystery of the boy's motivation through a series of therapy sessions. Alan's confusion results from mixed signals from his religious, middle-class mother and his socialist, working-class father. The boy worships horses. His crisis comes when Jill Mason, a girl who works with him at Harry Dalton's stables, attempts to seduce Alan one night in the presence of Alan's horse god, Equus. The mutilations follow as a consequence of Alan's guilt and shame. Dysart encourages Alan to remember and relive the experience in order to get over it, but he also questions his right to take an extraordinary boy and turn him into an ordinary one. At the end, Dysart appears to have taken over Alan's demons.

   The play, originally mounted by the National Theatre at the Old Vic in London, was a triumph of inventive theatrical design, and Shaffer incorporated John Dexter's set design, a square arena and a circle of wood that could be turned, in printed editions of the play. The play is not realistic. The horses are represented by actors wearing special clogs and horse masks. Understandably, Sidney Lumet decided to use real horses when faced with the challenge of filming it, but that, in addition to "opening up" the play to outdoor settings, violates the abstract theatrical design that had made the play so successfully inventive. The dialogue is almost entirely faithful to the source, however, and Dysart's long monologues remain intact. The film provides a record of Peter Firth's performance as Alan, as he played him both in London and in New York. Richard Burton was not the original Dysart but had played the role onstage, and his vocal imprint seems perfect for the role. Overall, the performances are excellent, but the realistic rendering of the bloody spectacle as Alan relives it is potentially repulsive on film, and much of the spirit of the play is lost as a consequence. The film retains the play's nude spectacle. *(J. M. W.)*

Resources: Stephen E. Bowles, *Sidney Lumet: A Guide to References and Resources* (Boston: G. K. Hall, 1979); Frank R. Cunningham, *Sidney Lumet: Film and Literary Vision* (Lexington: University Press of Kentucky, 1991); J. M. Welsh, "Dream Doctors as Healers in Drama and Film," *Literature & Medicine* 6 (1987): 117–127.

EVERYBODY COMES TO RICK'S (1940)
Murray Burnett and Joan Alison

Casablanca (1942)

Directed by Michael Curtiz

Adapted by Julius Epstein, Philip Epstein, and Howard Koch

Cast: Humphrey Bogart (Rick Blaine), Ingrid Bergman (Ilsa Lund), Paul Henreid (Victor Laszlo), Claude Rains (Capt. Louis Renault), Dooley Wilson (Sam)

Length: 102 minutes

Everybody Comes to Rick's is perhaps the most famous unproduced play in American cultural history. Written in 1940, it was bought by Warner Brothers in 1942 and quickly adapted into the much-loved film *Casablanca*. Burnett and Alison's play is set in Rick's Café, operated by the American Rick Blaine in Casablanca, French Morocco. The café has a clientele of many nationalities and is a center of political intrigue involving refugees from the Nazis. Rick, cynical and apolitical to begin with, eventually carries out a daring plan to allow Lois Meredith (once the love of his life) and Victor Laszlo (her husband, a prominent leader in the anti-Hitler underground) to leave Casablanca for Lisbon. At play's end, Rick surrenders to the authorities. The film opens up the play's setting, adding a flashback in Paris and several exterior and interior scenes around Casablanca. Scriptwriters Julius and Philip Epstein have added some witty lines, though much of the film's dialogue comes directly from the play. The plot remains almost intact, except for new character names—for example, Lois Meredith becomes Ilsa Lund—and a new ending. In the film's ending, Rick (Humphrey Bogart) engineers the escape of Ilsa (Ingrid Bergman) and Victor Laszlo

(Paul Henreid), then sets off with the French captain Renault (Claude Rains) to continue the fight against Nazism. This ending puts an optimistic spin on America's entry into World War II and gives hope that the Free French of General de Gaulle will win out over the Nazi puppets of Vichy France. Though *Casablanca* is a finely crafted work in all respects, its magic probably resides in the unique tone set by Hungarian-born director Michael Curtiz and the film's many European actors—Bergman, Henreid, Rains, Peter Lorre, Conrad Veidt, S. Z. Sakall, and so on. The film's atmosphere combines sadness for Europe, pleasure in things European, and fierce anti-Nazi sentiment, all linked to American patriotism in the months after Pearl Harbor. *Casablanca* remains one of the great classics of the American cinema. It was the second-ranked film on the American Film Institute's 1998 list of the best American films. *(P. A. L.)*

Resources: Charles Francisco, *You Must Remember This* (Englewood Cliffs, NJ: Prentice-Hall, 1980); Aljean Harmetz, *Round Up the Usual Suspects* (New York: Hyperion, 1992); Richard E. Osborne, *The Casablanca Companion* (Indianapolis: Riebel-Roque, 1997).

EVITA (1978)
Andrew Lloyd Webber; lyrics by Tim Rice

Evita (1996)

Directed by Alan Parker

Adapted by Alan Parker and Oliver Stone

Cast: Madonna (Eva Perón), Antonio Banderas (Ché), Jonathan Pryce (Juan Perón), Jimmy Nail (Agustin Magaldi), Victoria Sus (Dona Juana), Julian Littman (Brother Juan), Olga Merediz (Blanca)

Length: 134 minutes

Rated: PG

The London opening of this musical at the Prince Edward Theatre, directed by Harold Prince, coincided with the Faulklands War and was a smash hit that ran to 2,900 performances. A film was sure to follow, though not immediately. The play tells the story of Eva Perón, her rise to power from humble beginnings in Los Toldos, a village 200 miles west of Buenos Aires; her career as a tango singer and film actress; her affair with Colonel Juan Perón, whom she marries after his brief arrest following a populist revolt in 1945, and her role in her husband's government; her charitable work as political activist, which endeared her to her people; and her death caused by uterine cancer in 1952 at the age of thirty-three. Her story is narrated by Ché Guevara (Antonio Banderas in the film), who serves as an Everyman chorus. It was a contemporary opera, propelled to mass popularity by its signature song, "Don't Cry for Me, Argentina." Many directors, including Oliver Stone, were competing for the assignment, but Alan Parker was perhaps the best choice to direct the film in such a way that it would recall the stage production while at the same time extending the action to film and exterior settings. Though the framework remains theatrical and operatic, the musical is at the same time cinematic, effectively using flashbacks and flash-forwards to advance the plot efficiently. All of the lines are sung or delivered through recitative, a performance style exactly matching Madonna's talents. Although the film was nominated for several Academy Awards and won for Best Song, it grossed only a disappointing $23 million. It was probably too stylized to succeed with a mass popular audience, but it was impressively adapted to the screen. *(J. M. W.)*

Resources: Owen Gleiberman, "Phantom of the Opera," *Entertainment Weekly* No. 358 (20 December 1996): 49–50; Anthony Lane, "Immaterial Girls," *The New Yorker* (6 January 1997): 74–75; Peter Travers, "Madonna's Big Moment," *Rolling Stone* (23 January 1997): 71–72; Richard Zoglin, "Mad for Evita," *Time* 148.29 (30 December 1996): 134–137.

EXTREMITIES (1983)
William Mastrosimone

Extremities (1986)

Directed by Robert M. Young

Adapted by William Mastrosimone

Cast: Farrah Fawcett (Marjorie), James Russo (Joe), Alfre Woodard and Diana Scarwid (roommates)

Length: 89 minutes

Rated: R

This is the story of an attempted rape—actually, two attempted rapes in the film version—and the victim's rage and retribution. The first occurs when Marjorie (Farrah Fawcett) leaves a shopping mall one night and is attacked by a rapist wearing a ski mask and armed with a knife, hiding in the back seat of her car. She manages to escape but finds the police unresponsive and uncaring about her dilemma. Meanwhile, the would-be rapist has stolen her purse and her wallet and has her identification and address.

Shortly thereafter the rapist comes calling at her home, and this is the main action of the play, set "[b]etween Trenton and Princeton, New Jersey, where the cornfield meets the highway." The play is a marvel of construction and raw emotion, requiring only four players, the rapist, Joe (James Russo in the film), and the three women whose home he invades, played by Fawcett, Alfre Woodard, and Diana Scarwid. Marjorie is at home when the rapist arrives, entering the house without knocking, pretending first to be seeking a man named Joe, then pretending that he needs to use the telephone, but in no time he is beating up Marjorie and terrorizing her, until she retaliates, with a vengeance. She maces him in the face with insecticide, temporarily blinding him, then bashes him over the head, disabling him long enough to tie him up and imprison him in the fireplace. He has abused her and threatened her life, but since it is his word against hers, there being no witnesses, she concludes that it would be pointless to contact the police and decides to murder him. When they return home, her housemates disagree, and the moral choice that needs to be made becomes the central conflict of the play. There is no doubt that the man is a dangerous psychopath and killer, but would the evidence against him hold up in court? The main flaw in the play is that it does not really answer this question convincingly. Although Joe confesses to other crimes in the presence of all three women, the confession is exacted by questionable means. This is a civil libertarian's nightmare, interestingly dramatized. Farrah Fawcett came to the film after having played Marjorie in the New York off-Broadway production, again proving herself worthy of the role. Although the film's opening sequence shows Marjorie out in the world, the film is nearly as claustrophobic as the play, which, in this case, works to the film's advantage. *(J. M. W.)*

Resources: Stephen Farber, "A Serious Farrah Fawcett Takes Control in 'Extremities,'" *New York Times* (17 August 1986): 19; Jack Kroll, "Beauty and the Beast," *Newsweek* (1 September 1986): 86.

A FEW GOOD MEN (1989)
Aaron Sorkin

A Few Good Men (1992)

Directed by Rob Reiner

Adapted by Aaron Sorkin

Cast: Tom Cruise (Lt. Daniel A. Kaffee), Jack Nicholson (Col. Nathan Jessep), Demi Moore (Lt. Cmdr. Joanne Galloway), Kevin Bacon (Captain Jack Ross), J. T. Walsh (Lt. Col. Markinson)

Length: 138 minutes

Rated: R

After premiering at the University of Virginia Heritage Repertory Theatre, *A Few Good Men* appeared on 15 November 1989 at the John F. Kennedy Center for the Performing Arts. It was performed in two acts, with scenes often concluding by blending into the beginning of the next. The play dealt with the court-martial of two marines for the murder of a fellow soldier on Cuba's Guantanamo Bay and the concealed responsibility of base commander Col. Jessep for the deed. It originally operated in a distinctively formal manner by utilizing the theatrical equivalent of cinematic flashbacks and parallel editing, unlike Rob Reiner's pedestrian chronological direction, which uses only one flashback sequence. The film version also reduces the role of the murdered marine, Pvt. Santiago, who appears in the play via several flashbacks. Santiago now appears only in the precredits sequence and a voice-over flashback sequence documenting his various humiliations at the Marine Corps base. The film also omits the frequently ironic, choruslike marine chants that punctuate key moments in the theatrical narrative. Although including several new outside scenes, Reiner's version mainly follows the action of the original play and emphasizes the courtroom drama of act 2, thus making his version resemble a variant of *The Caine Mutiny Court-Martial*. Jessep's guilt-ridden subordinate officer Markinson initially reveals himself to Kaffee by appearing in shadows in the rear seat of his car in a manner resembling Deep Throat in *All the President's Men*. Reiner also casts Jack Nicholson as an older version of his theatrical original to emphasize the generational and attitudinal conflicts between the military warrior father figure and his younger antagonist Kaffee, who will attain manhood and responsibility by succeeding in the trial, rather than avoiding the challenge of living up to the foreboding image of his attorney general father. However, apart from the leading performances by Cruise, Nicholson, and Kevin Bacon, *A Few Good Men* is mostly routine and formulaic, lacking the inspirational techniques of its theatrical original. *(T. W.)*

Resource: Kim Newman, "*A Few Good Men,*" *Sight and Sound* 3.1 (1993): 46.

FOOL FOR LOVE (1983)
Sam Shepard

Fool for Love (1985)

Directed by Robert Altman

Adapted by Sam Shepard

Cast: Sam Shepard (Eddie), Kim Basinger (May), Harry Dean Stanton (Old Man), Randy Quaid (Martin), Deborah McNaughton (Countess)

Length: 106 minutes

Rated: R

Sam Shepard's 1983 play was generally hailed as a work by the "new" Shepard—the rugged, matinee-idol-ascendant whose appearances in films such as *The Right Stuff* were making him more of a household name than the "old" Shepard, the experimental/hallucinatory playwright, had ever been (DeRose 114). The themes and structures of *Fool for Love* had at least passing similarity to Shepard's previous work, though; the exercise of ideas such as the destructiveness and devotion of passionately felt love and the interplay between reality and illusion make the play of a piece with the Shepard of *Buried Child* and *True West*. Here the turmoil results from the reunion and resulting interpersonal collision of Eddie and May, lovers who are actually half siblings by different mothers and the same "Old Man" who may or may not be a figment of their imaginations. Eddie comes to the shabby motel where May has sought refuge from him, and in the course of their alternating arguments and seductions, both their collective past and their individual presents confront them. The "Old Man"—an abject figure relegated to a corner of the stage—confounds them with riddlelike exchanges and taunts them with the fact of their supposedly shared paternity. Meanwhile, the relationships they have tried to build in each other's absence—May with a hapless suitor named Martin, Eddie with a flamboyant and mysterious woman called the "Countess"—metaphorically explode in their faces as Martin pathetically attempts to deal with Eddie's abuse, and the vengeful Countess blows up Eddie's pickup truck. Shepard himself directed the play in its initial run, first in San Francisco and then off-Broadway in New York, with Ed Harris as Eddie and Kathy Baker as May. *Fool for Love* became the first of Shepard's plays to be made into a film when Robert Altman adapted the play as one of a series of "filmed plays" he made in the 1980s. Shepard also played one of his own characters on film for the first time when he assumed the role of Eddie. Kim Basinger's performance as May, among other problems, led Shepard scholar Don Shewey to characterize the film adaptation of *Fool for Love* as "misguided": "The director perversely took a play set in a tiny motel room made claustrophobic with erotic tension and spread it out over the desert sky" (191). Shepard's own performance was another problem, according to Shewey and the playwright himself. David Denby claimed that Shepard's awkward performance here ended any speculation as to Shepard's matinee-idol future (Shewey 191), and Shepard soundly criticized Altman's ability to work with, and understand, actors (194). Apart from the maligned attempt to "open up" the play's setting, Altman's treatment of the play also seems to have settled the question of the Old Man's reality, as Altman presents (and Stanton portrays) the figure as a fully human and integrated (if somewhat enigmatic) character within the film's single locale of the motel. Other changes in adaptation included the natural tendency to present realistically what the play had to imply (i.e., the explosion of Eddie's truck) and the inclusion of a country-western soundtrack. Reportedly, the negative experience that Shepard had with this film has prevented him from accepting other offers to have his plays adapted as films. *(C. M.)*

Resources: David J. DeRose, *Sam Shepard* (New York: Twayne, 1992); Don Shewey, *Sam Shepard* (New York: DeCapo Press, 1997).

FORBIDDEN PLANET

See THE TEMPEST

FORTUNE AND MEN'S EYES (1967)
John Herbert

Fortune and Men's Eyes (1971)

Directed by Harvey Hart

Adapted by John Herbert

Cast: Wendell Burton (Smitty), Michael Greer (Queenie), Zooey Hall (Rocky), Danny Freedman (Mona)

Length: 102 minutes

Rated: R

During the late 1960s, *Fortune and Men's Eyes* was regarded as one of the most successful plays to have emerged from Canada. After its initial off-Broadway run at New York's Actor's Playhouse on 23 February 1967, this hard-hitting prison drama gained appreciative audiences in many parts of the world. Based on its author's own experiences in an Ontario reformatory, the play is really about "the cruelty and stupidity of force and violence," not primarily about homosexuality or the corruption of a heterosexual. Smitty's moral decline results from institutional forces controlling his behavior. The play ends with Smitty rebuffed in his attempts to dominate sexually the ambiguously gendered alternative character of Mona and denying his responsibility for the suffering he causes. Mona attempts to make Smitty see another possible potential for human relationships in prison by speaking lines from Shakespeare's sonnet "Fortune and Men's Eyes" as a counsel to rely on inner resources rather than submit to the contaminating influences of prison life. However, after witnessing the railroading of Mona as a scapegoat, Smitty projects his guilt onto the guards, society, and fellow prisoners, resulting in his moral decline into a figure of hatred and resentment. However, the Los Angeles revival of the play (staged by Sal Mineo), subsequent theatrical productions, and the film version all emphasized homosexuality and sexual sensationalism, which marred Herbert's critical vision. Although the film's original director, Jules Schwerin, wished to retain Herbert's theatrical message, MGM replaced him with Harvey Hart and persuaded Herbert to adopt Mineo's stage interpretation. For Vito Russo, the final product "seemed like a story about a country club for sadomasochistic homosexuals." MGM wanted a picture about homosexuality that it could exploit and condemn. Although the film never explicitly shows Rocky's rape of Smitty, Hart does shoot a gang-rape scene in the exercise room, which serves no thematic purpose. When Schwerin attempted to show Queenie as a sympathetic and ultimately mutilated character, the producers wanted to emphasize "the funny drag queen quality" aided by the casting of Michael Greer. Russo notes that while the original play "focused on the dehumanization of all four principals by the emotional demands of their roles and their environment" (73) and ended with Rocky still alive, the film version showed Rocky committing suicide after his humiliation by Smitty. Schwerin told Vito Russo, "I was not interested in exploiting homosexuality" (75). Unfortunately, the film betrayed Schwerin's and Herbert's intentions. *(T. W.)*

Resources: Neil Carson, "Sexuality and Identity in *Fortune and Men's Eyes*," *Twentieth Century Literature* 18 (1970): 208–218; Vito Russo, *The Celluloid Closet: Homosexuality in the Movies* (New York: Harper and Row, 1987).

FRANKENSTEIN (1927)
Peggy Webling

Frankenstein (1931)

Directed by James Whale

Adapted by Garrett Fort and John L. Balderston

Cast: Boris Karloff (the Monster), Colin Clive (Henry Frankenstein), Edward Van Sloane, Dwight Frye, Mae Clarke, John Boles

Length: 71 minutes

Mary Shelley's classic novel, *Frankenstein; or, The Modern Prometheus*, had been in print less than six years when the first stage adaptation appeared, a three-act "opera" entitled *Presumption; or, The Fate of Frankenstein*. Playwright Richard Brinsley Peake confronted the same problems that would bedevil all future adaptors to stage and film—how to dramatize a complex narrative from multiple points of view that spanned much of the globe and presented fantastic laboratory transformation and chases across mountains and ice floes. Peake's version would serve as a blueprint for most future adaptations: its chronologically linear plot line reduced many scenes into a few key situations (the creation scene, the bridal night, and the destruction of the Monster), eliminated other scenes (notably, the

Monster's education at the De Lacey household), stripped the dialogue of philosophical and scientific musings, introduced Fritz, Frankenstein's servant, and exploited the hideousness of the Monster. A century later, after many other subsequent dramatizations, Peggy Webling's play was still following Peake's basic story formula. Her *Frankenstein* premiered in London at the Preston Theatre late in 1927. Webling's play added a few story elements that would influence the James Whale Universal film adaptation— a name change from "Victor" to "Henry" Frankenstein, the Monster's accidental drowning of a little girl, his fascination with sunlight, and his attempted rape of Frankenstein's fiancée. When Universal decided to follow up its successful *Dracula* (also adapted from a stage play version of the novel) with another horror vehicle, writers John L. Balderston and Garrett Fort were called in to adapt Webling's play. But while Webling's basic outline and overly talky drawing-room sequences were transferred intact, there were a few significant changes: director James Whale suggested that the Monster's violent nature was caused by his having been given the brain of a criminal. Makeup ace Jack Pierce contributed a new "look" to the creature, the flat-topped head, surgical scars, and neck electrodes, all suggesting the procedures that stitched him together and brought him to life. The play also deleted a scene in which the Monster demands a bride and a change in the circumstances of his death—from a fire in an old mill rather than from a lightning bolt in the laboratory. Regardless of the many alterations and departures from Shelley's original novel in this and other "Frankenstein" films, the basic thesis has remained intact: as Albert J. Lavelley notes, "In each [the Monster] carries the burden of similar conflicts: endowed with superhuman strength, he is also highly vulnerable, the crucible in which the struggle of joy and suffering, sympathy and revenge, passivity and destructiveness most clearly is worked out" (244). *(J. C. T.)*

Resources: Donald F. Glut, *The Frankenstein Legend* (Metuchen, NJ: Scarecrow Press, 1973); Albert J. Lavelley, "The Stage And Film Children of *Frankenstein*," in George Levine and U. C. Knoepflmacher, eds., *The Endurance of Frankenstein: Essays on Mary Shelley's Novel* (Berkeley: University of California Press, 1979): 243–289.

THE FRONT PAGE (1928)
Ben Hecht and Charles MacArthur

The Front Page (1931)

Directed by Lewis Milestone

Adapted by Bartlett Cormack and (uncredited) Ben Hecht and Charles Lederer

Cast: Adolphe Menjou (Walter Burns), Pat O'Brien (Hildy Johnson), Mary Brian (Peggy), Edward Everett Horton (Bensinger), George E. Stone (Earl Williams), Mae Clarke (Molly), Clarence Wilson (Sheriff Hartman), James Gordon (the Mayor), Maurice Black (Louis)

Length: 101 minutes

Hecht and MacArthur's play, which appeared in New York in 1928, is set in the pressroom of the Chicago Criminal Courts Building. A group of reporters is there to cover the hanging of Earl Williams, whose execution for the murder of a black policeman has been postponed so it will occur just before an important election and will provide the Mayor with a law-and-order campaign issue. Hildy Johnson, a star reporter for Walter Burns' newspaper, enters to announce his resignation and his plans to marry Peggy, leave town, and work in advertising. When Williams escapes, due to the ineptitude of Sheriff Hartman, who gave his gun to him so he could reenact the crime, he enters the pressroom and surrenders to Hildy, who takes advantage of everyone's absence and hides him in a rolltop desk. Because he has the scoop of his life, Hildy is reluctant to leave, a fact Walter uses to keep him working for the paper, despite Peggy's efforts to get him on the train. Eventually, Williams is found, and both Hildy and Walter, who has been trying to get the desk removed from the building, are arrested for harboring a fugitive. They turn the tables on the sheriff and Mayor because Walter has some incriminating evidence about the sheriff and also knows how Earl got the gun. With the assignment completed, Hildy leaves with Peggy, but not before Walter gives him a watch as a gift. To prevent Hildy from leaving the newspaper, Walter calls the police to report that Hildy has stolen his watch and is on the train to New York. The targets of the play's satire are the cynical, callous press, the corrupt local government, and psychoanalysis. What makes the play entertaining is the rapid, almost staccato pace of the dialogue and physical action, which is retained in the 1931 film adaptation. The film opens up the play by cutting back and forth from the pressroom to Walter's office and from the pressroom to the gallows below and by adding street scenes such as when Walter (Adolphe Menjou) pulls the fire alarm to make Hildy (Pat O'Brien) think there is a fire story to be covered. Walter's role is expanded, providing several examples of his resourcefulness: he has Louis (Maurice Black) kidnap Peggy's mother and give Hildy counterfeit money; and after he hires Bensinger (Edward Everett Horton), a rival reporter, to get him out of the room, he calls his newspaper and tells them to throw him out when he reports for work. Although the story concerns Hildy's struggle to marry Peggy (Mary Brian), the relationship between Hildy and Walter is so close that Peggy is understandably jealous in this misogynistic film about male bonding. Walter's "Tell her nothing; she's a woman" expresses his attitude;

and the reporters' cruel taunting of Molly (Mae Clarke), the prostitute who loves Earl, drives her to attempted suicide. Although the film is a comedy, it has its darker moments. *(T. L. E.)*

Resources: Joseph Millichap, *Lewis Milestone* (Boston: Twayne, 1981); David L. Parker and Burton J. Shapiro, "Lewis Milestone," in *Close Up: The Contract Film Director*, ed. Jon Tuska (Metuchen, NJ: Scarecrow, 1976): 299–350.

The Front Page (1974)

Directed by Billy Wilder

Adapted by Billy Wilder and I.A.L. Diamond

Cast: Jack Lemmon (Hildy Johnson), Walter Matthau (Walter Burns), Carol Burnett (Mollie Malloy), Susan Sarandon (Peggy Grant), Vincent Gardenia (Sheriff), David Wayne (Bensinger), Austin Pendleton (Earl Williams), Martin Gabel (Dr. Eggelhoffer), Harold Gould (the Mayor), Paul Benedict (Plunkett), Jon Korkes (Rudy Kepler)

Length: 105 minutes

Rated: PG

This remake of the Hecht-MacArthur play basically follows the same plot and is set in the same time period as its source (see plot summary in the 1931 adaptation), but in their efforts to update the film Wilder and Diamond make the dialogue more vulgar, the main characters more cynical and sexually suspect, and the additions gratuitous. Bensinger becomes a homosexual reporter obsessed with his own toilet paper; Hildy's girlfriend, Peggy, becomes an organist at a theatre; and Rudy, an added character who serves as a naive replacement for Hildy, wets his pants at the sound of gunshots and is told to change his diapers. Walter Burns' first effort at splitting up Hildy and Peggy consists of his impersonating Otto Fishbein, Hildy's supposed probation officer; Otto/Walter tells Peggy that Hildy is on probation for flashing young girls. Dr. Eggelhoffer, the Freudian psychologist who examines Earl and allows him to escape, provides a graphic phallic analysis of his subject; and in the film's postscript he is described as having written the *Joys of Impotence*, his coming to terms with his gunshot wound. Plunkett, who has the governor's reprieve that would free Earl, is not offered a job as in the original; he is sent with some cash to a Chinese brothel. Wilder's cynicism is demonstrated at the end of the film when the audience is informed about what happened to the characters: when Hildy and Peggy split up, she marries and names one of her children Hildy, while Hildy becomes the managing editor of a newspaper; and the amoral Walter Burns gives university lectures on the Ethics of Journalism. Despite the performances of Lemmon and Matthau, who had worked together so well in *The Fortune Cookie* (1966) and *The Odd Couple* (1968), the film updates the original but does not improve it. *(T. L. E.)*

Resources: Bernard Dick, *Billy Wilder* (Boston: Twayne, 1980); Leland Poague, *Wilder and McCarey* (New York: A. S. Barnes, 1980); Steve Seidman, *The Film Career of Billy Wilder* (Boston: G. K. Hall, 1977).

His Girl Friday (1940)

Directed by Howard Hawks

Adapted by Charles Lederer

Cast: Cary Grant (Walter Burns), Rosalind Russell (Hildy Johnson), Ralph Bellamy (Bruce Baldwin), John Qualen (Earl Williams)

Length: 92 minutes

Hecht and MacArthur's satiric dissection of the newspaper business has been filmed several times: by Lewis Milestone (1931, starring Pat O'Brien and Adolf Menjou) and Billy Wilder (1974, starring Jack Lemmon and Walter Matthau) and twice altered by Howard Hawks and, with a similar metamorphosis of gender, by Ted Kotcheff (1988, starring Burt Reynolds, Kathleen Turner, and Christopher Reeve) under the title *Switching Channels*. After asking a secretary to read aloud the part of *Morning Post* reporter Hildy Johnson, Hawks discovered that the part could be played more effectively by a woman. The authors agreed, and *His Girl Friday* was produced. Besides changing Hildy's gender, Hawks and scriptwriter Charles Lederer made some considerable changes in the material. They added a twenty-minute sequence set at the *Morning Post* to open the film and introduce Hildy Johnson (Rosalind Russell), her fiancé, Bruce Baldwin (Ralph Bellamy), and Walter Burns (Cary Grant). Like the play, the film is mainly set at the prison where convicted murderer Earl Williams (John Qualen) awaits hanging. After Williams escapes, Hildy finds him and becomes convinced of his innocence. Their conversation about using an insanity defense to avoid the gallows is not in the play. Hawks allows this exchange to move at a less-fevered pace than the dialogue in the rest of the picture, which, for the most part, is delivered in so hyped-up and syncopated a manner that the conversations at times sound like the verbal equivalent of a drum solo. Like the play, Hawks' film attacks the myths of journalistic objectivity and judicial fairness. However, the balance of the film, unlike the play, is affected significantly by the incorporation of Hildy as a woman. As a result, it is less a criticism of the press than a question of Hildy's choice of a husband. Despite the farcical fireworks and smart-aleck cynicism, *His Girl Friday* is basically a romance, but one with two almost equally unsuitable suitors. Robin Wood observes that not much of a choice is to be made between either Walter's "slick, cynical brilliance" or Bruce's "life of unadventurous respectability." Hildy comes across as a force of nature able to keep two diligent and committed men at bay while saving a demented, innocent man from the gallows. *(D. S.)*

Resources: Joseph McBride, *Hawks on Hawks* (Berkeley: University of California Press, 1982); Todd McCarthy, *Howard Hawks: The Grey Fox of Hollywood* (New York: Grove, 1997); Robin Wood, *Howard Hawks* (New York: Doubleday, 1968).

Switching Channels (1988)

Directed by Ted Kotcheff

Adapted by Jonathan Reynolds

Cast: Kathleen Turner (Christy Colleran), Burt Reynolds (Sully), Christopher Reeve (Blaine Bingham), Ned Beatty (Roy Ridnitz), Henry Gibson (Ike Roscoe), Ken James (Warden Terwilliger), Charles Kimbrough (Governor), Fiona Reid (Pamela Farbrother)

Length: 108 minutes

Rated: PG

The only set in the Hecht-MacArthur *Front Page* (1928) is the pressroom of the Chicago criminal courts building. The reporters are covering the impending execution of Earl Williams, convicted of shooting a black policeman. Earl's death is necessary for the reelection of the Mayor, who is running as a law-and-order candidate. Hildy Johnson, ace reporter for the *Herald Examiner*, enters the pressroom to announce that he is quitting his job, marrying Peggy, and leaving for New York. After Earl escapes because of Sheriff Hartman's incompetence, Hildy cannot resist the story and postpones his departure. Walter Burns, his editor, keeps Hildy on the story by having Peggy's mother kidnapped. When Pincus gives the sheriff Earl's reprieve, the sheriff and Mayor buy him off with the promise of a job. After finding Earl, Hildy hides him in a rolltop desk, but the sheriff eventually finds him and seems to have the upper hand. Pincus, however, returns with the reprieve, and the sheriff and mayor are exposed. In a goodwill gesture Walter gives Hildy a watch, but after Peggy and Hildy leave, he calls the authorities to claim Hildy stole it, thereby ensuring Hildy's return. *Switching Channels*, the fourth adaptation of the play, is derived from the play and from Howard Hawks' *His Girl Friday* (1940), which changed the sex of the star reporter. The Kotcheff remake contains much updating. Christy, Sully's ex-wife, is the star anchorwoman for Sully's cable news station; and the man she is quitting her job for is billionaire Blaine Bingham instead of the Albany insurance man of *His Girl Friday*. Ike, the convicted killer, is charged with the death of a drug-dealing policeman responsible for his son's death; and Roy Ridnitz, the law-and-order candidate, uses race riots as justification for moving up Ike's execution to forestall the Governor's last-minute (11:00 P.M. news) pardon. Ike's Houdini-like escape from the electric chair is aided by a power outage caused by television crews attending the "live" execution; and Christy hides him in a photocopying machine. The film is generally more upbeat than the play. When Pamela, Ike's lawyer and love, jumps out the window to divert attention from the photocopier, she is basically unhurt (in the play when prostitute Molly, Earl's love, jumps out the window, she survives but is absent from the rest of the play). Christy also succeeds in shaming the cynical, hard-bitten news reporters. At the end of the film, the warden and Ray are exposed not by a Pincus-like figure but by a television camera; and Blaine, vain and egotistical, breaks off the engagement—there is no stolen-watch gimmick. *(T. L. E.)*

Resources: Vincent Canby, "Film: Turner in *Switching Channels*," *New York Times* (4 March 1988): C10; Pauline Kael, "The Current Cinema: A Smooth Sail," *New Yorker* 64 (21 March 1988): 100–102.

THE FUGITIVE KIND

See ORPHEUS DESCENDING

A FUNNY THING HAPPENED ON THE WAY TO THE FORUM (1962)
Burt Shevelove and Larry Gelbart; music and lyrics by Stephen Sondheim

A Funny Thing Happened on the Way to the Forum (1966)

Directed by Richard Lester

Adapted by Melvin Frank and Michael Pertwee

Cast: Zero Mostel (Psuedolus), Phil Silvers (Lycus), Jack Gilford (Hysterium), Buster Keaton (Erronius), Michael Crawford (Hero), Annette Andre (Philia), Patricia Jessel (Domina), Michael Hordern (Senex)

Length: 99 minutes

The 1960s championed a decade of American musicals transferred to film with four films—*West Side Story* (1961), *My Fair Lady* (1964), *The Sound* of *Music* (1965), and *Oliver* (1968)—all receiving Academy Awards for Best Picture. Plopped in the middle of these warhorses is Stephen Sondheim's *A Funny Thing Happened on the Way to the Forum* (1966), which, unfortunately, did not fare as well. *Forum* is one of those chestnuts of American musical theatre that are constantly in performance. *Forum* was first presented by Harold Prince at the Alvin Theatre, New York, on 8 May 1962 and was directed by veteran George Abbott. While the film version of *Forum* may please many who find its slapstick and vaudeville humor simply hilarious, fans of Sondheim and purists of musical theatre will shake their heads in wonder as to why eight of the songs from the Broadway version were dropped from the film, retaining only five of the original songs, which has resulted in the film's being listed in some video movie guides under "comedy" rather than "musical." *Forum* centers around the antics of Pseudolus (Mostel), a Roman slave who yearns to have his freedom and will do anything to accomplish that end. To achieve his goal, Pseudolus promises his owner, Hero, that he will obtain for him Philia (Annette Andre), the Virgin, who resides next door in the house of Marcus Lycus (Silvers). Every possible situation of mistaken identity and slapstick humor is employed in following Pseudolus as he attempts to achieve his freedom. Instead of the obligatory car chase that Siskel and Ebert are fond of criticizing at the end of many films, the film substitutes a seven-minute chariot chase, which precedes the denouement. In spite of the lack of some Sondheim songs, the performance of Zero Mostel, Phil Silvers, Jack Gilford, and Buster Keaton make viewing *Forum* worthwhile. These are comic masters who know how to deliver a line and do a double take with the greatest of ease. Richard Lester keeps the action of the film moving quickly, and except for the 1960s female hairdos and eye shadow, *Forum* continues to maintain an ageless quality that should continue to delight audiences for many years. *(J. D.)*

Resources: Burt Shevelove and Larry Gelbart, *A Funny Thing Happened on the Way to the Forum* (New York: Applause Theatre Book, 1991); Neil Sinyard, *The Films of Richard Lester* (London: Croom Helm, 1985).

GHOSTS (1881)
Henrik Ibsen

Ghosts (1994)

Directed by David Cunliffe

Cast: Dorothy Tutin (Mrs. Alving), Richard Pasco (Pastor Manders), Donald Fraser (Engstrand), Brian Deacon (Oswald), Julia Foster (Regina)

Length: 90 minutes

Allegedly retaliating for *A Doll House*'s hostile reception two years earlier, Henrik Ibsen wrote *Ghosts* (1881) to reveal the devastation of a marriage based on lies. Instead of leaving her philandering husband, Mrs. Alving, for the sake of appearances and conventional morality, stays in a loveless marriage but sends son Oswald away at a young age. The play opens just as an orphanage is to be dedicated to her dead husband's memory and as Oswald has returned home to die from inherited syphilis, though disbelieving vehemently that his father could be the cause. Ibsen uses Mrs. Alving to condemn Pastor Manders, her longtime mentor, for her life of married hypocrisy. Additionally, Ibsen makes Pastor Manders the dupe of Engstrand, a carpenter, who helped to build and later secretly burned the orphanage. A further complication is that Engstrand has raised Regina, Mrs. Alving's house servant, as his daughter. In the final act Mrs. Alving tells both Regina and Oswald the long-hidden secret that Regina is really Oswald's half sister, thus squelching their romantic feelings for each other. Regretfully, Mrs. Alving admits that her role as a puritanical wife helped contribute to her husband's dissolution. The play ends as Oswald lapses into insanity, his mother hopelessly watching. Although directing essentially a filmed play, David Cunliffe is very faithful to the text, adding nothing but occasionally cutting dialogue. He omits a rather lengthy debate between Pastor Manders and Mrs. Alving concerning the need to insure the new orphanage. Filmed in period costume, the director is faithful to Ibsen's settings. The only change the director makes is to reverse the order of the opening scene so that Pastor Manders and Regina and her father argue; this opening starts the film on a less strident note. Dorothy Tutin as Mrs. Alving is somewhat better than the rest of the cast, who fail generally to engage each other in a convincing way. *(K. Z.)*

Resources: Michael Goldman, *Ibsen: The Dramaturgy of Fear* (New York: Columbia University Press, 1989); Frederick J. Marker, *Ibsen's Lively Art: A Performance Study of the Major Plays* (New York: Cambridge University Press, 1989).

THE GLASS MENAGERIE (1944)
Tennessee Williams

The Glass Menagerie (1950)

Directed by Irving Rapper

Adapted by Tennessee Williams and Peter Berneis

Cast: Jane Wyman (Laura), Kirk Douglas (Jim), Gertrude Lawrence (Amanda), Arthur Kennedy (Tom)

Length: 107 minutes

Despite its pessimistic message and ending, Williams' *The Glass Menagerie* survived its 1944 opening in Chicago and went on to New York, where it won its author his first New York Critics Award. In the play a domineering Amanda nags her children Laura and Tom until Laura escapes from reality by retreating into a fantasy world inhabited by glass animals, and Tom escapes by becoming a wandering sailor. The play, narrated by Tom, who is guilt-ridden because he abandoned Laura, occurs in Tom's memory and is the antithesis of realism. When it was filmed in 1950, however, it did not receive favorable reviews because the film was so different from the play. The pessimistic ending became a happy one. Rather than being destroyed by her discovery that her "gentleman caller" is already engaged,

Laura is portrayed as happily awaiting other "gentleman callers." To make that ending convincing, Laura is normalized, and her physical defect, a pronounced limp, and timid nature are altered accordingly. In the play she never attends typing classes; in the film she does but drops out because of a cruel teacher and a terrifying exam. When she then visits the zoo, she seems relatively happy, rather than sad and depressed. Likewise, the role of Jim O'Connor, the "gentleman caller," is altered: he is no longer a shallow young man who has failed to achieve his dreams but is instead an engaging hero who can manipulate his superiors. In the play Amanda also lived in a dream world, one inhabited by her seventeen "gentleman callers," but there is some doubt as to her story. When the visits of the "gentleman callers" are filmed, however, her story becomes real, and the illusory character of the play is destroyed. Other added "outside" scenes detract from the play's sense of confinement and the notion that the real world lies somewhere outside the play. Since Amanda, Tom, and Laura are shown (not described, as in the play) in outside scenes, the visit of Jim, an "emissary from the outside world," loses its thematic importance. In fact, Williams' original message about the impossibility of achieving one's dreams or overcoming one's limitations is completely subverted by the film, which Williams described as the most "dishonest" adaptation of his work. *(T. L. E.)*

Resources: Gene Phillips, *The Films of Tennessee Williams* (East Brunswick, NJ: Associated University Presses, 1980); Maurice Yacowar, *Tennessee Williams and Film* (New York: Frederick Ungar, 1977).

GLENGARRY GLEN ROSS (1984)
David Mamet

Glengarry Glen Ross (1992)

Directed by James Foley

Adapted by David Mamet

Cast: Jack Lemmon (Shelly Levene), Al Pacino (Ricky Roma), Ed Harris (Dave Moss), Alan Arkin (George Aaronow), Kevin Spacey (John Williamson), Alec Baldwin (Blake), Jonathan Pryce (James Lingk)

Length: 100 minutes

Rated: R

David Mamet adapted his own Pulitzer Prize–winning play, first produced in 1984 during the Reagan era. It criticizes the greed, desperation, and competitiveness of the American workplace by showing struggling real estate agents attempting to sell worthless land to gullible clients. The play is structured in two acts set in two locations, the real estate office and a Chinese restaurant across the street, which becomes an extension of the workplace. The salesmen are competing for their jobs and for the desirable "Glengarry" leads, which two of the salesmen steal to sell to a competing firm. In adapting the play Mamet made structural changes to open it up, in other words, to free it from the two set locations of the play by making more frequent shifts between those settings and taking the action outside, where it is usually raining. Mamet also added a character "from down-town," Blake (Alec Baldwin), to more clearly establish a motive for the theft and to demonstrate the extreme pressure placed on the salesmen. The restructuring distrubs the balance among the ensemble. An over-the-hill salesman, Shelly Levene (Jack Lemmon), and the energetic sales leader, Ricky Roma (Al Pacino), along with office manager John Williamson (Kevin Spacey), take the foreground, while Dave Moss (Ed Harris), who engineers the theft, and the weaker George Aaronow (Alan Arkin) are made less central. Levene, who turns out to be the thief, is given a clearer motive. Rather than simply struggling to prove himself and regain his manhood in this macho setting, in the film Levene is humanized and sentimentalized. As a father, he is worried about his daughter, who is in the hospital, and he is being pressured to pay the hospital bill. Instead of being merely vain, the character is pathetic, as Mamet makes the plot and motive more ob-vious for a mass audience. On the other hand, the play's tough dialogue is preserved and brilliantly enacted by a superior cast. The relative merits of the reinvented screenplay are perhaps debatable since the screenplay makes the salesmen mere victims, but the moral and economic climate had changed during the eight years required to get the film produced. The main themes of the play are retained, however, in this superior adaptation. *(J. M. W.)*

Resources: Rita Kempley, "Mamet's Moral Swamp," *Washington Post* (2 October 1992): C1, C5; John Lahr, "Fortress Mamet," *The New Yorker* (17 November 1997): 70–82; James Ryan, "Playing Mamet's Music," *Boston Sunday Globe* (27 September 1992): B33–34.

GLORIFYING THE AMERICAN GIRL
(1906)
Florenz Ziegfeld

Glorifying the American Girl (1929)

Directed by Millard Webb
Adapted by J. P. McEvoy

Cast: Mary Eaton (Gloria), Eddie Cantor, Helen Morgan, Rudy Vallee, Florenz Ziegfeld, and Texas Guinan (as themselves)

Length: 87 minutes

From the Anna Held production of *The Parisian Model* in 1906 to a succession of *Follies* throughout the next two decades, Florenz Ziegfeld glorified the American girl. Born out of a combination of opulent exoticism and studied elegance, the "Ziegfeld girl" was a more "respectable" stage creation than the standard, commonplace "chorus girl." Even if she did little more than strike "sculptural" poses and wear elaborate (and revealing) costumes, she was an essential element in some of the most imaginatively staged musical revues in the history of the American musical theatre. Paramount's *Glorifying the American Girl*, while not directly based on a particular Ziegfeld show, manages to convey the essential Ziegfeld style in a weird extravaganza that is uncertainly poised between "canned theatre" and "cinematic" spectacle. Modern commentators have not been kind to the film: "*Glorifying the America Girl* remains a glittery wreck," opines historian Richard Barrios, "a strange and sad fricassee of story lines and revue bits that collapses completely during its final reels" (197). This seems an unfair assessment. Admittedly, the backstage plot is pretty limp business, and the trouble-plagued production bombed at the box office, but as a fascinating document of the Ziegfeld revue, it is invaluable. Newsreel footage depicts an opening night at the Ziegfeld Theatre, with shots of attending luminaries like Fanny Brice, Texas Guinan, and Mayor James J. Walker. The last third of the picture is entirely taken up with a minirevue, with several lavishly staged, Ziegfeld-style *tableaux vivants*, or "living pictures" (shot in two-color Technicolor)—including a nautical scene with the showgirls immobilized within frames of fishnets, starfish, and seashells; and a "butterfly" scene featuring Eaton atop a high column, attended by showgirls wearing giant butterfly wings. The entire sequence appears to have been shot on a real proscenium stage. Framing the action are close-ups of audience members examining the program and shots of curtains opening and closing. The stage is seen only from the audience's vantage point; and several overhead perspectives and shifts in camera angle merely serve to approximate a variety of perspectives from different seats in the house. This is not to say that there are not effective cinematic moments. The most outstanding example is the imaginative, two-minute sequence that opens the picture: superimposed over a series of titles are images of "glorified" Ziegfeld girls. Shots of women in various "domestic poses"—ironing, washing, and so on—rapidly dissolve and transform into images of dazzling showgirls with fantastic headdresses and flowing gowns. Fragments of Ziegfeld songs—such as "A Pretty Girl Is Like a Melody"—blend in an aural montage on the soundtrack. *(J. C. T.)*

Resources: Richard Barrios, *A Song in the Dark: The Birth of the Musical Film* (New York: Oxford University Press, 1995); Randolph Carter, *The World of Flo Ziegfeld* (New York: Praeger, 1974); John C. Tibbetts, *The American Theatrical Film* (Bowling Green, OH: Popular Press, 1985).

GODSPELL (1971)
John-Michael Tebelak

Godspell (1973)

Directed by David Greene

Adapted by David Greene and John-Michael Tebelak

Cast: Victor Garber (Jesus), David Haskell (John the Baptist/Judas), Katie Hanley, Merrell Jackson, Joanne Jonas, Robin Lamont, Gilmer McCormick, Jeffrey Mylett, Jerry Sroka, Lynne Thigpen

Length: 101 minutes

Rated: G

For his M.F.A. thesis at Carnegie-Mellon University, John-Michael Tebelak wrote *Godspell*, a highly episodic, two-act play based on St. Matthew's account of the parables and Passion of Jesus. Inspired by the idea of "Christ as clown" in Harvey Cox's 1969 book *The Feast of Fools: A Theological Essay on Festivity and Fantasy*, Tebelak brought fresh imaginative and emotional power to the gospel stories with minimal sets and the basic theatrical devices of mime, slapstick, and vaudevillian humor. *Godspell* opened off-off-Broadway at the Cafe LaMama in early 1971. In a slightly altered version, the play moved to the off-Broadway Cherry Lane Theatre in May 1971, with a memorable score by Stephen Schwartz that would spawn the pop hit "Day by Day." *Godspell* was a runaway success (2,124 performances off-Broadway, 527 performances on Broadway) and a tempting film property. Production of the movie version, British director David Greene's first musical film, began the very next year. The studio suggested he cast rock stars and celebrities, but Greene chose instead to use members of *Godspell* troupes from New York (including four of the original members), Boston, Toronto, Washington, and Chicago. Greene considered the venture a "family" effort, like the original play, and and credited Schwartz and Tebelak with "a great many of the final ideas" in the film. It was Schwartz's idea, for example, to set the movie in a deserted Manhattan microcosm of island Earth. To this conceit, Greene and choreographer Sammy Bayes added a layer of invention Greene described as a "cross between *The Little Rascals* and *The Wizard of Oz*." Schwartz wanted a "slightly fantastical outlook" that would avoid the "artificiality" of most musical films, while seeking to maintain the play's childlike simplicity. The score is somewhat altered, omitting "Learn Your Lessons Well" and the country-flavored "We Beseech Thee," while adding the vacuous, saccharine "Beautiful City," Schwartz's (unsuccessful) attempt to create another pop hit. The song's placement, after we learn Judas will betray Jesus, beggars explanation. Aside from this and a few other miscalculations, the film and its cast are consistently engaging, and three episodes are especially fine. "Bless the Lord" becomes a full-fledged soul/Motown revue starring powerhouse Lynne Thigpen. The Parable of the Prodigal Son is retold against a hilarious backdrop of silent movies in the Cherry Lane Theatre, *Godspell*'s off-Broadway home. But the movie's showstopper is "All for the Best." Greene and his collaborators brilliantly realize the song's wry lyrics with dance routines atop the World Trade Center (then the world's tallest building) and a soft-shoe on a narrow scaffold high above Times Square, in which Jesus and Judas dance before their own giant images on the animated Bulova Accutron sign. Greene takes the original song's mixture of psalms and Rudy Vallee and adds a strong dash of what he called "incurable optimism *a là* Harold Lloyd"; the dizzying heights revealed by a series of zoom shots are nice visual symbols of the precarious life that the song both acknowledges and defies. By the 1990s the film may seem dated. Schwartz himself claimed Greene had "somewhat misinterpreted" the play by stressing the "hippie" elements, but others praised the film, preferring it to the pompous film version of the year's "other" Bible musical, *Jesus Christ Superstar*. Its fresh cast and inventive cinematic vocabulary preserve and extend the intimacy of the stage production. *(W. G. C.)*

Resources: *The Filming of Godspell* (CBS-TV Camera Three, 1973; reissued 1997 with *Parables from Godspell* by Creative Arts Television); Kurt Gänzel, *The Encyclopedia of the Musical Theatre* (New York: Schirmer/Macmillan, 1994); see also the Stephen Schwartz Web site (http://www.stephenschwartz.com).

GOLDEN BOY (1937)
Clifford Odets

Golden Boy (1939)

Directed by Rouben Mamoulian

Adapted by Lewis Meltzer, Daniel Taradash, Sarah Y. Mason, and Victor Heerman

Cast: Barbara Stanwyck (Lorna Moon), Adolphe Menjou (Tom Moody), William Holden (Joe Bonaparte), Lee J. Cobb (Mr. Bonaparte), Joseph Calleia (Eddie Fuseli), Beatrice Blinn (Anna)

Length: 98 minutes

Odets' *Golden Boy* opened on Broadway 4 November 1937 and was adapted to film in 1939. Odets notes that the settings (Moody's office, the Bonaparte home, a park bench, the gym, and a dressing room) are not to be "too realistic." In the play, Joe Bonaparte, an aspiring violinist who happens to be a good boxer, impresses Moody in his debut against the Baltimore Chocolate Drop and, despite the objections of his music-loving father, continues to fight. Since he is afraid of hurting his hands, Joe's success is more defensive than offensive. Moody uses Lorna, his girlfriend, to convince Joe to forget the violin and concentrate on boxing. Although he sees through Moody's strategy, Joe loves Lorna and, in order to get her, vows to let nothing stand in his way. When he breaks his hand defeating an opponent, Joe's course is determined. Unhappy at his lack of progress, he has gangster Eddie Fuseli get him a fight at Madison Square Garden against the Chocolate Drop Kid. When the Kid dies, Joe examines his behavior and, with Lorna, who can no longer deny her love for him, drives off to die in a car accident. At the end of the play, Frank, his straight-shooting brother, tells his father the tragic news. Mamoulian's film adaptation, which ends in reconciliation rather than death, thoroughly revamps Odets' play. Frank is eliminated, and Mr. Bonaparte's role is considerably strengthened, which sharpens the conflict between the violin and the boxing gloves. In one scene Joe finds the violin his father has purchased for $1,500, cannot resist playing it, and is then joined by Anna, his sister, who now plays the piano. In fact, the added scenes at the Bonaparte house strengthen the audience's sense of Joe's musical commitment while they also stress strong family ties. Mamoulian also adds a scene with Lorna at an outdoor concert; this convinces Lorna that Joe is a violinist, not a boxer. To heighten the conflict Eddie Fuseli, the gangster, has demonstrably more negative influence on Joe than he did in the play. In fact, in one scene they are dressed similarly. When he accidentally kills his opponent, Joe enters the dead boxer's dressing room and receives forgiveness from his opponent's father. After quitting boxing and Fuseli, he and Lorna return to a new life at the Bonaparte house, his real home. *(T. L. E.)*

Resources: Tom Milne, *Rouben Mamoulian* (London: Thomas Hudson, 1969); Bob Thomas, *Golden Boy: The Untold Story of William Holden* (New York: St. Martin's Press, 1983).

THE GREAT WHITE HOPE (1968)
Howard Sackler

The Great White Hope (1970)

Directed by Martin Ritt

Adapted by Howard Sackler

Cast: James Earl Jones (Jack Jefferson), Jane Alexander (Emma Bachman), Robert Webber (Dixon), Marlene Warfield (Clara), Hal Holbrook (Cameron), Larry Pennell (Brady), R. G. Armstrong (Cap'n Dan), Moses Gunn (Scipio)

Length: 103 minutes

Rated: R

When Howard Sackler adapted his prizewinning *The Great White Hope* to the screen, he retained all the scenes from the play, and Jane Alexander and James Earl Jones were hired to reenact their stage roles. Since Sackler's play already reads like a series of film sequences, the film adaptation ran the risk of being a photographed play; but the fluid camera work and close-ups of Alexander and Jones make this a faithful film adaptation and a fine film. Modeled closely on the life of Jack Johnson, heavyweight champion from 1908 to 1915, *The Great White Hope* covers the boxing career of Jack Jefferson, who defeats Frank Brady, a retired champion and the first of racist America's white hopes. As a black champion with a white mistress, Emma Bachman, he threatens white fears of black sexuality and becomes the symbol for a repressed race. Jack, however, is also a threat to the Uncle Toms of the black community. After Jack and Emma cross the state line, Dixon, a federal agent, uses the Mann Act to arrest Jack. When he is fined and sentenced to three years, he visits his mother, impersonates a baseball player, and escapes. Unable to fight in England or in France (he brutally beats one fighter, intimidating possible challengers), he is reduced to playing Uncle Tom in *Uncle Tom's Cabin*. He refuses to return and fight in exchange for a reduced sentence and retires to Mexico, where he and Emma sink into degradation. After he rejects her, she drowns herself; and he agrees to lose to the new white hope in Havana. He takes a beating, then decides to fight, and ultimately is knocked out. There are some omissions (two of Cap'n Dan's racist monologues) and some changes (Scipio's monologue about Jack's desire to be white becomes a confrontation between the Jeremiah-like Scipio and Jack) and one important addition, an idyllic river scene that precedes Jack's arrest and visually establishes Jack and Emma's love. *(T. L. E.)*

Resources: Carlton Jackson, *Picking up the Tab: The Life and Movies of Martin Ritt* (Bowling Green, OH: Bowling Green University Popular Press, 1994); Randy Roberts, *Papa Jack: Jack Johnson and the Era of White Hopes* (New York: Free Press, 1983).

THE GUEST

See THE CARETAKER

HAIR (1967)
Gerome Ragni and James Rado (play and lyrics);
music by Galt MacDermot

Hair (1979)

Directed by Miloš Forman

Adapted by Miloš Forman and Michael Weller

Cast: John Savage (Claude), Beverly D'Angelo (Sheila), Treat Williams (Berger), Nicholas Ray (General), Annie Golden, Dorsey Wright, Miles Chapin, Don Dacus, Cheryl Barnes, Melba Moore, Ronnie Dyson

Length: 121 minutes

Rated: PG

A protesting "tribe" of hippies protest conscription and burn their draft cards at a "be-in." Claude, who has received his draft notice, decides to be conscripted into the army and refuses to burn his draft card. His friends Berger and Sheila attempt to dissuade him, but to no avail. Sheila is with Claude on his final night of freedom. The next day, his hair is cut off when he is taken by the army. This first musical of the hippie movement offered a spectacle of nudity in the first act's finale. "Aquarius" became a sort of anthem for the protest generation. The play was revived on Broadway in 1977, but by the time Czech director Miloš Forman was able to get his film production cleared and organized, the Age of Aquarius had long since passed. Rather than simply photographing the stage play, Forman decided to make his own version, working with playwright Michael Weller (*Moonchildren* and *Loose Ends*), who also worked with Forman on the adaptation of E. L. Doctorow's *Ragtime*. Forman used only two people from the original cast (Melba Moore and Ronnie Dyson), and he cut three of the original songs. Composer Galt MacDermot, who played Berger onstage but was too old for the role by the time the film was made, did all the orchestrations. Twyla Tharp was the choreographer. Forman approached the film as a musical but developed a new story line that he claimed "was hidden in the original one." The film was shot in Central Park and other New York City locations and in Washington, D.C., at the Lincoln Memorial. *(J. M. W.)*

Resources: Miloš Forman and Jan Novak, *Turnaround: A Memoir* (New York: Villard, 1994); Todd McCarthy, "Miloš Forman Lets His Hair Down," *Film Comment* 15.2 (March 1979): 17–21.

HAMLET (1602)
William Shakespeare

Hamlet (1948)

Directed by Laurence Olivier

Adapted by Laurence Olivier and Alan Dent

Cast: Laurence Olivier (Hamlet), Basil Sydney (Claudius), Eileen Herlie (Gertrude), Jean Simmons (Ophelia), Felix Aylmer (Polonius), Terence Morgan (Laertes), Normand Wooland (Horatio), Peter Cushing (Osric), Anthony Quayle (Marcellus), Esmond Knight (Bernardo), John Laurie (Francisco), Harcourt Williams (First Player), Stanley Holloway (Gravedigger)

Length: 152 minutes

Prince Hamlet is melancholy when the play opens because he is grieving the recent death of his father and disturbed because his mother, Gertrude, has married his uncle, Claudius, who is now king of Denmark. The ghost of Hamlet's dead father tells the prince that he was murdered by his brother while sleeping in his orchard, giving Hamlet the responsibility of avenging his death. Hamlet is uncertain, however, whether this was truly the ghost of his father or an evil spirit sent to tempt him into committing murder. When a troupe of actors arrives at Elsinore, Hamlet requests that they perform a play called *The Murder of Gonzago* and inserts lines to make this play more closely resemble what the ghost had told him, in order to see if Claudius will register guilt when he sees the play, as is the case. In an angry confrontation with his mother, Hamlet discovers an eavesdropper in his mother's bedroom and kills him, thinking it was the king, but it was, in fact, Polonius, the king's adviser. Claudius sends Hamlet to England with Rosencrantz and Guildenstern, who carry instructions to the English king to have Hamlet put to death, but Hamlet arranges to be rescued at sea by pirates and returns to Denmark. Laertes, the son of Polonius, holds Hamlet responsible for the death of his father and his sister, Ophelia, who goes mad and commits suicide after her father's death. A duel is arranged between Hamlet and Laertes, rigged so that Hamlet will be killed by poison if scratched by his opponent's sword. Gertrude dies after unknowingly drinking poisoned wine intended for Hamlet. Hamlet dies after killing both Laertes and Claudius. Laurence Olivier's film set an early standard and was much admired in its time, though decades later it may seem seriously dated by the Freudian interpretation forced upon the text. A voice-over attempts to simplify the play by informing the audience, "This is the tragedy of a man who could not make up his mind," which puts rather too much emphasis on the issue of Hamlet's alleged procrastination. The framing conflict between Denmark and Norway, which poses a foreign policy threat, is hardly stressed at all, and young Fortinbras of Norway disappears entirely from the film. The film seems overwrought and belabored in its attempt to be cinematic, as in the absurdly flamboyant camera work used to film Hamlet's famous "To be, or not to be" soliloquy. Scenes are rearranged to make the play fit the conventions of film narrative. The film removes Polonius' servant Reynaldo, sent to Paris to spy on Laertes, and also Rosencrantz and Guildenstern, brought to Elsinore to spy on Hamlet. Of course, Olivier's performance is worth watching, but the play has been restructured to showcase his talents. By later standards, it seems dated and oddly stylized, however. *(J. M. W.)*

Resources: Jack J. Jorgens, *Shakespeare on Film* (Bloomington: Indiana University Press, 1977); Bernice W. Kliman, *Hamlet: Film, Television, and Audio Performances* (Rutherford, NJ: Fairleigh Dickinson University Press, 1988).

Hamlet (1969)

Directed and adapted by Tony Richardson
Cast: Nicol Williamson (Hamlet), Judy Parfitt (Gertrude), Anthony Hopkins (Claudius), Gordon Jackson (Horatio), Mark Dignam (Polonius), Michael Pennington (Laertes), Marianne Faithfull (Ophelia), Ben Aris (Rosencrantz), Clive Graham (Guildenstern), Peter Gale (Osric), John Carney (Player King), Roger Livesey (Lucianus, Gravedigger), Roger Lloyd-Pack (Reynaldo)
Length: 117 minutes
Rated: G

As an adaptation of the play, this film is superior to Olivier's in the way it has been restructured for cinema. Although nearly half of the text has been cut, more of the characters are preserved. The adaptation has been done as filmed theatre, replicating Richardson's London stage production at the Round House Theatre, where the film was shot. Though the approach is theatrical rather than cinematic, the film excels in the performances it captures, especially Nicol Williamson's impudent prince, which is far more lively and believable than Olivier's. It also marks Anthony Hopkins' first screen appearance, as an effectively devious King Claudius. Very little emphasis is placed on Fortinbras and the Norwegian threat in this version, which centers squarely on the character of Hamlet. When Hamlet dies in Act V, the film is over, but Richardson streamlines and simplifies the text agreeably, cutting individual lines rather than whole scenes. The theme of incest is stressed rather too vigorously, however, since Marianne Faithfull's Ophelia, a far more experienced woman than readers might expect, appears to be involved in an incestuous affair with her brother, Laertes, which does make his grieving at her graveside seem the more credible. The film is especially sensitive to images of disease, corruption, and perversion. The ghost is not seen in this film, only heard, while his presence is suggested by an illuminating spotlight. The method is to close in rather than open up the play, and most of the action is represented by medium shots and close-ups. The advantage of this approach is that it puts the emphasis squarely on the text and the actors. Richardson makes no attempt to conceal the fact that this is a film of a play and lets the play speak for itself. *(J. M. W.)*

Resources: Michael Mullin, "Tony Richardson's *Hamlet*: Script and Screen," *Literature/Film Quarterly* 4.2 (1976): 123–133; Don Radovich, *Tony Richardson: A Bio-Bibliography* (Westport, CT: Greenwood Press, 1995).

Hamlet (1990)

Directed by Franco Zeffirelli

Adapted by Franco Zeffirelli and Christopher DeVore

Cast: Mel Gibson (Hamlet), Glenn Close (Gertrude), Alan Bates (Claudius), Nathaniel Parker (Laertes, Paul Scofield (Ghost), Ian Holm (Polonius), Helena Bonham Carter (Ophelia), Stephen Dillane (Horatio), Sean Murray (Guildenstern), Michael Maloney (Rosencrantz), Trevor Peacock (Gravedigger), John McEnery (Osric), Pete Postlethwaite (Player King)

Length: 135 minutes

Rated: PG

This version of Shakespeare's revenge drama was clearly made for a mass audience and features several good, high-profile performances. Mel Gibson is quite good as the prince and is certainly capable of doing justice to the lines. His performance is energetic and well modulated. Likewise, Helena Bonham Carter excels as a fragile, but spirited, Ophelia, who will do her father's bidding by spying on Hamlet but who clearly dislikes the idea. Paul Scofield is stately as the Ghost, and Ian Holm presents a Polonius who is politically involved and not simply a dottering and senile fool. John McEnery gives a devious and evil shading to the role of Osric, clearly involved in the king's conspiracy to kill Hamlet. The film was shot on location in England and Scotland to provide an appropriate medieval atmosphere. Where the film goes seriously wrong, however, is in its serious butchering of the text, which is scrambled almost beyond recognition. Zeffirelli entirely dismisses Shakespeare's first scene on the battlements with Horatio and provides his own exposition by taking the viewer back in time to the dead king's funeral. Only a fraction of the second scene, which should be set in public at court, retains that public setting. Instead, the film takes the viewer into the king and queen's private chambers. As a consequence, the king's public criticism of Hamlet's behavior loses much of its sting. Hamlet deserves a worthy opponent, but the Claudius played by Alan Bates is weak, jovial, and slow-witted and not apparently dangerous. The character of Hamlet's loyal friend Horatio is also far diminished in importance. As Gertrude, Glenn Close dithers too much, like a schoolgirl in love. Ophelia's "Get thee to a nunnery" scene is absurdly abridged and misplaced in the Mousetrap scene. Shakespeare charts Hamlet's psychological progression through four major soliloquies, but the fourth of these is missing, so even Hamlet's movement toward resolution is impeded. The spectacle of the duel scene is nicely staged, however, as Zeffirelli puts his emphasis on action rather than thought. Though Ophelia's mad scenes are nicely presented and effectively portrayed, Hamlet's alleged madness is carried to new levels of lunacy. The play is not only streamlined and simplified but outrageously dumbed down. No one could fully appreciate the elegance of Shakespeare's construction nor the elegance of his language by simply watching this filmed production. *(J. M. W.)*

Resources: David Impastato, "Zeffirelli's *Hamlet*: Sunlight Makes Meaning," *Shakespeare on Film Newsletter* 16.1 (1991): 1–2; John P. McCombe, "The Problem of Desire in Franco Zeffirelli's *Hamlet*," *Literature/Film Quarterly* 25.2 (1997): 125–131; John Tibbetts, "Mel Gibson Takes On 'Hamlet,' " *Christian Science Monitor* (15 January 1991): 12.

Hamlet (1996)

Directed and adapted by Kenneth Branagh

Cast: Kenneth Branagh (Hamlet), Derek Jacobi (Claudius), Richard Briers (Polonius), Julie Christie (Gertrude), Kate Winslet (Ophelia), Michael Maloney (Laertes), Nicholas Farrell (Horatio), Brian Blessed (Ghost), Timothy Spall (Rosencrantz), Reece Dinsdale (Guildenstern), Billy Crystal (First Gravedigger), Simon Russell Beale (Second Gravedigger), Robin Williams (Osric), Gerard Depardieu (Reynaldo), Jack Lemmon (Marcellus), Charlton Heston (Player King), Rosemary Harris (Player Queen), Ian McElhinney (Bernardo), Ray Fearon (Francisco), Rufus Sewell (Fortinbras), John Mills (Old Norway), Richard Attenborough (English Ambassador), John Gielgud (Priam), Judi Dench (Hecuba), Ken Dodd (Yorick)

Length: 238 minutes

Rating: PG-13

This is the most complete and extravagant version of Shakespeare's play ever captured on film, as Branagh's intent was to include everything and omit nothing, nearly 4,000 lines of text from the quarto and folio versions of the play, including scenes that are often abridged or cut in both stage and screen productions. The miracle achieved here is that a film that runs to four hours is never boring, and even the most difficult lines are made understandable. The cast read like a who's who of British, American, and international talents making cameo appearances—Jack Lemmon, for example, as the spear-carrier Marcellus in the first scene, Gerard Depardieu as Reynaldo, instructed by Polonius to spy on Laertes in Paris, Charlton Heston as the Player King, with John Gielgud and Judi Dench visualizing the action of his speech about Priam, Robin Williams as young Osric, and so it goes. Derek Jacobi's Claudius makes a powerful and dangerous opponent for Branagh's Hamlet, whose treatment of Kate Winslet's Ophelia goes beyond the verbal abuse of the play to physical abuse. His treatment of her makes her later mad scenes all the more plausible. The hovering presence and threat of Fortinbras and his army have never been so effectively captured on film, moreover, and this film ends the way Shakespeare intended to end the play, as Fortinbras breaks into the royal palace, after Hamlet has dispatched both Laertes and Claudius and died next to his mother. To stress the universality of the play, Branagh moves the action forward in time to a nineteenth-century setting. Branagh's approach was built upon the following guidelines: "a commitment to international casting; a speaking style that attempts to set the story in a historical context that is resonant for a modern audience but allows a heightened language to sit comfortably," and, above all, "a full emotional commitment to the characters, springing from a belief that they can be understood in direct, accessible relation to modern life" (xv). Rather than an oddly stylized museum piece like the Olivier version or a fragmented simplification like the Zeffirelli, this production has contemporary relevance and constitutes pure cinema. *(J. M. W.)*

Resources: Kenneth Branagh, *Hamlet, by William Shakespeare: Screenplay and Introduction* (New York: W. W. Norton, 1996); Mark Thornton Burnett, "The 'Very Cunning of the Scene': Kenneth Branagh's *Hamlet,*" *Literature/Film Quarterly* 25.2 (1997): 78–82.

See also ROSENCRANTZ AND GUILDENSTERN ARE DEAD

HAMP (1962)
John Wilson, adapted from a story by James Landsdale Hodson

King and Country (1964)

Directed by Joseph Losey

Adapted by Evan Jones

Cast: Dirk Bogarde (Capt. Hargreaves), Tom Courtenay (Pvt. Hamp), Leo McKern (Capt. O'Sullivan), Barry Foster (Lt. Webb), James Villiers (Capt. Midgley), Peter Copley (Colonel), Vivian Matalon (Padre), Jeremy Spencer (Pvt. Sparrow)

Length: 86 minutes

Private Arthur Hamp (Tom Courtenay), twenty-three years old when court-martialed for desertion in 1917, had served three years in World War I and was the sole survivor of the company with whom he had gone to France. After his wife writes him confessing to an affair, he snaps under fire. Though well represented by Captain Hargreaves (Dirk Bogarde), he is found guilty and sentenced to death. An appeal for mercy is denied, and Hamp is executed by a firing squad in the interest of morale, since Hamp's battalion is about to be sent into battle. The play *Hamp* by John Wilson was based on a true story written by James Lansdale Hodson, a defense lawyer in the court-martial who shaped the story into a radio script before John Wilson restructured it as both a stage and television play. Evan Jones decided to work directly from the radio script to draft the screenplay, which was then revised by Losey and Bogarde. The film was praised for its message about the injustices of war and the unfairness of the English class system. It was selected as "Outstanding Film of the Year" at the London Film Festival. *(J. M. W.)*

Resources: David Caute, *Joseph Losey: A Revenge on Life* (London: Faber and Faber, 1994); James Palmer and Michael Riley, *The Films of Joseph Losey* (Cambridge, UK: Cambridge University Press, 1993).

HARVEY (1944)
Mary Coyle Chase

Harvey (1950)

Directed by Henry Koster

Adapted by Mary Coyle Chase and Oscar Brodney

Cast: James Stewart (Elwood P. Dowd), Josephine Hull (Vera Louise Simmons), Peggy Dow (Miss Kelly), Charles Drake (Dr. Sanderson), Cecil Kellaway (Dr. Chumley), Victoria Horne (Myrtle Mae), Jesse White (Wilson), Wallace Ford (Lofgren)

Length: 104 minutes

When this Mary Chase comedy about a "pooka" (a specter from Irish folklore), which opened in November 1944, won the Pulitzer Prize in 1945, it was, amazingly enough in retrospect, selected over Tennessee Williams' *The Glass Menagerie*. Because of the popular success of the play, Hollywood quickly became interested in Chase and her work. In the Broadway production Frank Fay played the delusional dipsomaniac Elwood P. Dowd, who has an imaginary friend, an invisible giant rabbit over six feet tall named Harvey, to the distress and embarrassment of Dowd's family. "I wrestled with reality for over 35 years," Elwood explains, "and I'm happy to say that I finally won out over it." James Stewart, who had substituted for Frank Fay onstage, actively campaigned for the role in the Universal Studios production and got it. Twenty years after the film, in 1970, Stewart and Helen Hayes headlined a successful stage revival of the play that was considered even more enjoyable than the original. Stewart's talents and likable screen presence were obviously well suited for the role, which won him an Oscar nomination, though Stewart later admitted that he had played Elwood "a little too cute-cute." Jesse White, Victoria Horne, and Josephine Hull all went from the original stage production to the Hollywood version, and Hull, who was well known for her portrayal of Penny Sycamore in Kaufman and Hart's *You Can't Take It with You* and for

Joseph Kesselring's *Arsenic and Old Lace*, won an Academy Award for Best Supporting Actress for her portrayal of the protagonist's distraught sister. *(J. M. W.)*

Resources: Brooks Atkinson, *Broadway* (New York: Proscenium/Limelight, 1985); Ty Burr, "Jimmy Stewart: The Richest Man in Hollywood," *Entertainment Weekly* No. 388 (18 July 1997): 36–48; Howard Thompson, *James Stewart* (New York: Pyramid, 1974).

HEAVEN CAN WAIT (1938)
Harry Segall

Heaven Can Wait (1978)

Directed by Warren Beatty and Buck Henry

Adapted by Warren Beatty and Elaine May

Cast: Warren Beatty (Joe Pendleton/Leo Farnsworth/Tom Jarrett), Julie Christie (Bette Logan), James Mason (Mr. Jordan), Jack Warden (Max Corkle), Charles Grodin (Tony Abbott), Dyan Cannon (Julia Farnsworth), Buck Henry (the Escort)

Length: 101 minutes

Rated: PG

This 1978 Warren Beatty vehicle is a remake of *Here Comes Mr. Jordan* (1941) and is based on an unproduced 1938 play by Harry Segall called *Heaven Can Wait* (it should not be confused with the 1943 Ernst Lubitsch film of the same name). The central figure in the play is Joe Pendleton, a young boxer who dies prematurely and, with the help of the angelic Mr. Jordan, is returned to life in the body of a murdered millionaire named Farnsworth. Pendleton, now in Farnsworth's body, strikes up a relationship with Bette Logan (whose father was wronged by the real Farnsworth), only to be remurdered. In order for Joe to fulfill his destiny, Mr. Jordan moves him into the body of boxer K. O. Murdoch, so that Joe can win the championship and be reunited with Bette. In the film's script by Beatty and Elaine May, football replaces boxing, and Farnsworth is a wealthy industrialist with environmentally destructive business practices. One frustrating aspect of both the play and film versions is the unexplained loss of Joe's spirit as his memory is wiped clean near the end of the story, and he is left with only the memories of the person he inhabits, in the case of the film, quarterback Tom Jarrett. Throughout the story we've been led to believe that Pendleton, more specifically, his "spirit," must be returned to earth in order to complete his destiny. Early in Segall's play, just before Joe enters Farnsworth's body, Jordan tells him that *"Spiritually*, there'll be no change in you! . . . *You'll always be yourself, Joe!* Nothing can change that—you'll merely be using his physical covering—like donning a new overcoat!" Why, then, does Jordan erase Joe's memory, instructing him to fulfill his destiny with only a vague recollection of his life as Joe Pendleton? Otherwise, the film is a light and breezy comedy with Beatty and Julie Christie well cast as the romantic leads. An excellent supporting cast led by Jack Warden, Dyan Cannon, and Charles Grodin ably supports the fantasy elements central to the film's success. As Frank Rich points out, "[T]hough the film is set almost entirely in modern Los Angeles, it never gives the audience time to question its fantastic premise or its hopelessly romantic conviction that love can triumph over class differences, physical metamorphoses and even death." *Heaven Can Wait* received nine Academy Award nominations, including Best Picture, and won an Oscar for Art Direction. *(M. G.)*

Resources: Frank Rich, "Warren Beatty Strikes Again," *Time* (3 July 1978): 70–74; Harry Segall, *Heaven Can Wait* (New York: Dramatists Play Service, 1969).

Here Comes Mr. Jordan (1941)

Directed by Alexander Hall

Adapted by Sidney Buchman and Seton I. Miller

Cast: Robert Montgomery (Joe Pendleton/Bruce Farnsworth/Ralph Murdoch), Evelyn Keyes (Bette Logan), Claude Rains (Mr. Jordan), James Gleason (Max Corkle), Edward Everett Horton (Messenger #7013)

Length: 94 minutes

Harry Segall's unproduced play *Heaven Can Wait* (1938) had success on the screen as *Here Comes Mr. Jordan* (1941) prior to being performed onstage under two different titles, *Halfway to Heaven* (1943) in London and *Wonderful Journey* (1946) in New York. Both theatrical productions were unsuccessful when compared to the film versions of *Here Comes Mr. Jordan* and the 1978 remake, *Heaven Can Wait*, with Warren Beatty. The story revolves around boxer Joe Pendleton, whose spirit is accidentally plucked from his body by the newly appointed Heavenly Messenger #7013. Angelic supervisor Mr. Jordan discovers the mistake and orders #7013 to return Pendleton to his earthly body, only to find that it has been cremated. Pendleton reluctantly accepts the body of Jonathan Farnsworth, a millionaire businessman who has just been murdered by his philandering wife, Julia, and his private secretary, Tony. As Joe works to unravel Farnsworth's shady business dealings, he begins a relationship with Bette Logan (whose father was framed by the real Farnsworth), only to be remurdered by Julia and Tony. Joe then enters the body of boxer K. O. Murdoch, who has just been murdered for refusing to take a dive during a fight. Joe, now inhabiting Murdoch's body, resumes the match and becomes the champion. He is then reunited with Bette, fulfilling his destiny. Except for a few minor changes, the film retains much of the basic plot structure of the play: Robert Montgomery's performance as Pendleton is self-assured and seamless. As critic Juliette Friedgen points out in *Magill's Survey of Cinema*, Montgomery's "sustaining sense of awe concerning all that is happening neither falters nor becomes overdone," allowing the audience to connect with the fantasy elements of the story. The supporting cast of characters, especially Claude Raines and James Gleason, is also excellent, and the film exudes a classic sense of charm and humor throughout. The film was nominated for seven Academy Awards and won an Oscar for Best Screenplay. According to William Leonard, "Segall reworked the Jordan-fantasy theme into *Angel on My Shoulder*, switching heaven to hell," with Paul Muni as a deceased gangster, and "Claude Rains' saintly Mr. Jordan became Nick, the devil himself." In 1947, *Down to Earth*, a musical remake/sequel to *Here Comes Mr. Jordan*, was released, starring Rita Hayworth, adapted by Edwin Blum and Don Hartman, and once again directed by Alexander Hall. Gleason and Horton also reprised their roles, but despite this link to the earlier film, *Down to Earth* met with limited success. *(M. G.)*

Resources: William Torbert Leonard, *Theatre: Stage to Screen to Television*, Vol. 1 (Metuchen, NJ: Scarecrow Press, 1981); Frank Magill, ed., *Magill's Survey of Cinema: English Language Films*, vol. 2 (Englewood Cliffs, NJ: Salem Press, 1980).

HELLO, DOLLY! (1964)
Jerry Herman and Michael Steward; adapted for the stage from Thornton Wilder's *The Matchmaker*; music and lyrics added by Jerry Herman

---

Hello, Dolly! (1969)

Directed by Gene Kelly

Adapted by Ernest Lehman

Cast: Barbra Streisand (Dolly Levi), Walter Matthau (Horace Vandergelder), Michael Crawford (Cornelius Hackl), Marianne McAndrew (Mrs. Molloy), E. J. Peaker (Minnie Fay), Tommy Tune (Ambrose Kemper), Louis Armstrong (as himself)

Length: 129 minutes

Composer/lyricist Jerry Herman's adaptation of the play *The Matchmaker* by Thornton Wilder (rewritten from his earlier version, called *The Merchant of Yonkers*) has a longer stage history than most plays adapted to film. The original story comes from a play by English author John Oxenford entitled *A Day Well Spent*; Johann Nestroy wrote a classic Viennese version of the story entitled *Einen Jux will er sich machen*; Tom Stoppard also wrote his own adaptation of the story, calling it *On the Razzle*. The musical *Hello, Dolly!* opened at the St. James Theater, New York, on 16 January 1964. The story takes place at the turn of the twentieth century and focuses upon the exploits of widow-turned-marriage-broker Dolly Gallagher Levi and her attempts to win the heart of Horace Vandergelder, the half-a-millionaire who owns a feedstore in Yonkers, New York. Mrs. Levi has been hired by the widower Mr. Vandergelder (Walter Matthau) to find him a new wife to cook and clean for him. Dolly sets Horace up with a pretty milliner, Mrs. Molloy (McAndrew), herself a widow, merely as a means of getting him to New York, where she can wine and dine him at the very elaborate Harmonia Gardens restaurant, where Mrs. Levi spent many blissful nights with her former husband, Ephraim. Dolly manages to get Mrs. Molloy and her cohort Minnie Fay out of the picture by introducing them to Vandergelder's two clerks, Cornelius Hackl (Michael Crawford) and Barnaby Tucker. All ends happily with a series of marriages and an elaborate wedding procession beautifully filmed on location in New York. The film version includes a new opening song for Streisand, "Just Leave Everything to Me," which replaces "I Put My Hand In" from the Broadway score. Most of the dialogue is retained from the original production, with occasional new lines more suited to Streisand's particular comedic gifts, reminiscent of her Fanny Brice performance in *Funny Girl*. Unlike other musicals starring Streisand, *Hello, Dolly!* permits the other members of the cast to sing. Director Gene Kelly borrows from his experience in past MGM musicals. Several sequences resemble other crowd-pleasing "business" from earlier musicals: "Before the Parade Passes By" recalls "Don't Rain on My Parade" from *Funny Girl*; "Put on Your Sunday Clothes" looks strikingly similar to "On the Atchison, Topeka and the Santa Fe" from *The Harvey Girls*; and, most importantly, the title song sung by Streisand and Louis Armstrong calls to mind his performance in *High Society* (1956). However, the obvious studio singing dubbed in after the fact is disappointing. The film also lacks effective chemistry between the two stars, while the charm of the original stage production gets lost in this anachronistic big-budget, old-fashioned extravaganza. Unique to the film version is an additional song for Dolly, the romantic ballad "Love Is Only Love." Mrs. Levi gets ready for her big evening on the town with Horace, while exploring in song the possibility of marrying again. *(J. S.)*

Resources: Kurt Ganzl, *The Encyclopedia of Musical Theatre* (New York: Schirmer, 1994); Gerald Mast, *Can't Help Singin': The American Musical on Stage and Screen* (New York: Overlook Press, 1987).

HENRY IV, PARTS I & II, HENRY V, RICHARD II, and THE MERRY WIVES OF WINDSOR

William Shakespeare (with additional narration based upon Raphael Holinshed's *Chronicles of England*)

Chimes at Midnight (Falstaff) (1965)

Directed and adapted by Orson Welles

Cast: Orson Welles (Falstaff), Keith Baxter (Prince Hal), John Gielgud (Henry IV), Norman Rodway (Henry Percy, "Hotspur"), Jeanne Moreau (Doll Tearsheet), Fernando Rey (Worcester), Marina Vlady (Kate Percy), Ralph Richardson (narrator)

Length: 115 minutes

Orson Welles' *Chimes at Midnight* is a brilliant alchemy of no less than five of Shakespeare's plays and, like the mystical process that creates something priceless from a strange admixture of materials, it transforms Shakespeare's passages into a masterwork of art unique unto itself. As with his *Othello*, this film has only recently been restored and reedited, with special attention paid to the synchronization of sound and image. As a result, Welles' study of the sometimes comic, often poignant, and ultimately tragic relationship between Falstaff and Prince Hal offers some of the most inspired interpretations of a number of Shakespeare's most celebrated scenes. Welles pays particular attention to the familial triangle between Henry IV, his son, and Falstaff, the comic "Lord of Misrule" who acts as a surrogate father to the prince. Hal is symbolically caught between the opposing worlds of his "fathers": court and tavern, duty and diversion, king and companions. Cinematically, Welles captures this external struggle for Hal's loyalties through his juxtaposition of the spacious, yet sterile, world of Henry's palace and Hotspur's castle (scenes dominated by high-angled long shots) with the cramped, yet carnivalesque, atmosphere of the Boar's Head tavern, home to Falstaff and his fellow roaring boys (in which the camera, like Falstaff's great girth, can barely maneuver through narrow hallways). The first half of the film follows Hal's movement between the two worlds and is highlighted by the "mock deposition" sequence from *Henry IV, Part I*, in which Hal and Falstaff role-play King Henry and the prince. Hal's famous retort to Falstaff's plea ("banish plump Jack, and banish all the world!")—"I do, I will"—provides the fulcrum around which the drama unfolds, a bittersweet portent of the film's final scenes. The justly renowned Battle of Shrewsbury sequence (the stylistic precursor to the Battle of Agincourt in Kenneth Branagh's film version of *Henry V*) pronounces Hal's inexorable movement away from Falstaff's festive world and into one of nationalistic prerogatives. From this point on, the tone of the film becomes increasingly somber, as Hal's confinement within his role of monarch-to-be grows increasingly absolute. By the time he succeeds to the throne and rejects Falstaff ("I know thee not, old man"), Welles photographs Hal almost exclusively through rows of pikes—symbolic of both his royal power and alienation from the world of his festive companions. According to Sidney Homan, Welles himself commented that he "directed everything and planned everything with a view of preparing for the last scene." Purists have long scoffed at the film for its obvious textual liberties, but *Chimes at Midnight* is a masterful elegy to a world of companionship and vitality sacrificed to the abstractions of duty and politics. It captures Shakespeare at his most contemplative, mourning Falstaff's death not just as the loss of a great comic figure but as a symbol of all humanity. *(R. R.)*

Resources: Michael Anderegg, *Orson Welles, Shakespeare, and Popular Culture* (New York: Columbia University Press, 1999); Sidney Homan, "*Henry IV, Part Two* on Stage and Screen," in *Henry IV Part II* (New York: Signet, 1988).

HENRY V (1599)
William Shakespeare

Henry V (1944)

Directed by Laurence Olivier

Adapted by Laurence Olivier, Reginald Beck, Alan Dent, and Dallas Bower

Cast: Laurence Olivier (King Henry V), Robert Newton (Pistol), Leslie Banks (Chorus), Renee Asherson (Princess Katherine), Esmond Knight (Fluellen), Leo Genn (Constable of France), Ralph Truman (Mountjoy), Felix Aylmer (Archbishop of Canterbury)

Length: 137 minutes

The film began as a propaganda exercise. Olivier was asked by Jack Beddington at the Ministry of Information to make it for the British cause in World War II. In his autobiography, Olivier provides a fascinating account of the practical difficulties. The battle sequences were shot in Ireland using extras who were paid an additional pound if they brought their own horses.

The film was completed in sixteen weeks of shooting at Denham Studios. The crew made use of the only Technicolor camera in England, and special effects had to be created using primitive means, particularly in the opening and closing shots using the model of the Globe Theatre. Half of the lines in the play were excised. However, the Battle of Agincourt is added, and so is the rejection of Falstaff from *Henry IV, Part 2* to explain the roles of Pistol and friends. Less attractive aspects of Henry are also excluded, including his decision to kill prisoners of war. Henry is seen as a consummate warrior, but a chivalrous one. It was the perfect embodiment of patriotic resolve for the Britain of 1944. "We few, we happy few, we band of brothers" had great resonance for a nation that had so recently lived through the Battle of Britain and was busy replacing "modest stillness and humility" with the "hard-favored rage" necessary to proceed "once more unto the breach." Today, the film seems much more stridently patriotic. Nevertheless, it is full of riches. The great variety of spoken styles is aptly reflected in the acting. In Henry's set-piece speeches, Olivier reverses the usual method of moving from wide shot to close-up in order to reflect Shakespeare's oratorical process. The minor roles are played by a cadre of fine actors, led by Robert Newton, whose interpretation of Pistol is delightful. The film's greatest triumph is its structure, which makes such effective use of the context of the Elizabethan theatre, seamlessly moving from apron stage to "reality" and back. Not only does this help in the presentation of difficult sequences such as the Archbishop of Canterbury's discourse on Salic law, but it also provides a luminous interpretation of the Chorus' opening lines: "Oh, for a Muse of fire, that would ascend / The brightest heaven of invention." It is not hard to believe that he had such a cinema in mind! *(W. L. H.)*

Resources: Anthony Davies, *Filming Shakespeare's Plays: The Adaptations of Laurence Olivier, Orson Welles and Akira Kurosawa* (Cambridge: Cambridge University Press, 1988); Harry M. Geduld, *Filmguide to Henry V* (Bloomington: Indiana University Press, 1973); Laurence Olivier, *Confessions of an Actor* (London: Weidenfeld and Nicolson, 1982).

Henry V (1989)

Directed and adapted by Kenneth Branagh

Cast: Kenneth Branagh (King Henry V), Robert Stephens (Pistol), Derek Jacobi (Chorus), Emma Thompson (Princess Katherine), Ian Holm (Fluellen), Brian Blessed (Exeter), Richard Briers (Bardolph), Paul Scofield (King of France), Judi Dench (Mistress Quickly)

Length: 137 minutes

Rated: PG

When it became known that, at the age of twenty-eight, Kenneth Branagh was to make a film of *Henry V*, some regarded him as brave, but others as merely foolhardy. In 1984 he had triumphed as the youngest actor ever cast in the role of Henry by the Royal Shakespeare Company in Adrian Noble's well-received production of the play. He brought much of that interpretation to his film. In 1986 he had created the Renaissance Theater Company to place a profound emphasis on the actor. Indeed, individuals like Judi Dench and Derek Jacobi, who directed plays for the company, were duly recruited to participate in its first film project. Branagh spent eighteen months convincing skeptical potential backers that they should risk their money on such an enterprise. Olivier's version of the play exercised such a powerful place in the pantheon that it was thought to be impossible to produce a successful new version. Branagh proved otherwise. He has argued that he wanted to reclaim the play from nationalism, yet his version is not as much antiwar as profoundly ambiguous and uncertain. Throughout, one is struck by the omnipresence of Olivier's conception. As the film begins, "the muse of fire" becomes Derek Jacobi's lighted match, giving way to the movie soundstage, in a clear reference to the earlier work. The roots of Olivier's film are theatrical; Branagh's will be naturalistic. Indeed, the latter film makes much greater use of intimate close-ups. Where Olivier's battle scenes are romantic, Branagh's are replete with mud and blood. Nowhere is the change more evident than in the more ruthless facets of the character excluded in the earlier film but exploited in the later work. Even Branagh felt unable to include Henry's most damning action: his decision to kill the French prisoners. But the hanging of Bardolph for stealing and the bloodcurdling threats used against Harfleur provide a decidedly more complex interpretation of leadership. Branagh effectively uses these incidents to present the ambiguities of character and the complexity of moral judgment about war. His Henry is a study in the hard-won achievement of leadership through bitter experience, in which triumph and tragedy are inextricably intertwined. *(W. L. H.)*

Resources: Kenneth Branagh, *Beginning* (New York: St. Martin's Press, 1991); Kenneth Branagh, *Henry V: Screenplay* (New York: W. W. Norton, 1997); James N. Loehlin, *Henry V* (Manchester: Manchester University Press, 1996).

See also HENRY IV, PARTS I & II, HENRY V, RICHARD II, and THE MERRY WIVES OF WINDSOR

HERE COMES MR. JORDAN

See HEAVEN CAN WAIT

HIS GIRL FRIDAY

See THE FRONT PAGE

HOBSON'S CHOICE (1915)
Harold Brighouse

Hobson's Choice (1954)

Directed by David Lean

Adapted by David Lean, Norman Spencer, and Wynyard Browne

Cast: Charles Laughton (Henry Horatio Hobson), John Mills (William Mossop), Brenda de Banzie (Maggie Hobson), Daphne Anderson (Alice Hobson), Prunella Scales (Vicky Hobson), Helen Hayes (Mrs. Hepworth)

Length: 107 minutes

Lean's film adaption is the third made of Brighouse's play, which was first staged in the United States in 1915. The play concerns Hobson, who runs his boot-making shop and his three daughters with a penny-pinching, iron hand. Maggie, his eldest daughter and accomplished saleswoman, rebels against his rule by literally forcing William Mossup, her father's accomplished boot maker, to marry her, securing financing from Mrs. Hepworth, and establishing a rival boot-making business that eventually gains most of the local business. When her father will not provide dowries for her two sisters, Maggie opportunistically uses her father's drunken trespassing to obtain an out-of-court settlement that provides dowries for her sisters. When her father's ailing business and chronic alcoholism force him to seek Maggie's help, she and William return, but only after her father agrees to their terms. Lean's adaptation adds several exterior scenes that provide glimpses of Hobson's blustering behavior in the Moonraker, the local pub, and of Maggie's drive and determination: she and William go to Mrs. Hepworth's; she visits William's "intended" and puts not only her but her formidable mother to rout; and she transforms the cellar rooms she and William work and live in. Lean's film also develops the relationship between Maggie and William and adds some comic touches. Maggie not only teaches William to read but also gives him the self-confidence and the "power" (William's word) to become a match for Hobson and Maggie herself. In the play Maggie takes William by the ear and leads him into the bedroom on their wedding night; in the film a hesitant William summons up his courage and with martial music marches into the bedroom. When Maggie demands a kiss in the street, William refuses; he kisses her when he effectively confronts her father. The most effective screen scenes involve Maggie's mixed feelings about William's growing independence and power, and the complexity of their relationship is mirrored in the relationship of Maggie and her father. She rebels, but at the end of the film, she wisely and lovingly lets him arrange the details of the partnership between Mossop and Hobson. *(T. L. E.)*

Resources: Michael A. Anderegg, *David Lean* (Boston: Twayne, 1984); Gerald Pratley, *The Cinema of David Lean* (South Brunswick, NJ: A. S. Barnes, 1974); Stephen M. Silverman, *David Lean* (New York: H. N. Abrams, 1992).

HOME OF THE BRAVE (1945)
Arthur Laurents

Home of the Brave (1949)

Directed by Mark Robson

Adapted by Carl Foreman

Cast: Frank Lovejoy (Mingo), Lloyd Bridges (Finch), James Edwards (Pvt. Moss), Steve Brodie (T. J.), Jeff Corey (Psychiatrist), Douglas Dick

Length: 86 minutes

Arthur Laurents' 1945 play was originally about anti-Semitism, but in adapting it for the screen, Carl Foreman and producer Stanley Kramer changed the role of the Jewish soldier to an African American or "Negro," to use the more common parlance of the time. In all other respects, the play and the film are essentially the same. Hollywood in the postwar 1940s was issue-oriented, producing a number of films that addressed, directly or indirectly, issues of prejudice and bigotry. *Home of the Brave* was particularly hard-hitting in its flagrant use of the word "nigger" and its premise that racial prejudice is more deeply embedded in the collective subconscious of white America than many who feel they have overcome it could have imagined. Both the play and the film are set in the Pacific islands during World War II. Three men are selected for a special mission: to survey an island prior to an invasion. The likable and fair-minded Mingo (Frank Lovejoy) is the sergeant in charge, but as the recent recipient of a "Dear John" letter, he is initially sullen and withdrawn. T. J. (Steve Brodie), a confirmed bigot, attempts to hide his malice behind a hypocritical friendliness, but the bitterness of his deep-seated bigotry soon becomes clear. Finch (Lloyd Bridges) is innocent and likable, with an outgoing friendliness that offsets the limitations of the other two. A fourth man, Private Moss (James Edwards), is essential to the mission because he has the necessary mapmaking training; to the initial shock of the others, he is black. Finch is surprised for a different reason, since he and Moss were best friends in high school. On the island the group is surrounded by Japanese. In attempting to escape, Finch is killed, but not before he and Moss, caught up in fear and tension, have a vicious argument. At the height of their conflict, Finch nearly uses the "N" word epithet but gets no further than the first syllable before he checks himself, but too late: Moss knows what he was about to say. Finch profusely apologizes but is killed before Moss can adequately respond. Moss is injured but rescued from the island. After a period of hospitalization, Moss is pronounced healthy but suffers from a psychosomatic paralysis of his legs. He is subsequently cured by an army psychiatrist (Jeff Corey), who leads Moss to confront the mixed guilt and hatred he feels as a result of Finch's death, as well as the sense of separation and self-hatred he feels because of his race. The message, the need to accept our differences and to learn to live and work together, may seem simplistic and reductive today but was hard-hitting and dynamic in its time. *(R. C. K.)*

Resources: Thomas Cripps, *Making Movies Black* (New York: Oxford University Press, 1993); Edward Mapp, *Blacks in American Film: Today and Yesterday* (Metuchen, NJ: Scarecrow, 1972).

HOOK

See PETER PAN

HURLYBURLY (1984)
David Rabe

Hurlyburly (1998)

Directed by Anthony Drazan

Adapted by David Rabe

Cast: Sean Penn (Eddie), Kevin Spacey (Mickey), Chazz Palminteri (Phil), Gary Shandling (Artie), Meg Ryan (Bonnie), Robin Wright (Darlene)

Length: 123 minutes
Rated: R

David Rabe's dissection of the morally bankrupt world of Hollywood debuted in 1984 in New York City at the Promenade Theater. Directed by
Mike Nichols, it featured an all-star cast, including Harvey Keitel, Christopher Walken, Judith Ivey, William Hurt, and Sigourney Weaver. Restricted to the claustrophobic confines of a casting office and a Hollywood
Hills residence, the male rivalries and interior tensions among four friends
explode into scenes of violence, anguish, and self-loathing (the "hurly-
burly" of the title stems from one of the witches' speeches in the first scene
in *Macbeth*). Eddie and Mickey, a casting director and his associate, respectively, share a condo. Artie is a struggling screenwriter, and Phil is an
out-of-work actor. Two incidents trigger episodes of confrontation and violence among the four—Phil's physical abuse leading to a broken marriage
and his frustrations over his damaged career; and the rivalry between Eddie
and Mickey over Darlene's affections. After Eddie loses Darlene and attempts suicide, he consoles himself with Donna, a prostitute. Phil is killed
in an auto "accident" that may have been suicide; Artie is perpetually lost
in a cocaine haze. Only the cool, suave Mickey manages to remain above
the fray. Accused of having no emotions, Mickey sardonically remarks that
he does have enough feelings "to get by." In bringing his play to the screen,
Rabe relocates many of the monologues and conversations in locations like
Mulholland Drive and Beverly Hills. Eddie's climatic suicide attempt has
also been altered from a pill-popping episode to an elaborate sequence in
his swimming pool. As the self-flagellating Eddie, Sean Penn indulges himself in a succession of over-the-top harangues and self-recriminations. Gary
Shandling as Artie is muffled in a drug-induced haze. Chazz Palminteri is
a ticking bomb waiting to explode, a bristling collection of brutish tics and
quirks. Kevin Spacey is the most frightening as the unflappable Mickey, for
he has most successfully accommodated himself to the situational ethics of
his times. While Eddie still searches for answers to life's enigmas, Mickey
has long since given up the quest. While Eddie tortures himself with the
presumption that Phil's mysterious suicide note possesses an interior meaning, Mickey coolly dismisses it. Eddie is obviously Rabe's tool to question
the workings of a pernicious society, and Mickey, ultimately, becomes that
society's chief emblem—and victim. However, the abstract nature of the
characters' problems, which may have played well onstage, is at odds with
the specificity of the camera. Against this very real and concretized world
the fuzzy existentialism just hovers like a dirty cloud. On the plus side,
Rabe's screenplay has kept relatively intact the play's dazzling verbal vir-
tuosity and the characters' ongoing semantic gamesmanship. Each character has his own sound, his own mantra—from Eddie's whine to Mickey's
urbane verbal chic. *(J. C. T.)*

Resources: Marcelle Clements, "A Dispatch from the War against Women," *New York Times* (15 November 1998): II-A, 28; David Savran, *In Their Own Words* (New York: Theatre Communications Group, 1988).

I AM A CAMERA (1951)
John Van Druten

I Am a Camera (1955)

Directed by Henry Cornelius

Adapted by John Collier

Cast: Julie Harris (Sally Bowles), Laurence Harvey (Christopher Isherwood), Shelley Winters (Natalia Landauer), Ron Randall (Clive), Lea Seidl (Fraulein Schneider), Anton Diffring (Fritz)

Length: 93 minutes

John van Druten's *I Am a Camera,* based on *The Berlin Stories* of Christopher Isherwood, appeared in New York in 1951. The play concerns Sally Bowles, an amoral chanteuse, and Christopher Isherwood (Chris), an aspiring writer; the two live in rooms in Fraulein Schneider's Berlin boardinghouse in 1930, just as the Nazis are coming to power. Sally's boyfriend Klaus has abandoned her after impregnating her, and she has an abortion so that she can continue her current affair with Clive, a rich American who plans to take Chris and Sally on a world tour. After Clive leaves her, Sally is visited by her mother, who believes Sally and Chris are engaged. Eventually, Chris tells Sally's mother that Sally has broken the engagement, and Sally's mother returns to England. At the end of the film Sally is off with a new lover to perhaps appear in his film, and Chris is off to write stories about Berlin. The play also concerns the relationship between Fritz, a gigolo, and Natalia, an English pupil of Chris' and daughter of a wealthy Jewish department store owner. Fritz, who has denied his Jewish heritage, finally reveals his identity to Natalia, and the two are married. Through the anti-Semitic threats that Natalia's father receives, the blow Natalia gets at a Nazi street-corner rally, and Fraulein Schneider's anti-Semitic remarks, the Nazi threat is depicted. When Collier adapted the play to film, he altered it radically. The film begins and ends at a cocktail party for writer Sally Bowles; Christopher Isherwood attends the party and tells the Sally Bowles story to his fellow journalists. In this "flashback" Chris describes in voice-over narration what happened twenty-five years ago. The audience sees Sally performing at the Windemere Club, the Nazis roughing up Jews, the dancing at the Landauer home, Chris' meeting with an editor who hires him, and the manic partying at the hotel. This last scene, inspired by Chris' hypochondria in the play, consists of Chris' being treated for a hangover by a variety of German medical practices: hydrotherapy, electric shock treatments, and so on. In light of information about Nazi medical research, these scenes are both comic and ominous. In fact, by using outside scenes the film stresses Nazi brutality: Chris is shown fighting Nazi thugs in the street. The political message is also more pronounced than in the play. Chris comments that Berlin is a "town to get out of." On the other hand, the film makes concessions to the censors: Sally does not have an abortion in the film; she only thinks she is pregnant. In addition, at the end of the flashback Chris has an essay published and has been hired to write more. His success is demonstrated at the end of the film when, as a successful writer, he leaves the cocktail party with Sally in a replay of their first meeting. *(T. L. E.)*

Resources: Linda Mizejewski, *Divine Decadence: Fascism, Female Spectacle, and the Makings of Sally Bowles* (Princeton: Princeton University Press, 1992); Hal Prince, *Contradictions: Notes on Twenty-six Years in the Theatre* (New York: Dodd, Mead, 1974).

See also CABARET

I NEVER SANG FOR MY FATHER (1968)
Robert Anderson

I Never Sang for My Father (1970)

Directed by Gilbert Cates
Adapted by Robert Anderson

Cast: Melvyn Douglas (Tom Garrison), Gene Hackman (Gene Garrison), Dorothy Stickney (Margaret Garrison), Estelle Parsons (Alice)
Length: 92 minutes
Rated: PG

Robert Anderson first conceived this autobiographical story as an original screenplay. His film script, which had not been produced, later became the basis for his play, which opened in 1968. Although it was not considered a success, Columbia Pictures obtained screen rights, and Anderson adapted the play back to film. The protagonist in the film is Gene Garrison (Gene Hackman), a middle-aged widower torn between his guilt-ridden sense of obligation to his father and his desire for independence. The father, Tom Garrison (Melvyn Douglas), is a domineering, inflexible individual who was deserted by his own father, whom he therefore hates. This hatred surfaces periodically and clearly has affected his relationship with his own son. Gene's sister, Alice (Estelle Parsons), is absent for the first part of the film, having been banished by her father years earlier for marrying a Jew. The mother, Margaret Garrison (Dorothy Stickney), is the pivotal person in the family. She provides the emotional support for each individual and serves as the conduit for family interaction. Through the opening scenes, Anderson provides the audience with an understanding of these complex family dynamics. The family equilibrium becomes unbalanced when the mother suddenly dies. Alice, Gene's sister, returns home and with Gene contemplates what to do about their aging father. Gene is overwhelmed with his conflicting emotions. He desires to remarry and move to the coast, yet he still yearns for a loving relationship with his father. Alice begs Gene to think about his own happiness. Forcing the issue, Alice confronts their father about his plans. When the conversation becomes ugly, Gene relents and accepts responsibility for his father. Absolving herself, Alice leaves. Faced with making decisions about his father's care, Gene embarks on a depressing tour of alternative living arrangements for his father. Convinced that he cannot force his father into any of these situations, he asks his father to move with him to California. Rigid in his expectations, the father accuses his son of being ungrateful and selfish. At an impasse, Gene leaves. The film ends much as it started, with a narrative describing the last years of an unresolved father-son relationship. *(N. I.)*

Resources: Thomas P. Adler, *Robert Anderson* (Boston: Twayne, 1978); *Variety Film Reviews* 12 (October 1970).

I REMEMBER MAMA (1944)
John Van Druten

I Remember Mama (1948)

Directed by George Stevens

Adapted by George Stevens and Harriet Parsons

Cast: Irene Dunne (Mama), Barbara Bel Geddes (Katrin), Oscar Homulka (Uncle Chris), Philip Dorn (Papa), Cedric Hardwicke (Mr. Hyde), Edgar Bergen (Mr. Thorkelson), Barbara O'Neil (Jessie Brown), Peggy McIntyre (Christine), June Hedin (Dagmar), Steve Brown (Nels), Ellen Corby (Aunt Trina), Hope Landin (Aunt Jenny), Edith Evanson (Aunt Sigrid), Florence Bates (Florence Dana Moorhead)

Length: 134 minutes

Van Druten's *I Remember Mama*, adapted from Kathryn Forbes' novel *Mama's Bank Account*, premiered in New York in 1944 with Marlon Brando playing young Nels. While Mama is the focus, the play also describes the developing career of Katrin, who reads her story, which is the play itself, at the beginning and end of the play, thus providing a framing device. Katrin, the "dramatic one," listens intently to the stories read by Mr. Hyde (the deadbeat boarder who leaves his library to the family), gets the role of Portia in *The Merchant of Venice*, and writes stories that are rejected until she writes not about what she has read but what she knows. Fortunately, she remembers a great deal about her mother, who oversees the family finances, dupes hospital authorities so she can see her daughter Dagmar, helps sister Trina get her a husband, tends the gruff, but generous, Uncle Chris, swaps recipes for writing advice from Miss Moorhead, trades her brooch, a family heirloom, for the graduation present Katrin thinks she wants, and brings "Uncle" Elizabeth, the cat, back from death.

All this action occurs on three sets: Uncle Chris' ranch, Mama's kitchen, and the hospital, though the play alternates foreground and background sets, which allows for fluid motion. The film adaptation is quite faithful to its source, keeping more of the dialogue and adding only those exterior shots related to the action—the children hiding outside when Uncle Chris arrives in his car, the front porch of his ranch, and the children entering and leaving buildings. Very little dialogue is omitted (Mama's reference to her dead son's grave) or altered (Uncle Chris teaches his nephew to "swear" in Norwegian, rather than English), a bow to censorship. Despite its fidelity to its source, the film adds some effective touches not suited to drama.

Katrin's voice-over narration and her image superimposed on the action remind the audience that she is the writer, and the camera's close shots of Katrin's first cup of coffee, a symbol of her maturity, and Chris' ceremonial deathbed drink give those two scenes an intimacy and a ritualistic quality not easily rendered on the stage. Stevens' adaptation is faithful and yet takes full advantage of the film medium. *(T. L. E.)*

Resources: Donald Ritchie, *George Stevens: An American Romantic* (New York: Museum of Modern Art, 1970); John Van Druten, *Playwright at Work* (New York: Harper, 1953).

THE IMPORTANCE OF BEING EARNEST (1895)
Oscar Wilde

The Importance of Being Earnest (1952)

Directed and adapted by Anthony Asquith

Cast: Michael Redgrave (Jack Worthing), Michael Denison (Algernon Moncrieff), Edith Evans (Lady Bracknell), Joan Greenwood (Gwendolen Fairfax), Dorothy Tutin (Cecily Cardew), Margaret Rutherford (Miss Prism)

Length: 95 minutes

Oscar Wilde's witty comedy became an immediate hit when it was first performed in 1895, but under the shadow of Wilde's imprisonment it was not published until 1899. In spite of its popularity onstage throughout the twentieth century, no one attempted to capture this effervescent play on film until 1952. Just as Wilde had, at the request of the producer, shortened the play from four acts to three for its original run, British director Anthony Asquith further streamlined the play in his film adaptation. Much repetition is eliminated; conversations with servants are shortened or omitted; and allusions to literary criticism and various contemporary issues are dropped. What remains are the frothy plot—which works through a series of mistaken identities to unite two young couples—and Wilde's incomparable epigrams. Those epigrams are delivered most memorably by Edith Evans, who reprised her renowned stage role as Lady Bracknell. Michael Redgrave turns in a solid performance as Jack Worthing, an orphan found in the cloakroom of Victoria Station, whose desire to marry Lady Bracknell's daughter Gwendolen is temporarily thwarted by the young woman's insistence that she will marry only a man named Earnest and by her mother's refusal to allow her to "form an alliance with a parcel." The film relies heavily on the actors' delivery of Wilde's smart dialogue, since Asquith believed that the "purely verbal" humor of this particular play could not be "translated into an image" (*Theatre Arts*). Asquith's intent to "allow Oscar Wilde to speak with his own voice" (*Theatre Arts*) led him to make a film that was in many ways a recorded stage play. Indeed, the film begins and ends with a red stage curtain, the first glimpse of Jack Worthing is through the opera glasses of a woman in a theatre box, and the credits take the form of a theatre program. With such framing, the film's few cinematic gestures seem misguided. Asquith's halfhearted attempts to open up the play result, for instance, in a scene in which Lady Bracknell is glimpsed on her journey to Hertfordshire cooped up in a train car—an image that spoils her surprise entrance without producing any real sense of an exterior world. Likewise, the visual pleasure promised by Technicolor and elaborate costumes is undercut by the film's camera work, primarily two shots, that serve to focus attention on the characters' talk. Asquith's film can be relished for its performances and for Wilde's wit, but it remains more a record of the play than a cinematic work. *(C. M. D.)*

Resources: Anthony Asquith, "The Importance of Being Faithful," *Theatre Arts* 37 (April 1953): 72–74; "The Importance of Being Earnest," *The Motion Picture Guide*, vol. 4, ed. Jay Robert Nash and Stanley Ralph Ross (Chicago: Cinebooks, 1986).

INDIANS (1969)
Arthur Kopit

Buffalo Bill and the Indians, or, Sitting Bull's History Lesson (1976)

Directed by Robert Altman

Adapted by Alan Rudolph and Robert Altman

Cast: Paul Newman (William F. Cody, a.k.a. Buffalo Bill), Joel Grey (Nate Salsbury), Kevin McCarthy (Major Arizona John Burke), Harvey Keitel (Ed Goodman), Geraldine Chaplin (Annie Oakley), Burt Lancaster (Ned Buntline), Frank Kaquitts (Sitting Bull), Will Sampson (William Halsey)

Length: 123 minutes

Rated: PG

Released during the year of the bicentennial, Robert Altman's adaptation of Arthur Kopit's 1969 play *Indians* continues the director's long-established proclivity for skewering national stereotypes and ingrained beliefs. In this case, the targets are the culture's obsession with celebrity and the horrific extermination of Native Americans. Altman uses Kopit's play as a template for the film; the credits assert that the film is merely "suggested by" the play. The 1960s counterculture production focused on the figures identified with its title, not the "heroic" William F. Cody. Like much theatrical work of its day drawn to the primitive and the natural, Kopit's play elevated the Native American characters above their Western antagonists in a schematic fashion that dramatized the conflict of cultures through ritual and evocative tableaux. Altman focuses instead on the figure of Cody (Paul Newman) and his collaborators in the "authentic business," as his producer Nate Salsbury (Joel Grey) refers to the Wild West show. In typical Altman fashion, a large cast of characters interplay within an elaborately drawn environment—in this case, the winter quarters of the company—that surpasses depth of character or, to the narrative's detriment, an assertive dramatic story line. *Buffalo Bill and the Indians* opposes the Native Americans' assumptions about the past with Cody's "better sense of history," as he calls it, articulated through spectacle and popular mythology. Sitting Bull (Frank Kaquitts), an unassuming and diminutive figure, has joined the stage show for the sole purpose of meeting the president, Grover Cleveland, and arguing the case of his people. In the meantime, he refuses, through his interpreter, William Halsey (Will Sampson), to acquiesce to Cody's plans for his participation, slyly demanding that his perception of the past override the egotistical Cody's fabrications. When the warrior dies off-camera, Cody remains haunted by him and all he and his people represent. In a climactic confrontation, Cody argues to the silent wraith, "Truth is whatever gets the loudest applause." Altman ends his film with a performance of Cody's triumphing over Sitting Bull, now enacted by Halsey. Although *Buffalo Bill and the Indians* is never dull, Altman's obeisance to the critique of genocide and to the subjugation of history to the demands of ideology override much that the audience can identify with. History may, in the end, be little more than, as Halsey argues, "disrespect for the dead," yet the film concerns the living. Critiquing the racism and self-aggrandizement of the characters makes for an effective argument but a stunted film. *(D. S.)*

Resource: Patrick McGilligan, *Robert Altman: Jumping Off the Cliff* (New York: St. Martin's Press, 1989).

INHERIT THE WIND (1955)
Jerome Lawrence and Robert E. Lee

Inherit the Wind (1960)

Directed by Stanley Kramer
Adapted by Nathan E. Douglas and Harold Jacob Smith

Cast: Spencer Tracy (Henry Drummond), Fredric March (Matthew Harrison Brady), Gene Kelly (E. K. Hornbeck), Dick York (Bertram Cates), Claude Akins (Reverend Brown), Donna Anderson (Rachel)

Length: 127 minutes

Based on the notorious "Scopes Monkey Trial" in 1925, Lawrence and Lee's 1955 play recasts defense attorney Clarence Darrow as "Henry Drummond," prosecutor William Jennings Bryan as "Matthew Harrison Brady," the defendant Henry Scopes as "Bertram Cates," and journalist H. L. Mencken as "E. K. Hornbeck." The action is transferred from Dayton, Tennessee, to the midwestern town of Hillsboro, where Cates is being tried for breaking a state criminal statute barring the teaching of evolution in public schools. In the climactic scene between the two attorneys, the wily Brady forces Drummond to admit that the Bible could be interpreted in a nonliteral fashion, thus making it possible to argue that evolution could be consistent with the biblical account of creation. Although Cates is found guilty, the judge imposes only a token fine. The humiliated Brady dies on the spot of a heart attack. Independent producer/director Stanley Kramer considered his film version the last of a trilogy of pictures, beginning with *The Defiant Ones* (1958) and *On the Beach* (1959), intended to deal with controversial racial and religious issues: "Enjoy them or not—agree with them or not—these are motion pictures that hit people hard, force people to see them, to think and to take a stand" (Spoto 223). In order to ensure commercial appeal, however, Kramer replaced the original Broadway stage actors with established movie stars—Ed Begley's Brady with Fredric March, Paul Muni's Drummond with Spencer Tracy, and Tony Randall's Hornbeck with Gene Kelly. Like the play, the film did not mention certain real-life facts, that is, that the American Civil Liberties Union (ACLU) participated in stage-managing the trial; that the accused teacher was really a sports coach and had never formally taught evolutionary theory; and that although the trial's outcome loosened restrictive teaching practices in some states, the Tennessee statute in question remained in effect for many years. Many scenes are added to open out the courtroom-bound drama: the arrivals in town of Drummond and Brady are separately depicted in a clever manner, establishing their respective characters, as Drummond arrives anonymously on a community bus, while Brady arrives in an entourage amid the hoopla of the cheering crowd. Other additions include a full-scale revival meeting, incidents among the demonstrators picketing in the town square outside the courtroom, a romance between Cates and his fiancée, Rachel (Donna Anderson), and several episodes in the boardinghouse where Drummond and Brady are staying. As if to counteract negative criticisms by fundamentalists that the film was "anti-Christ," Kramer persistently layers the soundtrack with hymns and folk songs, including "Gimme

That Old-Time Religion" and, at the very end, a full-scale choral rendition of "The Battle Hymn of the Republic" (with soloist Leslie Uggams). *(J. C. T.)*

Resources: Paul Bergman and Michael Asimow, *Reel Justice: The Courtroom Goes to the Movies* (Kansas City, MO: Andrews and McMeel, 1996); Thomas J. Harris, *Courtroom's Finest Hour in American Cinema* (Metuchen, NJ: Scarecrow Press, 1987); Donald Spoto, *Stanley Kramer: Film Maker* (New York: G. P. Putnam's Sons, 1978).

THE INSPECTOR GENERAL (1836)
Nikolai Gogol

The Inspector General (1949)

Directed by Henry Koster

Adapted by Philip Rapp and Harry Kurnitz

Cast: Danny Kaye (Khlestakov/Georgie, a.k.a. Farfel Knabe), Walter Slezak (Yakov), Alan Hale (Kovatch), Elsa Lanchester (Maria), Gene Lockhart (Mayor), Barbara Bates (Leza), Rhys Williams (Inspector General)

Length: 101 minutes

Nikolai Gogol's only full-length play premiered in the Aleksandrinsky Theater in St. Petersburg in April 1836 and in Moscow in May of the same year with the celebrated Shchepkin playing the mayor. The play was generally badly received. It was revised in 1841, and more was added and changed by Gogol in 1846 and in 1851. The screenplay for the Warner Brothers production, written by Philip Rapp and Harry Kurnitz, is credited as "suggested by the play by Nikolai Gogol." The film is a musical adaptation featuring very long, tongue-twisting musical numbers, slapstick, and Danny Kaye shenanigans. The foolish idler of the play, Khlestakov, is changed to Georgie, alias Farfel Knabe, an illiterate, itinerant assistant elixir salesman played by Danny Kaye. The servant character, Osip, becomes Yakov, the charlatan elixir salesman. The mayor and his council, remarkably similar in play and film, include boorish officials and bumpkin twin businessmen. The mayor receives word that the Inspector General probably has arrived incognito in their village of Brodny. There is a rush to clean up the town and erase traces of fraud. The fool, taken for the Inspector General, is invited on a tour of Brodny's facilities and brought to the mayor's house for dinner, where the wife (Elsa Lanchester) has an eye for him. In the stage version there's a daughter, and in the film, a maid is the

love interest. Yakov, posing as a servant, seizes on the economic possibilities of duping the crooked officials, who on his advice make large payments to his master, the fake Inspector General. In the play Khlestakov
takes the bribes and skips town just before the real Inspector General arrives. The screenplay, however, deviates substantially from the original
source, adding, among other things, a murder plot, a rescue of the church
organ by Danny Kaye, and a near execution. The film ends when the real
Inspector General makes Danny Kaye the new mayor. The film is enjoyable,
if silly, but it could take a word of advice from Chekhov, who wrote, "You
must not lower Gogol to the people, but raise the people to the level of
Gogol." David Thompson judged the film awful—"all Danny Kaye and no
Gogol." *(K. O.)*

Resources: Eric Bentley, *The Playwright as Thinker* (New York: Harcourt, Brace,
and World, 1946); Martin Gottfried, *Nobody's Fool: The Lives of Danny Kaye*
(New York: Simon and Schuster, 1994); David Thompson, *A Biographical
Dictionary of Film* (New York: William Morrow, 1976): 251.

IRMA LA DOUCE (1960)
Alexandre Breffort

Irma La Douce (1963)

Directed by Billy Wilder

Adapted by I. A. L. Diamond and Billy Wilder

Cast: Jack Lemmon (Nestor), Shirley MacLaine (Irma la Douce), Lou Jacobi
(Moustache), Bruce Yarnell (Hippolyte), Hope Holiday (Lolita), Joan Shawlee
(Amazon Annie)

Length: 147 minutes

Although based on a play by Alexandre Breffort, the musical version by
Marguerite Monnot, which ran several years in Paris, London, and Broadway, attracted Billy Wilder's attention. Attracted by the idea of a pimp
who became the patron of his hooker "only to become jealous of himself,"
Wilder threw out the original musical's sixteen numbers to concentrate on
a daring screen comedy. The original play involved the love of former policeman Nestor for prostitute Irma, who does not want him to work but
to follow in the footsteps of her former pimps. Nestor wishes to rescue
Irma from her chosen path and decides to masquerade as a wealthy client
(Lord X) who will provide enough money for her exclusive services. Irma
falls in love with the client, provoking Nestor's jealousy, "murder" of the

client, and his conviction. He escapes from prison, masquerades as the client for the last time, and marries Irma before she delivers their child, giving her a new occupation as wife and mother. Wilder moved the setting from Montmartre to Les Halles, evoking images of Emile Zola's *Le Ventre du Paris*, as well as the author's pleasure in scandalizing conventional morality, also shared by Europeans Wilder and coscenarist I. A. L. Diamond. The Halles "meat market" also applies to the prostitutes on display as well as Hollywood female commodification! Wilder intended to challenge contemporary Hollywood beliefs that screen comedy should be merely sweetness and light seeking to "strike a happy medium between Tennessee Williams and Walt Disney." Alexandre Trauner's sets soon became known as a "Disneyland for Adults" tourist attraction. Although *Irma la Douce* fails to match the qualities of Lemmon and MacLaine's teaming in *The Apartment*, this attempt at a sophisticated morality play message (ironically earning it a production seal of approval) also contains several key Wilder digs at American conformity. He subverts the Hays Code by making a comedy out of an otherwise taboo subject. Bistro-owner Moustache often counsels Nestor by using Marxist terminology in a Hollywood movie made during the Cold War! The Halles pimps form themselves into a union named MPPA, a play on the Motion Picture Producers Association. Slyly subverting censorship codes, Wilder and Diamond also undermine Hollywood narrative conventions. While the original play and musical ended with the birth of Irma's child, the film brings Lord X back to life at the same time as Nestor is with Irma. Seeing this impossible resurrection, Moustache can only finally exclaim to the audience, "[B]ut that's another story." *(T. W.)*

Resources: Bernard Dick, *Billy Wilder*. Rev. Ed. (New York: Da Capo Press, 1996); Tom Wood, *The Bright Side of Billy Wilder, Primarily* (New York: Doubleday, 1970).

THE JAZZ SINGER (1925)
Samson Raphaelson

The Jazz Singer (1927)

Directed by Alan Crosland

Adapted by Alfred A. Cohn

Cast: Al Jolson (Jakie Rabinowitz), Warner Oland (Cantor Rabinowitz), Eugenie Besserer (Sara Rabinowitz)

Length: 89 minutes

Samson Raphaelson's 1925 play (based on his short story "Day of Atonement") told the story of Jakie Rabinowitz, whose obsession with jazz music runs him afoul of his traditionalist cantor father. Taking the stage name of "Jack Robin," he runs away from home and becomes a popular singer. On the eve of his big break headlining a major Broadway revue, he learns his father is dying. Rushing to his father's bedside, Jakie is persuaded to return to the synagogue and follow in his father's footsteps. Although George Jessel starred in the play, there was no question that the real model for Jakie was Al Jolson, who also came from generations of cantors and established himself as a popular entertainer, contrary to their expectations. Warner Brothers studio bought the screen rights and rushed it into production in the summer of 1927 as a Vitaphone, synchronized-sound feature to be shot on the new Warners lot on Sunset Boulevard. Jessel, who had no experience with talkies, was replaced by superstar Jolson, who desperately wanted the part and had already appeared in several Vitaphone short films. Alan Crosland, who had directed Warners' first Vitaphone release, *Don Juan*, the year before, was assigned to direct. Raphaelson's play was a sincere portrait of a time of crisis in a Jewish family and contained melodramatic elements—the jazz singing, the old cantor's death, the religious pageantry—that occurred offstage, but the Warners' film dragged them center stage and bathed them in flagrant, sentimental eyewash, with mother love the dominating emotion. Eugenie Besserer's performance as Jakie's mother is nearly unwatchable, and Raphaelson described Jolson's acting as "lousy" (Jolson's vaunted "improvised dialogue" was probably planned in advance; and his line "You ain't heard nothin' yet" had already become his signature tag years before). In true Hollywood fashion, Jakie has it both ways in the end, leaving opening night to sing the "Kol Nidre" for his father but returning to the Winter Garden stage to resume his hit career. Raphaelson acknowledged that the film had some attractive location shots of New York's East Side but bitterly attacked everything else: "The whole damned thing—the dialogue, whatever they had taken from my innocent play was either distorted or broken up. I had a simple, corny, well-felt little melodrama, and they made an ill-felt, silly, maudlin, badly timed thing of it" (Carringer 20). In sum, Warners cashed in on the play not for its serious theme of adjustment (how the new generation finds its place in an established cultural tradition) but as a basis for integrating singing and talking sequences. Moreover, as Robert Carringer has observed, it was transformed into a typically American fable of success—"open revolt against tradition, westward movement, the expenditure of energy, triumph, and the replacement of the values of the old by the values of the new" (27). *The Jazz Singer* has been remade and updated twice, by Michael Curtiz in 1952, starring Danny Thomas in the Jolson role; and by Richard Fleischer in 1980, starring Neil Diamond. *(J. C. T.)*

Resources: Robert L. Carringer, ed., *The Jazz Singer* (Madison: University of Wisconsin Press, 1979); Charles Higham, *Warner Brothers* (New York: Charles Scribner's Sons, 1975).

JEFFREY (1993)
Paul Rudnick

Jeffrey (1995)

Directed by Christopher Ashley
Adapted by Paul Rudnick

Cast: Steven Weber (Jeffrey), Michael T. Weiss (Steve), Irma St. Paule (Mother Theresa), Patrick Stewart (Sterling), Bryan Batt (Darius), Sigourney Weaver (Debra Moorhouse), Robert Klein (Skip Winkley)

Length: 92 minutes

Rated: R

Paul Rudnick's *Jeffrey*, which appeared in New York City in 1993, is a blend of farce and tragedy involving gays and AIDS. The play opens with two men in bed. After Jeffrey discovers that his condom is broken, his partner is concerned, as are the rest of the cast, who all emerge from the bed, suggesting that lovers "sleep" with all their previous partners. Because sex has become potentially deadly (it's not "fun" anymore), Jeffrey decides "no more sex" for him. Unfortunately, after his vow, he meets Steve, an attractive bartender, who is HIV positive, and the play becomes a series of amusing skits all designed to bring Steve and Jeffrey together. The skits include *It's Just Sex*, a television game show with Steve and two other gay contestants; Hoedown for AIDS; a postmodern evangelist who solves the sexual problems of her audience; a meeting of Sexual Compulsives Anonymous, where Jeffrey "testifies" about his first gay sexual partner; a visit to St. Patrick's, where a priest makes sexual advances to Jeffrey; a gay and lesbian parade; and Steve's beating by "straights," who leave him to be consoled by Mother Theresa! The play also has its more somber moments: Sterling loses his lover, Darius, to AIDS and resents Jeffrey's attempts to console him because Jeffrey is fleeing to Wisconsin (a presumably safe place?) and avoiding the AIDS threat. When Darius reappears as an angel, he tells Jeffrey to "hate AIDS, not life." Armed with this message, Jeffrey leaves Steve a phone message to meet him at the Empire State Building, the clichéd romantic site of *An Affair to Remember* and *Sleepless in Seattle*. The play ends with the two batting a balloon around, keeping it from hitting the ground, a metaphor for life and love Jeffrey got from the priest. When Rudnick adapted his play to film, he made a few changes but stayed close to the original. Mother Theresa's role (Irma St. Paule) is expanded; she twice comforts Jeffrey (Steven Weber) and plays the piano during Jeffrey's reconciliation with Steve (Michael T. Weiss). Director Ashley uses the film's overhead shots in the hoedown scene, when the gay dancers are photographed from above in the manner of Busby Berkeley. Jeffrey's casting skit is enriched by showing not only Jeffrey's many takes but also a clip of his role as the gay neighbor in a detective series. On the other hand, there are some important omissions, such as the crowded bed in the play's opening scene and the Empire State Building conclusion, with all its romantic reverberations. *Jeffrey* is too faithful an adaptation, retaining even the intertitles for the skits, to be a good film. *(T. L. E.)*

Resources: Kenneth L. Geist, *"Jeffrey," Films in Review* (September–October 1995): 57; Peter Matthews, *"Jeffrey," Sight and Sound* (April 1996): 47.

JEZEBEL (1931)
Owen Davis, Sr.

Jezebel (1938)

Directed by William Wyler

Adapted by Clement Ripley, Abem Finkel, and John Huston

Cast: Bette Davis (Julie Morrison), Henry Fonda (Preston Dillard), Fay Bainter (Aunt Belle Massey), George Brent (Buck Cantrell), Henry O'Neill (General Bogardus), Margaret Lindsay (Amy Dillard)

Length: 103 minutes

Owen Davis' melodrama *Jezebel* played on Broadway with moderate success. The New York production starred Miriam Hopkins as the willful southern belle; however, when it came time for Warner Brothers to cast the film, they passed over Hopkins (despite her favorable reviews) in favor of Bette Davis, who had recently been passed over by David O. Selznick for the role of Scarlet O'Hara. Warner Brothers was determined to have *Jezebel* released prior to *Gone with the Wind*. They succeeded. Produced at the considerable cost of $1 million, the film was a financial and critical success. Davis won her second Oscar for Best Actress, and Fay Bainter won for Best Supporting Actress. Set in pre–Civil War New Orleans, the story centers on the youthfully headstrong, unmarried Julie Morrison (Davis), who, in a brazen act of social insolence, wears a red gown to the Olympus Ball instead of the customary, demure, white gown. In consequence, her fiancé (Fonda) breaks their engagement and leaves for Philadelphia. Three years pass, wherein Julie waits, in relative seclusion, for Preston's return. Pres reappears, and Julie, dressed all in white, delivers her tender, supplicating apology to him. It is too late. Pres has married a well-heeled, mannerly northerner. Shortly afterward, a yellow jack epidemic ensues. Pres contracts the deadly fever, and Julie, at her own considerable peril, accompanies him to a quarantine island, where she admirably aims to nurse him back to health and return Pres to his wife. Breaking mildly with the conventions of melodrama, *Jezebel*'s ending lacks closure, as it is uncertain whether Pres or Julie ever survives the epidemic. *Jezebel* is an elegant movie, a William Wyler paradigm of classical Hollywood cinema. The frames are beautifully balanced. The cinematic techniques (sound, lighting, shot composition, and continuity editing) all work, in lovely subtlety, as indiscernible threads that build, bind, and blend the constituent parts into a harmonious whole. Even Max Steiner's typically tonally inflated score somehow works. *(L. C. C.)*

Resources: Jan Herman, *A Talent for Trouble: The Life of Hollywood's Most Acclaimed Director, William Wyler* (New York: Putnam, 1996); Gene Ringgold, *The Complete Films of Bette Davis* (New York: Citadel Press, 1990).

JOHNNY BELINDA (1940)
Elmer Harris

Johnny Belinda (1948)

Directed by Jean Negulesco

Adapted by Irmgard von Cube and Allen Vincent

Cast: Jane Wyman (Belinda McDonald), Lew Ayres (Dr. Robert Richardson), Charles Bickford (Black McDonald), Agnes Moorhead (Aggie McDonald), Stephen McNally (Locky McCormick), Jan Sterling (Stella McGuire), Dan Seymour (Pacquet)

Length: 102 minutes

Despite controversy over its content (rape and an illegitimate child), Harris' play, first staged in New York City in 1940, became a Broadway hit; and when it was translated to film, it was also popular, providing Jane Wyman with an Academy Award–winning performance as Belinda. The play, set in 1900 on an island off Canada's maritime provinces, concerns Belinda, a deaf-mute who is brutally raped by Locky, a drunken bully who marries Stella to get the money to save his farm from foreclosure by Pacquet, the village storekeeper and usurer. Because he has kindly taught Belinda sign language, Dr. Richardson is suspected of being the father of Belinda's child and, through rumors spread by Pacquet and Mrs. McKee, the town gossip, loses his patients and is forced to find a position elsewhere. After Black McDonald, her father, is killed by lightning, Belinda and her aunt Aggie are destitute; and Locky, with the assistance of Pacquet and Mrs. McKee, uses their poverty and the child's illegitimacy as excuses to adopt Johnny. Despite Stella's objections, Locky goes to the McDonald place, knocks Belinda to the floor, and attempts to get his son. Belinda shoots him and is charged with murder. At the trial Dr. Richardson interprets Belinda's signing, but Belinda is acquitted only by Stella's testimony that Locky was the rapist/father. At the end of the play Belinda speaks Johnny's name, and she is reunited with her son and Dr. Richardson, who loves her. Much of Harris' dialogue is retained in the film adaptation, but the film adds several outside scenes to the three interior sets in the play. One added scene demonstrates Dr. Richardson's love and commitment to Belinda (he takes her to a doctor in a larger city); and another deepens Locky's villainy (he fights Black McDonald and lets him fall off the cliff to the rocks below). The film decreases the complicity of the town in allowing Locky to adopt Johnny and adds several scenes that demonstrate the doctor's increasing devotion to Belinda. At the end of the film Stella does not readily admit Locky's crime in the substantially extended, suspenseful trial; Stella's guilt and compassion, captured in several close-ups, finally convince her to tell the truth, winning acquittal for Belinda, who rides off into the sunset with her baby and Dr. Richardson. *(T. L. E.)*

Resources: Jean Negulesco, *Things I Did and Things I Think I Did* (New York: Simon and Schuster, 1984); Lawrence J. Quirk, *Jane Wyman: The Actress and the Woman* (New York: Dembner Books, 1986).

JULIUS CAESAR (1599)
William Shakespeare

Julius Caesar (1953)

Directed and adapted by Joseph L. Mankiewicz

Cast: Louis Calhern (Julius Caesar), Marlon Brando (Antony), Alan Napier (Cicero), James Mason (Brutus), John Gielgud (Cassius), Edmond O'Brien (Casca), Michael Pate (Flavius), Douglas Dumbrille (Lepidus), Greer Garson (Calpurnia), Deborah Kerr (Portia), Ian Wolfe (Ligarius)

Length: 120 minutes

In this century the most notable stage production to date has been the Orson Welles 1937, modern-dress, antifascist version, in which Welles played Brutus. In the Mankiewicz film (as in the play) Brutus (James Mason) and Cassius (John Gielgud) are leaders of a conspiracy to assassinate Julius Caesar (Louis Calhern), fearing that his growing power will lead to his dissolving the Republic and accepting the crown of Rome. Caesar, failing to heed the advice of the soothsayer who warns him of his peril on "the ides of March," is murdered in the Forum. Against the advice of Cassius, Brutus permits Antony to speak to the Roman populace, confident that by speaking first, he, Brutus, can convince the citizenry of the rightness and necessity of Caesar's death. Antony, however, turns the crowd against the conspirators, and they must flee for their lives. Brutus and Cassius commit suicide after their forces are defeated at Philippi by Antony, Octavian, and Lepidus, Roman leaders forming the second triumvirate.

Critics generally agree that the 1953 version is the best of the eight film productions, which include two silent versions in 1908. Marlon Brando (as Marc Antony) was approaching the zenith of his career, having drawn both critical and popular notice the year before in *A Streetcar Named Desire* and *Viva Zapata*. The intensity of his brooding style proved well suited to Shakespeare, and he more than held his own with such seasoned British actors as James Mason and John Gielgud. Antony's oration to the populace on the death of Caesar is an effective combination of sorrow, repressed anger, and Machiavellian pragmatism. It is effectively balanced by Brutus' quietly introspective soliloquies reflecting on the horror of the assassination and the altruistic conviction that made it necessary. Brutus' tragic flaw is that he listens to no one, relying on his own conscience and convictions. In particular, he fails to respond to the repeated advice of Cassius, his fellow conspirator, whose advice is always correct but always unheeded. Although it was photographed in black and white, Mankiewicz's film follows the continuity of the play and has lost none of its power and dramatic quality, even though the text may have been shortened; it forgoes the lavish spectacle characteristic of Hollywood's general treatment of such period pieces but did win an Academy Award for art direction and set decoration. (*R. C. K.*)

Resources: Oscar J. Campbell and Edward Quinn, eds., *The Reader's Encyclopedia of Shakespeare* (New York: Crowell, 1966); Jack J. Jorgens, *Shakespeare on Film* (Bloomington: Indiana University Press, 1977); Roger Manvell, *Shakespeare and the Film* (New York: Praeger, 1971).

Julius Caesar (1969)

Directed by Stuart Burge

Adapted by Robert Furnival

Cast: Charlton Heston (Antony), Jason Robards (Brutus), John Gielgud (Caesar), Richard Johnson (Cassius), Robert Vaughn (Casca), Richard Chamberlain (Octavius Caesar), Diana Rigg (Portia), Jill Bennett (Calpurnia), Christopher Lee (Artemidorus), Alan Browning (Marullus), Andrew Crawford (Volumnius), David Dodimead (Lepidus)

Length: 117 minutes

Director Stuart Burge had already directed an earlier BBC television production in 1959 and was certainly familiar with the play. Nonetheless, this film was made in the shadow of the earlier, superior Mankiewicz adaptation and, unfortunately, suffers by comparison. Some liberties were taken with the text, especially Calpurnia's dream, extended to incorporate the warnings of the poet Artemidorus, but in general Shakespeare's plot is followed well enough. The Forum scene takes place within minutes of Caesar's killing, with Caesar's blood still on the conspirators' hands, "exactly as Shakespeare's text has it," according to Roger Manvell. John Gielgud's Caesar is witty and urbane and one of the strengths of the production, but Gielgud objected to the way the film truncated "the natural cadences of Shakespeare." Charlton Heston chose to play Antony as a power-hungry opportunist, in contrast to the more thuggish earlier Brando treatment. Jason Robards played Brutus as though the character were deeply troubled by his involvement in the assassination. Where strength was needed, Robards brought instead a "worried intensity" to the role, in the words of one critic. Jason Robards was not the producer Peter Snell's first choice for the role and had never seen the play performed. His interpretation of the role was considered too "showy," if not downright eccentric. On the other hand, the performances by Charlton Heston, John Gielgud, and Diana Rigg were consistently praised. Overall, this film production has been judged adequate, but rather flat. (*J. M. W.*)

Resources: Roger Manvell, *Shakespeare and the Film* (New York: Praeger, 1971); Kenneth S. Rothwell and Annabelle Henkin Melzer, *Shakespeare on Screen* (New York: Neil-Schuman, 1990).

KEY LARGO (1939)
Maxwell Anderson

Key Largo (1948)

Directed by John Huston

Adapted by John Huston and Richard Brooks

Cast: Humphrey Bogart (Frank McCloud), Edward G. Robinson (Rocco), Lauren Bacall (Nora Temple), Lionel Barrymore (James Temple), Claire Trevor (Gaye Dawn)

Length: 101 minutes

When Huston adapted Anderson's pre–World War II verse play *Key Largo* (1939) to film, he changed characters, plot, and themes. Anderson's play concerned Frank McCloud, an American fighting fascists in the Spanish civil war. When McCloud sees that the war is futile, he decides to flee the battle. His companions stay and die, while he escapes and even helps the fascists in order to return to the States. Conscience-stricken, he seeks the forgiveness of his companions' families, one of whom (George Temple) lives in the Florida Keys. Eventually, he stands up to some crooked gamblers and a corrupt sheriff but dies in his effort to save two fugitive Indians. Except for a few outside scenes, notably, the climatic showdown at sea between McCloud and Rocco, Huston retains the closed setting of a resort hotel run by James Temple and his daughter-in-law Nora, wife to George Temple. Rather than seeking atonement, Frank seeks only to tell the Temples how George died. Rocco and his hoodlums, who are selling counterfeit money, have taken over the hotel. Frank, who seems disheartened by what he sees in postwar America, does not want to become involved, even after a deputy is killed; but he does display courage when he defies Rocco and gives Gaye a drink and when he dispatches Rocco and his minions on the boat trip to Cuba. The conflict between Frank and Rocco is a replay of the war: Frank and the democratic allies; Rocco and fascism. What Frank fought abroad he must fight at home, and fight he does. While he earlier said Rocco wasn't worth his trouble, Frank eventually learns that his history of engagement overrules his head, his ideas of appeasement. Since his transformation is partly effected by Nora, Bogart's role as cynic changed by love is similar to his role in *Casablanca* (1942). (*T. L. E.*)

Resources: Scott Hammen, *John Huston* (Boston: Twayne, 1985); John McCarty, *The Films of John Huston* (Secaucus, NJ: Citadel Publishing Group, 1987).

THE KILLING OF SISTER GEORGE (1965)
Frank Marcus

The Killing of Sister George (1968)

Directed by Robert Aldrich

Adapted by Lukas Heller

Cast: Beryl Reid (June Buckridge a.k.a. Sister George), Susannah York (Alice "Childie" NcNaught), Coral Browne (Mercy Croft)

Length: 135 minutes

Rated: X

While Robert Aldrich, director of *Kiss Me Deadly* (1955) and *The Dirty Dozen* (1966), is customarily thought of as a "man's man" director, his films have also centered on women characters, as in his 1968 adaptation of the English play *The Killing of Sister George* by Frank Marcus. Aldrich had used his considerable profits from *The Dirty Dozen* to open a movie studio in 1967; *Sister George* was that organization's initial release. The director perhaps considered the play's narrative of a lesbian couple and the tensions that fragment their relationship a commercial hook. June Buckridge (Beryl Reid) has played the role of district nurse Sister George on a popular television serial for some time. However, her popularity has waned because of the aging of her audience and the repercussions of her alcohol-driven tantrums; she has been in a long-term relationship with Alice "Childie" NcNaught (Susannah York), a wistful, childlike woman whom she dominates and whose affections for her now appear tenuous at best. The relationship fragments after Buckridge loses her job as Sister George and Alice's affections are stolen by the sexually predatory agent Mercy Croft (Coral Browne). The final shot of the film finds Buckridge alone and tormented, without either employment or affection. Aldrich opened up the play by adding the sequence in which Mercy Croft seduces Alice. This episode was unusual for its day, not only in its overt, if stereotyped, depiction of lesbianism but also for the brutal manner in which the seduction is portrayed. The MPAA gave the film an X rating, mainly because of this sequence. Aldrich attempted unsuccessfully and at great expense to have the decision overturned; the X rating, however, no doubt turned away some potential viewers. Some criticized Aldrich as abrasive or unnecessarily crude, willing to sacrifice effects over balanced emotions. The near hysteria in *The Killing of Sister George* would seem to validate such criticism, were it not for the affectionate depiction of Sister George as one of Aldrich's sympathetic monsters, victims as much of their own unmanageable desires as they are of social repression beyond their control. *(D. S.)*

Resources: Edward T. Arnold and Eugene L. Miller, *The Films and Career of Robert Aldrich* (Knoxville: University of Tennessee Press, 1986); Andrew Sarris, "Robert Aldrich," in *Cinema: A Critical Dictionary*, ed. Richard Roud, Vol. 2 (Norwich: Fletcher and Son, 1980): 21–23.

KING AND COUNTRY

See HAMP

KING LEAR (1605)
William Shakespeare

King Lear (1970)

Directed and adapted by Grigori Kozintsev

Cast: Yuri Jarvet (Lear), Valentina Shendrikova (Cordelia), Elza Radzins (Goneril), Galina Volchek (Regan), Oleg Dal (Fool), K. Sebris (Gloucester), I. Merzen (Edgar), R. Adomaitis (Edmund), V. Emelyanov (Kent), A. Vokach

(Cornwall), D. Banionis (Albany), A. Petrenko (Oswald), I. Budraitis (France)

Length: 140 minutes

The play begins in a fairy-tale setting in which an old King Lear has un-realistically decided to divide his kingdom among his three daughters, Go-neril, Regan, and Cordelia, his favorite, all of whom are asked to express in public their love for their father. The two older sisters are extravagant in expressing their affection, but Cordelia refuses to flatter her father, who disinherits her in a fit of rage and splits his kingdom between the other two sisters, with the provision that they will care for him in his old age. Cor-delia, meanwhile, is married to the King of France. Goneril and Regan soon decide that their father makes unreasonable demands and threaten to strip him of his retinue of riotous knights. Confronted about this, Lear's rage gets the better of him, and he finds himself disinherited and abandoned to the wilderness, save for the company of his loyal Fool and his faithful retainer Kent, who has angered the King but returns to serve him in dis-guise. In a parallel plot the Duke of Gloucester is disinherited by his bastard son Edmond, who turns him against his brother Edgar, who disguises him-self as a mad beggar. Gloucester is accused of treason, blinded, and cast into the wilderness, to be cared for by Edgar in disguise. After all this misery, Cordelia comes with the army of France to rescue her father, who has gone quite mad. Edmund, meanwhile, has seduced both Goneril and Regan but is challenged and killed by his brother, but not before he has given orders to have Cordelia killed. Lear dies at the end of a broken heart. Arguably and ironically, the best film version of *King Lear* was made in the Soviet Union, with director Grigori Kozintsev working from Boris Pas-ternak's Russian translation of the play, undertaking a bicultural transfor-mation of the play into a coherent structure of unforgettable images. Lear is played by a wizened old man, possessed of a quiet dignity in his moments of composure but capable of conveying and sustaining the building rage that dominates his moments of "hideous rashness." But Yuri Jarvet's Lear is also frail and defenseless against loneliness and isolation, a vulnerable man thrown off-balance by forces larger than himself. He has divided his kingdom, and he is divided within himself. The interpretation of the play is redemptive, resulting in what the director called in his book *Shakespeare: Time and Conscience*, "[a]n instant of harmony so beautiful that the rest of life is like utter darkness beside it. The optimism of *King Lear* does not only lie in the idea that evil men either are punished or kill one another; it lies mainly in the feeling of victory of the worthy over the unworthy, even though their moral victory be a factual defeat at the same time" (102). This interpretation is beautifully realized. *(J. M. W.)*

Resources: Grigori Kozintsev, *King Lear: The Space of Tragedy* (Berkeley: Univer-sity of California Press, 1977); Grigori Kozintsev, *Shakespeare: Time and Con-*

science. Trans. Joyce Vining (New York: Hill & Wang, 1967); James M. Welsh, " 'To See It Feelingly': *King Lear* through Russian Eyes," *Literature/Film Quarterly* 4.2 (1976): 153–158.

King Lear (1971)

Directed and adapted by Peter Brook

Cast: Paul Scofield (Lear), Irene Worth (Goneril), Susan Engel (Regan), Anne-Lise Gabold (Cordelia), Patrick Magee (Cornwall), Cyril Cusack (Albany), Tom Fleming (Kent), Alan Webb (Gloucester), Ian Hogg (Edmund), Robert Lloyd (Edgar), Jack MacGowran (Fool), Barry Stanton (Oswald)

Length: 137 minutes

Peter Brook follows Shakespeare's design but gives us a truly demented King of Britain who is defined by his rage and irrationality, senile or witless as he partitions his kingdom between undeserving daughters Goneril and Regan and disinherits his favorite Cordelia, thereby throwing the realm into chaos and discord. The selfish King is then disinherited by his selfish daughters and turned loose to face the elements. The world goes mad as Lear goes mad, and the film shows the viewer that world through the eyes of Lear. Brook takes his cue from the interpretation of Jan Kott's *Shakespeare, Our Contemporary,* in other words, *"King Lear,* or *Endgame,"* more epic grotesquerie than tragedy, reducing Shakespeare's play to an absurd satire in a world devoid of human compassion. Hence, the film reinvents the play in the context of the brutalities of the twentieth century, creating a heartless dramatic world of complete negation. As Lillian Wilds notes, Brook "deliberately and systematically cuts all lines and scenes which supply motivation or act to mitigate what otherwise must be gratuitous cruelty" (163). He removes all of Cordelia's self-questioning asides, for example, before she refuses to flatter her father by telling him how much she loves him. The King of France's speech explaining Cordelia's refusal is also gone. Brook is determined to place Lear within a cold and meaningless universe. Charles Marowitz found Brook's approach "more cerebral than moving" and lacking in human terms: "Lear the ruler is there, as is Lear the madman; but Lear the father and Lear in those supreme final moments where the play transcends itself, is only sketched out" (120). He considers Paul Scofield "the most intelligent actor working today," however, capable of a performance that is both powerful and frightening. This is a major film that has not received its due. *(J. M. W.)*

Resources: Jan Kott, *Shakespeare, Our Contemporary,* trans. Boleslaw Taborski (Garden City, NY: Doubleday Anchor, 1966); Charles Marowitz, "Lear Log," *Tulane Drama Review,* 8.2 (1963): 103–21; Lillian Wilds, "One *King Lear* for Our Time: A Bleak Film Vision by Peter Brook," *Literature/Film Quarterly* 4.2 (1976): 159–164.

King Lear (1984)

Directed and adapted by Michael Elliott

Cast: Laurence Olivier (Lear), Colin Blakely (Kent), Anna Calder-Marshall (Cordelia), John Hurt (Fool), Robert Lindsay (Edmund), Leo McKern (Gloucester), Diana Rigg (Regan), David Threlfall (Edgar), Dorothy Tutin (Goneril)

Length: 140 minutes

Olivier's version of *King Lear* constitutes one of the finest and most faithful of film adaptations of Shakespeare's tragedy, thanks largely to Olivier's stellar performance as the title character. A much younger Olivier had played the role of Lear in a highly praised production at the Old Vic in 1946, and his advanced age not only lends verisimilitude and pathos to the film version but imbues his portrayal with a notable urgency and dignity. As Olivier himself put it at the time, "when you get to my age, you *are* Lear. . . . Here I am, at the very end of myself, in both age and experience." He captures Lear's essentially infantile selfishness in demanding of his daughters the profession of love that precipitates the inevitable problems, his madness after having been rejected by Goneril (Dorothy Tutin) and Regan (Diana Rigg), and his despair after the death of Cordelia (Anna Calder-Marshall), the one daughter who truly loves him. Tutin and Rigg are appropriately viperish as Shakespeare's ungrateful daughters, and, with a few exceptions, the rest of the cast is equally strong. Leo McKern is adept as Gloucester, who comes to see more when blinded, just as Lear gains a greater measure of sanity when mad. The casting of the versatile John Hurt as Lear's wise fool is inspired, the delivery of his gnomic remarks ranging from the madcap to the brutally honest. Robert Lindsay's Edmund, the neglected bastard son of Gloucester, unfortunately lacks the slick urbanity and relish that make the character one of Shakespeare's more compelling villains, and David Threlfall's Edgar, especially when disguised as Poor Tom, unintentionally calls to mind a Monty Python parody of Shakespeare. Overall, though, this is a striking production: director Michael Elliot wisely chose to emphasize the primitive, pre-Christian setting so crucial to the Shakespeare *King Lear* and so provides plenty of decaying timber, barking dogs, and massive stones. The few cuts made to the Shakespearean original are seamed over flawlessly, and the film as a whole displays just how compelling an accurate film adaptation of Shakespeare's works can be. *(G. H.)*

Resources: Harold Bloom, *Shakespeare: The Invention of the Human* (New York: Riverhead, 1998); Anthony Holden, *Laurence Olivier* (New York: Atheneum, 1988).

Ran (1985)

Directed by Akira Kurosawa

Adapted by Hideo Oguni, Masato Ide, and Akira Kurosawa

Cast: Tatsuya Nakadai (Hidetora Ichimonji, the Great Lord), Peter (Kyoami, Hidetora's Fool), Akira Terao (Tarotakatora "Taro" Ichimonji, oldest son), Meiko Harada (Lady Kaede, Taro's wife), Jinpachi Nezu (Jiromasatora "Jiro" Ichimonji, middle son), Yoshiko Miyazaki (Lady Sué, Jiro's wife), Masayuki Yui (Tango, Hidetora's retainer), Daisuke Ryu (Saburonaotora "Saburo" Ichimonji, youngest son), Hirsashi Igawa

Length: 161 minutes

Rated: R

Akira Kurosawa's twenty-eighth film follows the main plot of Shakespeare's *King Lear* involving Lear's division of his kingdom among his daughters, which results in his disowning the youngest and most loyal, Cordelia, then being disappointed, enraged, and cast out by the other two, Goneril and Regan, after which he is accompanied in his madness into the wilderness by his loyal Fool, until Cordelia comes with her husband to rescue him and is hanged as a consequence, after being taken prisoner. Shakespeare's Gloucester "echo-plot," with Gloucester's illegitimate son Edmund plotting to deceive his father and get his brother Edgar disinherited, tends to get lost in *Ran*. The title of Kurosawa's film means "chaos" in Japanese. This free adaptation of *Lear* is set during the late sixteenth century in Japan, the "Period of the Warring States," before rival feudal domains were united under the Tokugawa shogunate. The Lear figure is Hidetora Ichimonji, a warlord with notions of retirement. Since the Japanese line of issue required all heirs to be male, Kurosawa makes the offspring male instead of female. Hidetora has three sons: Taro, the elder and rightful heir, who forces his father to sign a document yielding all his power; Jiro, the middle son, who has his elder brother assassinated during a battle; and Saburo, the youngest brother, who is outspoken in criticizing his father's decision. Taro's vengeful and ambitious wife, Lady Kaede, urges her husband to seize power and later seduces Jiro to maintain her position. Kyoami, Hidetora's loyal servant, is the only person allowed to mock his lord and functions here as Lear's Fool. He stays with his master, who goes mad during the chaos that results. Kyoami is played by a famous Japanese transvestite named Peter, trained in *Jiutamae*, a stylized, Noh-drama related dance form developed for women in fourteenth-century Kyoto. *Ran* comprises static takes, infrequent camera movement, and conservative editing. In a battle at Mt. Fuji, the camera remains stationary as the massacred fall into the frame. The sequence is silent, except for Toru, Takemitsu's dark and solemn music, and when the silence is broken by the gunshot of Terao, we are reminded of Kurosawa's greatest silent sequence, Watanabe's dawning realization in *Ikiru* (1952), as he walks down a city street, that he will soon die of stomach cancer. *Ran* is a powerful and moving film, but a very loose adaptation of Shakespeare's play. *(L. C. C. and J. M. W.)*

Resources: James Goodwin, *Akira Kurosawa and Intertextual Cinema* (Baltimore: Johns Hopkins University Press, 1994); Stanley Kauffmann, "A Grand Finale," *The New Republic* (6–13 January 1986): 26–28; Dave Kehr, "Samurai *Lear*," *American Film* 10.10 (September 1985): 20–26; Donald Richie, *The Films of Akira Kurosawa* (Berkeley: University of California Press, 1984).

KISS ME, KATE (1948)
Samuel and Bella Spewack; songs and lyrics
by Cole Porter

Kiss Me, Kate (1953)

Directed by George Sidney

Adapted by Dorothy Kingsley

Cast: Howard Keel (Fred Graham), Kathryn Grayson (Lilli Vanessi), Ann Miller (Lois Lane)

Length: 111 minutes

One of the high points of American musical theatre, premiering in late 1948 and going on to 1,070 performances and a Tony Award for the season's best musical, *Kiss Me, Kate* is also regarded as Cole Porter's masterwork. This play-within-a-play begins with actors Fred Graham and his ex-wife, Lilli Vanessi, preparing for the opening night of their musical version of Shakespeare's *The Taming of the Shrew*. Their romantic squabbles offstage complement the action between Petruchio and Kate onstage. Book and music join in a seamless union, and the songs—"Another Op'nin', Another Show," "Wunderbar," "So in Love," "Brush Up Your Shakespeare," and others—are witty and sophisticated. Many derive directly from Shakespeare's lines: "I Am Ashamed That Women Are So Simple" musically transcribes Katherine's final capitulation speech and "Where Is the Life That Late I Led?" derives from one of Petruchio's "catalog" speeches. For George Sidney's film version, Howard Keel and Kathryn Grayson replaced Alfred Drake and Patricia Morrison as Fred Graham and Lilli Vanessi, respectively. Hermes Pan and Bob Fosse took on the choreography. The action of the modern story was transported from its Baltimore setting to

New York City. A prologue was added, in which Cole Porter himself (portrayed by actor Ron Randell) talks Fred and Lilli into doing his play. Song lyrics thought to be too risqué for the Hollywood censors were altered. Porter himself added an important new number for Ann Miller, who, in the secondary role of Lois Lane, fairly stole the show out from under the principals: the classic "From This Moment On" sequence, which he had previously dropped from another stage show, *Out of This World* (1950). *Kiss Me, Kate* was the only major Hollywood musical to be filmed in the then-novel technique of 3-D. Alas, the fad died out quickly, and upon its release the film played only a few venues in that format. According to historian Michael B. Druxman, the film was not a box office hit: "Maybe, back in 1953 when it was first released, the idea of Shakespeare in any form was just too highbrow to attract a mass audience, particularly when television was still a novelty and, of course, free" (48). *(J. C. T.)*

Resources: Gerald Bordman, *American Musical Theatre: A Chronicle* (New York: Oxford University Press, 1978); Michael B. Druxman, *The Musical: From Broadway to Hollywood* (New York: A. S. Barnes, 1980); Gerald Mast, *Can't Help Singin'* (New York: Overlook Press, 1987).

See also THE TAMING OF THE SHREW

LA CAGE AUX FOLLES (1974)
Jean Poiret

La Cage aux Folles (1978)

Directed by Edouard Molinaro

Adapted by Edouard Molinaro, Francis Veber, Marcello Danon, and Jean Poiret

Cast: Ugo Tognazzi (Renato), Michel Serrault (Albin), Michel Galabro (Charrier), Benny Luke (Jacob)

Length: 99 minutes

Rated: R

Jean Poiret's French play established the flamboyant characters whose relatively normal existence as a gay couple running a drag show and nightclub is disturbed when they encounter some of the straight world's least tolerant people. This collision of types, played with sight gags and sexual humor, made the farce a long-running stage success. Poiret collaborated in adapting the story to screen as the 1978 film *La Cage aux Folles*, a French and Italian production in French. Like the sets, the leads, Tognazzi as Renato and Serrault reprising his stage role as Albin, are larger than life and so honest in being garish that they are likable. The ostentatious gayness, especially personified by Jacob, a petite black man who, as the maid, prances about in skimpy outfits, is highly comical material. The film is funny because, for all their outlandishness, Renato and Albin are caught in a dilemma that could have happened to any couple.

Renato runs the nightclub where his longtime lover, Albin, lives fully in character as the difficult diva, Zaza. Renato's son from a heterosexual dalliance, Laurent, announces his engagement to Andrea. Meanwhile, her father, the Secretary General of the Union of Moral Order, is politically embarrassed when the Union President is found dead with a prostitute. Andrea's parents, status-hungry prigs, hoping the wedding will establish them as proper and socially upright, are comforted when she describes Laurent's parents as being stately bureaucrats employed in "Cultural Affairs." When her parents come to meet Laurent's family, Renato agrees to act the part Andrea described, and, when Laurent's mother fails to arrive on time to play her part, Albin attempts it. Chaos ensues when Laurent's mother does appear. Eventually, Andrea's father has to dress in drag to avoid being recognized as he storms out.

The film became the highest grossing foreign-language feature released in the United States to that time. A moderately popular 1980 sequel, also directed by Molinaro, *La Cage aux Folles II*, featured the gay couple as fish out of water in a spy-thriller plot. Another sequel, the 1985 film *La Cage aux Folles 3: The Wedding*, was much less successful.

The story returned to stage as a 1983 Broadway musical with music and lyrics by Jerry Herman and book by Harvey Fierstein. The highlight song and theme of the show were "I am what I am." The musical made the most of the drag show nightclub premise, using spectacular productions of songs and choreography. The show likewise used the gay world for comic effect but also highlighted the celebration of individuality.

It was filmed again in 1996 as *The Birdcage*, an American film scripted by Elaine May and directed by Mike Nichols. Robin Williams and Nathan Lane played the couple with the club in Miami Beach. *(S. C. C.)*

Resources: Owen Glieberman, "Swish Fulfillment," *Entertainment Weekly* No. 318 (15 March 1996): 44–46; Pauline Kael, *Taking It All In* (Holt, Rinehart, and Winston, 1984).

LA RONDE

See REIGEN

THE LAUNDROMAT (1978)
Marsha Norman

The Laundromat (1978)

Directed and adapted by Robert Altman

Cast: Carol Burnett (Alberta), Amy Madigan (DeeDee), Michael Wright (Shooter)

Length: 60 minutes

One of playwright Marsha Norman's earliest works, *The Laundromat* was first performed onstage by the Actors Theater of Louisville in 1978 and has been considered a study for *'night Mother*, which Norman told the *New York Times* is "probably true." The play was based on a "fairly specific encounter" Norman had in a laundromat, the sort of "chance occurrence that saves your life." The play brings together three characters, DeeDee (Amy Madigan), unhappily married to a womanizing factory worker, Alberta (Carol Burnett), an older suburban housewife haunted by the memory of her dead husband, and a black disc jockey named Shooter (Michael Wright), at a twenty-four-hour laundromat in the dead of night. During an antagonistic conversation, the women transcend barriers of class and age to achieve personal insights that could change their lives. Norman claimed director Robert Altman was "on the horizon" of transforming one-act plays to television with "artistry and commitment." Carol Burnett admitted that a play about "two people just sitting in a laundromat talking" was potentially boring but added that Altman was able to make it "visually interesting" by knowing how to move the camera. Altman refused to "open up" the play by throwing in "a lot of cars and exteriors" because "the set becomes a character." Norman admitted that when she wrote the play, she did not yet "know how to hold a two-character play together for an entire evening," so she considered it necessary "to bring in that third character, Shooter, to mess things up in order to get the final confrontation between the two leads." Altman shot the film in ten days at Studios Eclair in Paris for Home Box Office. *(J. M. W.)*

Resources: Anne Tremblay, "Altman Makes a Cable Film Abroad," *New York Times* (20 January 1985): Sec. II: 26; Virginia Wright Wexman and Gretchen Bispinghoff, *Robert Altman: A Guide to References and Resources* (Boston: G. K. Hall, 1984).

LENNY (1971)
Julian Barry

Lenny (1974)

Directed by Bob Fosse

Adapted by Julian Barry

Cast: Dustin Hoffman (Lenny Bruce), Valerie Perrine (Honey Bruce), Jan Miner (Sally Marr, Lenny's mother)

Length: 111 minutes

Rated: R

Julian Barry's play *Lenny*, based on the life of the controversial and litigation-plagued comic Lenny Bruce, was presented on Broadway by director Tom O'Horgan. O'Horgan was most famous for the 1960s counterculture musical *Hair*, and *Lenny* starts from similar cultural roots. However, Barry's play has a much darker tone, as it describes how the stand-up comic is persecuted for his exploration of American taboos on sex, race, and language. Most of the film's spoken words come from Lenny Bruce's actual comic routines, but Barry and O'Horgan have dramatized them, sometimes splitting a monologue into several speaking parts. The playwright and director also provided a great deal of visual spectacle on a multileveled stage.

Bob Fosse's film version of *Lenny* places the same material in a more biographical or docudrama mode. In the film, Bruce's performances are given context by reenacted interviews (with actors playing his wife, mother, and manager) and by scenes of the comic's tormented private life and multiple court appearances. Black-and-white photography adds to the docudrama tone. Lenny Bruce's monologues are as central to the film as they were to the play, but the actor giving them has changed. Although Cliff Gorman's performance on Broadway was universally praised, United Artists wanted a Hollywood star to carry this "difficult" subject. Dustin Hoffman, an excellent choice, has the range and talent to embody the mercurial Lenny Bruce. *(P. A. L.)*

Resources: Albert Goldman, *Ladies and Gentlemen, Lenny Bruce!!* (New York: Random House, 1974); Kevin Boyd Grubb, *Razzle Dazzle: The Life and Work of Bob Fosse* (New York: St. Martin's, 1989).

LES LIAISONS DANGEREUSES (1985)
Christopher Hampton

Dangerous Liaisons (1988)

Directed by Stephen Frears

Adapted by Christopher Hampton

Cast: Glenn Close (Marquise de Merteuil), John Malkovich (Vicomte de Valmont), Michelle Pfeiffer (Madame de Tourvel), Swoosie Kurtz (Madame de Volanges), Keanu Reeves (Chevalier Danceny), Uma Thurman (Cécile de Volanges)

Length: 120 minutes

Rated: R

Christopher Hampton first adapted the epistolary novel by Choderlos de Laclos (published in 1782) to the stage at Stratford-upon-Avon in September 1985. The bad behavior of a thoroughly decadent society is set before the French Revolution in various châteaux and hôtels in and near Paris during the 1780s. The action is set in motion by Mme. la Marquise de Merteuil, a controlling demon who toys with the lives and reputations of others for her own amusement. Out of spite and malice, she challenges Valmont, a ruthless libertine, to deflower Cécile de Volanges, a sixteen-year-old virgin, before the girl is married to Merteuil's former lover, M. le Comte de Bastide, but Valmont thinks this unworthy of his talent. Instead, he proposes to seduce the virtuous Madame de Tourvel, a married woman famous for her moral scruples. If he succeeds, Merteuil will reward Valmont with a night of lust. The plot is cynical and repulsive in its deceit and debauchery. The Royal Shakespeare production was soon moved to London and was a considerable hit, running over 800 performances at the Ambassadors Theatre and earning four best play awards, including the prestigious Laurence Olivier Award for 1986. (Miloš Forman's *Valmont* [1989] is adapted from the original novel, not from Hampton's play.)

Hampton agreed with director Stephen Frears that the film should not simply follow the play but should also be drawn from the original novel. Both the writer and director viewed the play as an allegory. Though the story is set before the French Revolution, Hampton explained, to *Premiere* (51), "It also seems to relate very strongly to today. Recently, both in England and America, institutionalized selfishness has been encouraged, so the heartlessness of the characters' behavior seems to strike a chord." The play, he noted, was about "greed—not for money, since the characters are unbelievably rich—but for power." The film is different from the play, as is obvious from the play's conclusion, when the shadow of the guillotine falls over the stage. Frears believed that "plays are too long," so Hampton shortened his play by forty minutes, going back to the novel in order to rethink the dramatization. Although "the dialogue is from the play," Frears noted, "the story is more from the book." Both Valmont and Merteuil are made to suffer. Valmont dies willingly in a duel with the virgin's young lover, and Merteuil, who collects billes-doux as insurance for blackmail and reprisal, is finally betrayed by her own letters and publicly humiliated. Though conceding the film "is nasty, decadent fun," David Ansen was surprised by "how much anguished emotion seeps through its cool marble heart." *(J. M. W.)*

Resources: David Ansen, "Boudoir Battleground," *Newsweek* (26 December 1988): 63. Kathryn Carson, "*Les Liaisons Dangereuses* on Stage and Film," *Literature/Film Quarterly* 19.1 (1991): 35–40; Mark Hunter, "Marquise de Merteuil and Comte de Valmont Get Laid," *American Film* 4.3 (December 1988): 26–31; Pauline Kael, "The Comedy of Evil," *New Yorker* (9 January 1989): 78–80; Edmund White, "Before the Revolution," *Premiere* 2.5 (January 1989): 50–54.

LIFE WITH FATHER (1939)
Howard Lindsay and Russel Crouse, adapted for the stage from Clarence Day's book *Life with Father*

Life with Father (1947)

Directed by Michael Curtiz

Adapted by Donald Ogden Stewart

Cast: William Powell (Clarence Day, Sr.), Irene Dunne (Vinnie Day), Edmund Gwenn (Reverend Dr. Lloyd), ZaSu Pitts (Cora), Jimmy Lydon (Clarence Day, Jr.), Elizabeth Taylor (Mary Skinner), Martin Milner (John Day)

Length: 118 minutes

Life with Father was based on a series of family sketches written by Clarence Day, Jr., which became a successful Broadway play adapted by Howard Lindsay and Russel Crouse. It opened at New York's Empire Theatre on 8 November 1939, with Lindsay in the role of father. Although Jack Warner purchased the screen rights in 1945, Day's widow and the playwrights exercised a virtual contractual stranglehold on the film, involving casting, set design, costumes, and makeup. The film attempted to be faithful to the play. Set in New York City in 1883, it mainly consisted of a succession of comedy sketches in which father's attempt to run his household on business lines is perpetually thwarted by his wife, Vinnie. A subplot involved his dwindling resistance to undergoing baptism. Father's capitulation ends both play and film. Despite contractual restrictions, Curtiz attempted to make the play as cinematic as possible. Irene Dunne's understated performance ideally complements William Powell's blustering patriarch. The three-act play occurs entirely inside the Day household. Some exterior scenes are included in the movie: the opening street scenes outside the Day Home, following stereoscopic views of period photographs; father's visit to an employment office to replace a servant; father's revelation during dinner at Delmonico's that he has never been baptized. Viewers also see a church service referred to in the play when the reverend utters his baptism sermon, go outside the porch when Clarence and Mary talk privately, and witness a street scene when Cora and Mary depart in a cab. Even in interior scenes, Curtiz visually supplements the dialogue: the camera tilts down a vent in Vinnie's bedroom to reveal the two younger sons below, listening to the parental debate about father's nonbaptism. They both appear outside in the yard when one brother teases the other about his father's going to hell. Stewart also adds a running joke about successive maids employed at the Day household who all leave because of father's eccentricities. Curtiz uses a mobile camera and varied long, medium, and close-up shots. Despite the restrictions imposed by the play's copyright holders, who attempted to interfere in the film whenever possible, Michael Curtiz finally completed a worthy adaptation. After finishing thirty days over schedule, *Life with Father* became a big box office hit after its release in August 1947. *(T. W.)*

Resources: Howard Lindsay and Russel Crouse, *Clarence Day's Life with Father Made into a Play* (New York: Alfred A. Knopf, 1949); James C. Robertson, *The Casablanca Man: The Cinema of Michael Curtiz* (London: Routledge, 1993).

THE LION IN WINTER (1964/1966)
James Goldman

The Lion in Winter (1968)

Directed by Anthony Harvey

Adapted by James Goldman

Cast: Peter O'Toole (Henry II), Katharine Hepburn (Eleanor of Aquitaine), Jane Merrow (Alais Capet), Anthony Hopkins (Richard), Nigel Terry (John), Timothy Dalton (Philip II), John Castle (Geoffrey)

Length: 134 minutes
Rated: PG

Who is the only actor to have been twice nominated for an Academy Award for best performance for playing the same character? Answer: Peter O'Toole, for portraying Henry II in *Becket* opposite Richard Burton and Henry II in *The Lion in Winter*, opposite Katharine Hepburn. Both of these successful films are adaptations of stage plays. The blending of theatrical language and film images is quite successfully merged in the film adaptation of *The Lion in Winter*. Sometimes referred to as a medieval *Who's Afraid of Virginia Woolf?*, *The Lion in Winter* tells the story of King Henry II (O'Toole) and his wife, Eleanor of Aquitaine (Hepburn), and their personal verbal battles over which of their three sons will succeed the aging Henry to the throne of England. One historical note from Goldman's script indicates, "There were no laws of primogeniture in Henry's time. It was a rare thing when the King was followed by his eldest son. When kings died, it was open season on the English throne, a fact responsible for much that Henry did" (Goldman ix). Director Harvey gives us an opening scene of medieval battle to establish time and place and then proceeds to bring Goldman's script to full fruition. *Lion* won Academy Awards for Hepburn (Best Actress), Goldman (Screenplay), and John Barry (Original Score). *Lion* also marks the screen debuts of both Anthony Hopkins and Timothy Dalton, who took over the film role of Philip originally created onstage by Christopher Walken. O'Toole and Hepburn give powerful performances as an aging couple who both love and distrust one another with as much passion, fire, and honesty as have rarely been seen onscreen. Hepburn's Eleanor is determined that their eldest son, Richard (Hopkins), should succeed Henry to the throne, but Henry has other ideas. At first favoring John, his youngest son, Henry confronts Eleanor with the idea that he will marry Alais and begin a new family of future kings, to which Eleanor responds that Henry's new offspring might not live long enough to see adulthood. Beneath all their bickering, we see a love and a history shared by Henry and Eleanor, which leave the audience at the end of the film with the idea that perhaps these two powerful monarchs will somehow work out their differences and perhaps even find a way to reconcile themselves to one another in order to find peace in their final days. *(J. D.)*

Resources: Ronald Bergan, *Katharine Hepburn: An Independent Woman* (New York: Arcade, 1996); James Goldman, *The Lion in Winter* (New York: Penguin Books, 1983); Nicholas Watshott, *Peter O'Toole: A Biography* (New York: Beaufort Books, 1983).

THE LITTLE FOXES (1939)
Lillian Hellman

The Little Foxes (1941)

Directed by William Wyler

Adapted by Lillian Hellman

Cast: Bette Davis (Regina Giddens), Herbert Marshall (Horace Giddens), Teresa Wright (Alexandra Giddens), Richard Carlson (David Hewitt)

Length: 116 minutes

Lillian Hellman's stage drama about a turn-of-the-century southern family's struggle over money and power is one of the most notable American theatrical works of the twentieth century. Its unregenerate acidity is undiluted by any strains of romantic emotion or comic relief. The imperious Regina Giddens (played onstage by Tallulah Bankhead) dominates her chronically ill husband, Horace (Frank Conroy), and daughter Alexandra (Florence Williams). She collaborates with her brothers Oscar (Carl Benton Reid) and Benjamin (Charles Dingle) Hubbard to raise the funds to cement a merger with Chicago businessman William Marshall (Charles Dingle). Loath to invest his funds, Horace puts off his insistent wife, whose concern over her social position exceeds any worries about his health. Behind her back, Oscar's son Leo (Dan Duryea) absconds with bonds Horace owns to finance the deal. When Regina and Horace argue over the matter, he suffers a seizure, only to succumb to its effects when Regina deliberately withholds his medicine. The play concludes with Regina's controlling the family fortunes but losing her daughter's affections and falling prey to the manipulations of her unscrupulous siblings. Wyler's adaptation of the play was scripted by Hellman, who not only physically opened up the narrative but also transformed the insistent pessimism of the play by introducing David Hewitt (Richard Carlson) as a love interest for Alexandra (Teresa Wright). The moral and emotional complexity of Regina's character is undercut by Bette Davis' treatment of her as a termagant without any emotional shading, despite Wyler's insistence to the contrary. Nonetheless, Hellman considered the motion picture to be better than the original play itself. Wyler uses the camera to enhance dramatic intensity on several occasions. Two notable sequences in this regard are the conversation between Oscar and Leo (played as onstage by Reid and Duryea) in the bathroom. Wyler uses the two characters' reflections in a set of mirrors to underscore their duplicity. The other is the celebrated close-up (written about enthusiastically by the French film theoretician André Bazin) of Davis during the fatal seizure suffered by Horace (Herbert Marshall). Wyler and cinematographer Greg Toland skillfully use screen space and deep focus. Although nominated for nine Academy Awards, the film won none. *(D. S.)*

Resources: Michael Anderegg, *William Wyler* (Boston: Twayne, 1979); Jan Herman, *A Talent for Trouble: The Life of Hollywood's Most Acclaimed Director, William Wyler* (New York: G. P. Putnam's Sons, 1995).

LITTLE MURDERS (1967)
Jules Feiffer

Little Murders (1972)

Directed by Alan Arkin

Adapted by Jules Feiffer

Cast: Elliott Gould (Alfred Chamberlain), Marcia Rodd (Patsy Newquist), Vincent Gardenia (Mr. Newquist), Elizabeth Wilson (Mrs. Newquist), Jon Korkes (Kenny), Donald Sutherland (Minister), Lou Jacobi (Judge), Alan Arkin (Lieutenant Practice), John Randolph (Mr. Chamberlain), Doris Roberts (Mrs. Chamberlain)

Length: 110 minutes

Rated: R

After failing in New York in 1967, Feiffer's black comedy, which he described as a "post-assassination play," was a hit in London and then returned to critical acclaim in New York two years later. Set entirely in the Newquist apartment in New York City, *Little Murders* concerns Alfred, a successful photographer who passively submits to aggression, and Patsy Newquist, an aggressive, ambitious woman who marries him despite her father's disapproval. Shortly after their marriage, conducted by a Reverend Dupas, who abides by Alfred's strictures about God's not being mentioned in the ceremony, Patsy is shot dead by random gunfire. Six months later Alfred's behavior changes radically: he has been in several fights and brings a rifle into the Newquist apartment. Lieutenant Practice, who is investigating not only Patsy's murder but that of some 345 other victims, visits the Newquists but can offer only a paranoid conspiracy theory before his glass is shot out of his hand by more gunfire. After he leaves, Mr. Newquist loads Alfred's rifle, and he and Kenny, Patsy's homosexual brother, shoot from their apartment window and kill people on the street below. When

Alfred kills Lieutenant Practice, there is some male bonding and, thanks to Mrs. Newquist, a celebratory dinner. When Feiffer adapted the play to film, he added an introductory sequence in which Patsy (Marcia Rodd) observes a beating, calls the police (who fail to respond), and takes on the hoodlums who are attacking Alfred (Elliott Gould), enabling him to escape but causing the hoodlums to attack her. Despite this inauspicious beginning and Alfred's lack of interest in a variety of sports she excels in, Patsy decides to marry him. When he meets the Newquists, Alfred finds blackouts, gunfire from the streets, and hostile questions from Carol (Vincent Gardenia), Patsy's father. To open up the claustrophobic play, Feiffer adds Patsy's visit to Alfred's parents in Chicago; the Chamberlains are academics whose speech is dotted with phrases like the "dynamics of apathy." Carol also visits Lieutenant Practice (Alan Arkin), whose frustration and paranoia mirror America's response to the assassinations and violence of the 1960s. The most interesting sequence in the film features Donald Sutherland as the hippie minister of the First Existential Church: after he reveals Carol's bribe to include God and declares that most of the couples he's married are now divorced, the wedding ends in a battle. As in the play, Patsy is killed by gunfire, and a distraught Alfred returns to the Newquist apartment, where he, Carol, and Kenny indulge in some slaughter of their own. Mrs. Newquist (Elizabeth Wilson) cooks them a big dinner and asserts that it's good to hear the family laughing again. Although the play seemed out of step with American values when it first appeared, subsequent events reaffirmed Feiffer's vision. *(T. L. E.)*

Resources: Alan Arkin, *Halfway through the Door: An Actor's Journey toward the Self* (New York: Harper and Row, 1979); Pauline Kael, "Varieties of Paranoia," in her *Deeper into Movies* (Boston: Little, Brown, 1973): 253–259.

A LITTLE NIGHT MUSIC (1973)
Hugh Wheeler and Stephen Sondheim

A Little Night Music (1978)

Directed by Harold Prince

Adapted by Hugh Wheeler and Stephen Sondheim

Cast: Elizabeth Taylor (Desiree Armfelt), Diana Rigg (Charlotte Mittelheim), Len Cariou (Frederick Egerman), Lesley-Anne Down (Anne Egerman), Hermione Gingold (Madame Armfelt), Laurence Guittard (Carl-Magnus Mittelheim), Christopher Guard (Eric Egerman), Chloe Franks (Fredericka Armfelt)

Length: 124 minutes

Rated: PG

Seeking a property on which to base an operetta-like Broadway musical, Stephen Sondheim and Harold Prince settled on Ingmar Bergman's *Smiles of a Summer Night* (1955), then hired British playwright Hugh Wheeler (who has novel and screenplay credits as Patrick Quentin) to adapt Bergman's screenplay to the stage. The resulting libretto follows Bergman closely. Aging stage actress Desiree Armfelt decides to settle down with her former lover, the lawyer Frederick Egerman. Inconveniently, he has been married for eleven months to the young and still virgin Anne. Eric, Egerman's son by a former wife, is a divinity student secretly in love with his stepmother. Desiree's jealous and obtuse current lover is Carl-Magnus Mittelheim, married to the bitter, but tolerant, Charlotte. To break up this marriage standing in her way, Desiree invites the Egermans to a weekend at her mother's country estate. The jealous Mittelheim and his wife show up unannounced. In the course of an evening's action, Eric runs away with his stepmother, Desiree and Egerman accept both middle age and each other, and the Mittelheims rekindle their relationship. Sondheim's music is a glittering swirl of variations on three-quarter time, and his lyrics are witty, sardonic, tender. The original Broadway production opened on 25 February 1973 at the Shubert Theater, directed by Harold Prince, with orchestrations by Jonathan Tunick. It won Tony Awards for Best Musical, Best Music and Lyrics, Best Book, Best Costume Design in a Musical (Florence Klotz), Best Actress in a Musical (Glynnis Johns as Desiree), and Best Supporting Actress in a Musical (Patricia Elliott as Charlotte). It ran for 601 performances, earning a substantial profit. As the Broadway production wound down, Harold Prince and Hugh Wheeler pushed to translate the play into film; Sondheim was reluctant, believing the libretto too static for the screen. Prince centered the film version on Elizabeth Taylor as Desiree. Wheeler adapted his libretto in a straightforward way. Sondheim rewrote one of the musical numbers, "The Glamorous Life," reworked the opening waltz, and sharply edited "Liaisons." Prince dropped the quintet of singers who provided uninvolved commentary throughout the stage play and cut "The Miller's Son," a strong number in which the Egerman maid's practical view of love and marriage balances the sexual predation and absurd romanticism of the upper-class characters. The film reviews were almost all extremely negative. Prince had earned his substantial reputation as a director of stage musicals by mounting plays fluidly. On the movie set for *A Little Night Music*, his instincts for movement deserted him. The mise-en-scène is static, and the editing nervous. He also drowned the production in large hats, flowing gowns, and bric-a-brac. "Authentic" Viennese settings often overwhelm the actors, and the film's literalism renders ludicrous many of Sondheim's deftly interwoven juxtapositions in which competing characters sing complementary verses. The only passage that has filmic life is "A Weekend in the Country," where Prince's direction matches the fluidity of Sondheim's music. Len Cariou and Hermione Gingold recreate the roles they played onstage. Taylor as Desiree is unsuccessful. She cannot sing at all, so even Sondheim's one hit song, "Send in the Clowns," falls flat. She also suffered a range of minor injuries and ailments during filming that limited her physical movement. The film was nominated for two Oscars, costume design and best score in an adaptation. Jonathan Tunick won the Oscar for his score. *(W. K.)*

Resources: Joanne Gordon, *Art Isn't Easy: The Theater of Stephen Sondheim*, 2d ed. (New York: Da Capo, 1992); Meryle Secrest, *Stephen Sondheim, a Life* (New York: Random House, 1998); Craig Zadan, *Sondheim & Co.*, 2d ed. (New York: Harper and Row, 1989).

LITTLE SHOP OF HORRORS (1982)
Howard Ashman and Alan Menken

Little Shop of Horrors (1986)

Directed by Frank Oz

Adapted by Howard Ashman and Alan Menken

Cast: Rick Moranis (Seymour), Ellen Greene (Audrey), Vincent Gardenia (Mushnik), Steve Martin (Orin), John Candy (disk jockey)

Length: 93 minutes

Rated: PG-13

Roger Corman produced and directed Charles B. Griffith's script for the 1960 film *Little Shop of Horrors*, inaccurately infamous as a film shot in two days. Using this film, Howard Ashman wrote the book and lyrics, with music by Alan Menken, for the 1982 Off-Broadway musical *Little Shop of Horrors*. The musical was a hit and was reworked into the 1986 film *Little Shop of Horrors*. The basic story involves cartoonishly odd, but very human, characters from Mushnik's flower shop on Skid Row, including the nice, but incompetent, Seymour Krelborn, the sweet, but dizzy, Audrey, and their boss, Mr. Mushnik. As Seymour's development of a mysterious plant brings fame and fortune, Audrey comes to care for Seymour. But the plant thrives only on human flesh, which Seymour must acquire to maintain his newly found love and success. Seymour faces internal demons and the large, carnivorous external demon his plant becomes. The 1960 film was low-budget with sparse sets and comically low-tech props but clever dialogue and background characters. The dentist scene includes Jack Nicholson as the pain-loving patient. The movie works because the characters remain honest in their bizarreness. In this film, Seymour lives with his hypochondriac mother until he develops the plant. He hopes to marry Audrey and become Mushnik's adopted son and heir to the flower business. Oddly, Seymour is able to find bodies for plant food, but he can't bring himself to kill anyone. Eventually, he becomes so enraged he jumps into the plant to destroy it. Seymour finally appears eerily in a bloom crying his mantra: "I didn't mean it!" The 1982 musical's props and characters are bigger. There is a "Greek Chorus" of three girls in the Motown girl-group tradition. Comic characters are more developed, including Orin, the sadistic dentist. Audrey is made blond and buxom, but she also expresses the desire for a quiet life in a picturesque suburb, as she sings "Somewhere That's Green." Seymour's brush with greatness and his descent into evil are much enhanced. Still, the characters maintain what Ashman saw as the sincerity and intensity necessary for the story to work. The very theatrical ending had tendrils of the plant dropping down on the audience, as the chorus sang "Don't Feed the Plants."

The 1986 film is even bigger. Rick Moranis *looks* like Seymour, and Ellen Greene, who was also the Broadway Audrey, plays her part well. Steve Martin's Orin is a comic highlight, and John Candy as a disk jockey perfectly captures the wonderfully weird sense of the story. The original ending with Seymour and Audrey's being victims of the plant was not well received in tests. The revamped ending had the couple conquering the plant and moving to the perfect suburban house Audrey sang about, only to have a garden complete with a budding, smiling plant. *(S. C. C.)*

Resources: Dennis Fischer, "Roger Corman's Little Shop of Horrors," *Cinefantastique* (January 1987); Alan Jones, "The Lost Ending," *Cinefantastique* (September 1987); Mark Thomas McGee, *Roger Corman: The Best of the Cheap Acts* (Jefferson, NC: McFarland, 1988); Dan Scapperotti, "Horror Film Fan Howard Ashman Talks about Making Roger Corman's B-Film a Musical Comedy Phenomenon," *Cinefantastique* (January 1987).

LITTLE VOICE

See THE RISE AND FALL OF LITTLE VOICE

LONG DAY'S JOURNEY INTO NIGHT (1956)
Eugene O'Neill

Long Day's Journey into Night (1962)

Directed by Sidney Lumet

Cast: Katharine Hepburn (Mary Tyrone), Ralph Richardson (James Tyrone), Jason Robards (Jamie), Dean Stockwell (Edmund)

Length: 174 minutes

Written in 1940, Eugene O'Neill's autobiographical play was not published or performed until 1956, after the author's death. The acclaimed play, which quickly took its place as one of the classics of the American theatre, provided the script for Lumet's reverential 1962 film. Critics and scholars are divided on the merits of the film, some deriding it as merely filmed theatre and others praising it as a masterpiece. Certainly, Lumet was faithful to the play, which was not rewritten but only carefully cut (by 27 percent by Donald Costello's count) so as to preserve O'Neill's portrait of the "four haunted Tyrones" grappling with alcoholism, morphine addiction, and a lifetime's bitterness one long day in 1912. But Lumet also brought to the work his own considerable skills as a director. His camera, which follows Edmund to the beach and later tracks through an empty hallway to reveal James Tyrone sitting down to a lonely dinner, provides visual images that complement O'Neill's words. Likewise, he edited Jamie's scenes in "a staccato rhythm" to make him feel "disjointed" and shot Mary in sustained takes "to help us drift into her narcotized world" (Lumet 67). Moving the early scenes out onto a sunny lawn, he structured the film to fade over the course of the day from lightness to darkness. The director's approach, though, is primarily to reinforce O'Neill's work, not to reinterpret it or expand on it. Lumet even forgoes the chance to turn the fog, used repeatedly in the play as a verbal symbol, into a visual image. Moreover, the stately pace of the film and its somewhat theatrical performances keep it anchored to its origins on the stage. Katharine Hepburn's gripping performance as the addiction-plagued mother won her an Academy Award nomination and several acting awards, but some have criticized Hepburn as "too mannered and too conspicuously a star to be convincing as the only member of the Tyrone family who is not theatrical" (Cooper 83). Ralph Richardson's modulated tones and sometimes exaggerated facial expressions are more appropriate for his character, who is an actor. Dean Stockwell's performance, commonly regarded as the weakest of the four, may suffer by comparison, in part, because it is more naturalistic than the dramatic turns of the other three lead actors. But all in all, the actors' bravura performances, Lumet's impressive craftsmanship, and O'Neill's ravaging script add up to a memorable film. *(C. M. D.)*

Resources: Burton L. Cooper, "Some Problems in Adapting O'Neill for Film," in *Eugene O'Neill's Century*, ed. Richard F. Moorton, Jr. (New York: Greenwood, 1991): 73–86; Donald P. Costello, "Sidney Lumet's *Long Day's Journey into Night*," *Literature/Film Quarterly* 22, No. 2 (1994): 78–92; Sidney Lumet, *Making Movies* (New York: Vintage, 1996).

THE LONG STAY CUT SHORT/OR/THE UNSATISFACTORY SUPPER (1946) and 27 WAGONS FULL OF COTTON (1955)
Tennessee Williams

Baby Doll (1956)

Directed by Elia Kazan

Adapted by Tennessee Williams from two one-act plays

Cast: Karl Malden (Archie), Carroll Baker (Baby Doll), Eli Wallach (Silvia Vacarro), Mildred Dunnock (Aunt Rose Comfort)

Length: 114 minutes

The film *Baby Doll* (1956) was, in fact, based on two of Tennessee Williams' one-act plays, *27 Wagons Full of Cotton* and *The Unsatisfactory Supper*. Williams melded them into a single coherent story for the screen at the request of film director Elia Kazan. In the first play the heroine is the voluptuous wife of a seedy cotton gin owner many years her senior. The man burns down the cotton gin owned by Silvia Vacarro, in order to force Vacarro to use his facilities instead. This play is the driving force of *Baby Doll*. The other one-act play is a much less substantial character sketch of Aunt Rose, an elderly spinster who has worn out her welcome with her niece Baby Doll and the latter's husband, Archie Lee (the counterpart of the husband and wife in 27). Just how firmly the two one-acters solidified into one unified work of art is evidenced by the substantial amount of dialogue that Williams was able to retain from the two previously separate plays. In the film Baby Doll (Carroll Baker) is attracted to Vacarro (Eli Wallach) because he treats her less like a child—which is the approach Archie Lee takes to her—and more and more like the woman she really is. In the film's finale Archie Lee becomes hysterical when Vacarro informs him that he has wheedled evidence of the arson from Baby Doll and suggests that he has coaxed other favors from her as well. Archie Lee runs around the property drunkenly firing off his shotgun wildly and indiscriminately and is finally hauled off by the sheriff to spend the night in jail. Vacarro gallantly offers to take Aunt Rose in as his housekeeper, and Baby Doll decides to leave Archie for Vacarro. (Since her May–December marriage to Archie Lee was never consummated, it will not be difficult for her to obtain an annulment.) The movie's conclusion reflects a note of hope and optimism that is nowhere in sight in either of the two source plays. "I think of Baby Doll as a quiet little black comedy," Kazan told this writer; "and I've never been able to understand what all the fuss was about at the time of its release." In fact, Francis Cardinal Spellman, archbishop of New York, in an unprecedented action, denounced the picture from the pulpit of St. Patrick's Cathedral as a corruptive influence on American society. Presumably, Spellman and other church leaders who subsequently followed his lead mistakenly thought that some of the movie's images had a sexual intent, when they did not. For example, Baby Doll's sucking her thumb and licking an ice cream cone were not meant to depict the young girl's subconscious longing for fellatio, as some of the film's critics contended, but to show, as Kazan himself said, that "she's still a baby. She's not grown up. That's all I had in mind: arrested development." Perhaps Kazan said it all when he concluded, "If you see Baby Doll today, now that the controversy has long since then died down, you can see that it is a charming comedy, poetic and funny; and that is all it ever was." (G. D. P.)

Resources: Douglas Brode, The Films of the Fifties (New York: Carol, 1993); Gene D. Phillips, The Films of Tennessee Williams (Cranbury, NJ: Associated University Presses, 1980).

THE LONG VOYAGE HOME

See S.S. GLENCAIRN CYCLE OF PLAYS

LOOK BACK IN ANGER (1956)
John Osborne

Look Back in Anger (1959)

Directed by Tony Richardson

Adapted by Nigel Kneale

Cast: Richard Burton (Jimmy Porter), Claire Bloom (Helena Charles), Mary Ure (Alison Porter), Glen Byam Shaw (Colonel Redfern), Edith Evans (Mrs. Tanner), Gary Raymond (Cliff Lewis), Donald Pleasance (Hurst)

Length: 101 minutes

John Osborne's play rapidly came to epitomize a new movement in the English theatre involving "kitchen sink dramas" written by "angry young men." It was well received by most of the critics, calling it "the best young play of its decade." Kenneth Tynan even doubted that he could love anyone who did not want to see it! It became the first project for Woodfall Films, founded by John Osborne, Harry Saltzman, and Tony Richardson in 1958. Despite the objections of Saltzman, who later went on to coproduce James Bond films, Osborne insisted that Richardson serve as the film's director, "being the only possible commander to lead Woodfall's opening assault on the suburban vapidity of British film-making" (Osborne 107). Despite his reluctance to write the screenplay and his relief after Tynan suggested that Nigel Kneale, creator of the *Quatermass* series, adapt the screenplay, Osborne was less than happy with the changes. Indeed, he felt that the opening up of the play involved "ripping out its obsessive, personal heart" (Osborne 108). Clearly, in his first feature film, Richardson is not simply filming a play. He uses the original as raw material for the creation of a new work, involving new characters, such as Edith Evans' Mrs. Tanner, and new situations. Jimmy Porter's lengthy diatribes are severely cut in favor of cinematically establishing the context in which he exists. Jazz club, street market, and cemetery allowed for half of the eight-week shooting schedule to be outside the studio. Richardson was aided in these efforts by the expertise of his cinematographer, Oswald Morris, who made effective use of extreme facial close-ups and of a quietly restless, probing camera within the Porters' flat. Where the play is often a political and social manifesto, the film tends more toward realized personal drama, but this works to the long-term benefit of the film, which has a continuing resonance that the play, with its insufferable arch posturing, clearly lacks. In an interview that appeared in *Films and Filming*, Richardson pointed to the necessity of avoiding theatrical conventions in the creation of this film: "Stylisation to me almost always works against as utter a texture of life as I would like to have in the cinema" (February 1959: 25). *(W. L. H.)*

Resources: Roger Manvell, *New Cinema in Britain* (London: Studio Vista, 1969); John Osborne, *Almost a Gentleman* (London: Faber and Faber, 1991); Tony Richardson, *The Long Distance Runner: An Autobiography* (New York: Morrow, 1993).

LOOT (1966)
Joe Orton

Loot (1971)

Directed by Silvio Narizzano

Adapted by Ray Galton and Alan Simpson

Cast: Richard Attenborough (Inspector Truscott), Lee Remick (Fay), Hywel Bennet (Dennis), Roy Holder (Hal McLeavy), Milo O'Shea (Mr. McLeavy)

Length: 101 minutes

Loot was first performed at London's Jeanetta Cochrane Theatre on 29 September 1966. It was later revived as part of the "Joe Orton Festival" at London's Royal Court Theatre on 3 June 1975, directed by Albert Finney. The play begins with a quote from *Misalliance* by George Bernard Shaw where Lord Summerhays comments, "Anarchism is a game at which the Police can beat you," an axiom that "the British public . . . pretends not to believe." As embodied in Inspector Truscott, *Loot*'s scathing farce represents a comedy of language and social upheaval in which victims as well as corruptors form the target of Orton's satirical wit. The play involves attempts to conceal loot from a bank robbery in Hal's mother's coffin and schemes devised by serial killer nurse Fay and Inspector Truscott to gain access to it. Eventually, the one law-abiding figure in the film, Mr. Mc-Leavy, is unjustly arrested and scheduled for "accidental death" while in jail. After deciding to share the proceeds with the three accomplices—Hal, Dennis, and Fay—Truscott decides to take the entire loot into "protective custody." The screenplay was written by television writers Galton and Simpson, acclaimed for their innovative radio and comedy scripts for series such as *Hancock's Half-Hour* and *Steptoe and Son*. Although the screenplay lacks several examples of Orton's rapier-sharp satire and drops some of his outrageous lines, it does attempt some fidelity to the play. McLeavy's house is now a hotel. New incidents such as a police bulldozer's crushing a garden gnome appear, and the color scheme complements Orton's black-comedy verbal assaults on welfare state gentility. According to Joannides, Austin Dempster's photography renders the latter "in the garishness of a biscuit tin, with nauseating clashes between orange, mauve, lemon-yellow, and mismatching tones of green," and the hotel's ghastly setting "is the perfect physical equivalent of Orton's mental world, as artificial as Wilde's, where figures with the innocence of characters in Victorian pornography wander through labyrinths of Jonsonian corruption." (Ben Jonson was one of Orton's favorite playwrights.) In the film we see the actual bank robbery with gay duo Hal and Dennis naked to avoid incriminating dust on their clothes. The film, which also attempts a Brechtian use of songs recounting the action at various points of the film, was regarded as a successful adaptation and a fine film. *(T. W.)*

Resources: Paul Joannides, "Loot," *Monthly Film Bulletin* 38.444 (January 1971): 8–9; Susan Rusinko, *Joe Orton* (New York: Twayne, 1995).

LUV (1964)
Murray Schisgal

Luv (1967)

Directed by Clive Donner

Adapted by Elliott Baker

Cast: Jack Lemmon (Harry Berlin), Peter Falk (Milt Manville), Elaine May (Ellen Manville), Nina Wayne (Linda), Eddie Mayehoff (Attorney Goodhart)

Length: 93 minutes

Rated: PG

Schesgal's *Luv*, which premiered in New York City in 1964, takes place on a New York City bridge and has only three characters: Harry Berlin, Milt Manville, and Ellen Manville. In the first act of the comedy Milt talks Harry out of committing suicide and persuades him to marry Ellen, whom he wants to divorce in order to marry Linda. Among the comic bits are Ellen's chart of her sexual relations with Milt, Harry's real and faked paralysis and loss of hearing and sight, comparisons of unhappy childhoods, and "tests" of love. The action is at once intellectual and childish, the latter trait symbolized by the presence of a sandbox. In the second act Ellen and Milt meet on the bridge and discuss what has happened in the past months: Linda has walked out on Milt, and Ellen is disillusioned about Harry. Pledging their love for each other, Ellen and Milt promise they will change:

Milt will give up scavenging, his night job, and Ellen will "submerge her intelligence." To find happiness they must get rid of Harry, who wants to stay with Ellen. The solution is to push Harry off the bridge, but it is played for comedy, and it is Milt who is accidentally pushed over twice. Finally, Harry goes over the bridge but reappears to ask Milt, who leaves with Ellen, for the five dollars he owes him. At the end of both acts Harry is "treed" by a dog who chases him to a lamppost, the position he occupied at the end of the first act. The film adaptation adds several scenes and characters, but the cynical, sophisticated humor of the film comes primarily from the original stage dialogue. Since scenes at a bar, an amusement park, and even at Niagara Falls, where Harry weds Ellen, contain stage dialogue, nothing is gained by the change of scenery. The scenes at Milt and Ellen's house, which contains a basement where Milt keeps his trash and that Harry later converts to a doctor's office, contribute little to the film except to expand the role of the trashmen, with horse-drawn buggy, who buy Harry's stuff. Similarly, the film adds alimony payments and a greedy lawyer, but these additions seem too real in a surrealistic comedy. The film stresses sophomoric sexual humor with the addition of a voluptuous Linda and the bursting into song ("Love casts its shadow") whenever a breast is touched. Unlike the play, the film ends with Linda's saving Harry from drowning and being paired with him, while Milt and Ellen are reunited. *(T. L. E.)*

Resources: Alan Arkin, *Halfway through the Door: An Actor's Journey toward the Self* (New York: Harper and Row, 1979); Don Widener, *Lemmon: A Biography* (New York: Macmillan, 1975).

MACBETH (1606)
William Shakespeare

Macbeth (1948)

Directed and adapted by Orson Welles

Cast: Orson Welles (Narrator and Macbeth), Jeanette Nolan (Lady Macbeth), Dan O'Herlihy (Macduff), Edgar Barrier (Banquo), Roddy McDowall (Malcolm), Erskine Sanford (Duncan), Alan Napier (Holy Father), Peggy Webber (Lady Macduff and Witch)

Length: 104 minutes

Shakespeare's *Macbeth* begins with witches who approach Macbeth and Banquo, two of King Duncan's military leaders. Macbeth is hailed as thane of Glamis, thane of Cawdor, and king; Banquo is described as the father of kings. When Macbeth, already thane of Glamis, assumes the title of thane of Cawdor when that traitor is executed, he sees himself as having achieved two-thirds of the witches' prophecy. He and Lady Macbeth plot the murder of Duncan, who is soon to arrive at Macbeth's castle. Spurred on by his wife, Macbeth kills Duncan and the guards who have been drugged by Lady Macbeth. Macbeth stabs the guards, whom he accuses as murderers. When Malcolm and Donalbain, Duncan's two sons, who accompanied their father, flee for their lives, Macbeth brands them as murderers. As a relative of Duncan, Macbeth is crowned king, but he broods about Banquo's future as the father of kings and resolves to murder Banquo and his son, Fleance. Three murderers succeed in killing Banquo, but Fleance escapes. At the banquet that evening Banquo's ghost appears to Macbeth, who collapses in terror; Lady Macbeth dismisses the guests. A doubtful Macbeth seeks out the witches, who promise him that he cannot be slain by man of woman born and that he shall be king until Birnam Wood "come to Dunsinane," Macbeth's castle. Despite this reassurance Macbeth conducts a bloody campaign to eliminate all possible opponents. Lady Macduff and her family are slaughtered. When Macduff learns his family's fate, he joins forces with Malcolm, returns to Scotland from England, and marches on the castle. The soldiers, who carry branches of trees to disguise their number, bring Birnam Wood to Dunsinane; and Macduff, who was "ripped untimely from his mother's womb," kills Macbeth. Malcolm is proclaimed king. Welles' *Macbeth* is permeated by evil. It presents a conflict between Christianity, new to Scotland and symbolized by the Celtic cross, and the natural forces of chaos, symbolized by the trees, fog, primitive caves, shadows, and distortions. At the beginning of the film the audience sees the witches shape a lump of clay into an emblem of Macbeth, symbolically giving him birth. At the end of the play when Macduff beheads Macbeth, Welles cuts to the Macbeth emblem, which also has its head lopped off. The control of the church, represented by the Holy Father, an addition to the cast of the play, is tenuous—Macbeth kills the Holy Father. Even after Malcolm is proclaimed king, the forces of evil persist in the form of the witches, whose presence foreshadows another cycle of ambition, assassination, and destruction. *(T. L. E.)*

Resources: James Howard, *The Complete Films of Orson Welles* (Secaucus, NJ: Carol, 1991); Jack J. Jorgens, *Shakespeare on Film* (Bloomington: Indiana University Press, 1977).

Macbeth (1971)

Directed by Roman Polanski

Adapted by Kenneth Tynan

Cast: Jon Finch (Macbeth), Francesca Annis (Lady Macbeth), Martin Shaw (Banquo), Nicholas Selby (Duncan), John Stride (Ross), Stephan Chase (Malcolm), Paul Shelley (Donalbain), Terence Bayler (Macduff), Diane Fletcher (Lady Macduff), Keith Chegwin (Fleance), Noel Davis (Seyton)

Length: 139 minutes

Rated: R

Macbeth and his friend Banquo are hailed by three witches upon a "blasted heath" in Scotland who proclaim that Macbeth is destined to become king of Scotland. To hasten the prophecy, Lady Macbeth persuades her husband to murder King Duncan, who has already made him thane of Cawdor, when the king visits their castle. Following their father's death, the king's sons, Malcolm and Donalbain, flee for their safety, and Macbeth is proclaimed king. Because the witches predicted that Banquo "shall get kings," Macbeth also has him assassinated, but Banquo's son, Fleance, escapes. On a return visit to the witches, Macbeth is warned to "beware Macduff," who has gone to England with Malcolm, whereupon Macbeth has Lady Macduff and her children killed. Malcolm and Macduff and other Lords raise an army against Macbeth, whose own troops are defecting and whose wife goes mad and dies. In the climax Macduff challenges Macbeth and kills him, ending his murderous reign. Polanski's film is about as "bloody, bold, and resolute" as any production of this play could be. Macbeth and his lady are rather younger than one might expect them to be, but Jon Finch embodies the character's evil potential effectively. Polanski emphasizes the political deviousness of the plot by making Ross (John Stride) Macbeth's main henchman and the third murderer sent to dispatch Banquo and Fleance. Ross also visits Lady Macduff just before the murderers come to destroy her and her family. When Macbeth shows preference later to Seyton (Noel Davis), Ross defects to Malcolm and is there when Malcolm assumes the throne at the end. The film's final shots show Donalbain limping off to meet the witches, suggesting that the cycle of violence and murder is about to begin again. Polanski's cynical interpretation of the play seems to have been influenced by Jan Kott's *Shakespeare, Our Contemporary* (1966) and the director's own experiences in Poland during World War II. The film excels in its realistic spectacle and in its handling of the supernatural elements, especially the "Show of Kings" during Macbeth's second visit to the witches. The problem is that the bloody spectacle tends to overwhelm the poetry, but the images are unforgettable. *(J. M. W.)*

Resources: Bernice W. Kliman, *Shakespeare in Performance: Macbeth* (Manchester, U.K.: Manchester University Press, 1992); John Parker, *Polanski* (London: Victor Gollancz, 1993); Roman Polanski, *Roman by Polanski* (New York: William Morrow, 1984).

The Throne of Blood (The Castle of the Spider's Web/ Kumonosu-jo) (1957)

Directed by Akira Kurosawa

Adapted by Akira Kurosawa, Hideo Oguni, Shinobu Hashimoto, and Riyuzo Kikushima

Cast: Toshiro Mifune (Taketoki Washizu/Macbeth), Isuzu Yamada (Asaji/

Lady Macbeth), Takamaru Sasaki (Kuniharu Tsuzuki/Duncan), Minoru Chiaki (Yoshiaki Miki/Banquo), Akira Kubo (Yoshiteru/Fleance), Yoichi Tachikawa (Kunimaru/Malcolm), Chieko Naniwa (Spirit Woman/Witch), Takashi Shimura (Noriyasu Odagura)

Length: 105 minutes

Though set far from Scotland in feudal Japan, Kurosawa's film transformation of Shakespeare's play has been considered one of the very best adaptations of *Macbeth*. The film follows Shakespeare as closely as possible, minus the poetry. Several adjustments are made in this cultural transformation, which begins and ends with a meditation on evil ambition. Lost in a forest, General Washizu and his friend General Miki encounter a spirit, who tells Washizu that he will become king but that Miki's heirs will later rule. Like Macbeth, Washizu first murders his lord, then Miki, the Banquo figure. When Washizu visits the spirit a second time, she tells him that he will prevail until the forest moves, which gives him confidence, until Miki's son attacks his castle and uses cut boughs as camouflage for his army. At the end, Washizu's own men turn on him and skewer him with a barrage of arrows. Miki becomes the avenger rather than Macduff in this adaptation. Asaji, the Lady Macbeth figure, is an embodiment of pure evil, her performance influenced by the rituals of Noh-drama, which also influences the representation of the spirit world. Donald Richie notes that Lady Asaji is more evil than Lady Macbeth, "for she too is a kind of witch," and "she never entertains the slightest doubts." Unlike Shakespeare's character, she has a child that is stillborn, and her evil sustains her far longer than that of Lady Macbeth, who seems to develop a conscience. The Macbeth figure does not generate much sympathy. Ruled by greed and ambition, he lacks tragic grandeur as he follows his murderous trajectory until his evil deeds bring about his downfall. He is a criminal. His fate is just. The film is an often haunting and resonant cultural echo of Shakespeare's play. *(J. M. W.)*

Resources: J. Blumenthal, "*Macbeth* into *Throne of Blood*," *Sight & Sound* 34 (1965): 190–195; Donald Richie, *The Films of Akira Kurosawa* (Berkeley: University of California Press, 1970).

THE MADNESS OF GEORGE III (1991)
Alan Bennett

The Madness of King George (1994)

Directed by Nicholas Hytner
Adapted by Alan Bennett

Cast: Nigel Hawthorne (George III), Helen Mirren (Queen Charlotte), Rupert Everett (Prince of Wales), Julian Rhind Tutt (Duke of York), Rupert Graves (Greville), Amanda Donohoe (Lady Pembroke), Charlotte Curley (Amelia), Julian Wadham (Pitt), Ian Holm (Dr. Willis), Jim Carter (Fox), Barry Stanton (Sheridan)
Length: 110 minutes
Rated: R

Nicholas Hytner, associate director of the Royal National Theatre, first directed the National Theatre London production of this play before being asked to direct the film as well. Besides writing the screenplay, Alan Bennett played the role of a member of Parliament in the film, set in 1788, thirty years into the reign of George III (Nigel Hawthorne), who begins to show signs of bizarre behavior, hyperactive and babbling ceaselessly about the loss of his colonies in North America. While doctors attempt to diagnose the king's malady, Prime Minister Pitt (Julian Wadham) attempts to calm the House of Commons with false assurances of the king's good health. The Prince of Wales (Rupert Everett), however, wants his father declared unfit to rule and himself proclaimed regent and does not allow his Queen Mother access to her own husband. So isolated, the king's only sympathetic friend is his new equerry, Captain Greville (Rupert Graves). The only physician able to help the king is Dr. Willis (Ian Holm), who leaves the asylum in Lincolnshire he heads and travels to the court. Dr. Willis' therapy has the king enacting selections of Shakespeare's *King Lear*, which enables the king to recognize parallels between himself and Shakespeare's mad monarch. The therapy works, but as the king begins to improve, Parliament is preparing a bill to have the Prince of Wales declared regent. Shocked into action, the king is able to reassume his dignified demeanor and goes to Westminster to demonstrate that he is fit to rule. A delightful blend of tragedy and farce, the film was highly regarded by critics and earned multiple Academy Award nominations for Best Actor (Hawthorne), Best Supporting Actress (Helen Mirren), and Best Adapted Screenplay and won for Best Art Direction. Helen Mirren's compassionate portrayal of Queen Charlotte earned her the Best Actress award at the Cannes Film Festival of 1995. Parallels to the current royal family's problems and what Queen Elizabeth called the "annus horribilis" were quietly noticed and helped draw attention to this quality adaptation. *(J. M. W.)*

Resources: Brenda Scott Royce, *"The Madness of King George,"* in *Magill's Cinema Annual 1995*, ed. Beth A. Fhaner (Detroit: Gale Research VideoHound Reference, 1996): 372–374; Stephen Schiff, "The Poet of Embarrassment," *New Yorker* (6 September 1993): 92–101.

MAJOR BARBARA (1905)
George Bernard Shaw

Major Barbara (1941)

Directed and produced by Gabriel Pascal

Adapted by George Bernard Shaw

Cast: Wendy Hiller (Major Barbara), Rex Harrison (Adolphus Cusins), Robert Morley (Undershaft), Robert Newton (Bill Walker), Deborah Kerr (Jenny Hill), Marie Lohr (Lady Britomart), Walter Hudd (Stephen Undershaft)

Length: 131 minutes

Shaw's *Major Barbara* (1905) concerns the Undershaft family: Andrew Undershaft, a munitions millionaire intent on preserving tradition by passing his company on to a foundling like himself; Lady Britomart, his estranged wife and formidable foe, equally intent on having son Stephen inherit the company; Stephen, a gentleman and would-be politician; Barbara, a major in the Salvation Army who is in love with Cusins, a professor of Greek; and Sarah, about to marry an innocuous future millionaire. At a meeting in act 1 Undershaft promises to visit Major Barbara's headquarters if she will visit his. When he arrives at the West Ham shelter, Undershaft sees Major Barbara almost convert Bill Walker, a blustering rogue who is searching for his converted girlfriend. Determined to get his daughter out of the Salvation Army, Undershaft shows her that the army can be "bought" when the army general accepts donations from him and Bodger, the liquor millionaire. A disillusioned Barbara leaves the army and goes to visit her father's company, where she sees the munitions factory and the "beautifully situated," "almost smokeless town" where the employees live. Cusins solves the problem of a foundling inheriting the company when he explains that his parents' Australian marriage is not valid in England; and Undershaft offers to give him the company. Cusins' acceptance is endorsed by Barbara, who sees that she can continue her missionary work among the company employees.

Since Shaw adapted his play to the screen, he retains much of the script. For the most part, the changes involve showing the audience what was described in stage dialogue: Cusins' first meeting with Barbara and his joining the army to pursue her; Bill Walker's unsuccessful efforts to regain his girlfriend and to incite her new boyfriend to punch him; the Salvation Army meeting at Albert Hall, where the donations are announced. The most significant change from stage to screen occurs at the end of the film when Bill Walker, the religious skeptic, joins Cusins and Barbara as they march arm in arm through the company town. This religious reconciliation reflects the overall softening of Shaw's satiric look at the church and society. *(T. L. E.)*

Resources: Donald P. Costello, *The Serpent's Eye: Shaw and the Cinema* (Notre Dame, IN: University of Notre Dame Press, 1965); Valerie Pascal, *The Disciple and His Devil: Gabriel Pascal and Bernard Shaw* (New York: McGraw-Hill, 1970).

A MAN FOR ALL SEASONS (1960)
Robert Bolt

A Man for All Seasons (1966)

Directed by Fred Zinnemann

Adapted by Robert Bolt

Cast: Paul Scofield (Sir Thomas More), Wendy Hiller (Lady Alice), Robert Shaw (King Henry VIII), Leo McKern (Thomas Cromwell), Orson Welles (Cardinal Wolsey), Susannah York (Margaret More), John Hurt (Richard Rich), Nigel Davenport (Duke of Norfolk), Vanessa Redgrave (Anne Boleyn)

Length: 120 minutes

The play, written in two acts and published and produced in 1960, was introduced onstage by a character known as "the Common Man," who acted as commentator and stage manager. In the screen version, Zinnemann and Bolt delete the "Common Man" character and thereby dispense with much of the irony and wry humor in his commentary to a modern audience. The setting is sixteenth-century England in the years when Henry VIII (Robert Shaw), in need of an heir and frustrated by the failure of his wife, Catharine of Aragon, to conceive a male child, petitions the pope for a divorce so that he might remarry. When his petition is refused, Henry breaks with the Church of Rome, declaring himself the supreme head of the Church of England. Those who refuse to swear allegiance to the new Church and to the king as its leader are brought to trial for high treason and sentenced to death. The play's protagonist is Sir Thomas More (Paul Scofield), Henry's chancellor and adviser until he retires from his responsibilities to his country home, intent on avoiding the choice between his king and the Roman Catholic Church. His antagonists are Thomas Cromwell (Leo McKern), Henry's closest adviser, who fears More's character and integrity, and Richard Rich (John Hurt), a former student of More's but also a ruthless opportunist willing to sacrifice his benefactor to gain political favor. Surrounded by unprincipled men, More, a lawyer and a canny politician, is, above all, a man of conscience who cannot bring himself to sanction the political and practical expedient of the king's divorce and the establishment of the new church. The king, however, sees all who do not profess ardent support as enemies of the state. There is neither abstention nor neutrality. Although his wife (Wendy Hiller) and daughter (Susannah York) plead with him to do what is necessary to save his life, More is morally incapable of abandoning his principles. "I do no harm," More says before he is condemned, and "I think none harm. And if this be not enough to keep a man alive, in good faith I long not to live." A brief cameo appearance early in the film by the renowned Orson Welles as Cardinal Wolsey is disappointing. The film received six Academy Awards, including Scofield for Best Actor, Zinnemann for Best Director (and Best Picture), Bolt for the script adapted from his play, and Ted Moore for cinematography. *(R. C. K.)*

Resources: Myron Matlaw, *Modern World Drama* (New York: Dutton, 1972); Fred Zinnemann, *An Autobiography* (London: Bloomsbury, 1992).

A Man for All Seasons (1988)

Directed by Charlton Heston

Adapted by Robert Bolt

Cast: Roy Kinnear (the Common Man), Charlton Heston (Sir Thomas More), Vanessa Redgrave (Alice More), Adrienne Thomas (Margaret More), Sir John Gielgud (Cardinal Wolsey), Benjamin Whitrow (Thomas Cromwell), Richard Johnson (Duke of Norfolk), Jonathan Hackett (Richard Rich), John Hudson (William Roper), Nicholas Amer (Signor Chapuys), Martin Chamberlain (King Henry VIII)

Length: 150 minutes

This historical play, set during the reign of King Henry VIII in London, concerns the crisis of faith and of conscience for Sir Thomas More, a devout Roman Catholic who has been a friend and adviser to the king and chancellor after the death of Cardinal Wolsey. The king intends to divorce Catherine of Aragon and marry Anne Boleyn and wants More's support, but More refuses to cooperate. His response is to remain silent on the issue, even if that means giving up his government position, as he does in 1531. More has enemies at court, especially the pragmatist Thomas Cromwell and the opportunist Richard Rich, who will do anything to advance himself. More is imprisoned and is sent to the Tower after he refuses to take the oath mandated by Parliament in 1534 that would force him to acknowledge the supremacy of the English king over all foreign sovereigns, including the pope. In the trial that ensues Rich perjures himself giving false witness against More in order to please Cromwell and in order to be appointed attorney general for Wales. More is convicted of treason and executed in 1535, refusing to compromise his principles to the bitter end. The play had been already adapted by Fred Zinnemann in his Academy Award-winning film of 1960, but the Heston film is more faithful to the play and scrupulously retains Bolts' Common Man chorus, intended to comment on the action throughout. There are outstanding performances here by Vanessa Redgrave as Alice, Benjamin Whitrow as Cromwell, and Richard Johnson as Norfolk, in particular, but the approach is literal and not especially inventive or cinematic. *(J. M. W.)*

Resources: Peter Ackroyd, *The Life of Thomas More* (New York: Doubleday, 1998); Robert Bolt, "Preface," *A Man for All Seasons* (New York: Vintage, 1990).

THE MAN WHO CAME TO DINNER
(1939)
George S. Kaufman and Moss Hart

The Man Who Came to Dinner (1941)

Directed by William Keighley

Adapted by Julius and Philip Epstein from the Kaufman and Hart play

Cast: Monty Woolley (Sheridan Whiteside), Bette Davis (Maggie Cutler), Anne Sheridan (Lorraine Sheldon), Jimmy Durante (Banjo), Billie Burke (Mrs. Stanley), Russell Arms (Richard Stanley), Grant Mitchell (Mr. Stanley), Mary Wickes (Miss Preen), Elisabeth Fraser (June Stanley), Reginald Gardiner (Beverly Carlton)

Length: 112 minutes

This "comedy of bad manners" is an American classic, originally produced at the Music Box Theatre in New York in 1939 and dedicated to Alexander Woollcott, who served as the model for the central character, the pompous New York critic and radio personality Sheridan Whiteside. This New York celebrity, notorious for his biting wit, has visited the home of Mr. and Mrs. Ernest W. Stanley in a small Ohio town. A fall down the icy front steps has temporarily disabled the man, however, and the Stanleys find themselves trapped with an ill-tempered and unwelcome guest, as "portly Sheridan Whiteside, critic, lecturer, wit, radio orator, intimate friend of the great and near great" is stuck in Mesalia, Ohio. To cope with his provincial boredom, the man works out his frustrations on the Stanley family. Monty

Woolley first introduced the role of Sheridan Whiteside to the Broadway stage, and the film preserves a record of his performance, supported by Bette Davis, who played the celebrity's faithful secretary who falls in love with a local newspaperman, and Anne Sheridan as a Hollywood vamp and gold digger. Among the "great and near great" friends who come to visit Whiteside in Ohio is a crazy man named Banjo, played by Jimmy Durante in the film and based on Harpo Marx. The Beverly Carlton role in this theatrical roman à clef was based on playwright Noël Coward. The Stanleys soon discover that Whiteside takes a bit of getting used to, since, like Alexander Wollcott, he is the master of the insult. He even insults Maggie, his friend and secretary: "This aging debutante," he remarks in her presence, "I retain in my employ only because she is the sole support of her two-headed brother." He is even harder on his nurse, played by Mary Wickes in the film and on Broadway. After she admonishes him for eating candy, Whiteside snaps: "My great-aunt Jennifer ate a whole box of candy every day of her life. She lived to be a hundred and two, and when she had been dead three days, she looked better than you do now." After a month of nursing this curmudgeon and suffering this kind of verbal abuse, Miss Preen decides to leave her profession: "I am going to work in a munitions factory," she informs Whiteside. "From now on anything that I can do to help exterminate the human race will fill me with the greatest of pleasure." Though Monty Woolley, an erstwhile professor at Yale, made the Whiteside character a Broadway success (739 performances during the play's initial run), Woollcott himself played the character in Los Angeles and Santa Barbara. His friend Harpo Marx played the role of Banjo at the Bucks County Playhouse, taking his first speaking role in twenty-five years to do so. The Sheridan Whiteside character was also played variously by George S. Kaufman and by Moss Hart themselves in Bucks County. Clifton Webb played the role in Chicago. The play was like a magnet attracting talent. *(J. M. W.)*

Resources: Malcolm Goldstein, *George S. Kaufman: His Life, His Times* (New York: Oxford, 1979); Moss Hart, *Act One: An Autobiography* (New York: Modern Library, 1959).

MARAT/SADE (1964)
Peter Weiss; English version by Geoffrey Skelton; verse adaptation by Adrian Mitchell

---

Marat/Sade (1967)

Directed and adapted by Peter Brook

Cast: The Royal Shakespeare Company with Patrick Magee (Sade), Ian Rich-

ardson (Marat), Glenda Jackson (Charlotte Corday), Susan Williamson (Si-
monne Evrard)

Length: 115 minutes

The full title of the filmed play, almost always shortened, *The Persecution
and Assassination of Jean-Paul Marat as Performed by the Inmates of the
Asylum of Charenton under the Direction of the Marquis de Sade*, provides
a kind of plot summary. In a conceptual mood, Peter Brook turned Weiss'
Artaudian play into a "Theatre of Cruelty" experiment to worldwide acclaim, although Weiss dissociated himself from Brook's production, feeling
that much of his political content was de-emphasized. Brook's production
won awards in both Britain and the United States in 1964 and 1965, respectively. The play creates a fiction that proceeds from the historical fact
that Sade (Patrick Magee) was permitted to stage plays at Charenton during
the confinement of his final years. The play Sade is doing in 1808 concerns
the stabbing in 1793 of Marat (Ian Richardson), the Jacobin leader, by
Charlotte Corday (Glenda Jackson). The play/film brings together two significant figures of the French Revolutionary era fifteen years after the revolution and looks at opposing views of history and human nature. Sade,
the radical individualist, pursues his own pleasurable imagination and experience; Marat is the social activist who embodies the will of the revolution in action. The actors of the Royal Shakespeare Company, playing
inmates of the asylum, perform Sade's play, supposedly in the sanitarium's
bathhouse.

Brook's film was shot in seventeen days, and the director edited the
twenty hours of footage to the two-hour running time. The play, framed
as a play within a play within a play within a movie, includes an audience,
often seen in silhouette, dressed in twentieth-century garb. These fore-
grounded spectators sometimes rise to leave, and the audience for Brook's
film is, of course, another audience behind the filmed one on the screen.
David Watkins, the director of photography, uses his handheld camera
advantageously to achieve mobility within the claustrophobic madhouse.
Sometimes we as viewers look out from the point of view of the bathhouse
denizens at the onscreen audience, all of which gives a sense of participation
to the moviegoer. The adaptation's close-ups achieve a clarity often absent
in the stage production, where the chaos of the insane stage activity sometimes impaired the intelligibility of the text. The hallucinatory world of the
asylum receives more adequate detail on film than onstage with over-
exposed frames, "hot" shots of heavily madeup performers filmed against
stark white tiles, and out-of-focus studies of characters. Each principal is
treated individually by the camera, relative to shots and angles, or edited
differently with respect to rhythm. Sade, for example, is often seen in profile
at the extreme edge of the frame. Marat gets more frontal treatment. Sade

appears to have been shot with a longer lens than anyone else, thereby wiping out the background behind him in order perhaps to suggest his total self-involvement. Less successfully, Brook offers a blur of history in a montage sequence for what is a cleaner tableau onstage as "The Faces of Marat." As John Simon concluded, "All in all, there is something in this film version both for those who have seen the play and those who haven't, which cannot be said of many such undertakings." *(E. T. J.)*

Resources: Edward Trostle Jones, *Following Directions: A Study of Peter Brook* (New York: Peter Lang, 1985); John Simon, *Movies into Film: Film Criticism 1967–70* (New York: Dell, 1971).

MARTY (1953)
Paddy Chayefsky

Marty (1955)

Directed by Delbert Mann

Adapted by Paddy Chayefsky

Cast: Ernest Borgnine (Marty Pilletti), Betsy Blair (Clara Snyder), Esther Minciotti (Mrs. Pilletti), Joe Mantell (Angie)

Length: 91 minutes

Originally written as a television play, Chayefsky's screen adaptation garnered four Academy Awards, including Best Picture of 1955. The story revolves around Marty (Ernest Borgnine), a single man who lives alone with his mother (Esther Minciotti). While Marty is not physically attractive, he is a kindhearted, sensitive person. Marty is desperately lonely and has lost all hope of finding love. As the film opens, Marty is at work at the butcher shop. His last sibling has just been married, and he is being bombarded by cruel questions from his customers about why he is not married. Managing to divert these questions, he arrives at home to face the same question from his mother. Concerned, Mrs. Pilletti is determined that Marty will not remain a bachelor. She encourages him to attend a dance at the Stardust Ballroom, and Marty finally relents and goes to the dance with his pal, Angie. Standing on the sidelines, Marty notices a plain-looking girl, Clara Snyder (Betsy Blair), who has been abandoned by her blind date. His compassion for her overcomes his usual shyness, and he asks her to dance. In reaching out to comfort Clara, Marty finds the love he has been so desperately seeking. As the evening unfolds, the new friendship blossoms into romance, and the couple part with Marty promising to call the next day. Marty's and Clara's love immediately meets with obstacles. The following day, Marty finds unexpected opposition to his new relationship from his friends and, surprisingly, his mother. Succumbing to their pressure, Marty decides not to call Clara. Eventually, Marty's feelings from the previous evening triumph over his doubts, and he calls her. A sensitive and charming love story, *Marty* is a film of unforgettable performances. Rich characters and dialogue make this film a true classic. *(N. I.)*

Resources: Bosley Crowther, "Marty," *New York Times* (12 April 1955): 25; *Variety Film Reviews 1954–1958*, vol. 9 (23 March 1955).

MARVIN'S ROOM (1992)
Scott McPherson

Marvin's Room (1996)

Directed by Jerry Zaks

Adapted by Scott McPherson

Cast: Diane Keaton (Bessie), Meryl Streep (Lee), Leonardo DiCaprio (Hank), Robert De Niro (Dr. Wally), Hume Cronyn (Marvin), Gwen Verdon (Ruth), Dan Hedaya (Bob), Hal Scardino (Charlie)

Length: 98 minutes

Rated: PG-13

Scott McPherson's tragicomedy concerns "the gift of giving love" by being a caretaker to the dying. Bessie (Diane Keaton) is fatigued as a consequence of taking care of her aunt Ruth (Gwen Verdon) and her uncle Marvin (Hume Cronyn) in suburban Florida, but the cause of her fatigue is discovered to be leukemia, and she is advised by her doctor (Robert DeNiro) that her only hope is a bone-marrow transplant from her sister Lee (Meryl Streep), who works as a hairdresser in Ohio while trying to raise her two sons, Charlie (Hal Scardino) and his older brother, Hank (Leonardo DiCaprio), a troubled teen being held in a mental institution after burning down the family home. The two sisters have been estranged, but the real drama involves whether Hank will consent to be tested for the bone-marrow transplant. The dramatic conflict is between Bessie's dignity, compassion, and sense of humor and her sister's angry self-control, which begins to dissipate when she learns to care for someone other than herself. As one reviewer noted, the play seems determined to find humor and love in the face of tragedy. The playwright, who died of complications from AIDS in 1992, wrote: "My lover has AIDS. Our friends have AIDS. And we all take care of each other, the less sick caring for the more sick. At times, an unbelievably harsh fate is transcended by a simple act of love, by caring for one another." Producer Scott Rudin noted the crucial step in adapting the play to the screen is the process of opening up the play, in other words, "releasing the material from the constraints of a stage set." As he explained, "It's hard to open up a play without it seeming arbitrary. You can end up looking as if you took a 10-page scene and split it into three locations." For that reason the film had difficulty transcending its theatrical origins, but it earned Diane Keaton an Academy Award nomination for Best Actress and a Golden Globe nomination for Meryl Streep. *(J. M. W.)*

Resources: Sylviane Gold, "Going the Distance from Stage to Screen," *New York Times* (8 June 1997): Sec. II, 17, 27; Patricia Kowal, *"Marvin's Room," Magill's Cinema Annual 1997*, ed. Beth A. Fhaner (Detroit: Gale/VideoHound Reference, 1998): 347–348.

THE MATCHMAKER

See HELLO, DOLLY!

MEET JOE BLACK

See DEATH TAKES A HOLIDAY

THE MEMBER OF THE WEDDING (1950)
Carson McCullers

The Member of the Wedding (1952)

Directed by Fred Zinnemann

Adapted by Edward Anhalt and Edna Anhalt

Cast: Julie Harris (Frankie Addams), Ethel Waters (Berenice), Brandon de Wilde (John Henry), Arthur Franz (Jarvis), James Edwards (Honey), Dick Moore (Drunken Soldier).

Length: 91 minutes

Carson McCullers' coming-of-age novel, published in 1946, was successfully converted to the stage with the encouragement and help of Tennessee Williams in 1950. The stage adaptation, directed by Harold Clurman and featuring Julie Harris, Ethel Waters, and Brandon de Wilde, was a hit and named Best American Play of 1950 by the New York Drama Critics. Columbia Pictures producer Stanley Kramer commissioned Edward Anhalt and Edna Anhalt to adapt the McCullers play and signed on the principals from the Broadway production. Julie Harris played twelve-year-old Frankie Addams, who fantasizes that her brother and his new bride will want to include her in their honeymoon plans. Brandon de Wilde played John Henry, her seven-year-old cousin, whose illness causes Frankie to reflect upon her own trivial problems as she matures, and Ethel Waters plays the maternal cook, Berenice Sadie Brown, who has problems of her own with her stepbrother, Honey (James Edwards), who is in trouble with the law. Although Zinnemann was able to open up the play (to extend the action beyond the limited stage sets) by filming Frankie's nighttime venture into town, where she encounters a drunken soldier (Dick Moore) and realizes she may be out of her depth, the main setting, as in the play, is Berenice's kitchen, which serves to define Frankie's confinement and frustration. Frankie's mother is dead; her father is preoccupied with his work; her brother Jarvis (Arthur Franz) is in the military and usually away from home; Frankie yearns for a sense of "belonging." That is why she so desperately wants to be a "member" of her brother's wedding. By actually showing the wedding, Zinnemann's film dramatizes Frankie's disappointment in a way the play does not. The film also places more emphasis on Berenice, entrapped within the dominant white society, and her family problems, which are more strongly emphasized in the novel than in the play. Zinnemann would have preferred to adapt the novel, but budget constraints forced him to settle for the play. Though Zinnemann considered the film a "resounding flop" in his *Autobiography* (1992), it was also his personal favorite, and it should be considered a critical success as well as a remarkably faithful film adaptation. *(J. M. W.)*

Resources: Gene D. Phillips, *Exiles in Hollywood: Major European Film Directors in America* (Bethlehem, PA: Lehigh University Press, 1998); Fred Zinnemann, *An Autobiography* (London: Bloomsbury, 1992).

THE MERRY WIVES OF WINDSOR

See HENRY IV, PARTS I & II, HENRY V, RICHARD II, and THE MERRY WIVES OF WINDSOR

A MIDSUMMER NIGHT'S DREAM (1595)
William Shakespeare

A Midsummer Night's Dream (1935)

Directed by Max Reinhardt and William Dieterle

Adapted by Charles Kenyon and Mary McCall

Cast: Ian Hunter (Theseus), Victor Jory (Oberon), Anita Louise (Titania), Mickey Rooney (Puck), Grant Mitchell (Egeus), Verree Teasdale (Hippolyta), Dick Powell (Lysander), Ross Alexander (Demetrius), Olivia de Havilland (Hermia), Jean Muir (Helena), James Cagney (Bottom), Joe E. Brown (Flute), Hugh Herbert (Snout), Frank McHugh (Quince), Dewey Robinson (Snug)

Length: 117 minutes (but originally released at 132 minutes)

Theseus, the Duke of Athens, is about to marry the Amazon Queen Hippolyta after defeating her in battle and has advertised a competition for a wedding masque, which the weaver Bottom and his artisan friends hope to win. Theseus is asked to settle a matrimonial dispute. Egeus demands that his daughter Hermia marry Demetrius, though she loves Lysander, who loves Helena, who loves Demetrius. The young lovers flee Athens into an enchanted forest, ruled by Oberon, King of the Fairies, and his Queen, Titania, who are both involved in a dispute over a changeling boy. Angry with his wife, Oberon has his tricky servant Puck cast a spell over Titania so that she will fall madly in love with the first creature she meets. Meanwhile, Bottom and his friends have gone into the forest to rehearse their play about Pyramus and Thisby, and the mischievous Puck enchants him, giving him the head of an ass. Titania awakes to see this monstrosity and falls immediately in love with him. Puck also enchants the eloped lovers so that their affections are switched. Much confusion results. At the end, all the mortals emerge from the forest liberated, and the lovers are properly aligned. Bottom and crew get to perform their silly masque at court, and all ends happily. In this first major American treatment of Shakespeare, Warner Brothers spared no expense in mounting this fairy extravaganza. Max Reinhardt was brought from Germany to create the theatrical effects, with music, incidentally, from Felix Mendelssohn, and the cast reads liks a Hollywood who's who. Jimmy Cagney was over the top as Bottom, and so was Mickey Rooney as Puck, but Victor Jory's magisterial Oberon nearly steals the show. The emphasis is split between pure enchantment and farcical silliness. Although Shakespeare's design is closely followed, the text is abridged to allow time for the music, the ballet sequences, and the screen spectacle, which is impressive and magical. The film distances the world of Athens from the enchanted wood, as emphasized by gradual visual transitions, while the play attempts to draw the two together, as when one learns in Act II that Oberon has loved Hippolyta and that Titania has loved Theseus. Critic Jack Jorgens considered it "a remarkable interpretive film" that combined several traditions, its shortcomings offset by "sparkling virtues." For over thirty years it set the standard for Shakespeare's most famous comedy. (*J. M. W.*)

Resources: Jack C. Jorgens, *Shakespeare on Film* (Bloomington: Indiana University Press, 1977); Roger Manvell, *Shakespeare and the Film* (New York: Praeger, 1971).

A Midsummer Night's Dream (1999)

Directed and adapted by Michael Hoffman

Cast: Rupert Everett (Oberon), Michelle Pfeiffer (Titania), Stanley Tucci (Puck), David Strathairn (Theseus), Sophie Marceau (Hippolyta), Roger Rees (Peter Quince), Kevin Kline (Nick Bottom), Max Wright (Robin Starveling), Bill Irwin (Tom Snout), Sam Rockwell (Francis Flute), Calista Flockhart (Helena), Anna Friel (Hermia), Christian Bale (Demetrius), Dominic West (Lysander), Bernard Hill (Egeus), John Sessions (Philostrate)

Length: 115 minutes

Rated: PG-13

Michael Hoffman's main credential for making this adaptation is that he directed a production of the play while a Rhodes scholar at Oxford University. The novelty of the film's approach is to set the action at the turn of the twentieth century in northern Italy—Tuscany, circa 1900—at a country villa called "Monte Athena." The women wear fruity hats and bustles; the men wear straw hats and suspenders. A wind-up Victrola blats out the familiar strains of Mendelssohn's incidental music. Nuptials are in progress, but first Theseus and Hippolyta have to preside over a dispute concerning true love. Hermia is under strict instructions from her father to marry Demetrius, but she really loves Lysander. Helena is the odd woman out, and she dotes on Demetrius, who thinks he is in love with Hermia. When Hermia and Lysander elope into the forest, Demetrius follows, and is followed by ever-faithful Helena. An amateur theatre troupe directed by Peter Quince and dominated by that redoubtable ham Nick Bottom also seek refuge in the forest in order to rehearse their play "Pyramus and Thisby," which they hope to present as a wedding masque for Theseus and Hippolyta. All of these mortals come under the influence of Oberon and Titania, king and queen of the fairies, and Oberon's mischievous henchman, Robin Goodfellow, also known as Puck. The young lovers are bewitched by Puck, but there is some confusion about who should be in love with whom, though they all seem equally infatuated and foolish. Oberon sorts it out, finally, as he must do. Oberon also gets his petty revenge against Titania, his queen, with whom he has disputed the fate of a changeling boy, whom he wishes to claim as his own—for whatever purpose. Titania is bewitched and made to fall in love with the first creature she sees, a monstrously transformed Bottom, who has been given the ears of a donkey, but is not apparently embarrassed by this. He gets to sleep with Titania, but once the spell is lifted, cannot fully remember his "dream," which he vaguely recalls was "most strange." Back at "Monte Athena," Bottom and friends perform their absurd play of "Pyramus and Thisby," the rest of the mortals are matched and married, and Stanley Tucci's Puck appears in the guise of a streetsweeper to deliver his epilogue. In keeping with the Italian atmosphere, the film's music is an eclectic mix of Mendelssohn (over the main title) and opera arias from Massenet's *Thais*, Puccini's *La Boheme*, and Verdi's *La Traviata*, but, as David Denby protested, the additional music is rather oppressive. The role of Duke Theseus is cut way back; rather than a duke, he seems merely the manager of some odd resort hotel. Nor is Rupert Everett's Oberon particularly majestic, merely half-naked and a little befuddled. Stanley Tucci's oversized Puck is nicely executed, as is Kevin Kline's Bottom, though the actor seems to have been influenced by Jimmy Cagney's interpretation in the 1935 film version. Even so, Kline's presence stabilizes every scene he is in. Calista Flockhart is surprisingly good as the spunky Helena, as is Anna Friel as the much-abused Hermia. But Shakespeare deserves better than Hoffman is capable of delivering. "It's no fun at all," Joe Morgenstern wrote in *The Wall Street Journal*, "to see talented people trapped in a failed production," and this one "fails on all crucial counts, save visual grace." Although the reviews were disappointing, the film still has its charms. (*J. M. W. and J. C. T.*)

Resources: David Denby, "The Current Cinema," *The New Yorker* (17 May 1999): 96–99; Jack Kroll, "Midsummer Madness," *Newsweek* (24 May 1999): 74; Joe Morgenstern, *The Wall Street Journal* (14 May 1999): W5.

THE MIRACLE WORKER (1959)
William Gibson

The Miracle Worker (1962)

Directed by Arthur Penn
Adapted by William Gibson

Cast: Patty Duke (Helen Keller), Anne Bancroft (Annie Sullivan), Victor Jory (Captain Keller), Inga Swenson (Kate Keller)
Length: 106 minutes

William Gibson's 1959 play, fashioned from a drama he wrote for television a few years before, was based on the true story of the formative years of the deaf and blind Helen Keller, who grew up near the end of the last century in Tuscambia, Alabama. Because of the wild and uncontrollable behavior of their little girl, Helen's parents send for Annie Sullivan, a twenty-year-old teacher who herself is partially blind. Sullivan's disciplinary methods, which seem harsh at first, gradually take effect, and Helen begins to learn rudimentary spelling. But her ability to associate between words and objects comes only after a long struggle between teacher and student. At last, after the famous scene at the water pump, Helen is able to establish a link between herself and the outside world. The motion picture adaptation was in the sure hands of playwright William Gibson and director Arthur Penn (who had directed both the stage and television versions). The basic structure and dialogue were retained, although commentator Jean-Pierre Coursodon complains that Penn's mandate to bring a Broadway hit to the screen stifled his cinematic vision: "Penn did not realize that much of what may have been necessary on stage could be dispensed with on screen" (265). There is no doubting, however, that by means of powerful close-ups Penn was able to enhance visually the intensity and intimacy of the scenes between Sullivan and Keller. Critic Robin Wood attributes this to Penn's "intense awareness of, and emphasis on, physical expression" (Hochman 354). This is entirely in keeping with the thematic concerns of the play, that is, conceptualization through physical contact. For example, when Sullivan first introduces herself to Helen, she slams down her trunk on the step on which Helen is sitting. Helen feels the vibration, and Penn cuts to a close-up of Helen's grasping Sullivan's hands and raising them to her nose to smell. In the climatic sequence at the water pump, close-ups intensify Sullivan's urgency as she taps out the word "W-A-T-E-R" into Helen's palm. The emotional impact of this latter scene is overwhelming. As Coursodon says, "Woman, child, and water pump are a closed-circuit system through which meaning suddenly starts running, as though a switch had been thrown, and Helen's mouthing of the word, combined with the spurting of the water and the convulsive, passionate clasp of hand upon clenched fist is truly an orgasmic moment, dimly linking the scene to ancient myths of the creation as the ejaculation of a god" (265). Both Patty Duke and Anne Bancroft, as Keller and Sullivan, respectively, received Academy Awards for their roles. *(J. C. T.)*

Resources: Jean-Pierre Coursodon, *American Directors*, Vol. 2 (New York: McGraw-Hill, 1983); Stanley Hochman, ed., *American Film Directors* (New York: Frederick Ungar, 1974).

THE MISS FIRECRACKER CONTEST (1979)
Beth Henley

Miss Firecracker (1989)

Directed by Thomas Schlamme

Adapted by Beth Henley

Cast: Holly Hunter (Carnelle Scott), Mary Steenburgen (Elain Rutledge), Tim Robbins (Delmount Williams), Alfre Woodard (Popeye Jackson), Scott Glenn (Mac Sam), Veanne Cox (Tessy Mahoney), Ann Wedgeworth (Miss Blue)

Length: 102 minutes

Rated: PG

Carnelle Scott (Holly Hunter) hopes to reinvent herself and escape from Brookhaven, Mississippi, by entering and winning a beauty contest, but she finds herself competing with a number of girls who have had much more experience. They call Carnelle "Miss Hot Tamale" because she is considered the town slut, a reputation she is trying to lose. Carnelle works in a jewelry store (which becomes a fish factory in the film). Her cousin Elain (Mary Steenburgen), a former beauty and the most famous Miss Firecracker of recent memory, has returned to town to give a speech about "My Life as a Beauty," but she is not too supportive of Carnelle's ambitions. "I don't see why you are so interested in being Miss Firecracker; there's nothing to it," she advises. Elain's younger brother, Delmount (Tim Robbins), has just been released from an insane asylum and intends to sell the family home where Carnelle lives; he wants to go to college to study philosophy. Carnelle qualifies for the final round of the contest, but, unfortunately, she is not a winner. In fact, she comes in last as a finalist, perhaps, as Elain speculates, because of her soiled reputation. The play ends with Carnelle, Delmount, and Popeye, the dressmaker who fashioned Carnelle's costume, watching fireworks. The film sets the action in Yazoo City, Mississippi, and makes the romance between Delmount and Popeye interracial. In the play Popeye was intended to be warm and funny, but as Caryn James noted in her *New York Times* review, the film presents her as "a cruel caricature of a simple-minded person." Holly Hunter gives an energetic performance, but, as James notes, she cannot "give her character the depth Ms. Henley's script" failed to provide. *(J. M. W.)*

Resources: Hal Hinson, " 'Firecracker': Ignited by Hunter, Robbins," *Washington Post* (12 May 1989): D7; Caryn James, "Seeking Redemption in a Beauty Pageant," *New York Times* (28 April 1989): C12.

MISS JULIE (1888)
August Strindberg

Miss Julie (1950)

Directed by Alf Sjöberg

Cast: Anita Bjork (Miss Julie), Ulf Palme (Jean), Inger Borberg (young Julie), Jan Hagerman (young Jean), Marta Dorff (Kristin), Kurt-Olof Sundstrom (Julie's fiancé), Anders Henrikson (the Count)

Length: 87 minutes

The play is a psychological study of a woman who, as a child, was shaped by the influences of a socially ambitious and dominant mother and weak, aristocratic father. After her mother dies, Julie inappropriately flirts with her father's servant, Jean, with tragic results. This classic adaptation retains all the essential elements of Strindberg's *Miss Julie* but also makes some changes and additions while liberating the play from its confined setting, as when the camera moves out of the kitchen and into the drawing room, where the past misfortunes of the principals are recalled. But Sjöberg also takes his camera outdoors so that the libidinous spirit of midsummer's eve can be captured. The attraction of Anita Bjork's Julie toward her servant Jean (Ulf Palme) is therefore all the more plausible as they embrace in the atmosphere of the midsummer madness surrounding them. The film presents characters who are only named in the play, such as Julie's fiancé and especially, her father, the Count. Avoiding the more conventional filmed-theatre approach, this film is a genuine transformation. A great deal of screen time is devoted to the two central flashbacks that show the childhood experiences of Jean and Julie. The first is crucial to understand Jean's social conditioning and his habitual servitude; the second allows the viewer to understand better the way in which Julie herself is a divided character, torn between the common people and the aristocracy as well as between her father and mother. Sjöberg's camera makes fluid and unobtrusive transitions between past and present events, as the past is dramatized. A portrait of Julie's mother in the drawing room is dominant. As Julie begins to speak of her, the camera zooms into the face of the portrait, and when it pulls back to show the whole room, the viewer is taken into her past. Present reality is so dominated by the past that finally one sees characters, past and present, within the confines of the same frame, as time is made relative and psychological. The Count married a "common" woman who is a social reformer and a believer in woman's rights. She becomes master of the house and leads the estate into bankruptcy. When the Count finally asserts his authority, she burns the house down. She arranges for an interest-free loan from her friend and, as her husband does not then realize, her lover, reducing the husband to a position of dependence and servitude. She is cruel and lacks compassion for her daughter. All of this is better prepared for and better conveyed in the film than in the play, so as to understand Julie's fragmented character, her divided loyalties, her confusion about her place in society, and the confusion of gender. From her father she inherits the urge toward suicide, from her mother the resolution necessary to go through with it. Other details are filled in. Julie speculates that her father, when he discovers she has broken into his desk, stolen his money, and eloped with his servant, will "have a stroke and die," represented in a hypothetical flash-forward showing her father noticing the desk, reading her note, and then going into the next room to commit suicide. At the end of the play Julie "goes out resolutely," razor in hand, but readers are spared her suicide. The film shows the Count discovering Julie's slumped body, and the camera then moves to the razor she has dropped on the floor of the dining room, under the steely gaze of her mother's portrait. The play is wonderfully fleshed out for this filmed treatment. (J. M. W.)

Resources: Olof Langercrantz, *August Strindberg* (New York: Farrar, Straus, and Giroux, 1984); Michael Meyer, *Strindberg: A Biography* (New York: Random House, 1985); Neil Sinyard, *Filming Literature: The Art of Screen Adaptation* (London: Croom Helm, 1986).

THE MOON IS BLUE (1951)
F. Hugh Herbert

The Moon Is Blue (1953)

Directed by Otto Preminger

Adapted by F. Hugh Herbert

Cast: William Holden (Donald Gresham), Maggie McNamara (Patty O'Neil), David Niven (David Slater), Dawn Addams (Cynthia Slater)

Length: 99 minutes

A romantic comedy reminiscent of the screwball comedies of the late 1930s, *The Moon Is Blue* was one of the most controversial films released in the 1950s. Adapted by playwright F. Hugh Herbert from his highly successful Broadway play, the sophisticated and bold dialogue shocked the Hollywood censors. Otto Preminger, the director of the movie, refused to accept the suggestions of the Production Code Administration (PCA), and for the first time a major studio released a film for exhibition without a PCA seal of approval. The movie opens with central characters Donald Gresham (William Holden) and Patty O'Neil (Maggie McNamara) meeting on the observation platform of the Empire State Building. Gresham, a young architect, is set upon "picking up" the young woman. Patty, an aspiring actress, is seemingly naive but very outspoken. Stating emphatically that she is a "virgin," she demands to know Gresham's intentions. When he promises "not to take advantage of her," she agrees to accompany him first to his office and later to his apartment. Arriving at the apartment, the two decide that Patty will cook dinner. Gresham leaves for the grocery store, and the intrigue begins. Dropping by the apartment is David Slater (David Niven), the father of Gresham's former fiancée (Dawn Addams). The engagement ended the previous evening, and Slater, who conveniently lives upstairs, is there to confront Gresham about his daughter's spending the night at his apartment. Slater, an aging playboy, is immediately attracted to the "nice girl," Patty, and readily accepts her invitation to stay for dinner. Gresham is less than pleased with this prospect, but Patty will not be deterred. The remainder of the film is a series of hilarious misunderstandings, mishaps, and incidents engineered by Patty's overprotective father, the ex-fiancée, and Slater. The film follows a typical romantic comedy plot, where boy meets girl, boy loses girl, and in the end boy finds girl again. Although the dialogue and subject are mundane by today's standards, in 1953 the film produced significant controversy and a major legal battle, reaching the U.S. Supreme Court. Preminger artfully used the publicity to ensure box office success. *(N. I.)*

Resources: Gregory D. Black, *The Catholic Crusade against the Movies 1940–1975* (Cambridge, U.K.: Cambridge University Press, 1997): 119–128; Bosley Crowther, *"The Moon Is Blue," New York Times* (9 July 1953): 18; *Variety Film Reviews 1949–1953*, vol. 8 (3 June 1953).

MUCH ADO ABOUT NOTHING (1600)
William Shakespeare

Much Ado about Nothing (1993)

Directed and adapted by Kenneth Branagh
Cast: Kenneth Branagh (Benedick), Emma Thompson (Beatrice), Michael

Keaton (Dogberry), Robert Sean Leonard (Claudio), Keanu Reeves (Don John), Denzel Washington (Don Pedro), Richard Briers (Leonato), Kate Beckinsale (Hero), Brian Blessed (Antonio), Richard Clifford (Conrade), Ben Elton (Verges), Gerard Horan (Borachio), Phyllida Law (Ursula), Imelda Staunton (Margaret), Jimmy Yuill (Friar Francis), Patrick Doyle (Balthasar, a singer)

Length: 111 minutes

Rated: PG-13

Shakespeare's *Much Ado* is one of the bard's three "joyous" comedies (along with *As You Like It* and *Twelfth Night*), and Kenneth Branagh has brought it to the screen with the joy completely undiminished. He sacrifices nothing of the artistic integrity of the play in creating a bright and literally sunny film (much of it shot outdoors at the Villa Vignamaggio in Tuscany) that moves at a sprightly pace composed of equal parts of charm, alacrity, and beauty. The play offers two sets of lovers, the young, passionate, and innocent Hero and Claudio (Kate Beckinsale and Robert Sean Leonard) and the somewhat more worldly Beatrice and Benedick (Emma Thompson and Kenneth Branagh). Beatrice is perhaps Shakespeare's most clever heroine, but Benedick proves a nearly worthy adversary in the witty exchanges in which their professed enmity for each other unsuccessfully masks a mutual and growing attraction. Both Benedick and Claudio, soldiers in the service of Don Pedro, have recently returned from a battle in which they have captured Don Pedro's renegade brother, Don John, who is now seemingly reconciled with his former enemies. Claudio falls instantly in love with Hero, the daughter of Leonato (Richard Briers), the governor of Messina. Don John (Keanu Reeves), thirsting for revenge against his brother and his friends, concocts a plot with the help of his servants Borachio (Gerard Horan) and Conrade (Richard Clifford) to convince Claudio and Don Pedro that Hero has been unfaithful with Borachio. On his wedding day, Claudio denounces Hero before the wedding party. Until the matter can be resolved, Hero's proponents circulate the word that she has died from grief. Benedick, supporting Beatrice's loyalty to her cousin Hero, challenges Claudio to a duel. Matters are eventually set right by the comic night watchmen Dogberry (Michael Keaton) and Verges (Ben Elton), whose men have overheard Borachio and Conrade discussing their success and arrested them. Don John is again captured and subdued, Hero is "resurrected," and the play concludes happily with the dual marriages of Hero and Claudio, Beatrice and Benedick. The film is rich in splendid performances, especially Michael Keaton's comic brilliance as Dogberry. Branagh, who also brought *Henry V* and *Hamlet* to the screen, has rivaled Laurence Olivier as the twentieth century's definitive cinematic interpreter of Shakespeare. *(R. C. K.)*

Resources: Harold Bloom, *Shakespeare: The Invention of the Human* (New York: Riverhead, 1998); Oscar J. Campbell and Edward Quinn, eds., *The Reader's En-*

cyclopedia of Shakespeare (New York: Crowell, 1966); Anthony Lane, "Too Much Ado," New Yorker (19 May 1993): 97–99.

MY THREE ANGELS (1953)
Sam Spewack and Bella Spewack, based on
La Cuisine des Anges by Albert Husson

We're No Angels (1955)

Directed by Michael Curtiz

Adapted by Ranald MacDougall

Cast: Humphrey Bogart (Joseph), Aldo Ray (Albert), Peter Ustinov (Jules), Joan Bennett (Amelie Ducotel), Basil Rathbone (Andre Trochard), Leo G. Carroll (Felix Ducotel), John Baer (Paul Trochard), Gloria Talbott (Isabelle Ducotel), Lea Penman (Mme. Parole)

Length: 106 minutes

The Spewacks' play, which appeared in New York 11 March 1953, became a popular film adaptation in 1955. The play takes place in the Ducotels' living room at the back of their general store in a convict colony in Cayenne, French Guiana, at Christmastime. As three murderers on leave from the penal colony repair the roof, Felix Ducotel demonstrates his business ineptitude with Mme. Parole, who buys on credit. Amelie enters and starts to read a letter from her friend Suzanne as the convicts descend the ladder and watch her. When she faints at Suzanne's announcement of her engagement to Paul, the convicts read Suzanne's letter, revive Amelie and reassure her about Paul's love, and set about saving the Ducotels from romantic and financial ruin at the hands of Henri Trochard (Felix's cousin) and Paul, who appear at the Ducotel home after the convicts prepare a splendid Christmas dinner and decorate the Christmas tree, which has three small angels at its top. Although forger Joseph attempts to "revise" Felix's accounts to make him look like the honest man he is, Henri gets the "undoctored" books, warns Amelie to leave Paul alone, and goes to bed. The convicts arrange a meeting between Amelie and Paul; and when Henri interferes, they release Adolphe, their pet viper, into Henri's room. When Mme. Parole arrives to criticize Felix's managerial ability, the convicts frame her for Henri's murder and let her go only after she pays off her account. Paul, however, who has become like his uncle, suspects the will that Joseph forged is a fake and would arrest all of them, but he, too, is bitten by the handy Adolphe. Since Felix now will inherit Henri's money, the financial problem is solved, and when a young, unmarried ship's officer, whom the convicts see as Amelie's "future," enters the store, the romantic problem is resolved. The film adaptation changes the location to Devil's Island, provides a sequence establishing the convicts as escaped prisoners who offer to repair the roof, alters some names (Henri becomes Andre), omits the framing of Mme. Parole, and has the avaricious Andre and Paul die of Adolphe's bites when they put their hands where they don't belong: Andre claims that Adolphe's box is his and dies when he opens the box, and Paul finds Adolphe when he searches his dead uncle's pockets. Although the convicts have new clothes and a means of escape at the end of the film, they return to prison, where they will find a "better class of people." Curtiz opens up the film by including harbor shots, but the most effective cinematic touch is filming the charming Ducotels from the roof, where we share the convicts' perspective and understand their otherwise miraculous transformation into angels who sing "three angels came that night." This is one instance where the film is a decided improvement over the play. *(T. L. E.)*

Resources: Roy Kinnard and R. J. Vitone, *The American Films of Michael Curtiz* (Metuchen, NJ: Scarecrow Press, 1986); Judith Mayne, *Private Novels, Public Films* (Athens: University of Georgia Press, 1988).

We're No Angels (1989)

Directed by Neil Jordan

Adapted by David Mamet

Cast: Robert De Niro (Ned), Sean Penn (Jim), Demi Moore (Molly), James Russo (Bobby), Jessica Jickels (Rosie)

Length: 106 minutes

Rated: PG-13

Like the 1955 *We're No Angels*, Jordan's adaptation is loosely based on the Spewacks' *My Three Angels*, which appeared in New York in 1953. The film, however, owes more to the earlier film than to the play (the plot summary of which appears in the 1955 entry) in that the "angels" are escaped convicts intent on escaping, and at the end of the film one rejects freedom. Unlike the play and the earlier film, Jordan's film features convicts who become angels by chance rather than design. After Bobby (James Russo), a psychotic convict and the third angel(?), forces them to join him in a murderous prison break, Ned (Robert De Niro) and Jim (Sean Penn) attempt to cross the border into Canada and freedom. At the poverty-stricken border town (the film is set in 1935), they are mistaken for the scholar-priests expected at the monastery. Despite their limited intelligence and their biblical illiteracy, they manage to maintain their priestly roles:

Jim even preaches a comic, but touching, sermon at the Feast of Our Lady of Sorrows procession that crosses the bridge into Canada. Ned is also in the procession, which consists of priests shepherding disabled children to a shrine where they may be healed. His disabled charge is Rosie (Jessica Jickels), the deaf-and-mute daughter of Molly (Demi Moore), a prostitute who mocks Ned and the church for not answering her prayers. Also in the procession is Bobby, who, after being recaptured by the police, is freed by Ned, who doesn't want Bobby to reveal his and Ned's real identity. When the police spot Bobby, a gunfight ensues, Bobby takes Rosie hostage, and then the statue of the weeping Madonna and Rosie fall into the river below. Ned dives in to save Rosie and is "miraculously" helped by the hand of the statue. At the end of the film, Ned and Jim cross the bridge to Canada, but Jim, who has grown increasingly religious, returns to the monastery. Meanwhile, Molly and Rosie, who miraculously can now speak and hear, perhaps because of angelic or divine intervention, join Ned, who dissuades the now-religious Molly from taking holy orders and leads her and Rosie into Canada. The film, which was written by Mamet as a "buddy film" for friends Penn and De Niro, is one of the loosest adaptations in film history. However, it blends cynicism (the Madonna "weeps" because of a leaky church roof) with sentiment (Rosie's cure, the Madonna's helping hand) and farce (the priestly ineptitude of Ned and Jim) to produce a somewhat incongruous, but thoroughly enjoyable, film. *(T. L. E.)*

Resources: Gay Brewer, *David Mamet and Film* (Jefferson, NC: McFarland, 1993); Leslie Kane, ed., *David Mamet: A Casebook* (New York: Garland, 1992).

NEVER TOO LATE (1962)
Sumner Arthur Long

Never Too Late (1965)

Directed by Bud Yorkin

Adapted by Sumner Arthur Long

Cast: Paul Ford (Harry Lambert), Maureen O'Sullivan (Edith Lambert), Connie Stevens (Kate Clinton), Jim Hutton (Charlie Clinton), Jane Wyatt (Grace Kimbrough), Henry Jones (Dr. James Kimbrough), Lloyd Nolan (Mayor Crane)

Length: 105 minutes

Not rated

Never Too Late, directed by George Abbott, was first presented at the Playhouse, New York, on 27 November 1962. After a hugely successful run on Broadway, *Never Too Late* was immediately transferred to film, with its two major performances by Paul Ford and Maureen O'Sullivan being preserved for future generations to enjoy. Both Ford and director George Abbott were nominated for Tony awards in 1963 for their work. Two names missing from the 1963 Tony nominations were Jason Robards (Actor) and Fred Coe (Director) for *A Thousand Clowns*. This is an interesting comparison because both *Clowns* and *Never Too Late* were on the

Broadway stage during the 1962 season, and both plays transferred to film in 1965. The film version of *Never Too Late* seems to feel much less dated than the film version of *Clowns*, and part of this success might be due to the addition of color for *Never Too Late* and especially the performances of Ford and O'Sullivan. Aside from his role as Horace Vandergelder in *The Matchmaker*, the role of Harry Lambert is the one for which Paul Ford is probably most recognized. Harry Lambert owns the largest lumberyard in Calverton, Massachusetts, is in his early sixties, and, as we discover early in the film, his wife, Edith, who is in her early fifties, is pregnant. The first six minutes of the film establish Harry's working relationship with his son-in-law Charlie at the lumberyard, and then the film switches back into the primary script format of the play. Complications arise from Edith's enjoyment of the fact that she and Harry are bringing a new life into the world, while Harry resorts to buying dark glasses so people hopefully won't recognize him on the street and make fun of him with statements like "There must be life in the ole boy yet!" Further tensions arise when daughter Kate (Connie Stevens) has been forced to take over all of the household chores to give her mother a rest and decides that it would be more to her advantage to get pregnant herself rather than become a slave to chores. Major differences between the stage and film versions of *Never Too Late* include the fact that the play version covers only one week, while the film spans three seasons, so that by the end of the film Edith is quite visually pregnant. The stage version clues the audience in on the fact that Edith pretty much knows what's going on with her body even before she discusses it with the doctor, while the film has Edith leaving Dr. Kimbrough's office in total shock and disbelief. While the stage version of *Never Too Late* might not be produced as often as it once was, the film still holds up nicely and is worth the effort to seek out if for no other reason than the performances of Ford and O'Sullivan. *(J. D.)*

Resources: Sumner Arthur Long, *Never Too Late* (New York: Samuel French, 1963); Isabelle Stevenson, *The Tony Award* (New York: Crown, 1984).

'NIGHT, MOTHER (1982)
Marsha Norman

'night, Mother (1986)

Directed by Tom Moore

Adapted by Marsha Norman

Cast: Sissy Spacek (Jessie Cates), Anne Bancroft (Thelma Cates), Ed Berke (Dawson Cates), Carol Robbins (Loretta Cates), Sari Walker (Agnes Fletcher)

Length: 96 minutes

Rated: PG-13

'night, Mother had its first reading in 1981 and appeared in New York in 1983 after first being staged in Cambridge, Massachusetts, in 1982. Norman's play has two characters (Jessie Cates and her mother, Thelma Cates), one set (the interior of a house with Jessie's bedroom door being the focal point), and no intermission. Beginning at 8:15 P.M., the play uses synchronous time—that is, play time is real time, giving the omnipresent clocks almost a role in the play. Bent on suicide, which she eventually commits behind her locked bedroom door, Jessie prepares for her death, sets the house in order, disposes of her possessions, and tells her mother what to do after she shoots herself. Although her mother tries to dissuade her, Jessie does not change her mind. She has epilepsy, a broken marriage, a delinquent son, and no future. Since her play stresses Jessie's entrapment in the closed world of the house, Norman's film script stays close to the play. At the beginning of the film outside shots close in on the house, and at the end the process is reversed. Once the audience enters Jessie's world, the only outside scenes are those shot through the blinds on the window. The shot including the arrival of Dawson, Jessie's brother, and his family is especially significant, for the audience only partially sees the family, and their words are indistinguishable. Jessie's isolation and estrangement from her family are thereby established. As the film proceeds, close-ups of photographs of Jessie's father and the pipe-cleaner men he fashioned for her help explain her attachment to him and the reason Thelma was jealous of their close relationship. In fact, the close-ups of both women enable the audience to empathize with them and share their pain, as they slowly begin to reveal long-suppressed emotions. *(T. L. E.)*

Resource: Linda Ginter, ed., *Marsha Norman: A Casebook* (New York: Garland, 1996).

THE NIGHT OF THE IGUANA (1961)
Tennessee Williams

The Night of the Iguana (1964)

Directed by John Huston

Adapted by Anthony Veiller and John Huston

Cast: Richard Burton (Rev. T. Z. Shannon), Ava Gardner (Maxine), Deborah Kerr (Hannah Jelkes), Sue Lyon (Charlotte), Grayson Hall (Judith Fellowes), Cyril Delevanti (Nonno)
Length: 118 minutes

Despite a mediocre, pre-Broadway tour, Williams' *Night of the Iguana* was well received in New York; and John Huston's subsequent film adaptation was also a box office hit. The story concerns Shannon, a suspended priest who works as a guide for Blake's Tours in Mexico. His weakness for young women has caused his suspension and threatens his current job. In desperation he takes his Bible College women tourists to a hotel operated by Fred, who has died since Shannon's last visit, and Maxine, Fred's wife. Like the tied-up iguana in the play, Shannon is at the end of his rope. Within the stifling confines of Maxine's inn, Shannon must reconcile his spiritual and physical sides and learn to endure, "to live beyond despair and still live." His "salvation" comes from Hannah Jelkes, a sketcher of portraits, who is traveling with her grandfather, Nonno, a poet who completes his last poem before he dies. In the film adaptation Huston retains much of the claustrophobic atmosphere of the play. The only notable "outside" scene in the film occurs before the opening credits and depicts Shannon in the pulpit. His sermon degenerates into an attack on his parishioners, who know about his sexual encounter with a young woman. This scene explains his rejection of Charlotte, a nubile minor intent on seducing him. Because of the censors, Charlotte is unsuccessful in the film, and the relationship is essentially comic. Because Huston is more upbeat than Williams, there is no sex between the two. Though she is mean-spirited and strident, Miss Fellowes, a middle-aged latent lesbian, also does not pose the threat she does in the play. In addition, Huston eliminated the obnoxious Nazi tourists staying at the inn. At the end of the film, when Shannon, who has been trussed up because he attempted suicide, and the iguana are cut loose, Shannon has learned about the tolerance and self-acceptance he had earlier preached about. He is ready to accept Maxine's proposition about staying; and when he expresses perfunctory doubts, Maxine tells him, "I'll always get you back up." Aside from one lengthy, if necessary, exchange between Hannah and Shannon, Huston has made a truly cinematic film of Williams' play. *(T. L. E.)*

Resources: Gene Phillips, *The Films of Tennessee Williams* (East Brunswick, NJ: Associated University Presses, 1980); Maurice Yacowar, *Tennessee Williams and Film* (New York: Frederick Ungar, 1977).

NOISES OFF (1982)
Michael Frayn

Noises Off (1992)

Directed by Peter Bogdanovich

Adapted by Marty Kaplan

Cast: Michael Caine (Lloyd Fellowes), Carol Burnett (Dotty Otley/Mrs. Clackett), Christopher Reeve (Frederick Dallas/Philip Brent), Marilu Henner (Belinda Blair/Flavia Brent), John Ritter (Garry Lejeune/Roger Tramplemain), Nicolette Sheridan (Brooke Ashton/Vicky), Julie Hagerty (Poppy Taylor), Mark Linn-Baker (Tim Allgood), Denholm Elliott (Selsdon Mowbray/Burglar)

Length: 104 minutes

Rated: PG-13

Michael Frayn's highly successful 1982 comedy *Noises Off* has made an entertaining transition to screen in Peter Bogdanovich's 1992 release of the same name. This English farce is a play within a play, as we see the actors rehearse and perform in a touring production of a show called *Nothing On*. The play begins with the late-night final dress rehearsal, as a frazzled director attempts to coax a performance from an exhausted cast and crew. After being on the road for several weeks, things have begun to disintegrate at an alarming rate. The personal lives of the cast begin to have a decidedly negative impact on the performance, as lines are flubbed, and cues are missed. In the final act, some three months into the tour, the play spirals completely out of control as "behind-the-scenes" conflicts between cast and crew members spill over into the onstage action. All sense of a professional attitude is abandoned as the cast literally hangs from the curtain in an attempt to end the scene and salvage whatever dignity remains. Marty Kaplan's script, while Americanizing some references, keeps the dialogue and action intact, and Bogdanovich's direction keeps the pace fast and sharp, taking full advantage of the stage sets. As Armond White points out, "*Noises Off* was an ode to the theatre (and to valiant, resilient actors) made by a cineaste appreciative of the theatrical essence (human labor) at the heart of the cinema he loves" (62). The only real deviation between the play and film is Michael Caine's voice-over (as the director) leading up to the Broadway premiere. The final scene in the film, depicting a successful Broadway performance, does not appear in the original play and seems curiously out of place. Certainly, nothing in the play or the film up to this point has given us any indication that the performance will be anything but a failure. One critic who took exception to the film's treatment of the play is John Baxter, who states that although the film "has moments that recall Bogdanovich's earlier success with fast-paced farce (the delightful *What's Up Doc?*) . . . the film's only virtues derive from Frayn's play, whose commercial productions are far superior to this screen version" (82). This criticism aside, the film's cast, led by Caine and Carol Burnett, is enthusiastic and engaging. The film, as directed by Bogdanovich, succeeds in bringing this entertaining stage farce to the screen. *(M. G.)*

Resources: John Baxter, "Peter Bogdanovich," in *International Dictionary of Film and Filmmakers*, Vol. 2: *Directors*, Laurie Collier Hillstrom, ed. (Detroit: St. James Press, 1997): 80–82; Armond White, "Directed by Peter Bogdanovich," *Film Comment* 29.2 (March–April 1993): 61–64.

NUTS (1980)
Tom Topor

Nuts (1987)

Directed by Martin Ritt

Adapted by Tom Topor, Darryl Ponicsan, and Alvin Sargent

Cast: Barbra Streisand (Claudia Draper), Richard Dreyfuss (Aaron Levinsky), Maureen Stapleton (Rose Kirk), Karl Malden (Arthur Kirk), Eli Wallach (Dr. Herbert A. Morrison), Robert Webber (Francis MacMillan), James Whitmore (Judge Stanley Murdoch), Leslie Nielsen (Allen Green), William Prince (Clarence Middleton)

Length: 118 minutes

Rated: R

In this courtroom drama, high-society hooker Claudia Faith Draper (Streisand) is accused of murdering a client, Allen Green (Leslie Nielsen). Her parents have arranged for a high-profile lawyer to defend her by having her declared mentally incompetent and confined to psychiatric care, but Claudia rebels and punches him out at the hearing, breaking his nose. He therefore refuses to represent her, and the judge appoints public defender Levinsky (Richard Dreyfuss) to defend her. Claudia is at first hostile and uncooperative, especially after Levinsky goes to her apartment to bring her a sedate black dress and undergarments to wear in court. She feels her privacy has been violated. The film uses flashbacks to define her character, to her childhood when her stepfather molested her in her bathroom, which parallels and anticipates her encounter with the man she killed, clearly in self-defense. In the film Karl Malden plays her father (Arthur Kirk) as a more smooth and superficially civilized character than one would expect from the play, where he seems both crude and transparent, and his verbal breakdown while being cross-examined is not so complete in the film as in the play. Although Arthur Kirk is allowed more dignity in the film, he is still a perverse child-molester. The name of the self-defensive psychiatrist is changed to Dr. Herbert Morrison (Eli Wallach), but the essential character is left intact. Rose Kirk, the mother who pretended not to know that her second husband was molesting her daughter, no doubt for fear of losing him, is sympathetically played by Maureen Stapleton. In the play the hearing room is on the seventh-floor psychiatric wing of Bellevue Hospital. The film utilizes a more conventional courtroom setting and liberates the play from its limiting sets. In the film, for example, Dr. Morrison has Claudia sedated before she takes the stand, and when she returns to court, she is wearing her robe and pajamas, as in the play, but after the judge declares her competent, she waltzes out of the courtroom in her robe and pajamas into the streets of New York. Though clearly a Streisand vehicle, the play is well cast, well acted, and well directed. *(J. M. W.)*

Resources: David Ansen, "Down and Out in the Psycho Ward," *Newsweek* (23 November 1987): 83; Janet Maslin, "Streisand in 'Nuts,'" *New York Times* (20 November 1987): C17.

THE ODD COUPLE (1965)
Neil Simon

The Odd Couple (1968)

Directed by Gene Saks

Adapted by Neil Simon

Cast: Jack Lemmon (Felix Ungar), Walter Matthau (Oscar Madison), John Fiedler (Vinnie), Herbert Edelman (Murray), Monica Evans (Cecily), Carole Shelley (Gwendolyn)

Length: 116 minutes

Rated: G

The Odd Couple first appeared on Broadway in 1965 and was filmed three years later with Jack Lemmon and Walter Matthau costarring following their successful teaming in Billy Wilder's *The Fortune Cookie* (1966). Neil Simon originally envisaged it as "a black comedy" and wished to move beyond the simple comedy confines of *Come Blow Your Horn* and *Barefoot in the Park*. The entire play is set in Oscar Madison's Riverside Drive apartment over a period of nearly three weeks. Felix Ungar arrives late for his regular poker game at Oscar's, following his marital separation. Also divorced from his wife, Oscar allows the fastidious, hypochondriac Felix to move into his sloppy apartment. Two weeks later, to Oscar's chagrin

Felix has transformed the apartment into a model of domestic cleanliness. A few nights later Oscar arranges a double date with two English divorcées, the Pigeon sisters. Oscar arrives late, causing Felix to ruin his carefully prepared meal. Felix spoils the evening by delivering a morose monologue about his separation. He also refuses to continue the evening at the girls' apartment. The next evening Oscar tells Felix to move out. During the next card-game, Felix returns with the Pigeon sisters, who have invited him to share their apartment. The two men part amicably, calling each other by the names of their respective spouses. In adapting the play to film Simon retained the comic dialogue, while occasionally opening up the play. The credit sequence shows a disconsolate Felix walking around New York, moving into a seedy hotel, unsuccessfully failing to commit suicide by injuring his back, cricking his neck at a go-go joint, then going to Oscar's Riverside apartment. Other outside venues include a restaurant and a baseball game. Like the play, the film depicts both men's faults: Felix is anal-obsessive, narcissistic, and hypochondriac, while Oscar not only owes his ex-wife and poker players money but is equally selfish in not caring for the welfare of others. In both play and film each man thinks he is not as bad as the other, but they are both flawed, a point emphasized in the final lines where they call each other by the names of their supposedly erring spouses. Since both men learned nothing from the failure of their marriages, it was obvious that their new relationship would fail. They mirror each other. The play could also apply to women, an idea anticipated by the final credit sequence, which confuses and then corrects the names of the Pigeon sisters. In 1986 Simon rewrote his play as a female version costarring Rita Moreno and Sally Struthers, directed by Gene Saks. *(T. W.)*

Resources: Robert K. Johnston, *Neil Simon* (Boston: Twayne, 1983); Edythe M. McGovern, *Neil Simon: A Critical Study* (New York: Frederick Ungar, 1979).

OEDIPUS REX (C. 429 B.C.)
Sophocles

Oedipus Rex (1967)

Directed and adapted by Pier Paolo Pasolini

Cast: Franco Citti (Oedipus/Laius), Silvana Mangano (Jocasta), Alida Valli (Merope), Carmelo Bene (Creon), Julian Beck (Tiresias), Ninetto Davoli (young boy)

Length: 110 minutes

As originally staged, *Oedipus Rex* is set outside the royal house of Thebes. The play unfolds in chronological order. It begins many years after Oedipus has solved the riddle of the Sphinx and ascended the throne of Thebes by marrying Queen Jocasta, whose husband, Laius, has mysteriously disappeared. A plague has broken out in the city, and a procession of priests beg Oedipus to free them from this disaster as he once liberated them from the Sphinx. Gradually, Oedipus learns that he has caused the plague by unwittingly murdering his father and marrying his mother. After Jocasta commits suicide, Oedipus blinds himself and departs from Thebes to live the life of a beggar. Pasolini changes the order of the play in several significant ways. He opens with a prologue set in nineteenth-century Italy. The scene then changes to Morocco's desert landscape, where a servant takes baby Oedipus out to die. Pasolini's adaptation then chronologically depicts the story of Oedipus, showing his discovery by a Corinthian shepherd, his adoption by the childless King and Queen of Corinth, his pilgrimage to Delphi, and the events leading to the horrendous discovery of his past. The director emphasizes the visual nature of the desert landscape and Moorish architecture to reinforce the Freudian aspects of the Oedipus myth employed in the prologue. He also casts two major proponents of contemporary avant-garde theatre to illustrate the different mode of theatrical presentation operating in his adaptation. Noted film and theatre director Carmelo Bene appears as Creon, while New York director of the Living Theater, Julian Beck, plays Tiresias. Furthermore, Pasolini casts his favorite young actor, Ninetto Davoli, as the young boy who will accompany Oedipus throughout his travels, rather than his daughter Antigone in *Oedipus at Colonus*. After Oedipus leaves Thebes, the epilogue shows him in twentieth-century Rome playing a flute that the young boy has given him in Thebes. This instrument was earlier seen played by Tiresias and identifies the hero as both outcast and prophet. Although sightless in the climatic Thebes scenes, Oedipus appears with his eyes unmarred, but he is still blind. The epilogue shows Oedipus playing on the steps of one of Rome's most frequented architectural tourist spots, a factory representing industrialism, and finally, the location seen in the prologue. Eventually, Oedipus and the young boy reach a field, also seen in the earlier shots of the film, representing the mother earth to which he will soon return. *(T. W.)*

Resources: Pier Paolo Pasolini, *Heretical Empiricism*, ed. Louise K. Barnett (Bloomington: Indiana University Press, 1988); Oswald Stack, ed., *Pasolini on Pasolini: Interviews with Oswald Stack* (Bloomington: Indiana University Press, 1969).

OLEANNA (1992)
David Mamet

Oleanna (1995)

Directed and adapted by David Mamet

Cast: William H. Macy (John), Debra Eisenstadt (Carol)

Length: 90 minutes

Rated: R

Mamet's original play used two epigraphs absent in the film version. The first derived from Samuel Butler's *The Way of All Flesh,* dealing with the negative effects of an environment on impressionable young people, while the other came from a Pete Seeger folk song describing the failed Norwegian American nineteenth-century utopian colony Oleanna. Mamet sees academe as contaminated by disputes involving language and power, themes in his other plays. *Oleanna* is a nightmare version of Michel Foucault's power-knowledge battles, which contaminate both protagonists. Mamet, who directed the play 1 May 1992 in Cambridge, Massachusetts, opens up the theatrical text, which occurs entirely in John's office, by including adjoining rooms, corridors, and intermission scenes showing John in his new home and in a lonely hotel room. He also uses the camera to track the movements of both characters or to underline the key character in a particular scene, such as John at the opening of act 1 and Carol in act 2. In contrast to Pinter's British production, Mamet uses Jane Greenwood's costume design to emphasize the symbiotic duality existing between both protagonists in what is little more than a power struggle. John and Carol wear costumes that identify both protagonists: forty-something college professor John and twenty-something student Carol wear light olive green costumes. In the opening act Carol's combat jacket is the same color as John's casual shirt. In act 2, John and Carol both wear identically colored suits as their linguistic combat increasingly resembles a battle-zone version of Michel Foucault's power-knowledge conflict. John's book cover has a blood-red apple with revealingly ironic Garden of Eden and combat overtones. When John reaches into his desk drawer in act 3, a close-up reveals he has kept the paper dart he originally showed to Carol in act 1, thus suggesting a sadomasochistic relationship. Mamet's musical innovations include variations on the college refrain that begins the film: as the film progresses, the voice of the male singer is replaced by a female voice—this emphasizes the power struggle between the sexes. Like any classical Hollywood movie,

Oleanna evokes the cardinal rule of the beginning evoking the climax. The film opens with a long shot of a college and returns to that initial image with one significant difference. One male college student throws a football to another, thus highlighting Mamet's dark vision of academe as being just another debased version of that crippling American "House of Games" seen in other plays such as *American Buffalo* and *Glengarry Glen Ross*. *(T. W.)*

Resources: Verna Foster, "Sex, Power, and Pedagogy in Mamet's *Oleanna* and Ionesco's *The Lesson*," *American Drama* 5.1 (1995): 36–50; Christine MacLeod, "The Politics of Gender, Language and Hierarchy in Mamet's *Oleanna*," *Journal of American Studies* 29 (1995): 199–213.

ON A CLEAR DAY YOU CAN SEE FOREVER (1965)
Alan Jay Lerner; music by Burton Lane; lyrics and book by Alan Jay Lerner

On a Clear Day You Can See Forever (1970)

Directed by Vincente Minnelli

Adapted by Alan Jay Lerner

Cast: Barbra Streisand (Daisy Gamble), Yves Montand (Marc Chabot), Larry Blyden (Warren), Jack Nicholson (Tad), Bob Newhart (Dr. Mason Hume), Simon Oakland (Dr. Conrad Fuller)

Length: 129 minutes

Rated: G

This Alan Jay Lerner 1970 musical was considerably rewritten from the original Broadway production as a vehicle (and fashion show) for Barbra Streisand. The musical tells the story of a neurotic young girl named Daisy Gamble (Streisand), who engages the help of a psychiatric doctor/lecturer at a university, Marc Chabot (Yves Montand). Daisy has a problem. She is about to be married to a real stuffed shirt named Warren (Larry Blyden), who is concerned that she may not fit in with the Establishment because she is a five-pack-a-day smoker (curious, for a singer). The doctor discovers that Daisy has supernatural powers that allow her to make plants grow ("Hurry, It's Lovely Up Here"), give her extrasensory perception, and, most curious of all, when hypnotized, send her off into a past-life regression. Daisy soon begins to fall for the Doc ("Why I Can't Sleep," where Streisand sings a clever duet with herself), who, in turn, starts to fall for her previous incarnation (the haunting "Melinda," sung by Montand). Daisy finds out Marc is not in love with her (Daisy), but another her (Melinda) in Streisand's showstopping song "What Did I Have?" Marc tries to beckon her back through telepathy in a cut-and-paste version of "Come Back to Me" that has everyone from old women to dogs dubbed to sound like Montand. When she finally arrives, Montand sings the title song and helps Daisy understand that she is unique and special in her own right ("On a Clear Day"). The film effectively captures the past-life dream sequences, a device often used in musical theatre. Missing from the Broadway score are any songs that could not be reassigned to the film's two stars. The period costumes are beautifully designed by Cecil Beaton. Also of note is Nelson Riddle's orchestration. The curious addition of a young Jack Nicholson as Daisy's adopted brother Tad, a rival for her affections, seems superfluous to the plot; Nicholson's talent is wasted. The film neglects the stage subplot about a rich "Greek tycoon" who wants to finance the Doctor's research about past life so he can find a way to leave all his money to himself. The film garnered mixed reviews but has since become a cult classic for Streisand addicts. *(J. S.)*

Resources: Kurt Ganzl, *The Encyclopedia of Musical Theatre* (New York: Schirmer, 1994); Stanley Green, *Hollywood Musicals Year by Year* (New York: Hal Leonard, 1990).

ON GOLDEN POND (1979)
Ernest Thompson

On Golden Pond (1981)

Directed by Mark Rydell

Adapted by Ernest Thompson

Cast: Katharine Hepburn (Ethel Thayer), Henry Fonda (Norman Thayer, Jr.), Jane Fonda (Chelsea Thayer Wayne), Doug McKeon (Billy Ray), Dabney Coleman (Bill Ray), William Lanteau (Charlie Martin), Chris Rydell (Sumner Todd)

Length: 109 minutes

Rated: PG

In his Broadway play written in 1979, Ernest Thompson intended to portray "lakeside visitors who spend their summers, year after year, in New England. Life along the lake changes, but they remain the same, even while they're taken over by events." Norman Thayer is seventy-nine years old, as described by Thompson, and "flirting with senility, but he knows it and he plays it to the hilt," when the play opens "on Golden Pond, in the state of Maine." The first scene establishes the character of Norman and his patient, energetic wife, Ethel, sixty-nine years old, and married for forty-six years. Their forty-two-year-old daughter Chelsea arrives for a visit with her boyfriend, a dentist, and his son Billy toward the end of act 1 to celebrate Norman's birthday in July. Norman gets cantankerous with the dentist, but he enjoys the company of thirteen-year-old Billy. The action runs from June to mid-September. As they pack to leave, Norman has an attack of angina. Though Norman attempts to make light of his problem to Ethel, this could be their last summer vacation.

The play is a sentimental vehicle concerning aging, married love, and reconciliation. The film exploits those sentimental tendencies by adding movie nostalgia, with Henry Fonda and Katharine Hepburn working together for the first time ever onscreen. Family nostalgia is further enhanced by casting Jane Fonda as Chelsea, the daughter who never got along well with her father, since Fonda had alienated herself from her father during the Vietnam era. In fact, Jane Fonda, the driving force behind the production, purchased the rights to the play with the intention of costarring with her father. Filmed on a lake in Vermont, the adaptation opens up the play so the camera can follow Norman and Billy on their fishing expeditions, but the structure of the drama is tightened so as to sharpen the focus on Norman, Ethel, and Chelsea. There is nothing in the film to distract attention from the ultimate reconciliation between Chelsea and her father. As a young man, Norman was a diver on his college team, and young Chelsea had disappointed him because she would never attempt a back flip. In the film she swims to the float and executes her back flip to please her father. When she and her stepson Billy leave Golden Pond, Norman presents her with his college diving medal and Billy with a casting rod to complete the reconciliation motif. Since Norman has already given Billy the fishing rod, the film removes the later telephone conversation with Chelsea and Billy in California. It leaves a strong impression that because of Chelsea's reformation and the gift of a grandson in Billy, Norman has more of a reason to go on living. Henry Fonda, who died in August 1982, won an Academy Award for his portrayal of Norman. Thompson also won an Oscar for his adapted screenplay. Though some of the details are changed, the spirit of the play is wonderfully maintained. *(J. M. W.)*

Resources: Vincent Canby, "Henry Fonda's 'Effortless' Art," *New York Times* (22 August 1982): H1, H17; Fred Lawrence Guiles, *Jane Fonda: The Actress in Her Time* (Garden City, NY: Doubleday, 1982).

ORPHEUS DESCENDING (1957)
Tennessee Williams (from *Battle of Angels*, 1940)

The Fugitive Kind (1960)

Directed by Sidney Lumet

Adapted by Tennessee Williams and Meade Roberts

Cast: Marlon Brando (Val Xavier), Anna Magnani (Lady Torrence), Joanne Woodward (Carol Cutrere), Victor Jory (Jabe Torrence)

Length: 122 minutes

Early in his career Tennessee Williams reworked a play entitled *Battle of Angels* (1940) into a substantially revised version retitled *Orpheus Descending*, produced on Broadway in 1957. Val Xavier, the hero, is implicitly related to the legendary Orpheus, since he tries to liberate his beloved Eurydice (Lady Torrence in the play) from the clutches of Pluto, the ruler of the Kingdom of Death (Jabe, Lady's invalid husband), so that he and Lady can start a new life together. But Val fails just as Orpheus failed before him. The rewritten play also failed to win an audience. But Williams' belief in the play was vindicated when director Sidney Lumet brought it to the screen as *The Fugitive Kind* (1960). The stellar cast included Academy Award–winners Marlon Brando (Val), Anna Magnani (Lady), and Joanne Woodward (Carol, a wayward girl enamored with Val). Williams, who collaborated on the screenplay with Meade Roberts, added a precredit sequence set in New Orleans, which is solidly based on references within the play's exposition about how Val's wild existence in New Orleans forced him to leave there. Val then moves on to the little town of Marigold, Mississippi, where the play begins. Val soon falls in love with Lady, and their adulterous love affair stirs up the antipathy of the townsfolk. With Val's assistance, Lady opens a confectionery store, which is decorated like an orchard in full bloom. On the day of the grand opening Lady embraces Val in the store; they happen to look upward and see Jabe (Victor Jory). Like an Angel of Death Jabe descends the stairs from his sickroom over the store with a gun and kills his unfaithful wife. Then he sets a match to the tinsel and streamers and other decorations, and they immediately burst into flames. After Jabe dies in the blaze, a maddened mob forces Val back into the burning building with fire hoses to die with Lady. In the play Val is lynched on a tree and blowtorched. But having him together with Lady in death amid the conflagration is more symbolically right, because it visualizes in stunning images the ruined edifice, which they had erected to give substance to their romantic illusions, crashing down around them. Some critics maintained that Williams had been ill-advised to try to pump new blood into a tired old play about a group of unsympathetic riffraff by adapting it for the screen. On the contrary, the film presents the fugitive kind of the title as doomed creatures like Val and Lady, struggling to regain their footing in a hostile world that offers them no support or encouragement to be better than they are. As such, the film is worth the attention of serious viewers. *(G. D. P.)*

Resources: George Crandell, ed., *The Critical Response to Tennessee Williams* (Westport, CT: Greenwood Press, 1996); David Desser and Lester Friedman, *American Jewish Filmmakers: Sidney Lumet and Others* (Chicago: University of Illinois Press, 1993); Gene D. Phillips, *The Films of Tennessee Williams* (Cranbury, NJ: Associated University Presses, 1980).

OTHELLO (1604)
William Shakespeare

Othello (1965)

Directed by Stuart Burge

Adapted from John Dexter's National Theatre production

Cast: Laurence Olivier (Othello), Frank Finlay (Iago), Maggie Smith (Desdemona), Joyce Redman (Emilia), Derek Jacobi (Cassio), Robert Lang (Roderigo), Kenneth Mackintosh (Lodovico), Anthony Nicholls (Brabantio), Sheila Reid (Bianca), Michael Turner (Gratiano), Edward Hardwicke (Montano), Harry Lomax (Doge)

Length: 166 minutes

Othello, "the Moor of Venice," who loves fair Desdemona, is hated by his devious ensign, Iago, for reasons that are not clearly disclosed. The outwardly "honest," but inwardly malevolent and envious, Iago persuades Desdemona's foolish suitor Roderigo to inform her father, Brabantio, that Othello has stolen her, and Brabantio takes the issue to the Duke's council, which is mainly worried about a forthcoming Turkish attack on Cyprus. Othello defends himself successfully and is supported by Desdemona's testimony, whereupon Othello is sent to govern Cyprus with his newly appointed lieutenant, Michael Cassio. Desdemona, her servant Emilia, and Emilia's husband, Iago, are to follow. After the Turkish fleet is wrecked in a storm, there is a celebration, during which Iago gets Cassio involved in a drunken brawl. The disgraced Cassio loses his position, and Iago suggests

Cassio should have Desdemona plead his cause. Meanwhile, Iago insinuates to Othello that an affair is going on between Desdemona and Cassio and incriminates Cassio by planting a handkerchief in his house, a handkerchief that Othello once gave Desdemona. In a fit of jealous rage, Othello murders the innocent Desdemona in her bed. Emilia, who knows how Iago got the handkerchief, tells the truth about her husband and is killed by him. Othello stabs himself in grief; Iago is taken prisoner; Cassio becomes governor of Cyprus. The Stuart Burge film treatment follows the text as produced by the National Theatre and is an excellent example of filmed theatre, not especially cinematic in its approach but graced by distinctive performances by Maggie Smith as Desdemona, Frank Finlay as Iago, and Olivier as a flamboyant and idiosyncratic Othello, played as a swaggering, insolent black man with a distinctive and sometimes distracting Caribbean accent. Reviews of this controversial interpretation were mixed. Jonathan Miller objected to the portrayal of Othello as "a modern, show-biz Negro," drawing upon "all the ludicrous liberal cliche attitudes towards Negroes: beautiful skin, marvelous sense of thythm, wonderful way of walking, etc." According to Hirsch, American critics echoed Miller and regarded Othello as "a vaudeville darkie, a buffoon in blackface" (127). Olivier's voice control was remarkable, however, deeply modulated to capture "the vocal rhythms" of West Indians he had encountered in London. His Moor is smug, proud, and nonintellectual, a man of feeling easily swayed by Finlay's subtle Iago. "By any reasonable application of the requirements of film acting," Foster Hirsch notes, "this should be a ludicrous performance," but, to the contrary, "it is a great one," nonetheless (130). The production is shaped as a star vehicle for Olivier and is remarkable mainly for that reason. *(J. M. W.)*

Resources: Robert L. Daniels, *Laurence Olivier: Theatre and Cinema* (San Diego: A. S. Barnes, 1980); Foster Hirsch, *Laurence Olivier* (Boston: Twayne, 1979); Jonathan Miller, *Subsequent Performances* (New York: Viking, 1986).

Othello (1995)

Directed and adapted by Oliver Parker

Cast: Laurence Fishburne (Othello), Irene Jacob (Desdemona), Kenneth Branagh (Iago), Nathaniel Parker (Cassio), Michael Maloney (Roderigo), Anna Patrick (Emilia), Nicholas Farrell (Montano), Indra Ove (Bianca), Michael Sheen (Lodovico), Andre Oumansky (Gratiano), Pierre Vaneck (Brabantio), Gabriele Ferzetti (Duke of Venice), Philip Locke (First Senator), John Savident (Second Senator)

Length: 124 minutes

Rated: R

This adaptation follows Shakespeare's design but substantially reduces the text of the play. It was filmed on locations in Italy, including Venice, so the visual design of the film is appropriate. Just as Olivier played Othello in the theatrical film version directed by Stuart Burge, Kenneth Branagh in approaching the play left the direction to another talent, Oliver Parker, an actor turned director; but instead of playing the Moor in blackface, as Olivier had done, Branagh took the role of Ensign Iago, allowing a charismatic black actor, Laurence Fishburne, to take the lead, an important precedent, since never before had a black actor played the black protagonist on film. But since the villainy of Iago drives the play, Branagh is still front and center. Given the times, this was the right decision, since the film's release coincided with the O. J. Simpson murder trial, the trial of the decade, if not of the century, in America, involving a successful black man accused of murdering the beautiful white woman to whom he was married. Despite its thematic relevance at the time of its release, the film was judged unremarkable for several reasons. Although Fishburne was visually perfect for the role as a powerful and brooding exotic lover, the actor lacked classical theatrical training and had never before played a Shakespearean role. Likewise, Irene Jacob in the role of Desdemona was faulted as a French-speaking actress out of her depth in performing Shakespeare. Branagh, of course, was up to the challenge of playing Iago, but if the strongest actor in the production gets the role of Shakespeare's most enigmatic villain, the balance of the play is likely to be disturbed. Parker's adaptation cut at least 60 percent of the text in order to bring the running time down to about two hours, in comparison to the Stuart Burge–Laurence Olivier version, which was about forty minutes longer. The problem with simplifying the text in this way is that it tends to reduce the play to an erotic thriller, narrated from the villain's point of view. *(J. M. W.)*

Resources: Alex Albanese, "Sir Laurence," *Boxoffice* (December 1995): 10–11; Leslie Bennetts, "Catching Fishburne," *Vanity Fair* (December 1995): 172–180; Ken Tucker, "Homebard," *Entertainment Weekly* No. 306 (22 December 1995): 48.

The Tragedy of Othello: The Moor of Venice (1952)

Directed by Orson Welles

Adapted by Orson Welles and Jean Sacha (both uncredited)

Cast: Orson Welles (Othello), Michael MacLiammoir (Iago), Suzanne Cloutier (Desdemona), Robert Coote (Roderigo), Fay Compton (Emilia), Michael Lawrence (Cassio)

Length: 93 minutes

The 1997 restoration of *Othello*, complete with a freshly recorded sound track, resynchronized dialogue, and clear master negative, at long last allows audiences to experience the brilliance of Orson Welles' adaptation in a way the Cannes audience that granted it the Palme d'Or in 1952 must have only imagined. From its opening sequence, a depiction of Othello and Desdemona's funeral procession that juxtaposes extreme high- and low-angle camera shots amid the starkest of black-and-white contrast, to its penultimate shot of Cassio gazing down into the vaulted marriage chamber that has become their mutual tomb, Welles constructs a phantasmagoric canvas of images that brilliantly reflects both the Moor's psychological torment and Iago's coldly psychotic jealousy. Even after restoration, however, the narrative is difficult to follow, which, combined with the textual liberties common to Welles' adaptations, renders the film especially challenging to viewers not well versed in Shakespeare's play. Part of the difficulty is purely technical: the film was shot piecemeal over the course of several years, and Welles often had to dub the dialogue in later (making for some especially intriguing camera work in his attempts to avoid potential lip-synching problems). The result, however, is ultimately fortuitous, for Welles' financial limitations compelled him to confront the play as a visual experience rather than an aural one. With near-Eisensteinian power, the montage of images supplies an emotional drama that would otherwise be lost amid truncated speeches and scrambled dialogue. The attempted murder of Cassio in a Turkish bathhouse (improvised by Welles ostensibly because the costumes had not arrived on time) is a whirlwind of editing; the enormous shadow of Othello that obliterates Emilia as she shuts tight Desdemona's bedchamber is as viscerally stunning as the "It is the cause" speech that follows. The sight of the Moor, dwarfed by the gigantic iron gates separating him from Desdemona and the dying Amelia, hauntingly repeating, "She loved thee" over and over, devastatingly dramatizes Othello's utter alienation. Michael MacLiammoir's portrayal of Iago, curiously overlooked by many critics, is definitive, and Welles' over-the-top characterization provides the perfect counterpoint to MacLiammoir's restraint. The psychological symbiosis between the two is underscored by the film's expressionistic photography and set design: Othello is all close-ups and extreme-angle shots, whereas Iago lurks in the corners of compositions, always watching. By contrast, the women suffer substantially in Welles' adaptation, especially Desdemona, who is reduced to a naive and helpless caricature, capable only of a mute shake of the head to Emilia's refreshing diatribe on the faults of husbands. This may not be Welles' greatest film, nor is it the greatest of Shakespearean adaptations, but it is nonetheless a truly unique and inspired work. (R. R.)

Resources: Michael Anderegg, *Orson Welles, Shakespeare, and Popular Culture* (New York: Columbia University Press, 1999); Alfred Jacobs, "Orson Welles's *Othello*," in *Shakespeare and the 20th Century*, ed. Jonathan Bate, Jill L. Levinson, and Dieter Mehl (Newark: University of Delaware Press, 1999).

OTHER PEOPLE'S MONEY (1989)
Jerry Sterner

Other People's Money (1991)

Directed by Norman Jewison

Adapted by Alvin Sargent

Cast: Danny DeVito (Lawrence Garfinkle), Gregory Peck (Andrew Jorgenson), Penelope Ann Miller (Kate Sullivan), Piper Laurie (Bea Sullivan), Dean Jones (William J. Coles)

Length: 101 minutes

Rated: R

Sterner's play, which opened off-Broadway on 16 February 1989, is a cynical play with a serious theme: the selling of loyalty and friendship for money; Jewison's film adaptation is a comedy in which sexual battles parallel Wall Street ones. In the play Lawrence Garfinkle, Wall Street corporate raider, with the aid of Carmen, his computer, attempts to take over New England Wire and Cable, controlled by Andrew Jorgenson, sell the equipment, and close the plant. Bea Sullivan, his assistant and lover, persuades him to seek her lawyer daughter's assistance. While Kate uses legal stratagems against Garfinkle, she also is attracted to him. Jorgenson rejects her suggestions and those of Coles, his chief executive officer (CEO), who seeks a financial deal for himself. As the person who introduces the play and then provides the prologue, Coles is important as perhaps the most corrupt person in the play since he sells the voting rights to his stock to Garfinkle. In the proxy battle Jorgenson defends his traditional values, and Garfinkle espouses financial values and wins. In Coles' prologue the audience is told that Jorgenson died soon after he lost control and that Garfinkle and Kate married and have two children, "little bull" and "little bear." This cynical and downbeat ending is dropped from the film, which retains the clash in values and focuses more on the sexual antics of Garfinkle and Kate and turns Sterner's caustic play into a romantic comedy. One notable added scene at a Japanese restaurant demonstrates how Garfinkle and Kate spar verbally; he makes romantic, but raunchy, comments that she parries while purring a few double entendre lines herself. The two also play games—and Garfinkle comments that they both like the game better than the players—as Garfinkle, who requests a fork, reverts to using chopsticks and speaking Japanese after Kate leaves. In the film Garfinkle wins the proxy fight and is despondent. His mood changes when the resilient Kate offers him a chance to make more money by selling the plant, at a profit, to the workers, who will now manufacture air bags. After he accepts the deal and the lunch date, the jubilant Garfinkle knows, as the audience does, that he and Kate will, like corporations, merge. *(T. L. E.)*

Resources: Rita Kempley, "The Loot of All Evil," *Washington Post* (18 October 1991): D1–2; Richard Schickel, "A Ruthless Raider's Romance," *Time* (18 October 1991): 92.

OUR TOWN (1938)
Thornton Wilder

Our Town (1940)

Directed by Sam Wood

Adapted by Thornton Wilder, Frank Craven, and Harry Chandlee

Cast: Frank Craven (the Stage Manager), William Holden (George Gibbs), Martha Scott (Emily Webb)

Length: 90 minutes

Thornton Wilder's Pulitzer Prize–winning 1938 play is a turn-of-the-century idyll of small-town life in mythical Grover's Corners, New Hampshire. The Stage Manager appears on a bare stage to narrate the three-part drama—"daily life," "love and marriage," and "death and the meaning of life." The romance between young Emily Webb and George Gibbs is told by means of "blackout" sketches and flashbacks. The last act concludes with Emily's death during childbirth after nine years of marriage. Her spirit joins the mourners at her funeral and then revisits scenes of her life as a twelve-year old girl. After returning to her grave, Emily is saddened by how little the living appreciate their lives: "Do any human beings ever realize life while they live it?—every, every minute?" Wilder himself participated in writing the screenplay and agreed (albeit reluctantly) to make many substantial changes. Of course, the bare-stage abstractions and minimal use of props yielded to an opulently detailed set, designed by William Cameron Menzies and photographed in deep focus by Bert Glennon. The simple wedding sequence was inflated into a more sumptuous affair. Most importantly, the character of Emily was allowed to live (her death and ghostly visitation to the scenes of her youth were revealed to be a dream suffered during the birth of her second child). Those exceptions aside, however, the screenplay succeeds to a remarkable degree in preserving the basic structure and style of the original play. Frank Craven and Martha Scott repeat their roles as the Stage Manager (here called "Mr. Morgan") and Emily, respectively. The action is spread over twelve years, from 1901 to 1913, and is divided into three acts—the introduction of the Gibbs and Webb families, the marriage between George (William Holden) and Emily, and the graveyard scenes. Craven addresses the viewer directly and at one point solicits questions from an unseen "audience." Occasionally, voice-overs illuminate the inner thoughts of the characters, especially during the wedding scene. The penultimate graveyard scene abandons naturalistic staging and resorts to a more severely abstract conception, the characters standing stiffly in a void, illuminated by only two shafts of light. At the end, Craven reappears and, after wishing the viewer good night, departs. In sum, *Our Town* occupies an uneasy position between the naturalistic staging suited to the film medium and the stark abstractions more typical of experimental drama. Among its Academy Award nominations were a Best Picture nomination and nominations to Martha Scott for Best Actress and to Aaron Copland for Best Musical Score. *(J. C. T.)*

Resources: David Castronovo, *Thornton Wilder* (New York: Ungar, 1986); Ima Honaker Herron, *The Small Town in American Drama* (Dallas, TX: Southern Methodist University Press, 1969).

THE OUT-OF-TOWNERS (1970)
Neil Simon

The Out-of-Towners (1970)

Directed by Arthur Hiller

Adapted by Neil Simon

Cast: Jack Lemmon (George Kellerman), Sandy Dennis (Gwen Kellerman), Graham Jarvis (Murray), Billy Dee Williams (Lost and Found Position)

Length: 98 minutes

Rated: G

The Out-of-Towners was originally based on the first play Neil Simon cut out of *Plaza Suite* since it conflicted with the mood of the following play, *Visitors from Mamaroneck*. It also was influenced by Simon's experiences in flying to Boston to fix a floundering musical at the request of David Merrick. The usual relatively short flight from New York turned into a delayed travel nightmare in icy weather. Simon also altered his usual practice in tailoring the main role for Jack Lemmon. Whereas most Simon adaptations used the theatrical text as the basis for the narrative and cinematically extended the original into exterior locations, *The Out-of-Towners* is a film that combines both witty dialogue and cinematic extension in a balanced manner. It opens with a helicopter shot of the Kellermans' home in Twin Oaks, Ohio, and then cuts to exterior shots of the landscape, supposedly shot from a car, until the camera moves to reveal its objective position viewing the Kellermans inside the car. This initial camera strategy foreshadows the remainder of the film, which views the dilemma of the Kellermans both cinematically and objectively, rather than theatrically, as is the case of most Simon adaptations. After the Kellermans arrive at the Ohio airport, Hiller uses black comedy, showing their delayed plane journey to New York, their rerouted arrival in Boston, the train from Boston to New York, their walk in the rain from Grand Central to their fully booked hotel, their robbery outside the hotel, accidental involvement in a police chase, wanderings in Central Park at night, and their final destination at their original New York hotel before George decides to give up his prestigious New York job opportunity and return home to Ohio. Then, on their return journey, Cuban hijackers reroute their plane to Havana. *The Out-of-Towners* thus is better as a film than other Simon adaptations that reveal their original theatrical structures that dominate the cinematic versions and leave little room for visual flexibility. This is because Simon wrote several adaptations of the original one-act play, leaving its theatrical origins behind. (The play was also adapted for British television in the late 1960s, featuring Ed Begley and Margaret Johnston.) Although most reviewers thought the film lacked humor and that the Kellermans were largely responsible for their own misfortunes, *The Out-of-Towners* actually makes explicit several of the darker overtones that the comedic aspects of Simon's theatrical formats often overshadow. The film is best understood as a black, comedic, urban nightmare involving cultural and personal fears within the American Dream, usually treated humorously by Simon. *(T. W.)*

Resources: Robert K. Johnson, *Neil Simon* (Boston: Twayne, 1983); Neil Simon, *Rewrites: A Memoir* (New York: Simon and Schuster, 1996).

The Out-of-Towners (1999)

Directed by Sam Weisman

Adapted by Marc Lawrence

Cast: Steve Martin (Henry Clark), Goldie Hawn (Nancy Clark), Mark McKinney (Greg), John Cleese (Mr. Mersault), Mayor Rudolph Giuliani (himself)

Length: 91 minutes

Rated: PG-13

In this spin-off Simon retread, Henry Clark has been downsized from his advertising agency and is going to New York for an interview with another firm, but he is too ashamed to tell his wife that he has been fired. Wife Nancy, depressed and lonely because their son has gone to college, decides to go with Henry, and the farcical mishaps begin: their flight gets diverted to Boston, and they get separated from their luggage; they are not smart enough to catch the right train to New York and have to rent an expensive car, which they crash into the Fulton Fish Market; then they get mugged by a thief who claims to be Andrew Lloyd Webber; without cash or credit cards they are not permitted to check into their luxury hotel, so Nancy goes a-whoring to get them into a room while the fellow who has booked the room keeps an evening appointment, but they get caught before they can take advantage of room service; they blunder into a sex therapy session held in a church; and so it goes. Marc Lawrence unwisely presumes to rewrite and update Neil Simon's original, which critic Gray Arnold called "a ranting farcical pestilence," but he is not quite up to the challenge. Steve Martin and Goldie Hawn work an overly cute and dithering variant on the roles played by Jack Lemmon and Sandy Dennis in 1970. A comic highlight is the snobbish and unctious cross-dressing, kinky hotel manager at the Plaza, a new role played by John Cleese, who steals the show. The film was dismissed, with reason, by the *New York Times* as a "relentlessly silly mediocrity." *(J. M. W.)*

Resources: Gary Arnold, "New 'Out-of-Towners' Gets Lost, like Original," *Washington Times* (2 April 1999): C15; Lisa Schwarzbaum, "Nah, Voyagers," *Entertainment Weekly* No. 480 (9 April 1999): 47; Lawrence Van Gelder, "Still Not Such a Nice Place to Visit," *New York Times* (2 April 1999): B8.

PARFUMERIE (1937)
Miklos Laszlo

The Shop Around the Corner (1940)

Directed by Ernst Lubitsch

Adapted by Samson Raphaelson

Cast: Margaret Sullavan (Klara Novak), James Stewart (Alfred Kralik), Frank Morgan (Hugo Matuschek), Joseph Schildkraut (Ferenc Vadas)

Length: 97 minutes

Film director Ernst Lubitsch bought the rights to Miklos Laszlo's 1937 play *Parfumerie*, for $16,500. MGM, in turn, purchased it from Lubitsch for more than $62,000, thus making a tidy profit for the famed director. A native of Berlin, Lubitsch was attracted to the play's Old World sensibilities, its time period in the late 1920s, its setting of a novelty shop in Budapest, Hungary (which reminded him of his father's clothing store in Berlin), and opportunities for intimate ensemble casting. This was not the privileged world of aristocrats and the wealthy, as Lubitsch had depicted in his previous films, like *The Love Parade* (1929) and *The Merry Widow* (1935), but a cozy milieu of "everyday" folks—what biographer Herman Weinberg describes as "an evangel, lowly and wistful, of little people, their woes and happiness, as it concerned the shop which employed them, and their sorrows and joys outside of business" (74). Head clerk Alfred Kralik (James Stewart) has been corresponding anonymously in a "Lonely Hearts" newspaper column with a mysterious young lady (Margaret Sullavan). Little does he know that the new clerk in the store, Klara—to whom he conceives an instant aversion—is that very person. They bicker and squabble at first, each regarding the other as a competitive threat. But, shortly after Alfred is fired from the store (due to a misunderstanding with his boss), he meets his mystery woman at an arranged rendezvous over coffee and cake. Their identities revealed, antagonisms melt away, and after Alfred returns to the shop, they settle in for a happy marriage and prosperous business career. Historian Scott Eyman applauds the film's stagelike intimacy—claiming wrongly that no one and nothing are depicted outside the immediate confines of the shop: "[Lubitsch] gives the people at Matuschek and Company the full measure of his respect and affection. Through the dignity with which he treats them, the film becomes a celebration of the ordinary, gently honoring the extraordinary qualities that lie within the most common of us" (137). There have been three more versions of Laszlo's play, a 1949 musical film, *In the Good Old Summertime*; a 1963 Broadway adaptation by Jerry Bock and Sheldon Harnick, *She Loves Me*; and a Meg Ryan–Tom Hanks vehicle, *You've Got Mail* (1998). *(J. C. T.)*

Resources: Scott Eyman, *Ernst Lubitsch: Laughter in Paradise* (New York: Simon and Schuster, 1993); Herman G. Weinberg, *The Lubitsch Touch: A Critical Study* (New York: Dover, 1977).

You've Got Mail (1998)

Directed by Nora Ephron

Adapted by Nora and Delia Ephron

Cast: Tom Hanks (Joe Fox), Meg Ryan (Kathleen Kelly)

Length: 120 minutes

Rated: PG

Miklos Laszlo's 1937 play, *Parfumerie*, had already been adapted to the screen twice before—as a 1940 comedy by Ernst Lubitsch, *The Shop Around the Corner*, starring Jimmy Stewart and Margaret Sullavan; and as 1949 musical, *In the Good Old Summertime*, with Judy Garland and Van Johnson—when Nora Ephron decided to update it as a vehicle for Tom Hanks and Meg Ryan. The cozy story about a romance between two workers in a Budapest novelty shop, originally set in 1928, is updated to New York City in the present day. Joe Fox (Hanks) and Kathleen Kelly (Ryan) are rival bookstore proprietors. Joe's mammoth discount store has just opened, and it threatens to run Kathleen's little "Shop around the Corner" out of business. Little do these two antagonists know that each is, in reality, the "mystery person" with whom they've been corresponding anonymously on the Internet (in the play they contact each other in the "Lonely Hearts" newspaper column). Not until they meet in a prearranged rendezvous over coffee and cake (a scene lifted right out of the play), does he realize her true identity. *You've Got Mail* is a very talkie film—not as literate as another bookish romance, *84 Charing Cross Road*, but at the very least more articulate than *Mighty Joe Young*. Joe and Kathleen carry on their mutual seduction by tapping away at their respective keyboards in "dialogue" that is bright and literate, sprinkled with numerous fleeting references to books, particularly *Pride and Prejudice* (plainly alluding to Jane Austen's quirky romance between Darcy and Elizabeth). Whereas the Lubitsch version was a tribute to quaint old Budapest, Ephron's film takes to the streets of Old New York's lovable Upper West Side—with its picturesque shop fronts and homey brownstones, rainy streets, corner markets, bustling shoppers, and so on. Unfortunately, we grow a little annoyed at Joe and Kathleen's dunderheaded antagonism toward each other; and it takes far too long for hardhearted Joe to soften up and for sweet Kathleen to get some moxie. Meanwhile, Kathleen's Shop Around the Corner falls victim to Joe's big bad chain store. That's not the happy ending we were looking for. Yes, to be sure, Joe and Kathleen do fall in love (did you think they wouldn't?), but there's this other, harsher reality to contend with—a reality that is, well, crouching *around the corner*. (*J. C. T.*)

Resource: Lisa Schwarzbaum, "The Yule Tide," *Entertainment Weekly*, No. 463 (18 December 1998): 45–46.

THE PENTHOUSE/
THE METER MAN (1965)
C. Scott Forbes (*The Meter Man*)

The Penthouse (1967)

Directed and adapted by Peter Collinson

Cast: Terence Morgan (Bruce Victor), Suzy Kendall (Barbara Willason), Martine Beswick (Harry), Norman Rodway (Dick), Tony Beckley (Tom)

Length: 95 minutes

The Penthouse, which first appeared in London's fringe theatre during the mid-1960s, was adapted by British cult director Peter Collinson. The film retains the original play's claustrophobic dimensions by setting the events almost entirely in a penthouse suite of a yet-unfinished apartment building resembling Centre Point near Tottenham Court Road. (Left empty for more than a decade, Centre Point became symbolic of the wasteful excesses of the 1960s.) The film begins with a low-angle shot of the building with Tom and Dick looking upward to the inhabited penthouse and grinning in anticipated malicious satisfaction. Bruce and his mistress Barbara wake up inside at 8:15 A.M.; Barbara glances at her image in a mirror, an action she will repeat at the climax of the film after some twelve hours of mind games. Masquerading as meter men, Tom and Dick enter the apartment and overpower Bruce, hold a party, get Barbara drunk, and subject the couple to sadomasochistic sexual games while awaiting the arrival of the unseen Harry. At 5:15 P.M. they leave. But before Bruce and Barbara can recover from the ordeal, Tom and Dick's parole officer, Miss Harriet, arrives and persuades them to forgive Tom and Dick, who then break loose from their handcuffs and subject the couple to another ordeal. Permanently affected by their experiences, Barbara and Tom leave in opposite directions. Both play and film emphasize that Tom, Dick, and Harry represent demons from Bruce and Barbara's unconscious and unhealthy desires for their respective humiliations. Tom ends his five-minute monologue about discarded pet alligators that grow into dangerous threats in sewers by emphasizing that the alligators should not be blamed, but rather their original owners. This important scene hints at the nature of Britain's archetypal social masochism, which would explicitly emerge in the Thatcher era after the utopian liberalism of the swinging 1960s. Both play and film state that even the 1960s was characterized by dark elements within the British psyche. During Tom's monologue the camera slowly tracks into his face, a movement intermittently interrupted by close-ups of Bruce's fearful, yet cognizant, expression. Collinson opens up the original play by shooting scenes outside the penthouse; he also uses circular camera movements to express menace in scenes such as the binding of Bruce to a chair and the couple's final humiliation by Tom, Dick, and Harry. Although usually dismissed as a well-acted vulgar exercise in sadism and masochism, *The Penthouse* obliquely reveals the dark side of England's swinging 1960s and also recalls Joe Orton's plays, which dramatize psychopathic characters who were either wilfully destructive or blind to their own self-destructiveness. *(T. W.)*

Resource: Philip Barnes, *A Companion to Post-War British Theatre* (London: Croom Helm, 1986).

PERIOD OF ADJUSTMENT (1960)
Tennessee Williams

Period of Adjustment (1962)

Directed by George Roy Hill

Adapted by Isobel Lennart

Cast: Tony Franciosa (Ralph Bates), Jane Fonda (Isabel Haverstick), Jim Hutton (George Haverstick), John McGiver (Mr. McGillicuddy), Mabel Albertson (Mrs. McGillicuddy), Lois Nettleton (Dorothy Bates)

Length: 112 minutes

Period of Adjustment, which opened at New York's Helen Hayes Theatre on 10 November 1960, was directed by George Roy Hill after Elia Kazan withdrew. Hill also directed the 1962 film version, which was his first Hollywood venture. The title "period of adjustment" refers to the aftermath of a honeymoon period when couples must forgo romantic illusions and work at compromises to sustain their relationship. Both play and film focus on two married couples whose relationship is in jeopardy: the Bateses, who have been married for six years, and the newlywed Haversticks. Both Ralph Bates and George Haverstick are old army buddies who meet again in Ralph's home on Christmas Eve. Williams defined *Period of Adjustment* as a serious comedy, subtitled "High Point over a Cavern," in reference both to the shaky foundations of the Bates suburban home as well as to the shaky foundations upon which humans erect symbolic foundations of security. The film version stresses the comedic aspects of the play. Hill cinematically broadens the theatrical original beyond the one-set interior confines of the Bates home. Beginning with light, comic music, the fast-moving, precredit sequence shows George and Isabel meeting at the Veterans Hospital where she works as a nurse and then rapidly moves to their courtship and wedding. Isobel Lennart also includes an incongruous wedding supper at a trucker's café and Isabel's drenched arrival at her honeymoon hotel before moving to the play's opening at Ralph's house. Furthermore, the audience sees the symbolically ominous 1939 Cadillac hearse that George has bought secondhand for his honeymoon. It also becomes the location where the Bateses have their final quarrel. Ralph and Dorothy quarrel in the front seat, while the reconciled Haversticks overhear them in the back. Early in the film, Hill includes a scene emphasizing George's sexual insecurities, which are not in the play. After George initially leaves Isabel with Ralph, he passes a squabbling little boy and girl.

She walks off and leaves the boy alone. Shadows from the playground swing fall upon George's face, visually suggesting his personal feelings of inadequacy and entrapment. Finally, by presenting Ralph and George as opposites, respectively embodying practical compromise and the lures of fantasy, Hill depicts them as early sketches for the contrasting, but complementary, male roles he will later explore in *Butch Cassidy and the Sundance Kid* and *The Sting*. (T. W.)

Resources: Andrew Horton, *The Films of George Roy Hill* (New York: Columbia University Press, 1984); Maurice Yacowar, *Tennessee Williams and Film* (New York: Ungar, 1977).

PETER PAN (1904)
James M. Barrie

Hook (1991)

Directed by Steven Spielberg

Adapted by Jim V. Hart and Malia Scotch Marmo

Cast: Robin Williams (Peter Banning), Dustin Hoffman (James Hook), Julia Roberts (Tinkerbell), Maggie Smith (Gran-Wendy), Charlie Korsmo (Jack), Amber Scott (Maggie), Arthur Malet (Tootles), Bob Hoskins (Smee)

Length: 144 minutes

Rated: PG

As a filmmaker and artist who, in the opinion of some of his more acerbic critics, has never grown up, director Steven Spielberg might have seemed the ideal choice to make this full-scale screen adaptation of Sir James M. Barrie's five-act classic. Since the play's premiere on the London stage on 27 December 1904, it had endured as one of the great works of the imagination, yet Barrie himself had seen only one screen version in his lifetime, the Herbert Brenon 1924 silent film; and only Walt Disney's 1953 animated presentation had succeeded it. Thus, the Spielberg/Jim V. Hart/Malia Scotch Marmo adaptation was eagerly anticipated. Barrie's original plot outline was retained in only a tiny flashback section of the film, and the rest of the picture revealed that Pan had grown up to become Peter Banning, a cutthroat corporate lawyer who is too busy with his career to pay attention to his own children, Jack and Maggie. One of his clients is "Gran-Wendy," an old London lady who had adopted him as a baby. She lives in a picturesque old Victorian mansion with a servant and a strange old man named "Tootles." One night, when Peter and his wife join Wendy for dinner, the kids are kidnapped, and a note signed "Jas. Hook" is left behind. Sizing up the situation, Wendy informs the startled Peter that once upon a time he was Peter Pan, and she was his Wendy; that Peter had married her daughter, grown up, and forgotten his boyish legend; and that this "Jas. Hook" is none other than the legendary villain Captain Hook, returned to steal Peter's children. Later that night, Tinkerbell arrives and conducts the reluctant Peter to Never Land. Confronted by bloodthirsty pirates and their leader, Hook, Peter is humiliated at his inability to rescue his children. He has grown too old and forgotten how to be Peter Pan. Back with the Lost Boys, he remembers his past youth and gradually regains his ability to fly. His boyish vigor and strength renewed, he emerges the Pan of old and returns to the pirate ship to defeat Hook, who is killed when an enormous statue of a crocodile topples over and crushes him. Peter flies home with the children for a tearful reunion with his wife and Gran-Wendy. At the end, he wakes up in Kensington Gardens from what he thinks is a dream. On his way home he fails to vault the garden wall. "Out of pixie dust," he muses sardonically. Adopting the more mundane method of climbing the drainpipe, he clambers through the window and rejoins his waiting family. The film's box office performance was disappointing, and critics were generally unkind. Spielberg's film is a rich concatenation of many things—an autobiographical allusion to Spielberg's own experiences as a father, an allegorical warning against false father figures, and a complex and challenging postmodern meditation on the whole Peter Pan myth. However, this Pan has feet of clay. He has been allowed to grow up and resume his adult responsibilities and function as *both* father and child to his family. The original Pan's tragedy was that he could not—or, more precisely, *would not*—grow up. Here, Spielberg implies that both boy and man can commingle in some happy, fuzzy balance—doubtless an appealing notion to Spielberg but an appalling one to the tougher, more insightful, yet more sensitive Barrie. Other postmodernist attempts to inject modern elements and politically correct agendas into the story—and to erase the boundaries between imagination and reality—include a baseball game (with one team called "The Pirates"), references to pop culture icons like the Beatles, a troupe of skateboarding Lost Boys (who indulge in an *Animal House*–like food fight), the silly business with the crocodile statue, and a full-sized Julia Roberts as Tinkerbell. There are no Indians in sight, and Hook is no villain but merely a frustrated father figure who wants to make Peter's children love him. Similarly, Peter is another frustrated father who must cavort about in tights to regain his kids' love. In the end, this Pan declares that "to live must be an awfully big adventure," a reversal of the original play's most famous line. So be it. This Pan will live on as an adult-child, even if it means that the play must die in the process. *(J. C. T.)*

Resources: Douglas Brode, *The Films of Steven Spielberg* (New York: Citadel Press, 1995); Roger Lancelyn Green, *Fifty Years of Peter Pan* (London: Peter Davies, 1954).

Peter Pan (1924)

Directed and adapted by Herbert Brenon

Cast: Betty Bronson (Pan), Mary Brain (Wendy), Ernest Torrence (Captain Hook)

Length: 100 minutes

James M. Barrie's five-act play about a boy who refused to grow up and ran away to a life of adventure in Never Land was an instant international success since its first English production on 27 December 1904, with Nina Boucicault in the title role, and its first American presentation on 6 November 1905, with Maude Adams. It has been estimated that in its first half century in England alone it was presented over 10,000 times. The play's genesis is long and complex, drawing characters and incidents from Barrie's boyhood in Kirriemuir, Scotland; his relationships with the four children of Arthur and Sylvia Davies (whom he had met in 1898 in Kensington Gardens and with whom he remained closely associated the rest of his life); and two of his adult novels, *Tommy and Grizel* (1900) and *The Little White Bird* (1901). In *Peter and Wendy* (1911) Barrie rewrote the play into novel form. In the original play's first act the spritely Peter Pan arrives at the nursery of the Darling children—Wendy, John, Michael—and flies away with them to Never Land. In the second, the Lost Boys accept Wendy as their mother and build her a house. In the third, the villainous Captain Hook and his pirate gang abduct the children. In the fourth, Peter comes to the rescue and feeds Hook to a crocodile. In the last act, all the children have returned to the nursery, while Peter remains in Never Land, occasionally visiting the nursery as the years pass. The character of Peter Pan has been called the most famous person who never lived. That Barrie himself felt close to the character can be seen from a quotation from his early novel *Margaret Ogilvey* (1896), which describes his own youth: "The horror of my boyhood was that I knew a time would come when I also must give up the games, and how it was to be done I saw not. . . . I felt I must continue playing in secret." Director Herbert Brenon made the first and only silent film version, and he took pains to retain the flavor of a stage production. Apart from a magical special-effects shot of Peter's tipping out a pillowcase full of fairies (a suggestion from Barrie himself) and a few shots of a real pirate ship and a real sea (including a lovely image of seagulls gently circling around the ship's mast and shots of mermaids disporting about a beach), most of the action has a stage-bound quality (the parts of Nana the dog and the crocodile were obviously played by humans in animal costumes). A few of Barrie's lines were utilized in the intertitles, and he personally endorsed the casting of young Betty Bronson as Peter (continuing the English stage tradition that he be portrayed by a girl). Equally appealing was Ernest Torrence's Captain Hook, who delightfully indulged himself in grimaces and other attention-getting gestures. Barrie, however, was disappointed at the results. "It is only repeating what is done on the stage," he declared, "and the only reason for a film should be that it does the things the stage can't do." His own scenario, amounting to 15,000 words, which he sold to Paramount, was never used (but was reprinted in 1954 in Roger Lancelyn Green's *Fifty Years of Peter Pan*). (*J. C. T.*)

Resources: Andrew Birkin, *J. M. Barrie and the Lost Boys* (New York: Clarkson Potter, 1979); Joe Franklin, *Classics of the Silent Screen* (New York: The Citadel Press, 1959); Roger Lancelyn Green, *Fifty Years of Peter Pan* (London: Peter Davies, 1954).

Peter Pan (1953)

Supervised and adapted by Ben Sharpsteen, Hamilton Luske, and Wilfrid Jackson

Cast voices: Bobby Driscoll (Pan), Hans Conreid (Hook), Kathryn Beaumont (Wendy), Bill Thomson (Smee)

Length: 76 minutes

Walt Disney had wanted to make an animated version of Sir James M. Barrie's classic play as early as 1939, when he arranged with the Great Ormond Street Hospital in London (to whom Barrie had bequeathed rights to the play) to produce a film. But it wasn't until near the end of 1949 that actual production began. Including the costs for a live-action version, which was used as a model for the animators (in which dancer Roland Dupree portrayed Pan), it was to be one of his most expensive films to date, coming in at $4 million. The basic outlines of Barrie's five-act play (which had premiered in London on 27 December 1904) were retained, with the action beginning in the nursery of the Darling family; continuing with Pan's arrival; his teaching of the children—Wendy, Michael, and John—to fly; their departure to Never-Never Land; their encounters with mermaids, Indians, and the villainous Captain Hook; Hook's abduction of the children; and Pan's exciting last-minute rescue of the children and Hook's fate in the jaws of the crocodile. In a striking departure from the play—which brings the children back to the nursery, to be visited sporadically over the years by Pan—Hook's ship is sprinkled with Tinkerbell's pixie dust, and, now captained by Peter, it flies across the moon over London to the wondering eyes of the Darling household. As he gazes on the apparition, Mr. Darling gently murmurs that he seems to remember having seen it himself, long, long ago. Surprisingly, as historian Leonard Maltin points out, Disney's film was the first enactment of the play in which Pan was *not* played by a girl, where Nana was depicted as a real dog (as opposed to the theatrical tradition of a person in an animal suit), and where Tinkerbell was pictured as a tiny girlish sprite (as opposed to a mirror's reflected point of light). Moreover, one of the play's most famous moments was discarded—when Pan requests viewers to clap their hands to revive the dying Tinkerbell. The film did not do well at the box office, and Walt himself was displeased at its performance. Commentator Richard Schickel complains, perhaps with justification, that *Peter Pan* was another example of the "Disneyfication" process. Disney's name, not Barrie's appears over the title. Here, noted Schickel, was another example wherein Walt appropriated another person's work in order to gag it up and sentimentalize it: "The egotism that insists on making another man's work your own through wanton tampering and by advertising claim is not an attractive form of egotism, however it is rationalized" (296). However, to less jaundiced eyes, the film wears well, and there are many delightful moments, including the gags built around the relationship between Hook and Smee; the musical score by Oliver Wallace and songs by Sammy Cahn and Sammy Fain (especially "You Can Fly, You Can Fly," "Never Smile at a Crocodile," and "A Pirate's Life"); and the spectacular renderings of the London scenes, particularly when Pan and the children fly across night-shrouded London, the cityscape appearing through a break in the clouds below them. *(J. C. T.)*

Resources: Roger Lancelyn Green, *Fifty Years of Peter Pan* (London: Peter Davies, 1954); Leonard Maltin, *The Disney Films* (New York: Bonanza Books, 1973); Richard Schickel, *The Disney Version* (New York: Simon and Schuster, 1968).

THE PETRIFIED FOREST (1935)
Robert Sherwood

The Petrified Forest (1936)

Directed by Archie Mayo

Adapted by Charles Kenyon and Delmer Daves

Cast: Leslie Howard (Alan Squier), Bette Davis (Gabrielle "Gabby" Maple), Humphrey Bogart (Duke Mantee), Dick Foran (Boze Hertzlinger), Charley Grapewin (Gramp Maple), Genevieve Tobin (Mrs. Chisholm), Paul Harvey (Mr. Chisholm)

Length: 83 minutes

Sherwood's play, which opened at the Broadhurst Theater in New York City in January 1935, starred Leslie Howard, who also produced the play with Arthur Hopkins. The Broadway cast included Peggy Conklin (Gabby) and Humphrey Bogart (Mantee). In the movie version, which premiered the following 8 February, Bette Davis had the role of Gabby, and Howard and Bogart reprised their Broadway roles. Howard, in fact, insisted on Bogart for the part of Duke Mantee. The hero, Squier, an unsuccessful poet who is hitchhiking in the Arizona desert, stops at a roadside service station/lunchroom and meets a kindred spirit in the proprietor's François Villon-quoting daughter, Gabby. They immediately fall in love. She dreams of going to France. In Gabby, the disillusioned intellectual discovers something worth dying for. Others at the roadside stop include a young ex-fullback helper and the irritating Chrisholms, who arrive in their Duesenberg limousine. Squier believes he is one of the last individualists, like the pioneer and the gunman. (Dillinger and Bonnie and Clyde had died recently, which may have impressed playwright Sherwood, incorrectly, as the passing of the hoodlum.) Duke Mantee and his gang, subjects of a nationwide manhunt, hole up at the gas station, where the intellectual and the gangster converse. Squier gets Duke to agree to shoot him after he makes Gabby the beneficiary of his life insurance policy. She can collect and go to France, and he can make a noble gesture. Squier tells Gabby that they'll be together always in a funny sort of way. When the law arrives at the end and there is a shoot-out, Mantee shoots and kills Squier as prearranged. The film is truly a "photoplay," a filmed play. A remake, *Escape in the Desert*, was released in 1945, directed by Edward Blatt and introducing Nazi thematics. *(K. O.)*

Resources: *The Commonweal* (25 January 1935): 375 and (7 February 1936): 414; David Thomson, *A Biographical Dictionary of Film* (New York: Knopf, 1994).

THE PHILADELPHIA STORY (1938)
Philip Barry

The Philadelphia Story (1940)

Directed by George Cukor

Adapted by Donald Ogden Stewart

Cast: Katharine Hepburn (Tracy Lord), Cary Grant (C. K. Dexter Haven), Jimmy Stewart (Macaulay Connor)

Length: 112 minutes

Philip Barry's 1938 play, like his earlier work *Holiday* (filmed in 1930 and 1938, on the latter occasion directed by George Cukor), takes as its terrain the sumptuous world of the very rich. Rather than critiquing their position in the world, Barry postulates with a comic tone whether or not it is possible to have the world and retain one's sense of self, even sense of humor. Barry had written *The Philadelphia Story* for Katharine Hepburn, and it had played with enormous success (415 performances) on Broadway and throughout a national tour. This was the period of her Hollywood career when the actress was considered "box office poison," and, therefore, while a number of studios were eager to acquire the property, none were desirous of hiring her. MGM obtained the play and the stipulation that Hepburn play Tracy Lord when they discovered that Howard Hughes owned the rights in tandem with Hepburn. Hepburn stipulated that the screenplay required two leading men, and the play was therefore opened up with the addition of Stewart's character, journalist Macaulay Connor. He has been hired by Tracy's ex-husband, C. K. Dexter Haven (Cary Grant), to help him insinuate himself back into Tracy's life as she prepares to marry once again. Despite his abhorrence of the idle rich, Macaulay falls in love with Tracy, but she eventually rejects both him and her fiancé and rediscovers her devotion to her ex-spouse, Dexter. *The Philadelphia Story* is at once raucous and refined, memorably opening with the celebrated sequence in which Tracy throws Dexter out of the house, only to have him shove her back through the open door. As is typical of MGM films of the period, the production is lush and star-studded. *The Philadelphia Story* was nominated for several Academy Awards in 1940 and won two: James Stewart (his only Oscar) for Supporting Actor and Donald Ogden Stewart for Best Adaptation. *(D. S.)*

Resources: Patrick McGilligan, *George Cukor. A Double Life. A Biography of the Gentleman Director* (New York: St. Martin's Press, 1991); Gene D. Phillips, *George Cukor* (Boston: Twayne, 1982).

THE PIANO LESSON (1987)
August Wilson

The Piano Lesson (1994)

Directed by Lloyd Richards

Adapted by August Wilson

Cast: Carl Gordon (Doaker), Charles S. Dutton (Boy Willie), Courtney B. Vance (Lymon), Alfre Woodard (Berniece), Zelda Harris (Maretha), Tommy Hollis (Avery), Lou Myers (Wining Boy)

Length: 99 minutes
Rated: PG

Initially presented as a staged reading, *The Piano Lesson* opened at the
Yale Repertory Theatre in 1987. The set, Doaker's kitchen and parlor, is
dominated by an old upright piano with carvings of masklike figures resembling totems. In the course of the play Boy Willie is intent on having
his sister Berniece sell the piano so that he can buy some land that was
owned by the late Mr. Sutter, whose drowning may not have been accidental. Avery, a minister who wants to marry Berniece, also wants the
piano sold so that he can afford a bigger church. Berniece resists the pressure because she has seen Sutter's ghost, because she wants her daughter,
Maretha, to play it, and, most important, because the history of the family
has been carved into the piano, which her brother sees only as "wood."
The supernatural plays an important role in this play. Boy Willie and Lymon, a friend of his, cannot move the relatively small piano; and the climax
of the play occurs when Sutter's ghost and Boy Willie battle offstage as
Avery attempts to exorcize the ghost. Sutter's ghost departs, however, only
when Berniece, who has not played the piano since her mother died, asks
her dead mother for help and begins playing the piano "as an exorcism
and a dressing for battle." After Sutter's ghost leaves, Boy Willie gives up
his battle for the piano and plans to leave on the next train. August Wilson's film adaptation of his own play retains most of the dialogue and adds
a few outside scenes to open up the play. The audience sees events that
occur offstage in the play: Boy Willie and Lymon selling watermelons, Wining Boy going to a bar, Avery preparing for the exorcism, and, most important, the story of the carved piano and the family history. The end of
the film heightens the family concept as Berniece and Boy Willie are reconciled, and the last image is of Berniece and Maretha at the piano, suggesting the continuity of family history. *(T. L. E.)*

Resources: Kim Pereira, *August Wilson and the African-American Odyssey* (Ur-
bana: University of Illinois Press, 1995); Sandra Garnett Shannon, *The Dramatic
Vision of August Wilson* (Washington, DC: Howard University Press).

PICNIC (1953)
William Inge

Picnic (1955)

Directed by Joshua Logan
Adapted by Daniel Taradash

Cast: William Holden (Hal Carter), Kim Novak (Madge Owens), Susan Stras-
berg (Millie Owens), Betty Field (Flo Owens), Verna Felton (Helen Potts),
Cliff Robertson (Alan Seymour), Rosalind Russell (Rosemary Sydney), Arthur
O'Connell (Howard Bevans), Nick Adams (Bomber)
Length: 115 minutes

Lonely and beautiful Madge Owens lives with her sister Millie and her
mother, Flo, in an isolated Kansas town on the prairie, desperately wanting
to escape to a better life. She is being courted by Alan Seymour, whose
father controls the local granary, and is visited by a college friend, Hal
Carter, a onetime athlete who flunked out of college and has become a
drifter after trying his luck as an actor in Hollywood. Though presumably
engaged to Alan, Madge falls quickly in love with Hal at the town's Labor
Day picnic, which makes Alan both angry and jealous. A further complication in this sexually repressed situation is the attention Rosemary Sydney,
a middle-aged spinster schoolteacher, pays to Hal after getting drunk at
the picnic, which leads to embarrassing consequences for both of them. Hal
is also alienated from his friend Alan, whose father reports to the police
that Hal has stolen Alan's car, in order to help his son remove the intruder.
Madge consoles Hal; Rosemary finds consolation in the arms of local businessman Howard Bevans. After the couplings in act 3, Rosemary successfully puts pressure on Howard to marry her, and, counter to her mother's
wishes, Madge decides to elope with Hal to Tulsa, even though Hal has
admitted to her, "I'm just a no-good bum." They will live together in Tulsa,
where Hal plans to find work as a bellhop at the Hotel Mayo. Josh Logan,
who directed the play on Broadway, also directed the film version, filmed
in Salinas, Kansas, against an appropriate natural setting. In the play production Logan and Inge had fought over the proper ending, but Logan
apparently won, and the play and the film that followed were both very
successful. Hal Carter is a pretty crude loser in the play but is more sympathetic as William Holden represents him. Madge is hopeful about the
future, despite limited prospects in the play. Logan's film, which further
sentimentalizes the action, urges the viewer to conclude that Madge may
be headed toward future happiness and fulfillment in Tulsa. In the film
Madge, as portrayed by Kim Novak, a stereotyped 1950s female, will presumably achieve happiness because she has found a strong man to guide
and direct her life. Logan's Hal is more decent and has more potential than
the character Inge first imagined. Kim Novak is ravishing as Madge at the
dance pavilion, dancing seductively with Hal to Morris Stoloff's theme
music composed by George Duning, and as Rosemary Sydney, Rosalind
Russell gives the performance of a lifetime. The film takes a realistic drama
and treats it romantically and unforgettably. (J. M. W.)

Resources: Joshua Logan, *Josh: My Up and Down, In and Out Life* (New York:
Delacorte, 1976); Ralph F. Voss, *A Life of William Inge: The Strains of Triumph*
(Lawrence: University of Kansas Press, 1989).

PLAZA SUITE (1968)
Neil Simon

Plaza Suite (1971)

Directed by Arthur Hiller

Adapted by Neil Simon

Cast: Walter Matthau (Sam Nash/Jesse Kiplinger/Roy Hubley), Maureen Stapleton (Karen Nash), Barbara Harris (Muriel Tate), Lee Grant (Norma Hubley), Louise Sorel (Miss McCormack)

Length: 114 minutes

Rated: PG

Plaza Suite first appeared at New York City's Plymouth Theatre on 14 February 1968, directed by Mike Nichols, featuring George C. Scott and Maureen Stapleton playing Simon's three married couples. Arthur Hiller's film version retained Simon's original concept of the male lead playing three different parts but changed the female leads through each of the plays: *Visitors from Mamaroneck, Visitors from Hollywood,* and *Visitors from Forest Hills.* By the time the film version appeared, after the hit *Patton* (1970), George C. Scott was a major star and unavailable, so Walter Matthau duplicated his theatrical performances, while Maureen Stapleton now appeared only as Karen Nash in the opening play. Neil Simon critic Robert K. Johnson noted the tepid critical and public reaction to the film version, commenting that the "direction was heavy-handed" and that the major flaw was in the acting. Johnson also criticized casting three different women as lead actresses and making Walter Matthau ridiculous, as he floundered "beyond his range as a performer." These comments are unfair to the director and Matthau. As one of the few directors who have attempted to translate Simon cinematically, Hiller realized that the "acting tour de force" would not work onscreen and would confuse audiences, hence, the casting of three different lead actresses to provide varied complements to Matthau's leading performances. Furthermore, Matthau brings appropriate, accomplished performances to the film. The wigs he wears in acts 1 and 2 are visual complements to Simon's critiques of the artificial and performative nature of the failed masculinity in the original play. While Maureen Stapleton's performance reproduces some of the high-power theatrics of the original production, both Barbara Harris and Lee Grant deliver low-key acting styles more appropriate to the cinematic medium. As in *The Out-of-Towners,* Hiller does much more than merely open up the original play, using framing and camera movement to relate the story. In the first play,

Sam and Karen are frequently separated via mise-en-scène devices. When Karen becomes aware of her husband's infidelity, the camera swiftly dollies from behind her to a close-up of her anguished face. Finally, the play ends with Sam shot in deep focus at the end of the hotel corridor waiting for the lift with the bellboy, now, ironically, bringing the champagne meant to celebrate the twenty-fifth wedding anniversary and inquiring, "Is he coming back?" Hiller's innovative cinematic translations are often subtle, creating critical misunderstandings over how he moves Simon from drama into film. *(T. W.)*

Resources: Robert K. Johnson, *Neil Simon* (Boston: Twayne, 1983); Edythe M. McGovern, *Not-So-Simple Neil Simon: A Critical Study* (New York; Ungar 1979).

PLENTY (1978)
David Hare

Plenty (1985)

Directed by Fred Schepisi

Adapted by David Hare

Cast: Meryl Streep (Susan), Sam Neill (Lazar), Charles Dance (Raymond Brock), John Gielgud (Sir Leonard Darwin), Tracey Ullmann (Alice Park), Sting (Mick), Ian McKellen (Sir Andrew Charleson), Ian Wallace (Medlicott)

Length: 124 minutes

Rated: R

The play concerns Susan Traherne's attempt to find fulfillment in London during the postwar era of "plenty" and the promise of prosperity, but London seems rather dull in comparison to the excitement Susan experienced while working with the French Resistance during World War II. The play begins in 1962 in Knightsbridge, then shifts backward in time to 1943 in France, when Susan, at the age of seventeen, had a fleeting affair with a British agent code-named Lazar, who narrowly escapes capture by the Germans. The film version begins with this affair in the past to establish Susan's daring recklessness, then follows her into the more boring postwar era. She holds a job with a shipping company, then, after a fleeting affair with a working-class lover named Mick (Sting), she agrees to marry Raymond Brock, a career diplomat whose career she later destroys for no clearly explained reason other than her need for excitement. At the end of the play she is reunited with Lazar at a seaside resort in Blackpool, but even Lazar, who is now married after the war, seems rather ordinary in a peacetime setting. Susan's sanity seems to be an issue, but most likely she is mad with boredom. Hare notes that 75 percent of the women flown behind the lines for the Special Operations Executive during the war "were subsequently divorced after the war," and the play dramatizes Susan's restlessness in this context. Brock, a decent man who sincerely cares for his disturbed wife, cannot hold their marriage together. He is ruined by his dedication to an unworthy career in the Foreign Service, as seen from Hare's political perspective. Though the film puts the action of the play in chronological order and excises a few scenes, it is generally true to the spirit and intent of the original work. Performances by Meryl Streep as Susan, Charles Dance as Brock, Tracy Ullmann as Susan's Bohemian friend, and John Gielgud as Darwin are brilliantly accomplished in this well-directed adaptation. *(J. M. W.)*

Resources: David Ansen, "A Woman against Her Time," *Newsweek* (23 September 1985): 68; Stanley Kauffmann, "Revised Version," *The New Republic* (30 September 1985): 26–28; Steve Lawson, "Hare Apparent," *Film Comment* 21.5 (1985): 18–22; Gavin Millar, "The Habit of Lying," *Sight and Sound* 54.4 (1985): 299–300.

PRELUDE TO A KISS (1990)
Craig Lucas

Prelude to a Kiss (1992)

Directed by Norman Rene

Adapted by Craig Lucas

Cast: Alec Baldwin (Peter Hoskins), Meg Ryan (Rita Boyle), Kathy Bates (Leah Blier), Ned Beatty (Dr. Boyle), Patty Duke (Mrs. Boyle), Richard Riehle (Jerry Blier), Stanley Tucci (Taylor), Sydney Walker (Old Man)

Length: 110 minutes

Rated: PG-13

The play begins as a romantic comedy when Peter (Alec Baldwin), a Chicago publisher, meets Rita (Meg Ryan), a perky barmaid, at a party, falls in love, and decides to get married. An uninvited guest (Sydney Walker) turns up at the wedding and wants to kiss the bride. When a dark cloud blocks out the sun as they kiss, the viewer knows something has gone wrong. Rita's soul passes into the old man's body, and his soul, memory, and personality take over the bride, a bizarre turn of events. During the honeymoon in Jamaica, the puzzled groom notices that his bride is not quite herself and has understandable problems accepting the body switch. After the honeymoon he confronts "her," and "she" goes running home to mom and dad (Patty Duke and Ned Beatty). Peter then goes on a toot at the bar where his beloved used to work and meets the old geezer who is really the woman he loves and turns out to be dying of lung cancer and cirrhosis of the liver, so they have no time to waste in concocting a scheme to get the bodies switched back. The romantic comedy shifts into an AIDS allegory as the groom is put into a caring relationship with a man he loves who is slowly and surely dying. They love each other, but they cannot even hold hands in public, and Peter is unable to make physical contact with the woman (now an old man) he loves. When he finally plants a kiss on the old man's lips, that brings about the solution that returns Rita and the old man to their respective bodies. Everything that precedes is merely a "prelude" to that kiss of transforming love. This outlandish concept worked far better onstage than it could in the film, even though Norman Rene directed the stage production as well as the film, and Alec Baldwin had played Peter onstage in New York. Sydney Walker played the Old Man in the play's West Coast productions, yet what was made to seem believable onstage could not be effectively transformed into this movie, which makes the action seem far-fetched rather than magical. The play's New York setting was changed to Chicago and made realistic and literal but, at the same time, less supernatural. Although the language of the film script was very close to the play, this failed adaptation is an excellent demonstration of the idea that what works well enough onstage may not automatically work on film. Reviewers thought the film was well acted but agreed that Rene and Lucas were unable to transform the verbal into the visual agreeably enough to make the film a success. *(J. M. W.)*

Resources: Vincent Canby, "A Kiss Turns into the Unexpected," *New York Times* (10 July 1993): C10; Rita Kempley, "*Prelude*: Gooey Hooey," *Washington Post* (10 July 1993): B1, B6.

THE PRINCE AND THE SHOWGIRL

See THE SLEEPING PRINCE

THE PRISONER OF SECOND AVENUE (1971)
Neil Simon

The Prisoner of Second Avenue (1975)

Directed by Melvin Frank

Adapted by Neil Simon

Cast: Jack Lemmon (Mel Edison), Anne Bancroft (Edna Edison), Gene Saks (Harry Edison), Elizabeth Wilson (Pauline), Florence Stanley (Pearl), M. Emmett Walsh (Doorman), Ketty Lester (Unemployment Clerk), F. Murray Abraham (Taxi Driver), Sylvester Stallone (Youth in Park)

Length: 105 minutes

Rated: PG

The Prisoner of Second Avenue premiered at New York's Eugene O'Neill Theatre in 1971, directed by Mike Nichols, with Peter Falk, Lee Grant, and Vincent Gardenia in the leading roles. It presents a much darker comedy vision than most of Simon's plays. He once remarked that Mel and Edna are, "in some respect, those kids from *Barefoot in the Park* 20 years later." Set in the Edison's New York apartment, the play deals with the fears and insecurities affecting modern urban life with its fragile apartment dwellings, corporate downsizing, and the difficulties of marital readjustment. Simon has symbolically chosen the surname of a great American inventor for his twentieth-century couple living in a technologically wasteful, urban environment. After Mel loses his job, Edna becomes the breadwinner, and both gradually take on each other's former roles and personal attributes until the concluding scene, when Mel recovers from his mental breakdown. Like Mel, Edna later loses her job due to downsizing. Both decide to fight back and dump snow on the head of an upstairs neighbor who has twice drenched the verbally combative Mel with water. The film version opens out the play in several ways. Credit segments reveal Mel's humiliation: a bus driver throws him off the bus for not having the right fare; he acts paranoid when a lift is temporarily stuck, exits at the wrong floor, and enters an almost empty office, thus anticipating his approaching redundancy. The upstairs Unseen Neighbor who douses Mel with water now appears in several scenes viewed from the Edisons' balcony overlooking New York. New sequences especially invented for the film show Mel mistakenly pursuing a young man in Central Park for stealing his wallet, as well as encountering other distanced New Yorkers such as an unemployment clerk, taxi driver, and doorman, all played by either former pop stars (Ketty Lester) or future stars (Stallone, Abraham) and future major character actors (Walsh). Another new scene involves Mel and Edna's visit to Harry's affluent country residence. Despite both play and film concluding in an open-ended manner when Mel and Edna strike an *American Gothic* pose intimating the possibility of their making an effort to change by returning to a simpler lifestyle, Mel Frank's version does end on a more optimistic note. In the play, the radio announcer forecasts a record forty-three inches of snow, but in the film the announcer emphasizes that New Yorkers will collaborate as a group in facing the snowy weather. *(T. W.)*

Resources: Edythe McGovern, *Not-So-Simple Neil Simon: A Critical Study* (New York: Ungar, 1979); Neil Simon, *Rewrites: A Memoir* (New York: Simon and Schuster, 1996).

PROSPERO'S BOOKS

See THE TEMPEST

PYGMALION (1913)
George Bernard Shaw

Pygmalion (1938)

Directed by Anthony Asquith and Leslie Howard

Adapted by W. P. Lipscomb and Cecil Lewis

Cast: Wendy Hiller (Eliza), Leslie Howard (Higgins), Wilfred Lawson (Doolittle), Scott Sunderland (Col. Pickering), David Tree (Freddy), Esme Percy (Count Aristid Karpathy)

Length: 96 minutes

Shaw's *Pygmalion* updates the classical myth about a sculptor who rejects all women and sculpts a perfect woman who comes to life. In the play Professor Higgins, a linguist, is the Pygmalion figure, and Eliza Doolittle, a Cockney flower girl, is Galatea. After an encounter at Covent Garden, Eliza comes to Higgins' apartment and asks him to teach her how to speak like a lady. Higgins and Colonel Pickering, his genial colleague, transform Eliza's speech, manners, and behavior so much that she convinces another linguist that she is a Hungarian princess. Flushed with success, Higgins treats Eliza as a possession, and she turns to Freddy, who loves her. At the end of the play Eliza returns to Higgins but vows to marry Freddy. In a postscript Shaw explains why Eliza will indeed marry Freddy instead of Higgins. Gabriel Pascal, the producer of the film, believed that Shaw's ambiguous ending and his subsequent explanation were not suited to a film audience's expectations. When Shaw acquiesced to casting Leslie Howard, a romantic lead, as Higgins, the play was radically altered. (Howard also codirected the film.) In fact, Shaw agreed to several changes, all of which enhanced the developing relationship between Eliza and Higgins—many of these were included by Shaw in his 1941 revision of the original play (1913). In the film the audience sees Eliza's dismal Angel Court neighborhood, Higgins' elaborate phonetic equipment, Eliza's lessons in speech and dancing, and the Embassy Ball, where she totally takes in Karpathy, Higgins' former pupil and now linguistic rival. The major alterations, however, affect the Eliza-Higgins-Freddy love triangle. The film contains scenes with Eliza and Freddy; and the audience sees Higgins' anxiety when he discovers Eliza has left and his frantic search for her. At the end of the film the audience knows that Eliza's return to the kinder, gentler Higgins (Pascal softens Higgins in the film) is permanent. With the romantic additions, there are significant cuts, notably, in Eliza's father's diatribes about middle-class morality. The result is less Shaw but a successful film. *(T. L. E.)*

Resources: Donald P. Costello, *The Serpent's Eye: Shaw and the Cinema* (Notre Dame, IN: University of Notre Dame Press, 1965); Valerie Pascal, *The Disciple and His Devil: Gabriel Pascal and Bernard Shaw* (New York: McGraw-Hill, 1970).

A RAISIN IN THE SUN (1958)
Lorraine Hansberry

A Raisin in the Sun (1961)

Directed by Daniel Petrie

Adapted by Lorraine Hansberry

Cast: Sidney Poitier (Walter Lee Younger), Claudia McNeil (Lena Younger), Ruby Dee (Ruth Younger), Diana Sands (Beneatha Younger), Ivan Dixon (Joseph Asagai), Louis Gossett, Jr. (George Murchison), John Fiedler (Karl Lindner), Stephen Perry (Travis)

Length: 128 minutes

Lorraine Hansberry's *A Raisin in the Sun*, the first Broadway play by an African American woman, won both the New York Drama Critics Circle and Best Play of the Year Awards for 1958–1959. It was successfully transferred to a film version with director Daniel Petrie closely maintaining the intimacy of the Lloyd Richards stage production. The principals re-created their original stage roles on film. The movie focuses on a southside Chicago black ghetto family and its dreams for a better life, too long deferred, threatening to dry up, as the Langston Hughes poem expresses it, "like a raisin in the sun." The Younger family is to receive a $10,000 life insurance check from the recently deceased husband and father, Walter Lee Younger, Sr. The powerfully matriarchal Lena (Claudia McNeil) hopes to make a down payment on a house for the family to escape the entrapment of the urban apartment house where she and her husband brought up their children. Lena resides with her grown children: Walter Lee (Sidney Poitier), his wife, Ruth (Ruby Dee), and their young son, Travis, and Beneatha (Diana Sands), who has ambitions to become a doctor and who is increasingly drawn to her African American "roots." She has two suitors, Asagai (Ivan Dixon), a Nigerian, and George Murchison (Louis Gossett), scion of a prosperous African American capitalist family.

Walter is a chauffeur; his wife a cleaning woman. He is an opportunist who conflicts with his sister Beneatha, an idealist. Mother and children engage in a power struggle over control of the family and the inheritance. Lena finally confers trust in her son, who unfortunately loses much of the money in an unsuccessful bid to buy a liquor store. Thereafter, Walter comes close to yielding to the wishes of the Clybourne Park Improvement Association, represented by Mr. Lindner (John Fiedler), who wants to buy out the Youngers to prevent integration in their suburban subdivision; however, Walter ultimately repudiates the offer.

Hansberry presents a family of strong-willed women and a vulnerable male protagonist who measures up as a man by his final action. The lithe movements and expressive gestures of Poitier, memorable onstage, seem sometimes excessive on film. Mama's fragile plant in her tenement window endures from the stage production as chief symbol of the family's need for sunlight and nurture, growth, and maturity. She returns at the end of the film to retrieve it in a deep-focus shot of Walter on the stairs in the background.

The film's setting is consistent with the stage production, apart from three useful and plausible sequences away from the apartment. First, Walter, as a chauffeur, tends a large limousine and delivers his employer from a mansion to an urban appointment. Later, Mama retrieves Walter from a bar. A subsequent sequence takes the Younger family to their new house in Clybourne Park with a brief, but poignant, walk-through, culminating in the presentation of garden tools and garden hat to Mama in the backyard. In both the play and film, Hansberry offers more than a plea for racial tolerance; she universalizes the need to escape from grinding frustrations through familial love, respect, and dignity. (E. T. J.)

Resources: Anne Cheney, *Lorraine Hansberry* (Boston: G. K. Hall, 1984); Lorraine Hansberry, *To Be Young, Gifted, and Black: An Informal Biography* (New York: New American Library, 1970).

RAN

See KING LEAR

REIGEN (1920)
Arthur Schnitzler

La Ronde (1950)

Directed by Max Ophuls

Adapted by Jacques Natanson and Max Ophuls

Cast: Anton Walbrook (narrator), Simone Signoret (the prostitute), Serge Reggiani (Franz), Simone Simon (Marie), Daniel Gelin (Alfred), Danielle Darrieux (Emma Breitkopf)

Length: 97 minutes

Adapted from Arthur Schnitzler's play *Reigen*, *La Ronde* is Max Ophuls' first film made in Europe after spending nearly a decade in the United States. He had adapted the playwright's work before with his notable 1932 production of *Liebelei*. While Schnitzler's work is best known for its acidic dissections of the sexual mores of the European middle and upper classes, Ophuls invests the playwright's determinism with an equanimity that allows all the characters their reasons for being, however ill considered or misguided those reasons might be. As Andrew Sarris writes, "Even when he is most bitter, he never descends to caricature. His humor is never malicious, his irony never destructive" (70). *Reigen* follows the assignations of one set of characters after another, with the interplay between the individuals characterized by the recurrence of deception and deceit. Ophuls' *La Ronde* underscores the circularity of the narrative in two ways: first, the narrator, played by Anton Walbrook, explicitly connects the episodes and underscores their fusion by the carousel he commands; second, Ophuls' celebrated moving camera connects the physical actions of the characters with mesmerizing, tour-de-force elaborations of camera movement and placement. While some have criticized the visual character of his work as mere baroque decoration, here, as elsewhere, it visually underscores his sense of life's circularity and the impenetrability of fate. David Thomson comments, "Ophuls's is the cinema of movement because time and the heart die when they stand still. His films are not decorated by movement, they consists of it" (562). *La Ronde* as a consequence possesses a unity of structure, a beauty of visual organization, and an equanimity of tone rare in the cinema. Ophuls never condescends to his characters or trivializes either their actions or their motives. While Schnitzler may be seen as a cynic, Ophuls is a humanist. The brief moments of passion the characters in this film possess are never assigned any greater value or meaning than they deserve, but neither are they denied their substance or their proper sympathy. The inexorability of loss and the passage of time and the affections fill Ophuls' film with a sense of both the enormity of life and its inescapable limitations. *(D. S.)*

Resources: Andrew Sarris, *The American Cinema. Directors and Directions 1929–1968* (New York: Dutton, 1968); David Thompson, *A Biographical Dictionary of Film*, 3d ed. (New York: Knopf, 1994).

RICHARD II

See HENRY IV, PARTS I & II, HENRY V, RICHARD II, and THE MERRY WIVES OF WINDSOR

RICHARD III (1592)
William Shakespeare

Richard III (1955)

Directed by Laurence Olivier

Adapted by Laurence Olivier and Alan Dent

Cast: Laurence Olivier (Richard III), Cedric Hardwicke (Edward IV), John Gielgud (Clarence), Stanley Baker (Richmond), Ralph Richardson (Buckingham), John Phillips (Norfolk), Claire Bloom (Lady Anne), Alec Clunes (Hastings), Michael Gough and Michael Ripper (Murderers), Pamela Brown (Jane Shore)

Length: 139 minutes to 155 minutes (depending on cassette)

The title page of the First Quarto (1597) summarizes the action: "The Tragedy of King Richard the Third, containing his treacherous plots against his brother Clarence: the pittiefull murther of his innocent nephewes; his tyrannical usurpation; with the whole course of his detested life, and most deserved death." The 1955 screen version gave Laurence Olivier, who directed and played the title role, the opportunity to capture on film one of his most famous roles, performed at the Old Vic in London during and after World War II. Olivier first played Richard in 1944 to rave reviews. The film follows Shakespeare's somewhat skewed history of Richard, Duke of Gloucester, as he dispatches both friends and enemies in single-minded pursuit of the throne of England. The play opens with the slightly expanded "Now is the winter of our discontent" soliloquy, into which Olivier has integrated with telling effect lines spoken by Richard in *Henry VI, Part 3*. From this initial disclosure of his intent to have the crown by any and all means possible, Richard proceeds through a course of unhesitatingly evil and political intrigues to live up to his claim to "set the murderous Machiavel to school." Olivier plays Richard with a subtle mix of impish engagement and Tudor malice, balancing the two sides of a unique characterization to create the definitive performance of Richard—on film and stage—for the twentieth century. There is considerable emphasis on psychological intimacy between the title character and the film audience. Olivier's Richard, when he is not directly and intimately looking into the camera, using Shakespeare's soliloquies to share his murderous intrigue, keeps the audience attentive to his confidences with knowing nods, lifted eyebrows, and fleeting, but fixed, glances that reinforce a shared understanding of the pleasure and amusement he finds in his malevolence. Olivier made some significant changes to accommodate the length of the play to acceptable screen time, most notably, the regrettable omission of the role of Queen Margaret. The production design forgoes period-piece spectacle, unlike Olivier's earlier filmed treatments of *Henry V* (1944) and *Hamlet* (1948). Costumes and sets are minimal but sufficient to establish historical credibility. Olivier is supported in grand style by his most notable rivals for the title of the greatest Shakespearean actor of the century, Ralph Richardson as Buckingham and John Gielgud as the Duke of Clarence. Other distinguished performances include Claire Bloom as Lady Anne, Alec Clunes as Hastings, and Pamela Brown as Jane Shore, a nonspeaking role added by Olivier. *(R. C. K.)*

Resource: Roger Manvell, *Shakespeare and the Film* (New York: Praeger, 1971); Laurence Olivier, *On Acting* (New York: Simon and Schuster, 1986).

Richard III (1995)

Directed by Richard Loncraine

Adapted by Richard Loncraine and Ian McKellen

Cast: Ian McKellen (Richard III), Maggie Smith (Duchess of York), Nigel Hawthorne (Clarence), John Wood (Edward), Kristin Scott Thomas (Lady Anne), Annette Bening (Queen Elizabeth), Jim Broadbent (Buckingham)

Length: 105 minutes

Rated: R

Shakespeare's *Richard III* (1592) is the last in a series of history plays that chronicle England's political turmoil before the Tudors assumed the throne.

In order for the ambitious Richard, Duke of Gloucester, House of York—a man with a twisted spine and evil intent—to usurp his dying brother, Edward IV, he must first remove the rightful heir, his elder brother, the Duke of Clarence. Clarence's death triggers, in turn, Edward's death from grief. Next, Richard must woo Edward's widow, Lady Anne, and murder Edward's heirs, the Prince of Wales and the Duke of York. But no sooner does he gain the throne than he faces betrayal from his former ally, the Duke of Buckingham, who joins with Henry, Earl of Richmond, against him. At the battle of Bosworth Field, Richard is defeated and killed by Richmond, who then becomes Henry VII. Among earlier film versions, the most notable was Laurence Olivier's theatrical version of 1955. Instead of Olivier's respectful and deliberately paced approach to costume and setting, Richard Loncraine and Ian McKellen's film (based on a stage production directed by Richard Eyre) is a fast, stripped-down, modernized commentary on violence and tyranny in a 1930s England that seems to be veering toward Nazism. Despite the appearance of elegant cafés, airports, touring cars, glamorous fashions, and jackbooted thugs, the Elizabethan rhetoric remains intact. The opening scene at the House of York's Victory Ball is audacious. At the microphone, like a big band radio announcer, Richard (Ian McKellen) launches his "Now is the winter of our discontent" speech, while a female crooner sings a pop version of Marlowe's "The Passionate Shepherd to His Love" in the background. Moments later Richard is in the rest room, snarling, "I, that am not shap'd for sportive tricks," while doing his business at the urinal; then, turning to the camera, he declaims his glee at being a villain ("I am determined to prove a villain/And hate the idle pleasures of these days"). Turning to the camera, he crooks his finger at us and invites us to join in on the fun. This updated War of the Roses is an allegory clothed in brown shirts and leather. As Richard gets closer to the throne and his plots against Edward (John Wood), Clarence (Nigel Hawthorne), and Lady Anne (Kristin Scott Thomas) grow more treacherous, he and his henchmen exchange their graceful cloaks and sashes for black leather, riding crops, high boots, and visored hats. McKellen himself is a study in asymmetry, with the crooked back, uneven legs, and withered arm that Shakespeare had depicted. On the wall of his office hangs a gigantic painting of the Richard he imagines himself to be—a tall, erect figure berobed in a luxurious trousseau of leather and metal. The message is clear: behind the robes and scepters of the British monarchy lies the potential for tyranny, corruption, and fascism as ruthless and dictatorial as anything the Nazis could concoct. *(J. C. T.)*

Resources: Scott Colley, *Richard's Himself Again: A Stage History of* Richard III (Westport, CT: Greenwood Press, 1992); Deborah Mitchell, "*Richard III*: Tonypandy in the Twentieth Century," *Literature/Film Quarterly* 25.2 (1997): 133–145.

THE RISE AND FALL OF LITTLE VOICE
(1992)
Jim Cartwright

Little Voice (1998)

Directed: by Mark Herman

Adapted by Mark Herman

Cast: Jane Horrocks ("L. V."), Michael Caine (Ray Say), Brenda Blethyn (Mari), Jim Broadbent (Mr. Boo), Ewan McGregor (Billy)

Length: 99 minutes

Rated: R

Actress and voice impersonator Jane Horrocks rose to stardom on the London stage as Laura Voss, or "L. V." ("Little Voice"), in Jim Cartwright's 1992 cabaret play, *The Rise and Fall of Little Voice*. The action is divided between a sleazy cabaret platform and the tiny attic room of a sad, withdrawn young woman who barricades herself away from the outside world to worship in solitude the memory of her dead father by imitating the song stylings of his favorite singers—Marilyn Monroe, Judy Garland, Shirley Bassey, and others. Alternating with L. V.'s song renditions are conversations and monologues among the members of the cabaret audience that advance L. V.'s "back story" and the various subplots. Although Horrocks was a sensation in the role (which was created for her), she did not follow it to Broadway, where it flopped; rather, she has since become widely known to television audiences in the series *Absolutely Fabulous* and to moviegoers in Mike Leigh's *Life Is Sweet*. In adapting the play to the screen, Mark Herman's first priority was to get Horrocks to reprise her stage role and, second, to reconfigure the cabaret revue-style show into a more traditional linear narrative. The characters and subplots are amplified and the action "opened up" to reveal the details of life in a dingy northern English town (Scarborough served as the location). L. V. is surrounded by a loud, frowsy mother who lives downstairs (Brenda Blethyn), a sweet, but terminally shy, boyfriend who's a telephone repairman and carrier pigeon trainer (Ewan McGregor), and a brash and rather seedy small-time talent promoter named Ray Say (Michael Caine). While conducting a tawdry romance with L. V.'s mother, Ray overhears the girl singing a Judy Garland song. Convinced he has a gold mine of talent on his hands, he pushes her into performing at a local cabaret called Mr. Boo's. Although her singing creates a sensation, she lapses into a semicoma shortly thereafter, and Ray is unable to get her to repeat the performance. Instead, L. V.'s house is destroyed in a fire, and she is rescued by Billy, with whom she has fallen in love. They reunite at the end and, together, tend his prized pigeons. Despite strong performances by all concerned, the movie scants Horrocks in her singing sequences. Only in one scene, when she has her big night at the cabaret—the set piece of the film—is she permitted to cut loose and belt out a brief medley of Garland/Monroe/Bassey songs. Director Herman was determined to record the sound of the scene "live," eschewing the usual practice of lip-synching the songs to a playback. The results are electrifying, a tantalizing hint of how effective Horrocks must have been in the original stage presentation. In the narrow constrictions of a small stage, this offbeat fable of a timid, insecure woman finding her "voice" was quite engaging; but on the big screen, the fantasy is tied too securely to the trappings of reality, and the results are labored and strained. *(J. C. T.)*

Resource: Lisa Schwarzbaum. "Sing Out, Sister," *Entertainment Weekly* No. 462 (11 December 1998): 48, 50.

ROMEO AND JULIET (1595–1596)
William Shakespeare

Romeo and Juliet (1936)

Directed by George Cukor

Adapted by Talbot Jennings

Cast: Leslie Howard (Romeo), Norma Shearer (Juliet), John Barrymore (Mercutio), Basil Rathbone (Tybalt), Edna May Oliver (Nurse), C. Aubrey Smith (Capulet), Violet Cooper (Lady Capulet), Henry Kolker (Friar Laurence), Andy Devine (Peter)

Length 126 minutes

Romeo, of the house of Montague, believes himself to be in love with Rosalind and, hoping to see her, crashes a masked ball held by Lord Capulet, his father's enemy. While there, he meets Capulet's daughter Juliet and falls deeply in love with her. Friar Laurence agrees to marry them secretly, thinking that their marriage would end a long-standing family feud. The complication comes when Romeo is challenged by Juliet's cousin Tybalt, who kills Romeo's kinsman, Mercutio. Romeo then kills Tybalt and is exiled from Verona. Because her father demands that she marry another man, a desperate Juliet takes a sleeping potion that will create the illusion of her death. Friar Laurence sends Friar John to Mantua to inform

Romeo of this scheme, but Romeo's servant arrives there first with news of her death. Romeo goes to her crypt and takes poison, dying just as she awakens. When Juliet discovers Romeo's still warm body, she kills herself.

This was one of the first attempts by a major Hollywood studio to film Shakespeare and may be considered a groundbreaking effort and an interesting, though dated, attempt to transform theatre into film. MGM producer Irving Thalberg intended a faithful adaptation of Shakespeare's classic tragedy of the "star-crossed lovers" in this film dominated by production values, elaborate sets, and opulent costumes, but the film dates badly because of its artificiality and overly theatrical approach. The age of the principals would not pose an insurmountable problem onstage, where a convenient distance can be maintained between actors and audience, but the illusion is damaged by the cinema's use of close-ups. Consequently, at age forty-two Leslie Howard cannot be very convincing as Romeo. At age thirty-five Norma Shearer is also too old, even though she gives an extraordinary reading of Juliet's speech voicing her fears about taking the sleeping potion in act IV. Edna May Oliver's nurse is consistently strong. John Barrymore makes an eccentric Mercutio in his cups to explain the character's extravagance, but he is eclipsed by Basil Rathbone's intelligently restrained Tybalt. The casting reflects the popular culture of the 1930s; despite Barrymore's extravagance and Andy Devine's pratfalling rendering of Peter, the nurse's servant, the Hollywood cast represents top actors and stars of the time. However, the film is not especially inventive or cinematic in its approach. *(J. M. W.)*

Resources: Peter Morris, *Shakespeare on Film* (Ottawa: Canadian Film Institute, 1972); Gene D. Phillips, *George Cukor* (Boston: Twayne, 1982); Kenneth S. Rothwell and Annabelle Henkin Melzer, *Shakespeare on Screen: An International Filmography and Videography* (New York: Neal-Schuman, 1990).

Romeo and Juliet (1954)

Directed and adapted by Renato Castellani

Cast: Laurence Harvey (Romeo), Susan Shantall (Juliet), Flora Robson (Nurse), John Gielgud (Chorus), Mervyn Johns (Friar Laurence), Sebastian Cabot (Capulet), Lydia Sherwood (Lady Capulet)

Length: 138 minutes

Castellani's adaptation went to the opposite extreme from the earlier 1936 MGM treatment by filming on location in northern Italy, but it was also far more cavalier in its treatment of the text. Fidelity was not a primary concern, and many lines were cut, including Mercutio's famous "Queen Mab" speech. Peter Morris praises Castellani's "bold pruning" of the text in an effort to produce a film that would be visual rather than dramatic.

The Apothecary scene is dropped, as is the character of Balthazar in act 5, while a scene is added for Friar Laurence. "Anything that held up the essential action was as far as possible pruned away," Roger Manvell wrote, while "lines were cut without attention to rhythm, and speeches (regardless of their 'fame') were quite simply lost" (97). A miscast Laurence Harvey and an inexperienced Susan Shantall were considered more wooden than passionate, but the standout performance in this adaptation is Sebastian Cabot's rendering of Juliet's father, angry from beginning to end, who flies into a rage when he learns that Juliet is not willing to marry Paris after Romeo is forced into exile for slaying Tybalt. Dame Flora Robson chose to downplay the Nurse's vulgarity, but Mervyn Johns hit the mark playing Friar Laurence. The fight scenes involving Mercutio, Tybalt, and Romeo are brutal and short, involving knives rather than swords. The film excels in its representation of the "murderous and meaningless feud" between the Montagues and the Capulets, influenced, according to Bosley Crowther of the *New York Times* (22 December 1954), by the violent and "uncompromising style of the Italian neo-realists." The film was praised for its splendid color photography and its picturesque settings and costumes, but one would be hard-pressed to find a stronger interpretation of Lord Capulet than that provided by Sebastian Cabot. *(J. M. W.)*

Resources: Roger Manvell, *Shakespeare and the Film* (New York: Praeger, 1971); Peter Morris, *Shakespeare on Film* (Ottawa: Canadian Film Institute, 1972); Kenneth S. Rothwell and Annabelle Henkin Melzer, *Shakespeare on Screen: An International Filmography and Videography* (New York: Neal-Schuman, 1990).

Romeo and Juliet (1968)

Directed by Franco Zeffirelli

Adapted by Franco Brusati, Masolino D'Amico, and Franco Zeffirelli

Cast: Leonard Whiting (Romeo), Olivia Hussey (Juliet), John McEnery (Mercutio), Michael York (Tybalt), Milo O'Shea (Friar Laurence), Pat Heywood (Nurse), Paul Harwick (Capulet), Natasha Parry (Lady Capulet), Robert Stephens (Prince), Laurence Olivier (Chorus, voice-over)

Length: 152 minutes

Rated: PG

Zeffirelli took his lead from Renato Castellani by filming his adaptation in his native Italy, but his boldness had more to do with his determination to cast principals who were closer to the age of Shakespeare's star-crossed lovers than had ever been attempted on film. Coming from a background in opera, Zeffirelli orchestrated an emotional spectacle, getting outstanding performances from John McEnery as Mercutio and Michael York as Tybalt, on one hand, and from Pat Heywood as the busybody Nurse and

Milo O'Shea as the presumptive Friar Laurence. Purists were disturbed by Zeffirelli's manipulation of the text that cuts Romeo's scene with the Apothecary and his encounter with Paris at the Capulet crypt and the entire removal of Friar John's misadventures on his way to Mantua to inform Romeo of Friar Laurence's scheme. In this film, Balthazar, after witnessing Juliet's funeral, simply overtakes on horseback the slower Friar John, who travels by mule. An anachronistic song is added to Capulet's ball scene, sung by a young man while the two lovers attempt to find each other. Even so, these early encounters are quite charming, though Peter Morris objected to Olivia Hussey's "amateur theatrics in the climactic scenes," which he considered embarrassing. Against claims that this is not an actor's film are the strong performances that also extend to the Nurse and Lord Capulet, who seems in this version to be at odds with Lady Capulet, who appears to be intimate with Tybalt, which would help to explain her extreme demand that Romeo be executed. The film is gorgeously produced and earned Academy Awards for its costumes and cinematography by Alberto Testa. Despite its structural distortions, the film was the definitive version of the 1960s. *(J. M. W.)*

Resources: Jack J. Jorgens, *Shakespeare on Film* (Bloomington: Indiana University Press, 1977); Roger Manvell, *Shakespeare and the Film* (New York: Praeger, 1971); Peter Morris, *Shakespeare on Film* (Ottawa: Canadian Film Institute, 1972); Franco Zeffirelli, *Zeffirelli: The Autobiography of Franco Zeffirelli* (New York: Weidenfeld and Nicholson, 1986).

Shakespeare in Love (1998)

Directed by John Madden

Adapted partly from Shakespeare by Tom Stoppard and Marc Norman

Cast: Joseph Fiennes (Will Shakespeare), Gwyneth Paltrow (Viola de Lesseps), Geoffrey Rush (Philip Henslowe), Colin Firth (Lord Wessex), Simon Callow (Tilney the Master of the Revels), Judi Dench (Queen Elizabeth)

Length: 123 minutes

Rated: PG-13

This delightful fantasy whimsically alleges that an ill-starred love between young Will Shakespeare (Joseph Fiennes) and a beauteous young aristocrat named Viola de Lesseps (Gwyneth Paltrow) inspired the writing of the romantic tragedy *Romeo and Juliet*. This play-within-a-play-within-a-movie is cunningly written by Shakespeare veteran Tom Stoppard (*Rosencrantz and Guildenstern Are Dead*) and Marc Norman; and directed by John Madden. In London, the Lord Chamberlain's company and star playwright Kit Marlowe at the Curtain Theatre compete with the Admiral's Men and young Will Shakespeare at the Rose Theatre in 1593. Shakespeare promises manager Philip Henslowe (Geoffrey Rush), who is nearly bank-rupt, a sensational melodrama called *Romeo and Ethel, the Pirate's Daughter*, but poor ink-stained Will is suffering from writer's block. After he meets the dazzling, golden-tressed Viola (Gwyneth Paltrow), his inspiration returns, and their secretive, nocturnal lovemaking is transmuted into the action and dialogue of a new play, retitled *Romeo and Juliet*. As the play nears its premiere (with none other than Viola cross-dressed as Romeo!), Viola's intended husband, Lord Wessex, intervenes and carries her off to an arranged marriage, leaving behind a heartbroken Romeo. To his amaze-ment, she runs away from Wessex and appears at the theatre to play Juliet. Thus, Viola/Juliet and Will/Romeo reunite onstage to enact their frustrated love before the audience. None other than Queen Elizabeth blesses the performance, and, as Viola leaves with her chastened husband, Wessex, the disconsolate Romeo settles down to write *Twelfth Night*, featuring a her-oine named Viola. Never mind the historical fabrications of the film—not the least of which is the fiction that *Romeo and Juliet* grew out of a pirate melodrama; this is a fantasy, with virtually the entire play of *Romeo and Juliet* refracted into two parallel narratives that dominate action on- and offstage. The love between Will and Viola is nearly as star-crossed as that between Romeo and Juliet and attended by the same kinds of interfamilial rivalries (in this case, between the competing stage companies of the Cur-tain and Rose theatres). Moreover, the actions on-and offstage can scarcely be differentiated. The film's set piece is a long montage sequence wherein Will and Viola's nocturnal love scenes are crosscut with the daily stage rehearsals. A desperate embrace begins in the bedroom and in the next cut continues onstage; a whispered declaration of love begins onstage and in the next cut concludes in the bedroom. Similarly, in the extended scene of the play's premiere, the lovers enact their frustrations during a full-dress stage performance. Art and life, private passion and public performance conjoin. In sum, these two lovers have become actors in their own lives and participants in their own drama. *(J. C. T.)*

Resources: Marchette Chute, *Shakespeare of London* (New York: E. P. Dutton, 1949); Owen Gleiberman, "Bard to the Bone," *Entertainment Weekly* No. 462 (11 December 1998): 43–46.

William Shakespeare's Romeo + Juliet (1996)

Directed by Baz Luhrmann

Adapted by Craig Pearce and Baz Luhrmann

Cast: Leonardo DiCaprio (Romeo), Claire Danes (Juliet), Paul Sorvino (Ca-pulet), Diane Venora (Lady Capulet), Miriam Margolyes (Nurse), Pete Post-lethwaite (Father Laurence), John Leguizamo (Tybalt), Harold Perrineau (Mercutio), Brian Dennehy (Montague), Christina Pickles (Lady Montague),

Dash Mihok (Benvolio), Vondie Curtis-Hall (Prince), M. Emmet Walsh (Apothecary), Edwina Moore (Chorus-Anchorwoman)

Length: 113 minutes

Rated: PG-13

In this postmodern treatment, Baz Luhrmann updates the setting to a contemporary urban landscape called Verona Beach, and though the decor looks like *West Side Story* blended with Fellini's *Satyricon* and *Miami Vice*, the film is careful to retain Shakespeare's language. In fact, the complete title is *William Shakespeare's Romeo + Juliet*, but it is Shakespeare "plus." The casting is canny but peculiar: Mercutio is played by an African American in dreadlocks and drag who seems to be high and on a rave when he offers his thoughts about Queen Mab. The younger Capulets and Montagues are presented as urban street gangs, tattooed punksters, by and large. Tybalt could pass for a pimp or a drug dealer, and all the junior Capulets look like high-octane drug runners. Leonardo DiCaprio is a soulful Romeo, more sedate than his kinsmen, but Claire Danes is more at ease with Juliet's lines. Of the young men, only Romeo and peacemaking Benvolio (Dash Mihok) appear to be borderline-normal. The film pushes the envelope in the crypt scene, played in an ornate church in the center of the city. Fugitive Romeo is pursued by helicopter and sure to be caught, should he delay in taking the poison. In this version, Juliet begins to stir as Romeo administers the poison, and there is a brief moment of recognition before he dies. In general, Luhrmann gets the lines right, and, though many are cut, most of them are in the right place. The treatment is clearly over the top and not likely to please the purists, but the film was justly praised for its visual spectacle. (*J. M. W.*)

Resources: Stanley Kauffmann, "Blanking Verse," *New Republic* (2 December 1996): 40; J. Welsh, "Postmodern Shakespeare: Strictly Romeo," *Literature/Film Quarterly* 25.2 (1997): 152–153; W. B. Worthen, "Drama, Performativity, and Performance," *PMLA* 113.5 (1998): 1093–1107.

See also WEST SIDE STORY

ROPE (1935)
Patrick Hamilton

Rope (1948)

Directed by Alfred Hitchcock

Adapted by Arthur Laurents

Cast: James Stewart (Rupert Cadell), John Dall (Shaw Brandon), Farley Granger (Philip), Cedric Hardwicke (Mr. Kentley), Constance Collier (Mrs. Atwater)

Length: 80 minutes

The action of *Rope* (1948), which was derived from British playwright Patrick Hamilton's stage melodrama, unfolds not only in a single setting but in a single evening, so that the time span covered by the story corresponds to the running time of the finished film. To emphasize the plot's uncompromising unity of time and place, Alfred Hitchcock committed himself to shooting the eighty-minute movie in ten unbroken takes of approximately ten minutes apiece. This is the maximum amount of time a camera can run before it must be reloaded. Because each ten-minute reel was not broken up into a series of several individual shots while it was being photographed, there was ultimately little need to edit the picture once it was shot. The overall effect of all of this cinematic sleight-of-hand is to give the impression that the action moves along fluidly from beginning to end, without any discernible break, in one extended shot that runs the length of the entire movie. Based on the infamous Loeb-Leopold murder case, *Rope* opens with two homosexuals, Brandon (John Dall) and Philip (Farley Granger), using a rope to strangle David, an acquaintance from their prep school days, just for the thrill of it. After stowing the lad's corpse in an ornate antique chest, they prepare to serve an elaborate buffet supper to David's relatives and friends right on top of what is now the young man's coffin. Rupert Cadell (James Stewart), a former teacher of the two killers, attends the party. Gradually, his suspicions are aroused by the mysterious absence of David, who was expected to be present. Rupert returns to the boys' flat after all the other guests have gone and asks enough probing questions to give the two amateur murderers enough rope with which to hang themselves. When the moment of truth is finally at hand, Rupert throws open the chest to peer down on the corpse that he by now assumes he will find there. He then opens a window to summon the police with a gunshot. *Rope* was a pacesetter in its treatment of homosexuality in a way that was relatively forthright for American movies. Scriptwriter Arthur Laurents remembers that, while the industry film censor allowed the homosexual implications of some of the dialogue to slip by him undetected, he demanded the deletion of some innocuous phrases in the dialogue that Laurents had, in fact, brought over from the original English play. Expressions such as "dear boy" are commonly used by teachers and students in British boarding schools and do not necessarily carry homosexual connotations at all. Nonetheless, in spite of some censorial interference, Hitchcock depicted the homosexual ambience of the story in a satisfactory fashion. The two young men's overdecorated apartment, their "sympathetic" housekeeper, and their mutually resentful relationship with the dead lad's girlfriend all testify to the sexual orientation of the pair. All in all, *Rope* is a finely crafted film, worthy of a respected place in the Hitchcock canon. *(G. D. P.)*

Resources: Sidney Gottlieb (ed.), *Hitchcock on Hitchcock: Selected Writings and Interviews* (Los Angeles: University of California Press, 1997); John Russell Taylor, *Hitch: The Life and Times of Alfred Hitchcock* (New York: Da Capo, 1996).

THE ROSE TATTOO (1951)
Tennessee Williams

The Rose Tattoo (1955)

Directed by Daniel Mann

Adapted by Tennessee Williams and Hal Kanter

Cast: Anna Magnani (Serafina), Burt Lancaster (Alvaro), Marisa Pavan (Rosa), Ben Cooper (Jack Hunter), Virginia Grey (Estelle Hohengarten)

Length: 117 minutes

When Hal Wallis acquired Williams' *The Rose Tattoo* (1951), he hired Williams to coscript the film adaptation with Hal Kanter, and Daniel Mann, who had directed the stage play, as director. The play, because it celebrates passion and sexuality, had to be altered to get past the censors. Serafina, a Sicilian seamstress who lives in a fictional town near New Orleans, worships her husband, Rosario, who is killed when his truck with bootleg liquor turns over as he tries to escape the police. Fearful that her daughter Rosa will get pregnant by her boyfriend, Serafina ends their affair. Her extravagant mourning for Rosario changes when she discovers that he has been unfaithful with Estelle Hohengarten, who has a rose tattoo that matches Rosario's. Alvaro, a simple, younger man, is attracted to Serafina and gets his own rose tattoo. Serafina relents, and when Alvaro comes to her house, they have sexual relations. Transformed by sex, she allows Rosa her own sexual freedom. To circumvent censorship problems, in the film when Alvaro comes to Serafina's house, he is so drunk that he passes out. When Rosa discovers Alvaro and Serafina, the latter's protestations of innocence are true. This change reflects the film's overall focus on family and marriage rather than passion. When Serafina frees Rosa, she is matchmaking, not simply sympathizing with a young woman in love; and she herself is more interested in marriage than in pure passion. While the play is a kind of tragicomedy, the film stresses the comedy and loses sight of the passion that snatches eternity from fleeting moments. Although the tone and message of the film and play differ, the setting is essentially the same. Some outside scenes were added, but they usually involve characters other than Serafina, who has constructed her own love/worship prison. Showing Rosario, who does not appear in the play, removes the mystery shrouding the godlike character who was the object of Serafina's worship. The film does, however, succeed in showing Serafina's change of mind about Alvaro when she gives him Rosario's rose-colored shirt and plays "The Sheik of Araby," a song earlier associated with Rosario. Despite the change of tone and the concessions to censorship, the film had two Oscar winners: James Wong Howe for Cinematography and Anna Magnani for Best Actress. *(T. L. E.)*

Resources: Gene Phillips, *The Films of Tennessee Williams* (East Brunswick, NJ: Associated University Presses, 1980); Maurice Yacowar, *Tennessee Williams and Film* (New York: Frederick Ungar, 1977).

ROSENCRANTZ AND GUILDENSTERN ARE DEAD (1967)
Tom Stoppard

Rosencrantz and Guildenstern Are Dead (1990)

Directed and adapted by Tom Stoppard

Cast: Gary Oldman (Rosencrantz), Tim Roth (Guildenstern), Richard Dreyfuss (the Player), Joanna Roth, Iain Glen, Donald Sumpter, Joanna Miles, Ian Richardson (acting troupe)

Length: 117 minutes

Rated: PG

In this upside-down treatment of *Hamlet*, Shakespearean royalty yield center stage to three bit players: the Player, heading the acting troupe that evinces Claudius' guilt, and two lowly courtiers, who, before reaching an abrupt end, bumble through Elsinore castle, sidestepping clues that would demystify their mission and their lives. Neither Guildenstern's determination to "glean" and "delve" nor Rosencrantz's passivity brings either courtier a step closer to solving the mystery that circumscribes their lives—the Shakespearean myth apparent only to the audience and to the seemingly omniscient Player (a superb Dreyfuss). For the audience, knowledge of *Hamlet* imbues the "[d]eaths of kings, and princes . . . and nobodies!" with meaning—while the nobodies have, for answers, only the Player's breezy nihilism.

Despite the instant acclaim won by its National Theatre London debut, the play defied adaptation for nearly a quarter century. In rescripting it for film, Stoppard heavily cut dialogue to deflect the work's energy from language. Though the result won the Golden Lion Award for Best Film at the Venice Film Festival, it was not a popular success—perhaps because the two central nobodies neither invite identification nor achieve their goals, doubly defying Hollywood conventions.

Nevertheless, Stoppard's adaptations are consistently illuminating and occasionally ingenious. Some cleverly concretize abstractions—as when a badminton-game pantomime complements verbal repartee, or Oldman, in hammock-position atop a stone tomb, delivers Ros' surprisingly eloquent soliloquy on human intimations of mortality. The most striking is a series of scenes in which Ros comes within a heartbeat of making historic scientific discoveries. In the most comical of these, he constructs a paper biplane worthy of the Wright Brothers, only to have Guil crush it in an Oliver Hardy spasm of impatience; later, Rosencrantz just misses discovering Archimedes' principle and Newton's law of gravity—natural laws indicative of a design at work in the physical world.

The movie highlights the theme that—up to a point—"all-the-world's-a-stage." Loose printed pages—perhaps clue-yielding excerpts from a *Hamlet* folio—scuttle across the paths of an oblivious Ros and Guil, only to end up as crushed paper airplanes. Rosencrantz and Guildenstern, immersed in their baths, find themselves surrounded by bathing Tragedians who appear to accept them as two of their own troupe members. The lines between stage and reality blur further in the wheels-within-wheels "play within the play" scene, as the Player (now Lucianus in dress rehearsal for *The Murder of Gonzago*) announces Hamlet's "plan to catch the conscience of the King" by detonating a smoke bomb; when the mist clears to reveal the poison-in-the-ear puppet-mime being watched by the player-king and queen—whose masks cannot hide their Claudius-like uneasiness and Gertrude-like doubts—the camera cinches this intricate transition by cutting to a close-up of the player king losing his poker face, then jump-cutting to a matching close-up of Claudius as the final *Gonzago* performance provokes his cry for light. Later, we find the Player merely acting his King-of-England part at one moment, while actually executing the death order at the next. The curtain closes on Horatio's last eloquent lines, but the camera cuts to the Tragedians' cart lumbering through the wood at the spot where the summoned pair first encountered it—thereby suggesting that the entire story has been only a play staged by a seedy Renaissance acting troupe. Yet for Stoppard, all teasing interplay between art and life stops at the door of death—a theme underscored as the camera punctuates each noun in the Player's "[d]eaths of kings and princes . . . and nobodies!" line with cinematic images of *Hamlet*'s final bloodbath. *(T. M./I. M.)*

Resources: Paul Delaney, *Tom Stoppard: The Moral Vision of the Major Plays* (New York: St. Martin's Press, 1990); Paul Delaney, ed., *Tom Stoppard in Conversation* (Ann Arbor: University of Michigan Press, 1994); Tom Stoppard, *Rosencrantz and Guildenstern Are Dead: The Film* (London: Faber and Faber, 1991).

See also HAMLET

ROXANNE

See CYRANO DE BERGERAC

THE RULING CLASS (1968)
Peter Barnes

The Ruling Class (1972)

Directed by Peter Medak

Adapted by Peter Barnes

Cast: Peter O'Toole (Jack, 14th Earl of Gurney), Alastair Sim (Bishop Lampton), Arthur Lowe (Tucker), Coral Browne (Lady Claire Gurney), William Mervyn (Sir Charles Gurney), Carolyn Seymour (Grace Shelley), Michael Bryant (Dr. Herder).

Length: 138 minutes

Rated: PG

The Ruling Class was first performed on 6 November 1968 at the Nottingham Playhouse and transferred to London's Picadilly Theatre on 29 February 1969. Acclaimed by *Sunday Times* drama critic Harold Hobson as one of the major theatrical events of postwar British theatre, this biting satire by first-time playwright Peter Barnes combined wit, pathos, melodrama, horror, cynicism, and sentiment. Both play and film brilliantly depict the transition of "insane" heir Jack from harmless, hippie, God of Love figure to a "sane," normal, Jehovah-like, sadistic, Jack-the-Ripper member of the British Establishment. The film combines the play's original two-part structure and ensemble. Medak faithfully follows Barnes' original dialogue but also opens up the play to encompass exterior scenes, such as those in the garden of the Gurney stately home, Dr. Herder's clinic, and a reconstructed House of Lords for the final scene. Medak's cinematic extensions are few, but exceptional in their brevity. On his wedding morning, Jack leaps off his cross, and Medak freeze-frames his image to capture the character's transcendent simplicity. When Dr. Herder uses extreme methods to force Jack into Establishment normality, Medak's divides the audience perspective into two modes of vision, something impossible in the original play. The audience shares the family view of seeing Jack wrestle with an invisible being as well as Jack's internal view of the eight-foot Victorian beast who "cures" him of his benevolent feelings. When Jack first acts out his Jack the Ripper on seductive Aunt Claire, Medak photographs the 1888 Whitechapel surroundings, merely described in the play. Also, Jack makes his terrifying speech about the necessity for capital punishment and torture at a foxhunting meeting rather than the drawing room of the original play. This associates his speech with one of the most vicious surviving pursuits of the English ruling class. Finally, Medak extends the symbolic significance of Jack's maiden speech in the House of Lords by cutting back and forth between the real chamber and Jack's view of an environment totally populated by skeletons and decaying corpses, rather than the play's use of two tiers of moldering, cobwebbed dummies and three lords, one of whom drags a skeleton behind him. As in the play, the film ends with Jack's murdering his loving wife, formerly his uncle's mistress. But Medak visually concludes the sequence with an overhead shot of the Gurney Manor, Grace's scream, and the voice of the next heir speaking, "I'm Jack. I'm Jack." *(T. W.)*

Resources: Clive Barker, "On Class, Christianity, and Questions of Comedy," *New Theatre Quarterly* 6.21 (1990): 5–24; Peter Barnes, *Plays: One* (London: Methuen Drama, 1989).

SABRINA FAIR; OR A WOMAN OF THE WORLD (1953)
Samuel Albert Taylor

Sabrina (1954)

Directed by Billy Wilder

Adapted by Billy Wilder, Ernest Lehman, and Samuel Taylor

Cast: Humphrey Bogart (Linus Larrabee), William Holden (David Larrabee), Audrey Hepburn (Sabrina Fairchild), Walter Hampden (Oliver Larrabee), John Williams (Thomas Fairchild), Martha Hyer (Elizabeth Tyson), Ruth Woods (Gretchen), Marcel Dalio (Baron), Nella Walker (Maude Larrabee)

Length: 113 minutes

Samuel Taylor's *Sabrina Fair* opened on Broadway in 1953 and was adapted to film in 1954 by Billy Wilder and Ernest Lehman, who added sets, changed the plot, and omitted some characters. In the play, Sabrina, daughter of the chauffeur on the Larrabee estate, returns home after five years in Paris, where she has met Paul D'Argenson, a wealthy Frenchman who wants to marry her. Although Mr. Larrabee remembers her as a mousy, intelligent graduate of a small women's college, Sabrina's years in Paris have transformed her into a sophisticated, attractive young woman who attracts the attention of David, whom she has loved since her childhood. After a midnight cruise, David wants to marry Sabrina, but his parents oppose the match. Linus, David's brother, is a workaholic businessman who does not believe in romantic love and delights in teasing David by dating Gretchen, David's ex-wife. The verbal exchanges between Linus and Sabrina about the difference between being domestic and domesticated and the necessity of refusing commitment in order to pursue freedom suggest that they belong together. Paul's arrival at the Larrabee home further complicates matters, but the romantic Paul is diverted by Linus, who promises him a business deal. When Sabrina discovers that David has discussed his marriage proposal with his entire family before he asks her to marry him, she realizes he is not the man for her. Linus, who has been encouraging the David-Sabrina match, finally realizes, with the advice of Maude's friend, Julia, that he loves Sabrina, who is herself a millionaire, due to her father's wise investments. Wilder omits Gretchen and Julia, substitutes an aging, harmless baron for Paul, but retains the fairy-tale opening of the play (Sabrina's "Once upon a time . . ." introduction). Wilder, however, begins with a Larrabee party. Sabrina, hiding in a tree, observes the party and David's customary practice of sending a young woman to the indoor tennis court while he gets a bottle of champagne and puts two champagne glasses in his back pocket. On his way to the tennis court, he meets Sabrina but scarcely notices her. Despondent, she attempts suicide by exhaust fumes in the garage but is rescued by Linus. Wilder then photographs Sabrina's year in Paris, where she studies cooking and is transformed into a sophisticated young woman by an elderly baron. Upon her return, David falls in love with her, despite his engagement to Elizabeth Tyson, whose father runs the plastic company Linus wants to merge with. Mr. and Mrs. Larrabee and Linus do not want the merger/marriage ruined, so Linus incapacitates David, who sits on the champagne glasses he was taking to Sabrina at the tennis court. While David recovers, Linus wins Sabrina's love and convinces her to go by boat with him to Paris, but he does not intend to board the ship. Ashamed of what he has done, he gives his ship ticket to David, whom he wishes to join Sabrina on the ship. David, however, realizes that Sabrina and Linus belong together and arranges for Linus to meet Sabrina on the ship. *(T. L. E.)*

Resources: Bernard F. Dick, *Billy Wilder* (Boston: Twayne, 1980); Axel Madsen, *Billy Wilder* (Bloomington: Indiana University Press, 1969).

Sabrina (1995)

Directed by Sydney Pollack

Adapted by Barbara Benedek and David Rayfield

Cast: Harrison Ford (Linus Larrabee), Julia Ormond (Sabrina Fairchild), Greg Kinnear (David Larrabee), Nancy Marchand (Maude Larrabee), John Wood

(Fairchild), Richard Crenna (Patrick Tyson), Angie Dickinson (Ingrid Tyson), Lauren Holly (Elizabeth Tyson)

Length: 127 minutes

Rated: PG

Pollack's *Sabrina* is based not only on Samuel Taylor's *Sabrina Fair* (1953) but also on Billy Wilder's 1954 film adaptation of the play. In fact, Pollack's film, with relatively minor changes, mostly updates, is a remake of the film. (See entry on Wilder's film for plot summary of Taylor's play.) Pollack's opening sequence at the Larrabee party closely parallels Wilder's, but Pollack's omission of Sabrina's attempted suicide does make the film more "wholesome." When Sabrina goes to Paris, she is a "gofer" with *Vogue* magazine rather than a cooking student; this change with its fashion emphasis is, in Linus' words elsewhere in the film, more "nineties" in its focus on materialism and glamour. While in Paris, Sabrina is intent on "finding herself," also a 1990s preoccupation; and her developing skill at photography makes her an independent woman with career potential. As she finds herself, David's photograph, mounted on her apartment wall in Paris, becomes covered by material that reflects her growth; her obsession with him decreases, and her eventual choice seems more logical. David's situation is also changed. He is engaged to Elizabeth Tyson, now a pediatrician rather than a debutante; and Elizabeth's father is in electronics rather than plastics. Elizabeth is absent from much of Pollack's film, and the roles of her father and mother, a former flight attendant (another update), are enhanced. Linus' courtship of Sabrina is not conducted on a sailboat but, via helicopter and private jet, on the family's island retreat. When Linus actually donates a building on the island (he has told Sabrina he has given it to the town to use as a halfway house) to the town council and disregards the tax implications, the audience knows, if he does not, that he is changing. The ending in the films is almost identical. Instead of going to Paris by boat as Linus plans in the Wilder film, the trip is by plane, which means that Linus cannot travel with her—he flies by Concorde and is waiting for her at her Paris apartment. In Linus' absence, David takes over the company; it seems he has kept current on all company business! His parting words to Linus are, "It's time you ran away from home." At the end of the film Linus and Sabrina embrace against a Parisian backdrop. This romantic ending is parallel to the romantic fate Pollack provides for Sabrina's father; he marries another Larrabee employee. Although the film updates the material, the concern about social class seems dated, especially for the 1990s. *(T. L. E.)*

Resources: P. Travers, *"Sabrina," Rolling Stone* No. 726 (25 January 1996): 66; C. Vivani, *"Sabrina," Positif* No. 420 (February 1996): 27–28.

SAINT JOAN (1923)
George Bernard Shaw

Saint Joan (1957)

Directed and produced by Otto Preminger

Adapted by Graham Greene

Cast: Jean Seberg (Saint Joan), Richard Widmark (the Dauphin), Richard Todd (Dunois), John Gielgud (the Earl of Warwick)

Length: 110 minutes

Shaw's *Saint Joan* traces Joan's short-lived military career, trial, execution, and canonization twenty-five years after her death. In the play she first wins the support of Robert de Baudricourt, castle commander, after she demonstrates her control over the egg-laying abilities of the castle's chickens. With three soldiers she crosses the English-infiltrated countryside and arrives at Chinon, where she then gains the support of the cowardly Dauphin, heir to the French throne. She then goes to the camp of Dunois, whose soldiers need a west wind to cross the Loire River and defeat the English at Orleans. Her prayers bring the wind and the victory; but when she wants to carry the fight to Paris, the Dauphin, who has been crowned as Charles at Rheims following the Orleans victory, turns her down. When she continues the fight, she is captured; and after several months of political infighting and religious interrogation she is taken by English troops and burned at the stake. The six scenes of the play are followed by an epilogue that takes place twenty-five years later in Charles' royal chamber. Charles learns of Joan's canonization, falls asleep, and in his dream many of the leading players in the drama appear to justify their part in the drama.

In his film script Graham Greene begins as the play ends, twenty-five years after Joan's death and in Charles' royal chambers. As a result, the film consists of flashbacks to earlier action. The first flashback covers Joan's meeting with Robert de Baudricourt, the Dauphin, and Dunois and then her rejection by the newly crowned Charles, whom Dunois supports. The second flashback occurs after the Earl of Warwick joins the dream and recounts her interrogation, her exposure to the instruments of torture, the charges and trial, the political strife between the French and the English, and her burning at the stake by the English, with the passive collusion of the French clergy. After the two major flashbacks, additional characters appear in the dream: Cauchon, one of her persecutors, describes his excommunication; Dunois justifies his decision to back Charles, and a "saint from hell," the English soldier who gave her the makeshift wooden cross, explains that his actions give him one day off from Hell each year. The film ends with the observation that a dead saint is safer for the church than a live one, a high-angle shot of Joan asking, "How long, oh Lord?" and Charles covering his head with his bedding. Greene's changes, most of which involve cutting lengthy speeches, retain much of Shaw's satiric edge, but the changed ending leaves the audience on a comic, rather than serious, note. *(T. L. E.)*

Resources: Gerald Pratley, *The Cinema of Otto Preminger* (New York: A. S. Barnes, 1971); Otto Preminger, *Preminger: An Autobiography* (Garden City, NY: Doubleday, 1977).

SAME TIME NEXT YEAR (1975)
Bernard Slade

Same Time Next Year (1975)

Directed by Robert Mulligan

Adapted by Bernard Slade

Cast: Alan Alda (George), Ellen Burstyn (Doris), Ivan Bonar (Chalmers), Bernie Kuby (Waiter), Cosmo Sardo (2d Waiter)

Length: 119 minutes

Rated: PG

A romantic comedy, *Same Time Next Year* is the story of a unique love affair between a young housewife and an accountant. Bernard Slade's characters, George (Alan Alda) and Doris (Ellen Burstyn), provide a warm and humorous look at love, adultery, and life. The film begins with the couple's chance meeting at a country inn. At the end of the evening, George and Doris end up spending the night together. Feeling guilty the next morning, they acknowledge they are happily married to wonderful people. Despite their guilt, the pair still feel drawn to each other. Realizing they both come to the inn on the same weekend each year, George and Doris embark on their love affair. The film traces the lives of the two lovers over three decades through their annual romantic rendezvous. As the years pass, George and Doris share their dreams, triumphs, disappointments, and tragedies. Warm and wonderful characters, a major source of their charm flows not from their relationship but from the feelings they express for their unsuspecting spouses. Both George and Doris never completely leave their families behind. Through delightful stories, they introduce Helen and Harry, their spouses, as silent members of the cast. The dimension of the absent spouses firmly establishes the parameters of the love affair. George and Doris are clearly committed to each other, but for only one weekend each year. Robert Mulligan, the director, uses news footage to provide skillful transitions between the years and to place each weekend within the context of time. These scenes connect the changing attitudes and personal development of George and Doris to the current issues and events of the world. As the relationship evolves, George and Doris often appear to be traveling divergent paths. Within the confines of each weekend, the couple struggles to support their relationship through mutual understanding and compromise. Although they meet only once a year, George and Doris find that nurturing their love requires the same type of work as their respective marriages. By the end of the film, the characters, in many ways, have transformed their love affair into a second marriage. Alan Alda and Ellen Burstyn give outstanding performances in portraying two ordinary people who by chance find extraordinary love and friendship. *(N. I.)*

Resources: Gary Arnold, "Wry, with a Twist," *Washington Post* (9 February 1979): C1, C11; *New Yorker* (4 December 1978): 195; *Variety Film Reviews 1978–1980*, 15 (22 November 1978).

THE SEARCH FOR SIGNS OF INTELLIGENT LIFE IN THE UNIVERSE (1985)
Jane Wagner

The Search for Signs of Intelligent Life in the Universe (1991)

Directed by John Bailey
Adapted by Jane Wagner
Cast: Lily Tomlin
Length: 106 minutes
Rated: PG-13

The Search for Signs of Intelligent Life in the Universe was the most successful—commercially and artistically—of several collaborations between comedian-actress Lily Tomlin and writer Jane Wagner. After *Appearing Nitely* and *Moment by Moment*, *The Search for Signs* represented the height of Tomlin's talent for one-woman performances and of Wagner's skill in providing the words for those performances. *The Search for Signs* was the result of a lengthy process of trial and error, revision and rewriting, and a series of "work shows" in which the two women refined their ideas in front of paying and nonpaying audiences. The finished Broadway version of the play debuted in the fall of 1985, and Tomlin won the 1986 Best Actress Tony for her multicharacter performance. For the stage production, Tomlin went through no costume changes yet portrayed approximately a dozen separate characters in the course of the relatively free-form drama. With Tomlin shifting instantaneously from one character to the next, the play's dramatic vignettes range from the crass to the sublime. Acting as a sort of moderator is Trudy, a wizened bag lady who claims to be the medium for a group of extraterrestrials who are mounting the search that gives the play its title. Additional characters include Agnus Angst, a rebellious and belligerent young teen whose attitude matches her last name; Lud and Marie, Agnus' exasperated and quarrelsome grandparents; Chrissy, an anxiety-laden health-club aficionado; and Kate, a bored and cynical socialite. At the center of the play are Lyn, Edie, and Marge, a trio of feminist friends who reminisce and relive their roles as part of the women's movement. Throughout the play, Tomlin switched back and forth among characters at a moment's notice, using only her voice and her body to differentiate one from the others. These momentary transformations were motivated by the idea that the glimpses of the various characters came courtesy of the channeling abilities of Trudy. A 1986 documentary film, entitled *Lily Tomlin*, highlighted the preproduction process the play went through and included several onstage segments of the play itself. In 1991 the entire play was filmed, with many of the more imaginative elements of the stage production given more concrete treatment. Rather than forming a continuous series of vignettes connected solely by virtue of Tomlin's talents, director John Bailey used the capabilities of film to put the characters into more realistic settings. Thus, Trudy and Agnus Angst (among others) were given the full costumes that Tomlin's stage performance only suggested. This tactic of making the imaginary elements concrete disrupted the seamless flow of Tomlin's performance and was not well received. According to critic Mary E. Belles, "The filmmakers did not recognize that the cosmic glue holding the nebulous work together resides in Tomlin's instantaneous transformations . . . everything designed to open [the play] up to the screen is more distracting than enhancing" (352–353). *(C. M.)*

Resources: Mary E. Belles, "*The Search for Signs of Intelligent Life in the Universe*," in *Magill's Cinema Annual 1992*, ed. Frank Magill (Pasadena, CA: Salem Press, 1992); Jeff Sorenson, *Lily Tomlin: Woman of a Thousand Faces* (New York: St. Martin's Press, 1989).

SECRET HONOR: THE LAST TESTAMENT OF RICHARD M. NIXON (1983)
Donald Freed and Arnold M. Stone

Secret Honor (1984)

Directed and adapted by Robert Altman

Cast: Philip Baker Hall (Richard Nixon)

Length: 90 minutes

Rated: PG

At about 10 P.M. a suicidal and fictional character named Richard Milhous Nixon enters his study with a loaded pistol, intending to set the record straight before shuffling off this mortal coil and to defend his administration, while drinking himself into a stupor as he rants and discourses in what becomes, in the words of Vincent Canby, "an increasingly manic tangle of self-serving apologies, personal reminiscences, hilarious attacks on colleagues and, finally, a wild explanation for Watergate." This deftly filmed, one-man show is unique and tremendously complex rather than a mere comic impersonation. In his *New York Times* review Canby called it "the most eccentric film of the year," but Stanley Kauffmann dismissed it as a "lurid fantasy" that "misses the mark." Kauffmann praised Altman, however, "keeping his confined film visually alive" but felt that Philip Baker Hall in the solo lead deserved a better-written role. *(J. M. W.)*

Resources: Vincent Canby, "Five Movies that Make Demands on Audiences," *New York Times* (30 June 1985): Sec II, 15–16; Stanley Kauffmann, "Poor Richard's Almanack," *The New Republic* (15–22 July 1985): 32–33.

SEPARATE TABLES

See TABLE BY THE WINDOW and TABLE NUMBER SEVEN

THE SEVEN YEAR ITCH (1953)
George Axelrod

The Seven Year Itch (1955)

Directed by Billy Wilder

Adapted by George Axelrod and Billy Wilder

Cast: Marilyn Monroe (the Girl), Tom Ewell (Richard Sherman), Evelyn Keyes (Helen Sherman)

Length: 105 minutes

George Axelrod, after a decade of writing over 400 radio and television scripts, stormed Broadway with the smash comedy *The Seven Year Itch* (1953). Starring Tom Ewell as publisher Richard Sherman, who has been married for seven years and suddenly finds himself a summer bachelor, the play deals with Sherman's fantasies of an affair with "the girl" who has moved into the upstairs apartment. With his wife and son out of town for an extended vacation, Sherman's opportunity "to play while the cat's away" looms large. In the end, however, Sherman's flights of fancy are held in check by his conscience and his comic apprehensions of the consequences of such a dalliance. In adapting the play to film, Axelrod and director Billy Wilder, while largely adhering to the contours and settings of the original, toned down the play's more suggestive dialogue. However, with the glamour casting of blond bombshell Marilyn Monroe as "the girl," replacing the play's girl-next-door type essayed on stage by Vanessa Brown, the film tended to transform Sherman's Walter Mittyish longings into leering, animalistic lust. Playing against Monroe, Ewell's Sherman, while still an effective caricature of the era's gray-flanneled executive, moved from languorous fantasizing, to predatory wolfishness. Instead of the more gentle and sympathetic comic observations of the play, with the casting of Monroe, the film tended toward a more sexually explicit kind of burlesque. In spite of the changes brought about by Monroe's casting and the infusions of Wilder's famed Continental wit, the film remains a highly entertaining and revealing look into 1950s American popular culture. In Sherman's capacity as a publisher, for instance, the film capitalizes on the period's fascination with sexual psychology. Indeed, we catch Sherman in the midst of editing "The Repressed Urges of the Middle-Aged Male," a chapter from a forthcoming work titled *Man and the Unconscious*, a bit of business counterpointing Sherman's own potentially adulterous dilemma. Sherman's identification as a paperback publisher is likewise significant in that paperbacks soared to popularity during the decade. The film also stands as an important work in the oeuvre of one of Hollywood's master directors, Billy Wilder, and a companion to another equally memorable Wilder-Monroe sex comedy, *Some Like It Hot* (1959). Finally, *The Seven Year Itch* is arguably Monroe's best performance as "Marilyn Monroe," the 1950s quintessential sex symbol, the perfectly constructed "Girl" of everyman's dreams. In fact, the scene in which a rush of cool air from a subway grating sends her dress flying up past her waist remains the defining image of Monroe, an image in which her fleshy sensuality is tantalizingly juxtaposed against her childlike impish eyes and mien. *(C. M. B.)*

Resources: Peter Biskind, *Seeing Is Believing: How Hollywood Taught Us to Stop Worrying and Love the Fifties* (New York: Random House, 1983); Axel Madsen, *Billy Wilder* (Bloomington: University of Indiana Press, 1969).

SEXUAL PERVERSITY IN CHICAGO
(1974)
David Mamet

About Last Night . . . (1986)

Directed by Edward Zwick

Adapted by Tim Kazurinsky and Denise DeClure

Cast: Rob Lowe (Danny), Demi Moore (Debbie), Jim Belushi (Bernie), Elizabeth Perkins (Joan), George DiCenzo (Mr. Favio), Michael Alldredge (Mother Malone), Robin Thomas (Steve Carlson), Donna Gibbons (Alex), Megan Mullally (Pat), Patricia Duff (Leslie), Rosana De Soto (Mrs. Lyons), Sachi Parker (Carrie), Robert Neches (Gary), Ada Maris (Carmen), Joe Greco (Gus), Rebeca Arthur (Crystal), Tim Kazurinsky (Colin)

Length: 113 minutes

Rated: R

In David Mamet's one-act play, two friends, Danny and Bernie, and their female counterparts, Debbie and her roommate, Joan, are pretty cynical about love, marriage, and relationships. Danny and Debbie meet in a singles bar and end up spending the night together. They are bewildered the morning after, wondering what "last night" was all "about." These are not typical romantics but confused innocents tumbling down the freeway of life. Before long, they are having a full-fledged affair, and Debbie is moving in with Danny, while Joan and Bernie form a cynical chorus to frame their romantic expectations. After Debbie moves out to live with Danny, Joan gets involved with a lawyer, who ultimately leaves her to return to his wife, a wife Joan did not know existed. Elizabeth Perkins is splendid as the cynical, but vulnerable, roommate who simply cannot stand Danny's friend Bernie, played as a foulmouthed hedonist by Jim Belushi. After Danny and Debbie have a spat and separate, Joan and Bernie work to get the primary lovers back together, so that the film can reach its conclusion with an upbeat sense of reconciliation. Rob Lowe and Demi Moore show their early star potential in this boy-meets-girl fable, set in a swamp of contemporary cynicism. The filmmakers ditched the play's nasty title, extended the action, opened up the play to the outer world of Chicago, and made the story seem more hopeful. The film is less bleak than the play, but traces remain of the emptiness, sleaziness, and spiritual poverty of the singles scene, a breeding ground for AIDS, herpes, and emotional misery. The film is well directed and well acted by an impressive ensemble cast. *(J. M. W.)*

Resources: Leslie Bennetts, "To Be or Not to Be Committed: 'Last Night' Tackles Love in the 80's," *New York Times* (13 July 1986): II, 19–22; Jack Kroll, " 'Love' Is a Four-Letter Word," *Newsweek* (14 July 1986): 69.

SHADOWLANDS (1989)
William Nicholson

Shadowlands (1993)

Directed by Richard Attenborough

Adapted by William Nicholson

Cast: Anthony Hopkins (Jack Lewis), Edward Hardwicke (Warnie Lewis), Debra Winger (Joy Gresham), Joseph Mazzello (Douglas Gresham), James Frain (Peter Whistler)

Length: 170 minutes

Rated: PG

Shadowlands first existed as a BBC teleplay; Nicholson in 1989 adapted it to a play, which made its American debut in 1990. Set in Oxford in the 1950s, the play concerns the love story of C. S. Lewis (Jack), an Oxford don, author of children's books, and Renaissance scholar, and Joy Gresham, who describes herself as a Jew, converted Christian, and communist but who also is a prizewinning poet. Jack, who lives with his brother Warnie, is a popular lecturer on Christianity, and the play opens with his addressing the problem of pain, which he somewhat smugly suggests is

"God's megaphone to rouse a deaf world." His moral complacency and intellectual life are shaken by the arrival of Joy and her son Douglas. Although she is a fan of his, she occasionally confronts him; and her blunt manner and lack of tact alienate Jack's academic friends. After her divorce from her alcoholic husband, Joy returns to England; and she and Jack become close friends. In fact, he marries her so that she can stay in England. When she becomes ill with cancer, the marriage of convenience ripens into a real union. After Joy's death, Jack learns that experience is a hard teacher, and he alters the "pain" lecture he gave at the beginning of the play. When he and Douglas sit together in the attic, they both sob and experience "the pain that cries like a child." When he adapted his play to film, Nicholson added a prologue in Oxford (where Jack's academic life is portrayed), tutorials, book signings, lectures (all about the nature of pain), two trips to the Golden Valley, and a dawn celebration. The Golden Valley trips and dawn celebration (the first time he had ever seen it) serve to demonstrate how Joy opens up his emotional life, and the lectures, which culminate in his telling about Joy's illness, reveal his spiritual development. In the tutorial Jack encounters Whistler, a bright student Jack initially dismisses; but he learns from the student and modifies "we read not to be alone" to "we love to know we're not alone." Hopkins, who played a similarly repressed character in *Remains of the Day* (also 1993), does a convincing job of demonstrating how one is awakened to love and life through suffering. At the end of the film Jack reaches out to the despondent Douglas, and the last shots show them walking in the Golden Valley, the Herefordshire of Jack's youth. *(T. L. E.)*

Resources: W. M. Hagen, "*Shadowlands* and the Redemption of Light," *Literature/ Film Quarterly* 26.1 (1998): 10–15; Stanley Kauffmann, "Soft Focus," *New Republic* 211 (7 February 1994): 26.

SHAKESPEARE IN LOVE

See ROMEO AND JULIET

THE SHANGHAI GESTURE (1926)
John Colton

The Shanghai Gesture (1941)

Directed by Josef von Sternberg
Adapted by Josef von Sternberg, Karl Vollmoeller, Geza Herczeg, and Jules Furthman

Cast: Gene Tierney (Poppy), Walter Huston (Sir Guy Charteris), Victor Mature (Dr. Omar), Phyllis Brooks (Dixie Pomeroy), Albert Basserman (Commissioner), Ona Munson (Mother Gin Sling)
Length: 98 minutes

The Shanghai Gesture is based on a 1926 play written by Colton, who describes himself as "A Play Boy of the Eastern World" in the published edition. It deals with the revenge of brothel owner Mother God Damn on Sir Guy Charteris, who deserted her years before and arranged for her to be sold into white slavery. Unknown to him, she bore a daughter whom she substituted for Charteris' Caucasian baby before her humiliating life as a prostitute living in Chinese junks. Mother was the daughter of a rich Manchu official, and Charteris used her money to develop his present status as head of the British China Trading Company. Mother plans her revenge on New Year's Day by corrupting Charteris' officially recognized daughter, Poppy, and threatening to sell his Caucasian daughter, Ni-Pau (from another marriage), into slavery. However, she decides to restore Ni-Pau to her father and kill the now totally unredeemable Poppy. The Hays Office naturally rejected thirty-two earlier screenplay versions of his provocative play before von Sternberg and his adapters gained approval. The film basically follows the original plot but modifies taboo racial and sexual overtones according to censorship requirements. Mother God Damn now becomes casino owner Mother Gin Sling. Poppy's Japanese lover Prince Oshima is now Victor Mature's Dr. Omar, "doctor of nothing." Although lacking Marlene Dietrich and exotically photographing Gene Tierney, Ona Munson, and Phyllis Brooks in several scenes, von Sternberg appears to have lavished much visual attention on Victor Mature playing a male version of the Marlene Dietrich role model. Ni-Pau plays no part in the film, and the junk owners' bidding for the caged girls in the theatrical version becomes just a tourist attraction. Walter Huston's Charteris claims he had no knowledge of his lover's fate and states that the money he supposedly stole from her resides in a Chinese bank under his name. In the movie, unlike the theatrical play, Mother Gin Sling does not know that Poppy is her daughter until the end and shoots her now totally corrupt offspring. No reference is made to Poppy's drug addiction. Her problems arise from bad blood, bad sex, and overindulgence in drink. However, despite the restrictions of Hollywood censorship codes, von Sternberg's visual iconography speaks for itself. The whole film is a masterpiece of visual decadence centered around the huge gambling arena set presided over by Marcel Dalio's "Master of the Spinning Wheel." This shot concludes the entire film. *(T. W.)*

Resources: John Baxter, *The Cinema of Josef von Sternberg* (New York: A. S. Barnes, 1971); Peter Baxter, ed., *Sternberg* (London: BFI, 1981).

SHIRLEY VALENTINE (1986)
Willy Russell

Shirley Valentine (1989)

Directed by Lewis Gilbert

Adapted by Willy Russell from his play

Cast: Pauline Collins (Shirley Valentine-Bradshaw), Bernard Hill (Joe Bradshaw), Alison Steadman (Jane), Julia McKenzie (Gillian), Tom Conti (Costas Caldes)

Length: 108 minutes

Rated: R

Like the central character of Russell's earlier success, *Educating Rita*, Shirley Bradshaw wants more out of life than her humdrum existence as homemaker for her overworked husband, Joe, and longs to visit Greece, but Joe does not share her fantasy. The play consist of two monologues given to Pauline Collins, who played Shirley on stage in London and who also plays her in the film. In act 1 she speaks to the audience from her kitchen while she is preparing Joe's supper. In act 2 she continues while relaxing on a rock on the Greek coast, explaining how she got there with the help of her friend Jane, how she had an affair with a local gigolo named Costas, how she intends to stay there, and how she might react when her husband comes looking for her. Of course, the film involves more than a single actress. Collins begins her monologue in the kitchen, as in the play, but as she tells about her life, the film utilizes a flashback structure to dramatize and visualize her dealings with her husband, her children, and her friends and neighbors, all of whom are represented. When she goes to Greece, Shirley Bradshaw becomes Shirley Valentine (her maiden name) as she achieves self-fulfillment and is liberated from household drudgery. Like Rita in Russell's earlier play, Shirley takes control of her life and becomes a more interesting person. The film succeeds mainly because of the brilliance of Pauline Collins. *(J. M. W.)*

Resources: Georgia Brown, "Grecian Formula," *The Village Voice* (5 September 1989): 75; Rita Kempley, "Sweetheart Shirley Valentine," *Washington Post* (15 September 1989): C1, C9; Mervyn Rothstein, "Now Pauline Collins Puts Her Valentine's Message on Film," *New York Times* (27 August 1989): 15.

THE SHOP AROUND THE CORNER

See PARFUMERIE

SHOW BOAT (1927)
Music by Jerome Kern and book and lyrics by Oscar Hammerstein II (adapted from Edna Ferber's novel)

Show Boat (1929)

Directed by Harry A. Pollard

Adapted by Charles Kenyon

Cast: Laura La Plante (Magnolia), Joseph Schildkraut (Gaylord Ravenal), Alma Rubens (Julie), Otis Harlan (Cap'n Andy), Stepin Fetchit (Joe)

Length: 126 minutes

Edna Ferber's novel *Show Boat* (1926) has reached the screen three times, but always via the 1927 Kern-Hammerstein musical production. This landmark of the American musical theatre, with its integrated book and music, its sprawling fifty-year time span, and its controversial themes of miscegenation and desertion, premiered at the Ziegfeld Theatre on 27 December 1927. The story begins in the 1880s aboard the riverboat *Cotton Blossom*, where a troupe of performers have arrived in Natchez to put on a show. But when the racist sheriff discovers that the leading lady, Julie, is a half-caste, he moves to stop the show. Intervening is Magnolia, daughter of the ship's captain, and her lover, the handsome gambler Gaylord Ravenal. Later, Magnolia and Ravenal marry and relocate to Chicago, where Gaylord's dissolute life and gambling losses lead to his desertion of his wife and daughter, Kim. Magnolia finds work singing at the Trocadero. Years later, she and her daughter, now radio stars, attend a reunion with the old showboat troupe, including the now-reformed Ravenal. Universal Studios originally wanted to adapt Ferber's novel to the screen, but with the success of the musical stage version and the advent of the talking picture, it decided to retool the almost-completed silent film into a part talkie incorporating elements of the Kern-Hammerstein production. Universal stars Laura La Plante, Alma Rubens, and Joseph Schildkraut were brought in. The scenario includes most of the key moments of novel and play (although the theme of miscegenation is dropped), even if, as historian Miles Kreuger has pointed out, the characterizations are thin and events exaggerated. Of particular historical interest is the addition of a filmed prologue featuring original cast members performing numbers from the show—including Helen Morgan singing "Bill" and "Can't Help Lovin' Dat Man," Jules Bledsoe singing "Ol' Man River," and Tess "Aunt Jemima" Gardella singing "C'mon Folks" and "Hey, Feller!" Critics were generally unimpressed with the finished film, and they complained that the stagy prologue did not mesh at all well with the more "realistic" treatment of the main story. *(J. C. T.)*

Resources: Miles Kreuger, *Show Boat: The Story of a Classic American Musical* (New York: Oxford University Press, 1977); John Tibbetts, "John McGlinn: Restoring the American Musical theater,"*The World and I* 10.4 (April 1995): 112–117.

Show Boat (1936)

Directed by James Whale

Adapted by Oscar Hammerstein II

Cast: Irene Dunne (Magnolia), Allan Jones (Gaylord Ravenal), Helen Morgan (Julie), Charles Winninger (Cap'n Andy), Paul Robeson (Joe), Sammy White (Frank)

Length: 110 minutes

As early as 1934 Universal Pictures wanted to remake *Show Boat*, which it had first brought to the screen in 1929 in a part-talking version, a wobbly mixture of plot points from the book and songs and incidents from the musical stage show. In an effort to pay homage to the Broadway original, several principals were signed on to re-create their original stage roles, including Helen Morgan (Julie), Charles Winninger (Cap'n Andy), and Sammy White (Frank). Also brought on board were the original conductor Victor Baravalle, orchestrator Robert Russell Bennett, and Oscar Hammerstein himself, who wrote the scenario. From the London premiere came Paul Robeson as Joe. Otherwise, the key roles of Gaylord Ravenal went to newcomer Allan Jones, a classically trained tenor; and of Magnolia to Irene Dunne, a veteran of musical comedy. British émigré director James Whale (*Frankenstein, The Invisible Man, The Bride of Frankenstein*) seemed at first an odd choice to helm the project, but, as historian Miles Kreuger notes, "Whale manages to blend perfectly his finely crafted sketch of social mores, architectural and interior decor, costume design, and geographic atmosphere with the inherent conventions of the musical" (117–118). The film's exposition, sequence by sequence—especially the events of act 1, scene 1, concluding with Robeson's rendition of "Ol' Man River"—follows Hammerstein's original 1927 libretto very closely until the end, when a modern-dress sequence alters events and brings Magnolia and Kim to Hollywood. Among the other alterations from the stage production are a new wedding scene to replace the World Fair scene; the elimination of the song "Why Do I Love You?"; the addition of an extra song for Robeson; and the reunion of Magnolia and Ravenal, which occurs at the Trocadero rather than back at the *Cotton Blossom*. Among the many highlights is the delicious sequence in which Charles Winninger re-creates his original stage business of enacting all the parts in the rehearsal of *The Parson's Bride*; and when Joe sings "Ol' Man River" while the camera makes a 360-degree pan around him, moving into a tight close-up as the picture dissolves into a series of expressionist scenes. Although Helen Morgan appears relatively briefly—a handful of scenes that barely total twenty minutes of screen time—her rendition of "My Bill" ranks among the great moments in the history of the musical film. It would be Morgan's last film; she died in 1941 at the age of forty-one. The film opened to rapturous reviews and has remained ever since an outstanding example of the conjunction of the Broadway musical and the Hollywood film. *(J. C. T.)*

Resources: James Curtis, *James Whale* (Metuchen, NJ: Scarecrow Press, 1982); Miles Kreuger, *Show Boat: The Story of a Classic American Musical* (New York: Oxford University Press, 1977).

Show Boat (1951)

Directed by George Sidney

Adapted by John Lee Mahin

Cast: Kathryn Grayson (Magnolia), Howard Keel (Gaylord Ravenal), Ava Gardner (Julie), Joe E. Brown (Cap'n Andy), William Warfield (Joe)

Length: 108 minutes

The third and, to date, last version of the 1927 Kern-Hammerstein stage musical was produced for MGM in 1951 by ace musical impresario Arthur Freed. A great admirer of Jerome Kern, Freed had already incorporated several numbers from the stage show into his lavish screen biography of Kern, *Till the Clouds Roll By* (1946). George Sidney, director of the film's splashy finale, was brought in to helm the new adaptation, freshly conceived by John Lee Mahin. Robert Alton and Charles Rosher provided the dance choreography and the vivid Technicolor photography, respectively. Despite the all-star cast and lavish production values—and spectacular box office—purists have dismissed the overall results. Mahin reduced the time span of the sprawling story from fifty years to a mere decade, so that Magnolia and Ravenal are reunited while still young lovers (and their daughter, Kim, still just a child). Almost all of Hammerstein's dialogue was scrapped, and a whole new story line is introduced after Magnolia's triumphal debut at the Trocadero. Now, instead of going on to fame in New York, Magnolia (Kathryn Grayson) returns to the *Cotton Blossom* to raise her little girl and wait for the return of Ravenal (Howard Keel). Julie (Ava Gardner), meanwhile, returns to the story just in time to encourage Ravenal to return to the show boat and his wife and child (of whose existence he is unaware). As Magnolia and Ravenal embrace, the boat pulls away to the sounds of an offscreen choir singing "Ol' Man River." Julie, looking pathetically worn and alone, remains on the pier and silently blows them a kiss. While historian Miles Kreuger applauds the inclusion of one more scene for Julie, he sarcastically deplores how this vulnerable waif—a role originally intended for Judy Garland—is transformed by Ava Gardner's performance into a sensuous, strapping woman: "She is a glamour queen trying valiantly to break out of her mould [sic] to become a serious actress. Yet apparently neither she nor the studio is quite sure how to manage the transition" (183). Gardner's vocalizations can be heard on the MGM sound-track album, but her singing onscreen is dubbed by Annette Warren. In general, continues Kreuger, the film is sadly lacking in humor. All the *Cotton Blossom* stage performances have been excised (including Cap'n Andy's showstopping rendering of the roles in *The Parson's Bride*), along with the World's Fair scenes and the banter between Joe (William Warfield) and Queenie. "Can't Help Lovin' Dat Man of Mine," rendered authentically in the stage and 1936 version in a spirited quartet of voices, is here transformed into a slow, mournful soliloquy for Julie. Most of "Ol Man River," except for its refrain, is eliminated—perhaps, argues Kreuger, because it was felt the deleted lyrics placed too much emphasis on the toil of the black dockhands. As for the *Cotton Blossom* itself, it was constructed as a steam-driven, back-wheel paddleboat—a grievous error, since all show boats were simply barges with no power whatever of their own (they were pushed by towboats). *(J. C. T.)*

Resources: Hugh Fordin, *The World of Entertainment: The Freed Unit at MGM* (Garden City, NY: Doubleday, 1975); Miles Kreuger, *Show Boat: The Story of a Classic American Musical* (New York: Oxford University Press, 1977).

SIX DEGREES OF SEPARATION (1990)
John Guare

Six Degrees of Separation (1994)

Directed by Fred Schepisi

Adapted by John Guare

Cast: Stockard Channing (Ouisa), Will Smith (Paul), Donald Sutherland (Flan), Ian McKellen (Geoffrey), Anthony Michael Hall (Trent), Heather Graham (Elizabeth), Eric Thal (Rick)

Length: 102 minutes

Rated: R

John Guare's *Six Degrees of Separation* was a hit in 1990, when it appeared on Broadway. The set for the play is expressionistic: locations of action are indicated by stage lights; characters speak directly to the audience; there are few props; and telephone conversations are conducted without telephones. Flan, an art dealer, and his wife, Ouisa, are entertaining Geoffrey, a South African millionaire who may help them on a $2 million Cézanne sale, when Paul, a young African American, enters their apartment. Wounded in a Central Park mugging, he convinces them he is a friend of their children at Harvard. His glib talk, his cooking, and his coy reference to his father, Sidney Poitier, prompt Fran and Ouisa to have him spend the night. In the morning when Ouisa finds Paul with a naked young man, Flan has both men thrown out. When they find that other people in their set have had similar experiences with Paul, they realize that Paul is a con man who has learned about their lives and homes from Trent, a homosexual prep-school classmate of their children. Flan and Ouisa also discover that Paul has befriended a naive Utah couple, Rick and Elizabeth, whom he tells that Flan is his father. Paul cons Rick, has sex with him, and abandons him. Rick commits suicide. Since Elizabeth presses theft charges, Paul is wanted by the police and calls Ouisa for help. She urges him to give himself up, promises to meet him, and calls the police. Delayed by traffic, Ouisa and Flan are too late to meet him, and because they are not family and do not know his name, they never see him again. When Ouisa reads about the suicide of a jailed young African American, she wonders if it was Paul. Schepisi's sets are realistic, and instead of having characters address the audience, Flan and Ouisa tell their story to their friends and associates at various Manhattan venues. Perhaps because Guare adapted his own play, the dialogue is taken almost verbatim from the play; and the themes of generational conflict, phoniness, impersonation, and materialism are maintained. In both film and play a Kandinsky painting, painted on both sides, symbolizes the two sides that Flan and Ouisa's set experiences, order and chaos; and, indeed, Flan is living on the edge. The added statue of the dog in Central Park becomes another symbol: it represents rescue and safety, the latter a constant concern, yet acts of violence occur there. In the play Ouisa "sees" Paul as she leaves the apartment; in the film Ouisa, appalled at their experience with Paul, leaves a business luncheon, tells Flan they are badly matched, "sees" Paul in a storefront window, and walks toward a new life. *(T. L. E.)*

Resources: David Denby, "Unlikely Hero," *New York* 26 (13 December 1993): 82–85; Stanley Kauffmann, "The Hustlers," *New Republic* 209 (27 December 1993): 24.

THE SLEEPING PRINCE (1953)
Terence Rattigan

The Prince and the Showgirl (1957)

Directed by Laurence Olivier

Adapted by Terence Rattigan

Cast: Laurence Olivier (the Regent), Marilyn Monroe (Elsie Marina), Sybil Thorndike (Queen Dowager), Richard Wattis (Peter Northbrook), Jeremy Spencer (King Nicolas), Esmond Knight (Col. Hoffman), David Horne (Foreign Service Officer), Maxine Audley (Lady Maidenhead)

Length: 117 minutes

The Prince and the Showgirl first appeared as *The Sleeping Prince* at London's Phoenix Theatre on 5 November 1953. Laurence Olivier directed and starred in the leading role, then produced and directed the film version with Richard Wattis and Jeremy Spencer repeating their original roles. Rattigan's original play is a satire on "The Sleeping Beauty" fairy tale. But this time a *Sleeping* (Ruritanian) *Prince* of Carpathia is awakened into becoming a more human and loving person by his brief encounter with an American showgirl. The teaming of Olivier and Monroe, both at their creative peaks, was promising, but the film failed to integrate their acting styles into complementary performances. Both play and film are set during the coronation of King George V in 1911, an unstable period before World War I. The Prince Regent is concerned about his son's involvement in internal Carpathian politics, which Germany may use to its advantage. Censorship considerations also resulted in changes. After his first wife (the Queen of Carpathia) dies, the Hungarian-born Regent enters into a diplomatic marriage of convenience with an Austrian aristocrat to reinforce a trade agreement. In the play, Martita Hunt's Grand Duchess clearly knows, but does not care about, her husband's extramarital affairs. The film changes the character to Sybil Thorndike's undiscerning Queen Dowager to avoid offending unsophisticated American audiences. Although the play is set exclusively in a single room in the Carpathian Embassy, the film opens up the action, beginning with Foreign Office official Peter Northbrook discussing the implications of the Carpathian visit with his superior (David Horne). After introducing the Carpathian aristocrats riding along Hyde Park, another new scene shows the Prince Regent visiting the cast of *The Coconut Girl* and meeting Elsie, who attracts his attention by snapping her gown strap as she bows. Olivier uses theatrical devices such as closing doors as transitions between scenes but includes cinematic elements, such as the carriage procession to the coronation. Although we do not see the actual coronation, the viewers read Elsie's program with her and see her gaze in awe at the abbey's stained-glass windows. Olivier also includes the Coronation Ball scene, showing Elsie with Nicolas and the Regent attempting an ill-fated liaison with another mistress, Lady Maidenhead (Maxine Audley). Carpathian security chief Col. Hoffman (Esmond Knight) does not appear in the play but provides one of several excellent cameo roles. *(T. W.)*

Resources: Mark Ricci and Michael Conway, *The Complete Films of Marilyn Monroe* (New York: Citadel Press, 1964); Carl E. Rollyson, Jr., *Marilyn Monroe: A Life of the Actress* (Ann Arbor, MI: UMI Research Press, 1986).

A SOLDIER'S PLAY (1982)
Charles Fuller

A Soldier's Story (1984)

Directed by Norman Jewison

Adapted by Charles Fuller

Cast: Howard E. Rollins, Jr. (Capt. Davenport), Adolph Caesar (Sgt. Waters), Larry Riley (C. J. Memphis), Denzel Washington (Peterson), Art Evans (Wilkie), Robert Townsend (Ellis), David Alan Grier (Cobb), Dennis Lipscomb (Capt. Taylor), David Harris (Smalls), Wings Hauser (Byrd), Scott Paulin (Wilcox)

Length: 102 minutes

Rated: PG

When Columbia Pictures decided to adapt Charles Fuller's Pulitzer Prize–winning *A Soldier's Play* to the screen, it was a gamble, since it was essentially a story about African Americans, and there was no clear indication that it would win the crossover audience that finally materialized. Several actors from the original Negro Ensemble Company production were cast in the film, notably, Adolph Caesar as Sergeant Waters, Larry Riley as C. J. Memphis, and Denzel Washington as Peterson in the three of the play's major roles. Set on an army base in Louisiana in 1944, the play traces a murder investigation by Captain Richard Davenport (Howard E. Rollins, Jr.), a lawyer who was sent from Washington, D.C. Everyone on the base thinks Sgt. Waters was murdered by the Ku Klux Klan, but over time Davenport discovers otherwise. Waters was responsible for the death of the popular C. J. Memphis, a star baseball player and blues singer whom Waters considered a disgrace to the race because of his servile behavior around white officers. The enlisted men hated Waters because of the way he treated them and held him responsible for the death of C. J., whom he throws into the stockade on a trumped-up, fabricated charge. Waters wanted to teach C. J. a lesson in order to modify his behavior, but he miscalculates C. J.'s strength. Though C. J. is physically strong and a splendid athlete, he cannot stand being confined and commits suicide. Afterward, Waters, who was "all spit and polish," becomes a pathetic alcoholic and is murdered one night as he returns drunk to the base from Tynan, Louisiana, by Peterson, who is on guard duty. Davenport has reason to suspect two white officers, Byrd (Wings Hauser) and Wilcox (Scott Paulin), who also encountered Waters that night, and he has to fight for the right of interrogating them, but he finally gets his man after interrogating Wilkie (Art Evans) and Private Smalls (David Harris), who was on guard duty with Peterson that night. In the play, Davenport's final monologue explains that Peterson was arrested a week later in Alabama, but in the film Peterson and Smalls are both arrested on the base and brought before Davenport, so there can be a final dramatic confrontation between them, allowing Davenport to ask Peterson, "Who gave you the right to judge, to determine who is fit to be a Negro, and who is not?" Peterson's presumption is no worse than that of Waters, who was making similar demands of C. J. Memphis. In contrast to the film's upbeat ending, with the black troops marching off to war, the play ends with a final monologue in which Davenport tells the audience that all the men were wiped out in the Ruhr Valley after having been given the opportunity to fight. Hence, the film presents a serious shift in tone, but the central conflict involving criminal and racial justice is preserved and maintained. The racial tension is toned down; the sceenplay creates more sympathy for Waters and adds comic relief, as well as hope for future race relations. Though not an entirely faithful adaptation, the film is generally faithful, though simplified. *(J. M. W.)*

Resources: Carol Cooper, "*Soldier's Story* Salute," *Film Comment* 22.6 (December 1984): 17–19; Pauline Kael, "The Current Cinema," *The New Yorker* 26 November 1984): 117–119; John Nagle, "*A Soldier's Story,*" *Films in Review* 35.10 (December 1984): 621–622; Peter Roffman and Bev Simpson, "*A Soldier's Story,*" *Cineaste* 14.1 (1985): 42–43; J. M. Welsh, "*A Soldier's Story*: A Paradign for Justice," in *Columbia Pictures: Portrait of a Studio,* ed. Bernard F. Dick (Lexington: University Press of Kentucky, 1992): 208–217.

SORRY, WRONG NUMBER (1943)
Lucille Fletcher

Sorry, Wrong Number (1948)

Directed by Anatole Litvak

Adapted by Lucille Fletcher

Cast: Barbara Stanwyck (Leona Stevenson), Burt Lancaster (Henry Steven-son), Ann Richards (Sally Lord Dodge), Wendell Corey (Dr. Alexander), Ed Begley (James Cotterell), William Conrad (Morano)

Length: 89 minutes

Sorry, Wrong Number began as a twenty-two-minute radio script written by Lucille Fletcher in 1943. Frequently performed on radio with Agnes Moorehead in the role of Leona Stevenson between 1943 and 1948, the play was also performed in theatrical surroundings as well as film. Fletcher originally conceived it "as an experiment in sound and not just as a murder story, with the telephone as its chief protagonsit. . . . However, in the hands of a fine actress like Agnes Moorehead, the script turned out to be more the character study of a woman than a technical experiment, and the plot itself . . . fell into the thriller category." The original radio play is tightly structured, with the emphasis falling on Mrs. Stevenson's developing anx-iety as she realizes that she is the intended murder victim discussed in the phone conversation she has overheard. Like the film, the play ends with her murderer on the phone replying to the police department, "Sorry. Wrong number." Other background voices such as telephone operators and a police sergeant become subsidiary to Leona's dilemma. The film version opens up the play by providing background information concerning Leona's confinement, the reason for the contract on her life, and cinematic film noir devices that visually emphasize her alienation and link her with other 1940s "femme fatales." Stanwyck's Leona is a selfish woman with a nerve disorder who manipulates and marries her mild, working-class hus-band, Henry, as a substitute for the father she cannot possess. Aggravated by his emasculated role, Henry takes out a contract on Leona's life and falls into the menacing film noir world represented by William Conrad in his archetypal persona from *The Killers*. Unlike the original play, the film uses several flashbacks to fill in information about Leona's past history as well as supplementary characters such as her father, physician, and Henry's former girlfriend. The film ends with Henry's attempting to warn Leona in vain before her murder. After the contract killer has picked up her phone and answered, "Sorry. Wrong number," the police arrest Henry as he leaves a telephone booth. *(T. W.)*

Resources: Lucille Fletcher, *Sorry, Wrong Number and the Hitch-Hiker* (New York: Dramatist's Play Service, 1980); Matthew Solomon, "Adapting 'Radio's Perfect Script': 'Sorry, Wrong Number' and *Sorry, Wrong Number*," *Quarterly Review of Film Studies* 16.1 (1995): 23–39.

S.S. GLENCAIRN CYCLE OF PLAYS (1914–1917)
Eugene O'Neill

The Long Voyage Home (1940)

Directed by John Ford

Adapted by Dudley Nichols

Cast: John Wayne (Ole), Barry Fitzgerald (Cocky), Thomas Mitchell (Driscoll), Ian Hunter (Smitty), Wilfred Lawson (Captain), Ward Bond (Yank), Arthur Shields (Donkeyman), John Qualen (Axel), Mildred Natwick (Freda)

Length: 105 minutes

The Long Voyage Home is a Hollywood art movie developed from Eugene O'Neill's *S.S. Glencairn* cycle of one-act plays: *Bound East for Cardiff, In the Zone, The Long Voyage Home,* and *The Moon of Caribees,* written between 1914 and 1917. O'Neill discussed the adaptation with John Ford and Dudley Nichols during February 1940 and praised the film as the best screen adaptation of his work. Nichols reversed the order of the original plays and set them in the contemporary period of World War II, when German planes and U-boats threatened merchant shipping. The adaptation transfers the brooding melancholy and tragedy of the *S.S. Glencairn* quartet admirably to the screen, because of the collaborative efforts of the director, scenarist, cinematographer, and actors, all working together in the best traditions of theatrical ensemble. Cinematographer Gregg Toland's moody, pessimistic, expressionist lighting visually develops the tragic overtones of the plays. Working under Hollywood censorship codes, Ford and Nichols begin the film with an adaptation of *The Moon of the Caribees*. Although the original play's sexual references remain implicit in the film, Toland's opening cinematography subtly conveys the message that the sailors are deprived of both sex and alcohol, a message reproduced in silent-cinema fashion with intercut shots of sensual señoritas and sex-starved sailors. Due to censorship requirements, the West Indian Negresses of the play now become lusty Latinas accompanied by an obvious "Madam" figure. The film also enlarges the original roles of Ole and Smitty. No longer a middle-aged sailor who fails to return home in *The Long Voyage Home*, John Wayne's role is now an idealistic youngster whom the wandering sailors take a fatherly interest in sending home to Sweden. Although Ole is shanghaied as in the original play, the *Glencairn* sailors rescue him but lose Driscoll to the brutal *S.S. Amindra*, which is torpedoed the following day. The film gives Smitty's dilemma broader wartime connotations. He is an ex-officer who has been cashiered from the navy due to drunkenness and, ashamed, has abandoned his family. However, he dies heroically when a German plane strafes the *S.S. Glencairn*. When they reach London, the sailors silently watch a tragic night scene of Smitty's wife and family, escorted by officers of the Royal Navy, who have now accepted the deceased wandering hero back into their ranks. *(T. W.)*

Resources: Matthew Bernstein, "Hollywood's 'Arty' Cinema: John Ford's *The Long Voyage Home*," *Wide Angle* 10.1 (1988) : 30–45; Steven E. Colburn, "Illusion and the Tragic Pattern of Fate in O'Neill's *S. S. Glencairn Cycle*," in *Critical Essays on Eugene O'Neill*, ed. James J. Martine (Boston: G. K. Hall, 1984): 55–65.

STAGE DOOR (1936)
Edna Ferber and George S. Kaufman

Stage Door (1937)

Directed by Gregory La Cava

Adapted by Morrie Riskind and Anthony Veiller

Cast: Katharine Hepburn (Terry Randall), Ginger Rogers (Jean Maitland), Adolphe Menjou (Tony Powell)

Length: 92 minutes

Stage Door was first produced at New York's Music Box Theatre on 22 October 1936, with Margaret Sullavan and Phyllis Brooks in the leading roles of Terry Randall and Jean Maitland. Set entirely at the Footlights Club theatrical boardinghouse for actresses, the original play reflects the disdain of coauthor George S. Kaufman for Hollywood and its idyllic depiction of the theatrical world. In the original play, middle-class hopeful Terry Randall finally gains theatrical stardom as a reward for her moralistic qualities in avoiding the material traps of Hollywood and remaining true to her ideals. Terry steps into the theatrical role that her former boardinghouse acquaintance Jean Maitland cannot fulfill due to her contamination by Hollywood performance styles. She has also seen her former playwright/

boyfriend, Keith Burgess, leave her for Hollywood, after she has helped him rewrite a play that succeeds on Broadway. Terry's ideals are encouraged by David Kingsley, a character obviously modeled on Kaufman, who forsakes Hollywood to return to his former theatrical love. The film version retains the emphasis on the Footlights Club but drops Kaufman's didactic premises, as well as the characters of Burgess and Kingsley, and rewrites the play to emphasize the 1930s star persona of Katharine Hepburn. Now emerging from a rich family, Hepburn's Terry has decided to leave her inherited wealth to succeed as an actress on Broadway. Although Ginger Rogers' Jean Maitland initially resents Terry's personality and class background, the film affirms a female friendship and solidarity not just common to them but unique to the women in the boardinghouse. Unlike in the play, female desires are not centered on males, who are generally regarded as irrelevant or necessary evils toward making it in the theatrical world. Instead, the inhabitants of the Footlights Club aim at common goals and solidarity for the less fortunate. Although Terry's father manipulates Powell into producing a play to ridicule his daughter's lack of acting technique in the hope she will return home, the attempt backfires when Terry becomes an actress on the first night by sublimating into her performance the spirit of Kaye, who has committed suicide. Terry has gained the role Kaye originally wanted, and Jean angrily condemns her before the performance. However, Terry's touching performance brings tears to the Footlights Club females who attend the play and makes her name on Broadway. Despite her fame, Terry decides to stay in the Footlights Club with Jean, now her best friend, and act as supportive presence to her fellow boarders. Although the film drastically alters the original source, the changes result in a much better version that strongly affirms Katharine Hepburn's 1930s star persona. *(T. W.)*

Resources: Andrew Britton, *Katharine Hepburn: The Thirties and After* (Newcastle upon Tyne, England: Tyneside Cinema, 1984); Edna Ferber and George S. Kaufman, *Stage Door* (New York: Doubleday, Doran, 1936).

STALAG 17 (1951)
Donald Bevan and Edmund Trzcinski

Stalag 17 (1953)

Directed by Billy Wilder

Adapted by Billy Wilder and Edwin Blum

Cast: William Holden (Sefton), Don Taylor (Lt. Dunbar), Otto Preminger (Oberst Von Scherbach), Robert Strauss ("Animal" Stosh), Harvey Lembeck (Harry), Richard Erdman (Hoffy), Peter Graves (Price), Neville Brand (Duke), Sig Rumann (Schultz), Gil Stratton (Cookie)

Length: 120 minutes

Bevan and Trzcinski called their play *Stalag 17* "[a] comedy melodrama in three acts," and they dedicated it to their fellow prisoners of war. The drama and humor come from the tension that develops in a claustrophobic barracks full of American sergeants in a World War II German prisoner of war camp when the Americans realize that one among them is an informant. The men cope with hunger, cold, and boredom. However, after a well-planned escape results in two men being killed, and the radio covertly used by prisoners is confiscated, fear and anger surface. When it is clear that the Germans know details of sabotage carried out by Dunbar, a newly arrived prisoner, the group blames Sefton, a loner who has alienated his barracks-mates by constantly looking to profit in transactions with them and with German guards. After he has been completely ostracized and severely beaten, Sefton uses his ingenuity and concern for self preservation to discover who is informing the Germans and how it is being done. The play was first produced and staged by José Ferrer on 8 May 1951, just seven years after the time when the story is set. It was very well received. Within two years, Billy Wilder had collaborated on a screenplay and then produced and directed the film.

All the action of the play takes place over three days, culminating on Christmas Day 1944. Everything happens on one set, a Spartan, dark barracks crammed with bunks and soldiers. The set creates the tone, and the dialogue creates the characters; together they create the tension. The intimacy of the stage allows the dialogue to be more realistic, more coarse than it is in the film. The compressed time of the action accentuates the tension. The film expands the time and space of the action. It introduces a narrator, Sefton's minion Cookie (Gil Stratton), a new character. He recounts episodes that define the characters and provide comic relief. Otto Preminger plays the commandant, as a take on Stroheim in *La Grande Illusion*. Trzcinski appears briefly as himself. Strauss and Lembeck reprise their Broadway roles. What the film lacks in realism, it makes up in humorous or clever turns. In the play, the Americans capitalize on the Christmas drunkenness of the German guards. The film's soldiers outwit the Germans, finding an impossible hiding place for Dunbar, a threatened prisoner, and devising gadgets. The film uses different settings—Commandant's office, Russian compound, and stalag yard—but retains the cooped-up feeling. Each work is a wonderful study of the complexities of human will, motivation, and spirit. The story, in a very simplified form, became the inspiration for the popular television sitcom *Hogan's Heroes*. (S. C. C.)

Resources: Axel Madsen, *Billy Wilder* (Bloomington: Indiana University Press, 1969); Maurice Zolotow, *Billy Wilder in Hollywood* (New York: Putnam, 1977).

STEAMING (1981)
Nell Dunn

Steaming (1985)

Directed by Joseph Losey

Adapted by Patricia Losey

Cast: Vanessa Redgrave (Nancy), Sarah Miles (Sarah), Diana Dors (Violet), Pattie Love (Josie), Brenda Bruce (Mrs. Meadows), Felicity Dean (Dawn), Sally Sagoe (Celia)

Length: 15 minutes

Rated: R

Longtime friend and producer John Heyman asked Joseph Losey to direct a film of Nell Dunn's first play. In *Steaming*, an all-woman cast bond together to prevent the proposed destruction of their community bathhouse. Despite class conflicts between middle-class and working-class women, the women unite to save the bathhouse, which is a haven for them. The "steaming" refers to the bathhouse and their anger about a patriarchial society.

Patricia Losey actively petitioned her husband to allow her to write the screenplay. Despite the fact that Heyman hated the first draft, she remained the screenwriter. According to Sarah Miles, Losey told her before shooting began that he was dying, and his strong support for his wife's new role may well have involved concern about her future. When the film began production at Pinewood in February 1984, it was surrounded by an aura of impending doom. Losey was evidently very sick, a condition further aggravated by a knee injury on the set that mandated that he be hoisted onto the stage by a forklift truck and direct from a wheelchair (de Rham 281). Diana Dors was fighting cancer and died before the film opened. Even Losey's longtime continuity girl, Pamela Davies, was suffering from a condition subsequently diagnosed as terminal cancer. Compounded by the sheer unpleasantness of ubiquitous steam and mildew, this was far from a happy production. Losey has always been accused of lacking a sense of humor. Edith de Rham quotes the *Guardian* critic's remark that "a Losey joke book would be a slim volume indeed" (282). In this film, the lack of a light comic touch proves fatal. However, there are positive aspects to the work. In his initial written notes to the cast, Losey maintained that the cinema can be used "to increase enclosure rather than the Hollywood cliché of 'opening up' "(Ciment 387). At its best, the film presents the bathhouse as a flawed and decaying retreat but also a place of rebirth. He also elicits some fine performances from his actresses. Nevertheless, the opening up of the set to include exercise rooms and the like weakens the impact of the film. The change to a happy ending, a governmental reprieve for the baths, insisted upon by Heyman, further undermines a work that, even in its theatrical manifestation, is slight at best. Many of the reviewers of Losey's film betrayed a genuine sadness that such a competent, if uneven, director should end his life with such a flawed piece of work. *(W. L. H.)*

Resources: David Caute, *Joseph Losey: A Revenge on Life* (London: Faber and Faber, 1994); Michael Ciment, *Conversations with Losey* (London: Methuen, 1985); Edith de Rham, *Joseph Losey* (London: André Deutsch, 1991).

STEEL MAGNOLIAS (1986)
Robert Harling

Steel Magnolias (1989)

Directed by Herbert Ross

Adapted by Robert Harling

Cast: Sally Field (M'Lynn Eatenton), Dolly Parton (Truvy Jones), Shirley MacLaine (Ouiser), Daryl Hannah (Annelle), Olympia Dukakis (Clairee), Julia Roberts (Shelby), Tom Skerritt (Drum Eatenton), Sam Shepard (Spud Jones)

Length: 118 minutes

Rated: PG

Harling's play is set in a small town in Louisiana, and the action is restricted to one set, Truvy's Beauty Shop, where a tight circle of women meet to gossip and, more importantly, to support each other. In the course of the play M'Lynn's diabetic daughter, Shelby, marries, has a baby (despite her condition and her mother's misgivings), undergoes a kidney transplant (the donor is her mother), and then dies when her body eventually rejects the organ. Besides this main plot, there are several subplots: Annelle, a religious fundamentalist who gains employment at Truvy's, meets and marries a local, and has a child; Truvy experiences some problems with her husband, an unsuccessful contractor; and feuding friends Clairee and Ouiser exchange wisecracks. At the end of the play M'Lynn's friends help her come to terms with her daughter's death, and the birth of Annelle's baby reinforces the idea that life can and must go on if one has tough southern women friends, or "steel magnolias." Harling's screenplay takes the action outside to a wedding, to Shelby's house, to the hospital, to a festival, and so on, and those scenes include the men, who are never seen but who are discussed in the play. Though the audience sees Drum, M'Lynn's husband, firing at birds, and Spud, Truvy's husband, returning to open a second Truvy's Beauty Shop and making her a "chain," the focus is always on the women. The men are secondary characters who, as M'Lynn observes, are supposed to be "men of steel" but who, as Shelby's deathbed scene demonstrates, are really weak, as opposed to the steel magnolias. *(T. L. E.)*

Resources: Shirley MacLaine, *My Lucky Stars: A Hollywood Memoir* (New York: Bantam Books, 1995); Jim Welsh, "*Steel Magnolias,*" *Films in Review* 41.3 (March 1990): 169–170.

STILL LIFE (1936)
Noël Coward

Brief Encounter (1945)

Directed by David Lean

Adapted by David Lean and Ronald Neame

Cast: Celia Johnson (Laura Jesson), Trevor Howard (Alex Harvey), Joyce Carey (Myrtle Bagot), Stanley Holloway (Alberg Godby), Cyril Raymond (Fred Jesson)

Length: 85 minutes

Brief Encounter first appeared as a short theatrical play, *Still Life*, performed at London's Phoenix Theatre on 22 May 1936, with Gertrude Lawrence and Noël Coward in the leading roles. Although released in 1945, the film is set in the winter of 1938–1939 and indirectly treats the contemporary fascinating topic of wartime romances as "brief encounters," which contributed to its success in Britain. Although hailed as a realistic film at the time, Robert Krasker's cinematography employs elements of film noir in certain scenes to highlight the psychological guilt of two middle-class people falling into romantic temptation before finally submitting to repression. When Alec leaves, Laura rushes outside and attempts suicide by throwing herself under an express train. Krasker presents this sequence by using noirish lighting and canted angle shots later developed in *The Third Man*. *Brief Encounter* retained most of the significant roles from the original play but introduced the originally unseen figure of Laura's husband, Fred, in the framing narrative. Joyce Carey also reprised her original stage role as the fussy refreshment-room proprietress. David Lean's film version compressed the time period of Coward's five-scene play, which began in April and concluded the following March, to six successive Thursdays. The play was set entirely in Milford Junction Station's refreshment room. Lean cinematically expanded Coward's original theatrical setting by presenting most of the action as a memory mediated by two flashbacks remembered by Laura from her fireside at home. As Antonia Lant comments, "This temporal reduction accentuates both the brevity of the encounter and the couple's relative innocence by comparison with their stage predecessors. Time is further manipulated in the film by the use of two flashbacks and a fantasy sequence. These make it structurally more convoluted than the temporally linear play" (57). Lean also expanded *Still Life*'s fifty-five minute theatrical running time to eighty-five minutes of screen time. *Brief Encounter* stresses the limited nature of time by both visually emphasizing timetables and watches as well as using bells announcing the arrival of trains. Lean also suggests that Laura's husband, Fred, intuitively realizes the nature of the temptation she has undergone at the climax. Like the 1940s woman's film, *Brief Encounter* uses Laura's voice-over as if conscious of the narrative's implications for contemporary female audiences. Like *Mildred Pierce*, *Brief Encounter* deals with the dangers facing the independent woman and ideologically restores her to the home at the climax. *(T. W.)*

Resources: Richard Dyer, *Brief Encounter* (London: BFI, 1993); Antonia Lant, *Blackout: Reinventing Women for Wartime British Cinema* (Princeton: Princeton University Press, 1991).

STREET SCENE (1929)
Elmer Rice

Street Scene (1931)

Directed by King Vidor

Adapted by Elmer Rice

Cast: Sylvia Sidney (Rose Maurrant), William Collier (Sam Kaplan), Estelle Taylor (Anna Maurrant), Beulah Bondi (Emma Jones), Max Montor (Abe Kaplan), David Landau (Frank Maurrant), Matt McHugh (Vincent Jones), Russell Hopton (Steve Sankey), Anna Konstant (Shirley Kaplan), Lambert Rogers (Willie Maurrant)

Length: 80 minutes

When he adapted his *Street Scene*, which appeared in New York in 1929, to the screen, Rice kept most of the dialogue and maintained the claustrophobic setting of the play. Eight actors reprised their stage roles in a play about lower-middle-class life in New York tenements. In the play Anna Maurrant, who is married to a stern male chauvinist, has an affair with Steve Sankey; and all her neighbors gossip about it. Frank Maurrant, her husband, who said he was going to spend the day in Connecticut, returns to find Anna and Steve together and kills them both. In the third act, Rose Maurrant examines her future after her father is captured by the police. Sam Kaplan, an ambitious student bent on law school, is in love with her; but his sister makes her understand that she would only jeopardize Sam's future. A friendly coworker who also cares about her is willing to finance her as a mistress, but she also turns him down. At the end of the play she and her younger brother leave the apartment, and the couple who take their apartment listen to Mrs. Jones, the landlady, speculate darkly about Rose's future. Rose's belief in a better life in a place where one can "breathe" is juxtaposed to the intolerance, bigotry, and inflexibility of the other apartment dwellers, who are a mix of nationalities, religions, and values. In the film Rice takes some of the action away from the front steps of the building, but only to show men accosting women and youngsters fighting. In such an environment, the sensitive, intellectual Sam (William Collier) is ineffective, and predators rule the street. Sam's father (Abe Kaplan) quotes Karl Marx but is the butt of jokes and anti-Semitic comments. At the end of the film, Rose (Sylvia Sidney), who seems to be Rice's spokesperson, is undaunted by the oppressive environment and her neighbors and heads independently for an uncertain future. Sidney's performance established her as a star. *(T. L. E.)*

Resources: John Baxter, *King Vidor* (New York: Monarch Press, 1976); Raymond Durgnat, *King Vidor, American* (Berkeley: University of California Press, 1988).

A STREETCAR NAMED DESIRE (1947)
Tennessee Williams

A Streetcar Named Desire (1952)

Directed by Elia Kazan

Adapted by Tennessee Williams

Cast: Vivian Leigh (Blanche DuBois), Marlon Brando (Stanley Kowalski), Kim Hunter (Stella Kowalski), Karl Malden (Harold Mitchell)

Length: 122 minutes

A Streetcar Named Desire first appeared at New York's Barrymore Theatre on 3 December 1947, directed by Elia Kazan. In the play Blanche DuBois visits her sister, Stella, and Stella's husband, Stanley. The tension between Blanche, who represents the values of the old rural South, and Stanley, who embodies Northern industrialization, increases until he finally rapes her and she leaves for a mental institution at the play's end.

The film version used most of the original cast with the key exception of Jessica Tandy, who was replaced by the better-known Vivian Leigh. As well as opening out the New Orleans stage location, Kazan's film version faced the problem of contemporary censorship codes. The explicit homosexual features of Blanche's lost love contained in her confession to Mitch in scene 7 become diluted in substituted lines containing the condemnation that led to her young husband's suicide: "You are weak. I've no respect for you. I despise you." In contrast to the play's limited set, the misty lakeside where Blanche confesses her past to Mitch evokes the original scene where her sexually tormented husband killed himself. After Stella witnesses Blanche's departure at the climax, she does not return to Stanley "with inhuman abandon" as in the play but takes her baby and seeks refuge in Eunice's upstairs apartment. Although she utters moralistic lines about never returning to Stanley in compliance with contemporary censorship restrictions, most viewers would speculate about how definitive her actual decision is. Unlike in the play, Stanley utters the line, "I never touched her" after he pushes Mitch back in scene 11. But the looks of his cardplaying friends visually represent the silent condemnation of Hays Code ideology, rather than the reactions contained in the original play. Kazan also extends the film by having Stanley reveal Blanche's past to Mitch in an added factory scene. This not only supplements the original play but also foreshadows the final scene, when Mitch hits Stanley for what he has done to Blanche. Kazan also represents Stanley's rape of Blanche at the end of scene 10 with a shot of a mirror's cracking, a metaphoric signifier of both violence and the heroine's final descent into insanity. The film opens with Blanche's arrival by train in New Orleans and her asking directions from a young, handsome sailor. Although this character does not appear in the original play, the addition represents another coded reference to the dark secret in both Blanche's past and the sexuality of the playwright, both of which could not be represented explicitly in 1952. The role of the sailor in gay iconography was also commonly known within the celluloid closet at the time. *(T. W.)*

Resources: Elia Kazan, *Elia Kazan: A Life* (New York: Alfred A. Knopf, 1988); Philip C. Kolin, ed., *Confronting Tenesseee Williams's A Streetcar Named Desire: Essays in Cultural Pluralism* (Westport, CT: Greenwood Press, 1993).

SUDDENLY, LAST SUMMER (1958)
Tennessee Williams

Suddenly, Last Summer (1959)

Directed by Joseph L. Mankiewicz

Adapted by Gore Vidal and Tennessee Williams

Cast: Elizabeth Taylor (Catherine Holly), Katharine Hepburn (Mrs. Venable), Montgomery Clift (Dr. Cukrowicz), Albert Dekker (Dr. Hockstader), Mercedes McCambridge (Mrs. Holly), Gary Raymond (George Holly), Mavis Villiers) (Miss Foxhill), Patricia Marmont (Nurse Benson)

Length: 114 minutes

Poet Sebastian Venable has died under mysterious circumstances in Amalfi. After using Catherine Holly (Elizabeth Taylor) to attract homosexual lovers, he apparently was cannibalized by a gang of young boys. His mother, Violet Venable (Katharine Hepburn) wants Dr. Cukrowicz (Montgomery Cliff) to lobotomize Catherine at a local mental asylum in order to erase this memory from the young woman's mind and offers a substantial donation to the asylum if the operation is performed. The hospital is badly in need of funding, but Dr. Cukrowicz is not convinced that such a radical and invasive procedure is appropriate. Despite the homosexual content, as well as evocations of nymphomania and cannibalism, the Legion of Decency approved the film's moral purpose. The source was a one-act play originally paired with another short play, *Something Unspoken*, performed under the collective title *Garden District* in 1958. Therefore, the original play had to be expanded in order to be transformed into a feature-length film, which results in a great deal of gothic elaboration and considerable expansion of the Cukrowicz character to emphasize his ethical dilemma. In the play Cukrowicz is the doctor in control, but in the film he has to deal with a pragmatic superior, Dr. Hockstader, the hospital administrator, who wants to accept Mrs. Venable's bribe. Moreover, in the film a romantic attachment develops between Catherine and Cukrowicz. The climax comes when Catherine remembers the bizarre events surrounding Sebastian's death. The film ends with Mrs. Venable going mad. Tennessee Williams objected that his allegorical drama had been turned into a literal and unbelievable film, but the adaptation was later praised by critic Maurice Yacowar as "one of the best 'free' adaptations of modern drama" ever captured on film. The performances are outstanding. *(J. M. W.)*

Resources: James M. Welsh, "Dream Doctors as Healers in Drama and Film: A Paradigm, an Antecedent, and an Imitation," *Literature & Medicine* 6 (1987): 117–127; Maurice Yacowar, *Tennessee Williams and Film* (New York: Frederick Ungar, 1977).

SUMMER AND SMOKE (1948)
Tennessee Williams

Summer and Smoke (1961)

Directed by Peter Glenville

Adapted by James Poe and Meade Roberts

Cast: Laurence Harvey (John Buchanan), Geraldine Page (Alma Winemiller), Rita Moreno (Rosa), Pamela Tiffin (Nellie), John McIntire (Dr. Buchanan), Malcolm Atterbury (Rev. Winemiller)

Length: 118 minutes

After opening in Dallas, *Summer and Smoke* had only a brief run on Broadway in 1948, but when Jose Quintero revived it Off-Broadway in 1952 in an arena-theatre format, it was quite successful. Williams' expressionistic sets (fragments of walls, overhead blue sky, and looming Statue of Eternity) posed problems for film director Glenville, who had directed the play in London, because film is extremely realistic. The play, which focused on a body (John)–soul (Alma, which means soul) conflict, used only two interiors to heighten that contrast. Glenville could not replicate the expressionistic settings and added exterior scenes for contrast: he cuts back and forth between John's crap game and whiskey drinking and Alma's cultural club and lemonade sipping in the rectory. John is a complete hedonist who represents physical nature; Alma, the minister's daughter, represents spiritual nature. John tried to convert Alma to his philosophy, but when he fails, he decides to marry Rosa. Frustrated and jealous, Alma informs Dr. Buchanan, who is killed by Rosa's father when he arrives to prevent a wedding. As the play and film progress, John reforms and assumes his father's responsibilities, while Alma eventually realizes the limitations of her spiritual life. She goes to John, but when she discovers he is engaged to Nellie, she is last seen picking up a traveling salesman in the park. Besides adding settings to open up the film, Glenville uses lighting to contrast characters: Alma is softly lit, giving her radiance; Rosa and Nellie are photographed in bright light, suggesting their physical appeal. Glenville also extends the body/soul, instinct and conscience contrasts to Alma's parents and examines the parent-child relationships in more depth. All of the changes heighten Williams' theme of the necessity of the interlocking, not separation, of body and soul. *(T. L. E.)*

Resources: Gene Phillips, *The Films of Tennessee Williams* (East Brunswick, NJ: Associated University Presses, 1980); Maurice Yacowar, *Tennessee Williams and Film* (New York: Frederick Ungar, 1977).

SUMMER HOLIDAY

See AH, WILDERNESS!

SUMMERTIME

See THE TIME OF THE CUCKOO

SUNRISE AT CAMPOBELLO (1958)
Dore Schary

Sunrise at Campobello (1960)

Directed by Vincent J. Donehue

Adapted by Dore Schary

Cast: Ralph Bellamy (Franklin D. Roosevelt), Greer Garson (Eleanor Roosevelt), Hume Cronyn (Louis Howe), Jean Hagen (Missy Le Hand)

Length: 144 minutes

After a distinguished career as a Hollywood film producer, Dore Schary moved to New York to pursue an old ambition—to write for the Broadway stage. Schary, a liberal Democrat, focused his dramatic attention on the real-life crisis faced by Franklin D. Roosevelt when the president-to-be contracted polio. The result was a poignant theatrical docudrama, *Sunrise at Campobello*. The 1958 hit play scored with the public and critics and won the prestigious Antoinette Perry Award. In producing his adaptation for Warner Brothers, Schary used key members of his Broadway team. Foremost among these was the magnificent Ralph Bellamy, whose warm re-creation of FDR had won plaudits on Broadway. Director Vincent J.

Donehue was another critical carryover from the Broadway troupe. There were two other key casting decisions, Greer Garson as Eleanor Roosevelt and Hume Cronyn as Louis McHenry Howe, FDR's longtime friend and political adviser. As the film opens, it is 1921, and we are introduced to the patrician Roosevelt as they loll leisurely about the family retreat at Campobello, an isle off the coast of Maine belonging to the Canadian province of New Brunswick. Life is easy, although FDR's mother wishes that her son would pursue a career in a field less demanding than politics. Suddenly, tragedy strikes. After a day of sailing, Roosevelt, feeling chilled, retreats to bed. His legs become paralyzed, and a doctor is called. The symptoms are unmistakable. The diagnosis is poliomyelitis. The prognosis is that Roosevelt will never walk again. The rest of the film chronicles FDR's hard-won victories over both depression and disability. With the help of family and friends, Roosevelt pulls himself up out of despair. At the film's dramatic conclusion, with his zest for life and political ambition restored, a triumphant FDR stands on crutches to nominate Al Smith for president at the 1924 Democratic National Convention. Critical and box office response was positive. Bellamy again won raves as FDR. Greer Garson, fitted with prosthetic teeth to more accurately depict Eleanor Roosevelt, earned an Oscar nomination for Best Actress. The film also made the *New York Times* "Ten Best" list. Since it had been released in September 1960, just as the Kennedy-Nixon presidential race was heating up, and Schary had made the anti-Catholic sentiment faced by Al Smith a key part of his scenario, the film has been credited for having minimalized the issue of Kennedy's Catholicism in the 1960 presidential race. Significantly, *Sunrise at Campobello* was also one of the last Hollywood films to view politics in a positive light, as an admirable pursuit in which good people fight to overcome personal adversity in order to serve the public good. *(C. M. B.)*

Resources: James Monaco, *The Movie Guide* (New York: Putnam, 1992); Dore Schary, *Heyday* (Boston: Little, Brown, 1979).

THE SUNSHINE BOYS (1972)
Neil Simon

The Sunshine Boys (1997)

Directed by John Erman

Adapted by Neil Simon

Cast: Woody Allen (Al Lewis), Peter Falk (Willie Clark), Sarah Jessica Parker (Nancy Clark)

Length: 110 minutes

The plot involves two protagonists in their seventies, cantankerous, absent-minded, and possibly senile Al Lewis and Willie Clark, who worked together in vaudeville for forty-three years as "the Sunshine Boys" but who have not spoken to each other for a dozen years. Willie's nephew, Ben Silverman, wants them to resurrect one of their vaudeville routines for a television special. After they finally agree to a studio rehearsal, the cranky Lewis walks out, and Clark has a heart attack. This adaptation was updated by Neil Simon for Hallmark Entertainment in that the geriatric "Odd Couple" that drive the comedy, the show-business team of Lewis and Clark, were now comics in their prime during the Ed Sullivan era of television rather than former vaudevillians and are now being asked to appear in a movie. Woody Allen and Peter Falk are younger incarnations of Lewis and Clark than were George Burns and Walter Matthau in the feature film adaptation directed by Herbert Ross in 1975, but they may seem mismatched, since Peter Falk was sixty-eight when the film was made, while Allen was eight years younger. More serious than chronology, however, is the mismatching of comic talent. Allen seems better suited to his role than Falk, an imbalance that hampers the production. A gender change is made, turning Clark's nephew, who is also his agent, into a niece, played agreeably by Sarah Jessica Parker, a change that does not damage the play's meaning substantially. Simon's play is usually considered foolproof, but Caryn James found the pacing seriously off and described John Erman's direction as "pedestrian" and "uneven." The television adaptation was on the shelf for two years before being broadcast, despite a well-paced and nicely delivered performance by Woody Allen. *(J. M. W.)*

Resources: Caryn James, "Younger and Hipper, but Still Cranky," *New York Times* (26 December 1997): B39; Edythe M. McGovern, *Neil Simon: A Critical Study* (New York: Frederick Ungar, 1978).

SWITCHING CHANNELS

See THE FRONT PAGE

TABLE BY THE WINDOW and TABLE NUMBER SEVEN (1954)
Terence Rattigan

Separate Tables (1958)

Directed by Delbert Mann

Adapted by Terence Rattigan and John Gay

Cast: Burt Lancaster (John Malcolm), Rita Hayworth (Mrs. Shankland), Wendy Hiller (Miss Cooper), Deborah Kerr (Sibyl), David Niven (Major Pollock), Gladys Cooper (Mrs. Railton-Bell)

Length: 99 minutes

Terence Rattigan's play combined two plays, *Table by the Window* and *Table Number Seven*. It was first produced in London's St. James Theatre on 22 September 1954 and was published in 1995. In New York, it was first presented by the Producers Theatre in association with Hecht-Lancaster at the Music Box on 25 October 1956, directed by Peter Glenville. It has been made into two films. Laurence Olivier, originally assigned to direct the 1958 version, was replaced by Delbert Mann, who had worked with Paddy Chayefsky on both *Marty* (1955) and *The Bachelor Party* (1957). In Mann's version the two plays are radically changed and combined into a Hollywood movie complete with the title song, "Separate Tables," by Harry Warner and Harold Adamson. In its rearranged form the principals do not play two parts, as they did in the stage version, where in the New York production Eric Portman played both Malcolm and Pollock, and Margaret Leighton played both Mrs. Shankland and Sibyl. Because the 1958 film blends the stories, the characters encounter each other, and different actors must play the lead roles. A down-and-out American writer, John Malcolm (in the play an Englishman, a former junior Member of Parliament), is living at a quiet English seaside hotel populated by "characters," most notably, Mrs. Railton-Bell, who dominates her troubled, grown daughter. The residents sit at separate tables in the dining room but talk across to each other in a comfortable social matrix. Miss Cooper, the proprietress, is having a quiet affair with Malcolm when his ex, Mrs. Shankland, shows up under a pretense. With the sensitive Miss Cooper's help and against all odds, the estranged couple finally decide to give their relationship another try. Miss Cooper also encourages the Major to face his problems when the resident harridan, Mrs. Railton-Bell, and company discover his secrets: he is really only a retired lieutenant, and he has recently been charged with indecency. Sibyl Railton-Bell, introverted and prone to "spells," has formed a friendship with the Major, and the revelation of the truth about him has come as a shock. The pivotal role of Miss Cooper is diluted in the film; however, she influences Sibyl to be more independent and the Major to stay and face his problems. In the touching, if overstated, final scene, the residents make a point of greeting the Major when he courageously sits at his usual table, much to the disgust of Mrs. Railton-Bell. With the Major staying on and even her own daughter refusing to leave the dining room with her, the powerful lady is defeated, and the relationship between the Major and Sibyl has begun to heal. *(K. O.)*

Resources: Terence Rattigan, *Separate Tables: Two Plays* (New York: Random House, 1955); John Wakeman, "Delbert Mann," in *World Film Directors*, vol. 2 (New York: H. W. Wilson, 1985): 646–649.

Separate Tables (1983)

Directed and adapted by John Schlesinger

Cast: Alan Bates (John Malcolm, Major Pollock), Julie Christie (Mrs. Shankland, Sibyl), Claire Bloom (Miss Cooper), Irene Worth (Mrs. Railton-Bell)

Length: 50 minutes

Rated: PG

Like the stage version, this production is composed of two separate plays, *Table by the Window* and *Table Number Seven*. Schlesinger's favorite actor combination, Bates and Christie, play the leads, which are different characters in each play. The supporting cast remains the same in both the play and film. This made-for-television film version is quite deliberately a filmed play. Although it leaves out a minor subplot, is slightly rearranged, and has some updated dialogue, it is far more faithful to the original than the 1958 movie. This sensitive film retains the importance of the fair-minded Miss Cooper as a catalyst. The relationship between Malcolm and Mrs. Shankland is stormy and complex. The display of courage by Major Pollock and Sibyl at the end is played straight and unembellished, maintaining the exquisite and touching close of the original play. *(K. O.)*

Resources: Geoffrey Wansell, *Terence Rattigan* (New York: St. Martin's Press, 1991); Bertram A. Young, *The Rattigan Version: Terence Rattigan and the Theatre of Character* (New York: Atheneum, 1986).

TALK RADIO (1985)
Eric Bogosian

Talk Radio (1988)

Directed by Oliver Stone

Adapted by Eric Bogosian and Oliver Stone

Cast: Eric Bogosian (Barry Champlain), Alec Baldwin (Dan), Ellen Greene (Ellen), Leslie Hope (Laura)

Length: 110 minutes

Rated: R

Monologist Bogosian first staged *Talk Radio* in 1985 in Portland, Oregon, and the following year performed an expanded version in New York. The play takes place in a stripped-down version of a radio studio, and aside from a few illuminating comments by Dan Woodruff, the executive producer; Stu Noonan, Barry's operator; and Linda MacArthur, Barry's assistant, the show consists of Barry's abusive phone conversations with an assortment of losers. Among the callers is Kent, who subsequently appears at the station and joins Barry behind the microphones. When he gives a caller Barry-like advice to commit suicide, Barry is appalled and tells Linda to get him out. Kent turns abruptly around and points what turns out to be a camera at Barry and then takes a flash photo of him. When Bogosian and Stone adapted the play for the screen, they inserted material relating to the 1984 murder of Alan Berg, a Denver talk show host, by neo-Nazis. The film begins with night shots of Dallas, a city associated with assassination, and the sequence ends with a shot of a parked car in the radio station's parking lot. In the course of the film, which includes the Kent episode, there are calls about Jews, a delivered package containing a dead rat and anti-Semitic threats, and an anti-Semitic death-threat letter. This anti-Semitic motif runs throughout both shows (the play unfolds in ninety minutes of real time). Adding to the tension is the presence of a radio executive who wants to make Barry's show national. Dan, the producer, wants to establish guidelines for Barry, who continues to test the limits. Ellen, his ex-wife, has come to Dallas to visit Barry and is so concerned about the way the show is going that she becomes a caller. In this blending of professional and personal, she tells Barry she loves him, but he self-destructively puts on his role as caustic, cynical talk show host and rejects her love. Her appearance in the film triggers a flashback to Barry's past but does not account for his manic behavior, refusal to accept limits, and deliberate efforts to put himself at risk. After he leaves the studio with his producer/lover Laura and bids her good night, the film returns to the Berg/ Barry parallel when a bigoted assassin guns him down. The film does not end with Barry's death, for against a backdrop of downtown Dallas his associates and callers react offscreen to the news of his death. *(T. L. E.)*

Resources: Frank Eugene Beaver, *Oliver Stone: Wakeup Cinema* (New York: Max-well Macmillan International, 1994); Norman Kagan, *The Cinema of Oliver Stone* (New York: Continuum, 1995).

THE TAMING OF THE SHREW
(1593–1594)
William Shakespeare

The Taming of the Shrew (1929)

Directed and adapted by Sam Taylor

Cast: Douglas Fairbanks, Sr. (Petruchio), Mary Pickford (Kate), Edwin Max-well (Baptista Minola), Joseph Cawthorn (Gremio), Clyde Cook (Grumio), Geoffrey Wardwell (Hortensio), Dorothy Jordan (Bianca)

Length: 73 minutes (reissued in 1966 in a shortened version of 66 minutes)

The action is presented as a play within a play that starts with an "Intro-duction" involving a drunken tinker, Christopher Sly, on whom a practical joke is played by a nobleman. Ensconced in luxury, Sly is told that he has been dreaming for fifteen years. A group of players then perform the Italianate story that is the main action, concerning Baptista Minola's problem in marrying off his shrewish daughter, Katharine (Kate). Her father will not allow her younger sister Bianca to marry until Katharine is married first. A swaggering adventurer from Verona, Petruchio, who needs a dowry as much as he needs a wife, takes the challenge, weds Katharine, and takes her to his country house, where she is abused, humiliated, and, finally, "tamed." Thereafter, Petruchio takes Katharine back to Padua for the wedding of her sister Bianca to Lucentio. A contest takes place during the wedding feast to demonstrate the obedience of wives. Katharine is the most obedient and lectures her sister about why a wife should be subservient to her husband's every command. This early comedy invites exactly the broad and farcical treatment given it by matinee idol Doug Fairbanks and his Hollywood wife, "America's Sweetheart," Mary Pickford. The project started as a silent film, but a sound version was released. Completely gone are the Sly Induction and almost all of the Bianca subplot and Lucentio's scheming to get Kate married so he can claim Bianca. Act 1 is compressed into a few minutes, and the play is restructured to get the popular Fairbanks before the camera as quickly as possible. The film suggests that Bianca loves Hortensio (who, in the play, decides to marry a rich widow instead). With the disintegration of the subplot, the characters of Lucentio and Hortensio are compressed into a single character. Though much is lost here, the wedding in act III is close in spirit to Shakespeare. The action of act IV is compressed into a single night. (In the play Kate is not allowed to eat or sleep for days, until she learns obedience.) Because the plot is changed, the film omits the 100-crown wager that Kate is now more obedient than Bianca or the widow whom Hortensio has married (in the play). The play is transformed into a comic romp with broad physical humor as a star vehicle for Fairbanks and Pickford. The story that the film was originally released with the credit "Written by William Shakespeare, with additional dialogue by Sam Taylor" is apocryphal and probably began as a joke, according to Robert Hamilton Ball, who knew Sam Taylor and who wrote years ago that Roger Manvell had got the story wrong by depending on the memory of Lawrence Irving, who worked with set director William Cameron Menzies. *(J. M. W.)*

Resources: Roger Manvell, *Shakespeare and the Film* (New York: Praeger, 1971); John C. Tibbetts and James M. Welsh, *His Majesty the American: The Cinema of Douglas Fairbanks, Sr.* (Cranbury, NJ: A. S. Barnes, 1977).

The Taming of the Shrew (1966)

Directed by Franco Zeffirelli

Adapted by Suso Cecci D'Amico, Paul Dehn, and Franco Zeffirelli

Cast: Richard Burton (Petruchio), Elizabeth Taylor (Katharine), Michael Hordern (Baptista), Cyril Cusack (Grumio), Michael York (Lucentio), Alfred Lynch (Tranio), Natasha Pyne (Bianca), Alan Webb (Gremio), Victor Spinetti (Hortensio), Mark Dignam (Vincentio), Giancarlo Cobelli (Priest), Vernon Dobtcheff (Pedant), Roy Holder (Biondello), Gianni Magni (Curtis), Alberto Bonucci (Alberto), Bice Valori (Widow)

Length: 126 minutes

In Padua Baptista Minola will not allow his younger daughter Bianca to wed until a husband has been found for his elder daughter Katharine, notorious for her bad temper and shrewishness. A candidate is found in Petruchio, who woos and weds the surly Kate, mainly for her dowry, and then meets the challenge of "taming" her. Franco Zeffirelli's film was a commercial venture, a star vehicle for Richard Burton and his wife, Elizabeth Taylor, and their sizzling performances make this character-driven comedy memorable. Zeffirelli's film is twice as long as the earlier 1929 Sam Taylor version, which also exploited the celebrity status of a famous Hollywood couple, but it is far more cinematic. It gives more attention to the Bianca subplot, and it suggests that Petruchio is smitten by Katharine's beauty, though his motive is still mercenary at first. Burton's Petruchio pretends not to notice Kate's initial hostility and sullenness, and his rooftop pursuit of her when he first comes courting is great fun to watch. His rudeness and ill temper at the wedding and his cantankerous strategy to turn her into an obedient wife after the ceremony reveal some affection behind his feigned brutality, as he seems determined to beat Kate at her own game. Though Zeffirelli removes the Sly Induction, the spirit of Sly is captured by Burton's conception of Petruchio—a vulgar, boorish, drunken lout whose mannerisms and apparel are curiously at odds with his diction and verbal facility. This film is less cynical than the play, as it demonstrates that the couple has a great deal in common and is not exactly mismatched. They seem to understand each other. Taylor's later Kate is sentimentalized in a way her earlier one is not. She hates her sneaking, prissy sister; she wants a man as spirited as Petruchio who is willing to take her seriously and as she is. Her eyes linger upon Petruchio as she views him surreptitiously from a stained-glass window after her outrageous and humiliating encounter with him on the rooftops of Padua. The process of Kate's taming in the 1929 version was unconvincingly brief; Zeffirelli takes more time to humanize Petruchio and provide a motive for Katharine's transformation at the end, when she is absolutely loyal to her domineering husband, as romantic comedy overtakes farcical action. The film was a popular success and led the way for Zeffirelli's later adaptation of *Romeo and Juliet*. The Italian setting and art direction open up the play brilliantly. *(J. M. W.)*

Resources: Roger Manvell, *Shakespeare and the Film* (New York: Praeger, 1971); Franco Zeffirelli, *Zeffirelli: An Autobiography* (New York: Weidenfeld and Nicholson, 1986).

See also KISS ME, KATE

TEA AND SYMPATHY (1953)
Robert Anderson

Tea and Sympathy (1956)

Directed by Vincente Minnelli

Adapted by Robert Anderson

Cast: Deborah Kerr (Laura Reynolds), John Kerr (Tom Lee), Leif Erickson (Bill Reynolds), Edward Andrews (Herbert Lee)

Length: 123 minutes

Robert Anderson's 1953 Broadway hit, *Tea and Sympathy*, immediately attracted the interest of MGM, which retained Anderson to write the adaptation and hired original cast members Deborah Kerr, John Kerr (no relation), and Leif Erickson to re-create their stage performances. The story, set at a New England boys' school, opens with the principal character, Tom Lee (John Kerr), returning for his ten-year class reunion. In a flashback, Tom recalls his school experiences. A quiet, sensitive young man, he would rather listen to classical music than participate in "manly" sporting activities. Being different, he fails to conform to the "regular guy" image accepted by the other boys. Concluding that he is gay, the boys label him "sister-boy." His only source of support is the housemaster's wife, Laura Reynolds (Deborah Kerr), with whom he falls in love. She befriends him partly because of the overt hostility directed at him by her husband, Bill (Leif Erickson). This hostility stems from Bill's own feelings of repressed homosexuality. As the harassment of Tom intensifies, he resolves to prove his manhood by visiting Ellie, a local prostitute. Overhearing his plans, Laura attempts to stop him. When he abruptly kisses her, she pulls back and sends him away. He keeps his date with Ellie but fails sexually. Believing this confirms his homosexuality, he attempts suicide. Learning about the suicide attempt, Laura confronts Bill about his responsibility for Tom's action. She relates the events of the previous evening and regrets sending Tom away, not just out of sympathy but because of her loneliness and frustration in her marriage. Bill storms out, leaving the question of their marriage unresolved. Concerned about Tom, Laura follows him to a secluded spot in the country. Failing to convince Tom that his inability to have sex with Ellie did not make him unmanly, Laura decides to make love with Tom. The scene ends as Laura and Tom kiss and embrace. As the film reverts back to the present, Tom reads a letter left by Laura renouncing the wrong they committed. This final scene provides moral compensation to satisfy the Production Code Administration (PCA). *Tea and Sympathy*, a box office success, was significantly altered from the original play to accommodate PCA objections regarding the screen portrayal of homosexuality and infidelity. The film sped the removal of restrictions on screen homosexuality. *(N. I.)*

Resources: David Gerstner, "The Production and Display of the Closet: Making Minnelli's *Tea and Sympathy*," *Film Quarterly* (September 1997): 13; *Variety Film Reviews 1954–1958*, 9 (26 September 1956).

THE TEMPEST (1611)
William Shakespeare

Forbidden Planet (1956)

Directed by Fred McLeod Wilcox

Adapted by Irving Block and Allen Adler, with a script by Cyril Hume

Cast: Walter Pidgeon (Dr. Morbius), Anne Francis (Altaira), Leslie Nielsen (Commander Adams), Warren Stevens (Doc Ostrow), Jack Kelly (Lt. Farman), Richard Anderson (Chief Quinn), Earl Holliman (Cook), Robby the Robot (himself)

Length: 98 minutes

William Shakespeare's *The Tempest* has been the subject of a number of rewrites and transformations, and this science-fiction film resets the play's action to the distant planet of Altair-4 in the year A.D. 2257. In the film, a United Planets Cruiser is on a mission to find the survivors of the lost ship *Bellerophon*, which carried an expedition team from Earth. However, upon reaching the planet, the crewmen find that the only survivor is Dr. Morbius (Walter Pidgeon), a doctor of linguistics who has taken control of the planet through his understanding and use of the Krell technology that he found on the planet when he first arrived. With him on Altair-4 are his daughter Altaira (Anne Francis), born after the expedition landed, and his mechanical servant, Robby the Robot. Led by Commander Adams (Leslie Nielsen), the United Planets representatives try to bring the estranged scientist and his daughter back to Earth, but the enigmatic and aloof Morbius refuses, and he insists the crew leave the planet immediately.

Morbius' use of Krell technology, the men discover, has unleashed a creature of his subconscious, which attacks them. The Id-monster threatens to destroy all, and Morbius, realizing his error, faces up to his own inner fears and perishes with the creature, as Shakespeare meets Freud. Adams destroys the planet and blasts off for space with his new bride, Altaira. Many Shakespearean parallels are obvious: Morbius is Prospero, with science replacing his magic; Altaira is Miranda; Adams is Ferdinand; even the drunk Cook evokes Stephano. The popular Robby the Robot, who goes on to appear in a variety of films and television episodes, is the science-fiction analogue to the spritely Ariel, a relic of the planet's past, whom Morbius controls, as well as a sort of pseudo-Caliban, servant of the island's new master. Caliban is more directly manifested as the Id-creature who menaces the travelers. The film also evokes other classics, including *Dr. Jekyll and Mr. Hyde* and *Dr. Faustus*, as well as Edenic allusions. Highly regarded since its release, *Forbidden Planet* has even prompted a sequel, *Return to the Forbidden Planet*, a rock-musical filled with Shakespearean allusions, which returns the science-fiction film to the stage, where it began with Shakespeare. Although Wilcox's film is not a traditional representation of the text, *Forbidden Planet* is an exciting and inventive transformation that illuminates the rich possibilities inherent with *The Tempest*. (H. H. D.)

Resources: Frederick S. Clarke and Steve Rubin, "Making *Forbidden Planet*," *Cinefantastique* 8.2–3 (Spring 1979): 4–66; Frederick Pohl, *Science Fiction: Studies in Film* (New York: Ace Books, 1981); Virginia Mason Vaughan and Alden T. Vaughan, "Tampering with *The Tempest*," *Shakespeare Bulletin* 10.1 (Winter 1992): 16–17.

Prospero's Books (1991)

Directed and adapted by Peter Greenaway

Cast: John Gielgud (Prospero), Michael Clark (Caliban), Isabelle Pasco (Miranda), Michael Blanc (Alonso), Erland Josephson (Gonzalo), Mark Rylance (Ferdinand), Tom Bell (Antonio), Kenneth Cranham (Sebastian), Orpheo/Paul Russell/James Thierree/Emil Wolk (Ariel), Jim van der Woude (Trinculo)

Length: 127 minutes

Rated: R

In this bold and fascinating adaptation, Peter Greenaway deconstructs and reenvisions Shakespeare's final play, transposing scenes and lines in a film that considers the nature of texts and authorship. John Gielgud's Prospero is a controlling figure who speaks all of the film's dialogue (although it is mechanically altered at times, all lines are spoken, and thus all parts are played, by Gielgud), thus creating the text, as Prospero (as envisioned by both director Greenaway and iconic actor Gielgud) conflates with Shakespeare as playwright and artist. Greenaway's focus is specifically on the twenty-four books of knowledge that the wizard possesses (the number twenty-four perhaps serves as a reminder of either the twenty-four hours a day of the dramatic unities or the twenty-four frames per second of film). The film is divided into sections denoting the different books, such as *The Book of Water, The Book of Mirrors*, and *Love of Ruins*, which deconstruct and reset *The Tempest* as Prospero imagines it. In the film's storm-driven final scene, the magus breaks his staff and destroys his books. Caliban (Michael Clark), however, rescues his former master's final two books: a collection of Shakespeare's thirty-five plays, written in Prospero's hand, and the final play, the still-unfinished *Tempest*. Thus, the slave is the preserver of culture, although this culture is recorded and imagined by Prospero, who creates and maintains art through manipulation and dissection of text(s). Greenaway's film is an artistic and cinematic spectacle, which departs from the play text while, at the same time, respecting Shakespeare's original words. Viewers must have a solid knowledge of the play in order to follow this pastiche of scenes and lines, for *Prospero's Books* is a film embedded in *The Tempest*; the play is the starting point for the film, as it develops as a sort of cinematic spin-off, building on, and re-inforcing, the concepts within the play. The phrase "visual feast" may be a cliché in the discussion of Greenaway's pictures, but that description fits this film. Words appear on the screen as they are spoken; pictures are framed within frames; images are superimposed over faces. Orally, Prospero's voice-overs dominate the film, as he creates the film text through his storytelling magic. Peter Greenaway's film suggests rich and considerable possibilities for the play through its positioning of Prospero as creator and dominator of both island and text. With its unconventional filmmaking methods, its radical textual emendations, and its use of nudity, this film will rankle purists, but, with its inventive consideration of the role of Prospero/Shakespeare in the very creation of the text, *Prospero's Books* is an intriguing and radical adaptation of Shakespeare's final play. *(H. H. D.)*

Resources: Vincent Canby, "Review of *Prospero's Books*," *New York Times Film Reviews, 1991–92* (New York: Arno, 1993): 174–175; Mariacristina Cavecchi, "Peter Greenaway's *Prospero's Books*: A Tempest between Word and Image," *Literature/Film Quarterly* 25.2 (1997): 83–89; Peggy Phelan, "Numbering *Prospero's Books*," *Performing Arts Journal* 14.2 (May 1992): 43–50; Leon Steinmetz and Peter Greenaway, *The World of Peter Greenaway* (Boston: Journey Editions, 1995).

Tempest (1982)

Directed by Paul Mazursky

Adapted by Paul Mazursky and Leon Capetanos

Cast: John Cassavetes (Phillip/Prospero), Gena Rowlands (Antonia), Susan

Sarandon (Aretha/Ariel), Vittorio Gassman (Alonzo), Raul Julia (Kalibanos), Molly Ringwald (Miranda), Sam Robards (Freddy), Paul Stewart (Phillip's Father), Jackie Gayle (Trinc), Anthony Holland (Sebastian), Jerry Hardin (Harry Gondorf)

Length: 140 minutes

Rated: PG

The film has been freely adapted to capture the spirit of Shakespeare's *The Tempest* as a contemporary comedy that begins on one island, Manhattan, and moves to another, in the Aegean Sea. Phillip (Cassavetes), a successful architect, leaves New York and a tempestuous marriage and takes his daughter, Miranda, to live on a deserted, idyllic Greek island. While Phillip lusts after perfection, the randy goatherd Kalibanos lusts after Miranda, until a tempest brings to Phillip's fantasy island the Manhattan people he thought he could live without, and ultimately the characters are reconciled, as in Shakespeare's play. Details are changed. In the film Phillip's telescope replaces Prospero's staff. In New York Phillip commands, "Show me the magic," but the storm has already started outside his picture window. In Greece, closer to nature, Phillip seems able to conjure up a storm at will, even though the storm has been forecast. The benign enchantment of the film is closer in spirit to *A Midsummer Night's Dream* than to *The Tempest*. The Caliban figure is fully and humorously humanized. His bestial nature is suggested merely by his lust, his banality, and his materialism. According to Leon Capetanos, Mazursky "wanted to do a version of *The Tempest* as if it were done by the Marx Brothers" (8). The main focus was on the father-daughter relationship. Mazursky and Capetanos decided the play was not about magic but about "a person who people believe has magic." Mazursky "loved the magic," however, and "loved the idea of forgiveness." Ultimately, he decided not to use the language of Shakespeare because he felt that "it would be inaccessible to a mass audience." Mazursky was blocked for a number of years because he was "trying too hard to make a Shakespearean film." Then he realized that what appealed to him was the plot: "A man and his daughter on an island. A man consumed with negative feelings about his past. A man who felt that terrible things had been done to him and who in the end would put down his magic and forgive" (6). Capetanos explained that "Phillip doesn't really have any power." No one does: "You only have the power to forgive people for their mistakes and become friends with them and see them as human beings and see yourself as a human being" (92). The film, therefore, is not exactly Shakespeare, but it is awfully close to Shakespeare's denouement of reconciliation, forgiveness, and sacrifice, as Phillip gives up his hold on Miranda to Freddy, Arethia (Ariel) is "released," and Antonia and Alonzo are forgiven. The film is certainly a pleasure to watch. *(J. M. W.)*

Resources: Paul Mazursky and Leon Capetanos, *Tempest: A Screenplay* (New York: Performing Arts Journal Publications, 1982); Geoffrey Taylor, *Paul Mazursky's Tempest* (New York: New York Zoetrope, 1982).

The Tempest (1979)

Directed and adapted by Derek Jarman

Cast: Heathcote Williams (Prospero), Toyah Willcox (Miranda), Karl Johnson (Ariel), Jack Birkett (Caliban), David Meyer (Ferdinand), Peter Bull (Alonso), Richard Warwick (Antonio), Ken Campbell (Gonzalo), Neil Cunningham (Sebastian), Claire Davenport (Sycorax), Elisabeth Welsh (Goddess)

Length: 96 minutes

Rated: R

In this highly stylized film, Derek Jarman rearranges Shakespeare's text into an imaginative, original vision. The film begins and ends with shots of a sleeping Prospero, indicating that this *Tempest* is all the wizard's dream vision. Here the island has been transformed into a Palladian mansion, creating with its outsize corridors and eccentric decor an out-of-time setting that contributes to the dream-vision motif. Heathcote Williams is an unusually youthful Prospero, representing a combination of a Byronic figure and a Beethoven-like mad genius with the enigmatic Elizabethan magus Dr. John Dee, for whom Jarman holds a long-standing fascination. The controlling Prospero, whose unconscious mind creates the events that unfold, presents a boilersuited Ariel (Karl Johnson) who magically escapes at the film's end, although Prospero never directly frees him, and a Miranda (Toyah Willcox) who at once evokes punk rock style while remaining an obedient daughter. Played by the blind actor Jack Birkett (a.k.a. "The Great Orlando"), Caliban is a revolting, grotesque figure, but he is not a menacing one, for he is easily chased away by Miranda when he attempts to rape her; her response is to laugh at the odd servant. In an added scene, Caliban suckles from Sycorax's massive breast. Jarman's other textual addition is even more striking; the final sequence is a dazzling and campy reworking of the masque scene, with black blues singer Elisabeth Welsh singing Harold Arlen's "Stormy Weather." The song's refrain, "Keeps raining all the time," serves as a coda to Prospero's dream and his storm-inducing magic, and it also recalls the refrain from Shakespeare's own song that appears in both *Twelfth Night* and *King Lear*: "the rain it raineth everyday." Thus, this romance falls between the earlier comedy and tragedy, presenting a seemingly bright version of Shakespeare's final play while hinting, through the presence of an all-controlling Prospero, at a darker undercurrent. Jarman's film is a bold revisioning of the original text, transposing lines and scenes while maintaining the illusionary qualities of a dream. Although it first opened to mixed reviews and has since been some-what forgotten, Derek Jarman's film remains a unique and dynamic ad-aptation that transforms the play into a radical cinematic experience. *(H. H. D.)*

Resources: Walter Coppedge, "Derek Jarman's *The Tempest*," *Creative Screen-writing* (April 1998): 12–15; Diana Harris and MacDonald Jackson, "Stormy Weather: Derek Jarman's *The Tempest*," *Literature/Film Quarterly* 25.2 (1997): 90–98; Derek Jarman, *Dancing Ledge* (London: Quartet, 1984): 186–206.

THE TENDER TRAP (1954)
Max Shulman and Robert Paul Smith

The Tender Trap (1955)

Directed by Charles Walters

Adapted by Julius Epstein

Cast: Frank Sinatra (Charlie Reader), Debbie Reynolds (Julie Gillis), David Wayne (Joe McCall), Celeste Holm (Sylvia Crewes), Jarma Lewis (Jessica Collins), Lola Albright (Poppy Matson), Carolyn Jones (Helen)

Length: 107 minutes

Not rated

The Tender Trap was first presented by Clinton Wilder at the Longacre Theatre in New York on 13 October 1954 and was directed by Michael Gordon. The original Broadway cast included Robert Preston (Joe), Julia Meade (Jessica), and Kim Hunter (Sylvia). The play is written in the tra-ditional three-act format of the 1950s and gives an innocent sense of the morals and values of the period. The transfer to film holds up quite well, and the play itself was tremendously enhanced by the film's addition of the star power of Frank Sinatra and Debbie Reynolds. Sinatra's character of Charlie is transformed from a chemist lab technician in the play to a New York talent agent in the film, and this subtle change in story line is just the right touch for Sinatra and Hollywood. Sinatra is a New York bachelor who has women coming and going from his apartment as though it were a brothel. His best friend, Joe (David Wayne), shows up on Charlie's door-step one day and is amazed at Charlie's prowess with women. Many fem-inists and liberated women of the 1990s will find Debbie Reynolds' character of Julie just a bit much with her attitudes toward men and mar-riage. As far as Julie is concerned, a career is fine, but "it's no substitute for marriage. I mean, a woman isn't really a woman at all until she's married and had children" (Shulman and Smith 32). The age-old "boy-meets-girl, boy-loses-girl, boy-gets-girl" scenario is set in motion with Sinatra the louse eventually becoming Sinatra the married man. While Julie's ideas may seem somewhat antiquated in these later days of the twentieth-century, the film version of *The Tender Trap* gives us a nostalgic reminder of what the 1950s was all about. All of the secondary performers in the film are well defined and give good support to Sinatra and Reynolds. The film begins with Sinatra walking out from the horizon singing the title song, and the finale comes full circle with the four principal characters repeating the singing of the title song and taking a bow at the end of the film. *(J. D.)*

Resources: Gene Ringgold, *The Films of Frank Sinatra* (New York: Citadel Press, 1971); Max Shulman and Robert Paul Smith, *The Tender Trap* (New York: Dramatists Play Service, 1955).

THAT CHAMPIONSHIP SEASON (1972)
Jason Miller

That Championship Season (1982)

Directed and adapted by Jason Miller

Cast: Bruce Dern (George Sitkowski), Stacy Keach (James Daley), Robert Mitchum (Coach Delaney), Martin Sheen (Tom Daley), Paul Sorvino (Phil Romano)

Length: 108 minutes

Rated: R

Jason Miller's *That Championship Season* (1972) has one set, the Coach's house, where four former high school basketball players have a yearly reunion to celebrate their championship season. In the course of an evening the players reveal their true characters, turn on each other, and ultimately reunite for a common cause, the mayoral campaign. George, the mayor, has a face for all occasions, has put the city in debt, and has helped his friends. Phil, a lecher not above sleeping with George's wife, is the recipient of George's largesse and George's principal financial backer. James, the brother who sacrifices but gets no respect, suggests that Phil support him for mayor. Tom, James' alcoholic brother, resorts to cynical comments before signing on as George's speechwriter. The Coach, "retired" for striking one of his players, is a racist whose focus on winning has prevented his players from maturing. Throughout the play he serves as the surrogate "father" who has one-on-one "confessional" meetings with his "boys." At the end of the play he manages to pull the boys together to hear the radio coverage of the final game and to pose for another group photo. When he adapted his play to film, Miller tried to open up the play by creating more outside scenes. The best of these occurs at the beginning of the film when George is conducting an apolitical political rally complete with cheerleaders, speeches, and George's gift to the city, Tilly the elephant. The subsequent death of Tilly, the disposal and funeral problem, the city council response—this sequence is effective political satire. Miller was not as fortunate with the anticommunist campaign George and the Coach plan to wage against Sharmen, George's political opponent. The anticommunist material had more relevance when the play was staged ten years earlier. Another outside set occurs in the old high school gymnasium, which is closed like most of downtown Scranton, where the film is set. The "closed" nature of Scranton suggests change, loss, and the passage of time. Caught in the grip of memory, the four players and the Coach fail to age gracefully and to adapt. They can ignore adultery, betrayal, and loss, even the knowledge that the championship is tainted by the Coach's instructions to hurt the black scorer for the opposition. After the black player's ribs are broken, Martin, the only player never to attend the reunion, scores the winning basket but cannot celebrate the victory. Miller has retained almost all of the dialogue from the play, even the obscene comments, ethnic slurs, and anti-Semitic barbs; and the long speeches and enclosed set at the Coach's house make this seem more like filmed theatre than a film. *(T. L. E.)*

Resources: Brooks Atkinson, *Broadway*, rev. ed. (New York: Limelight, 1985); David Denby, "Movies: One of the Boys Is One of the Girls," *New York* 16 (27 December/3 January 1982/1983): 76–78.

THESE THREE

See THE CHILDREN'S HOUR

THIS HAPPY BREED (1943)
Noël Coward

This Happy Breed (1945)

Directed by David Lean

Adapted by David Lean, Ronald Neame, and Anthony Havelock-Ellis

Cast: Robert Newton (Frank Gibbons), Celia Johnson (Ethel Gibbons), Kay Walsh (Queenie Gibbons), Stanley Holloway (Bob Mitchell), John Mills (Billy Mitchell)

Length: 114 minutes

First produced in London at the Haymarket Theatre on 30 April 1943, with Noël Coward and Judy Campbell in the leading roles of Frank and Ethel Gibbons, *This Happy Breed* appeared two years later after the end of World War II and the Labour Party's landslide victory over Winston Churchill's Conservative Party. The film generally follows the chronological pattern of Coward's original stage production by focusing upon the lives of the lower-middle-class Gibbons family and the historical events from 1919 to 1939 affecting them. Both play and novel reproduce Coward's conservative, status quo ideology of lower classes content with their place in society and antithetical toward any radical changes in their lives, whether political or sexual. Lean cinematically extends the play in several ways. He begins his film with a shot of the river Thames before dissolving to Clapham's terraced houses and moving into the interior of Number 17 Sycamore Road, where the play's events occur. He concludes the film with reverse imagery. Major family sequences in the Gibbons household usually conclude with the camera tracking out before the image dissolves into another sequence, a cinematic parallel to theatrical lights dimming before the next scene. The film also includes several significantly historical external scenes. Frank, Ethel, and Bob celebrate British Empire Day in 1924 and view a pageant of military glory. Other scenes show the 1926 General Strike with Frank and Bob "naturally" helping the government against striking miners. After the family hears King Edward VIII's abdication broadcast on 10 December 1936, Lean departs from the original play by showing Ethel removing a royal calendar from the wall, presumably taking it to the trash can. Like their runaway daughter, Queenie, Edward has placed sexual fulfillment above British codes of duty and restraint. In 1937 Frank and Bob witness Conservative Stanley Baldwin's election victory. In response to Baldwin's nonrearmament poster, Bob remarks, ironically, "That's the face of a man you can trust." Later, Neville Chamberlain appears waving the 1938 Munich peace agreement before cheering crowds, as a prelude to Frank's critical speech against the appeasement mentality. Finally, the camera also tracks out to conclude the scene of Queenie leaving to join Bob in Singapore in 1938. Although Queenie finally admits the error of her ways and returns to the fold as wife and mother, she will ironically receive further punishment as a prisoner of the Japanese after 1941. Lean's film reinforces the conservative imagery of Coward's play and reveals that traditional British ideology was not completely routed by Labour's postwar electoral victory. *(T. W.)*

Resources: Kevin Brownlow, *David Lean* (New York: St. Martin's Press, 1996); Andrew Higson, *Waving the Flag: Constructing a National Identity in Britain* (Oxford: Clarendon Press, 1993).

THIS PROPERTY IS CONDEMNED (1942)
Tennessee Williams

This Property Is Condemned (1966)

Directed by Sidney Pollack

Adapted by Francis Ford Coppola, Fred Coe, and Edith Sommer

Cast: Natalie Wood (Alva Starr), Robert Redford (Owen Legate), Mary Badham (Willie Starr), Kate Reid (Hazel Starr), Charles Bronson (J. J. Nichols)

Length: 110 minutes

Filmmaker Sidney Pollack based his film on a one-act play by Tennessee Williams, which can be acted on the stage in about twenty minutes. An enormous amount of expansion was imposed on the play's slender plot to bloat it into nearly two hours of screen time, which is fairly obvious when one views the movie. The play simply presents a thirteen-year-old girl named Willie Starr, who has been deserted by her parents. Willie recounts for a lad named Tom the sad story of her sister Alva, who took care of her until Alva's untimely death from lung cancer. So it is Alva whom Willie idolizes and wants to imitate. Unfortunately, since Alva was a prostitute in her mother's boardinghouse-brothel for railroad men, Willie naively but firmly believes that the kind of life that Alva led is the only truly glamorous existence for any girl. Consequently, there is little doubt by play's end that Willie is condemned to take up her sister's sordid way of life. The three principal authors of the 1966 film version—including writer-director Francis Ford Coppola—elaborated Williams' slender little tale far beyond his original conception. The basic format that the screenwriters hit upon was to make Williams' play the framing device for the picture. Accordingly, they broke the one-act roughly in half, presenting the first portion as a prologue to the film and the remaining segment as an epilogue. In this way they utilized almost all of the play's original dialogue in their screenplay. In the prologue of the film Willie (Mary Badham) describes her family and present situation to the boy Tom, and in the epilogue she wraps things up by telling Tom what happened to each of them. The scriptwriters then had to devise a full-blown story told in flashback to fit between the prologue and the epilogue. Several of the characters in the picture are derived from people to whom Willie refers in the one-act play. The one character who is cut from whole cloth in the movie and who has no discernible counterpart in the play is Owen Legate (Robert Redford). He is a railroad inspector who stays long enough in the Starr boardinghouse to make Alva (Natalie Wood) dissatisfied with her dead-end existence there and to beckon her to a cleaner life in New Orleans as his wife. But before Owen can make an honest woman of Alva, her life is tragically cut short by lung cancer. The film then closes with the epilogue in which Willie is left with the grim prospect of coping with life alone. *This Property* was shot in rural Mississippi and New Orleans and greatly benefited from the location photography of veteran cinematographer James Wong Howe. Still, Williams was understandably disappointed with the finished product. Indeed, he accurately assessed the film as a "vastly expanded and hardly related film with the title taken from a very delicate one-act play. The film was hardly deserving of the talents of Robert Redford and Natalie Wood." Or, one might add, the talents of Sidney Pollack, Francis Coppola, and cinematographer James Wong Howe. *(G. D. P.)*

Resources: Peter Cowie, *Coppola: A Biography*, rev. ed. (New York: Da Capo, 1994); Gene D. Phillips, *The Films of Tennessee Williams* (Cranbury, NJ: Associated University Presses, 1980).

A THOUSAND CLOWNS (1962)
Herb Gardner

A Thousand Clowns (1965)

Directed by Fred Coe

Adapted by Herb Gardner

Cast: Jason Robards (Murray Burns), Barry Gordon (Nick Burns), Barbara Harris (Sandra Markowitz), William Daniels (Albert Amundson), Martin Balsam (Arnold Burns), Gene Saks (Leo Herman)

Length: 118 minutes

A Thousand Clowns was first presented on 5 April 1962 at the Eugene O'Neill Theatre, New York. The production was directed by Fred Coe. *A Thousand Clowns* is the touching story of Murray Burns, who, as an unemployed television comedy writer, has become the guardian of his twelve-year-old nephew Nick after his sister Elaine disappears one day with, as Murray explains it, "a tall chap with sun-glasses who was born to be her fifth divorce." Complications arise immediately as Nick announces to his uncle Murray that their homelife is about to be investigated by social workers representing his school. When social worker Albert Amundson later announces that Murray's lifestyle does not provide the proper atmosphere for bringing up a young boy such as Nick, Murray is left with only two choices. Murray must either get a job immediately or lose Nick. Unfortunately for Murray, the only real job possibility available to him is going back to his old job of writing for the Saturday morning children's show *Chuckles the Chipmunk*. Murray's life is further complicated when Sandra abandons her position as an official investigator on his case and impetuously spends the night with him, which begins the setup for a "boy meets girl, boy loses girl, boy gets girl" scenario. In the end, Murray does get the girl, and he does get to keep his nephew, but only after many of the usual complications one would expect from a light comedy of the 1960s. While current stage productions of *Clowns* still hold up well and are quite popular throughout the community theatre circuit, the transfer to film has a very 1960s feel to it. The plus side of the film is the re-creation of the stage performances of Jason Robards and Barry Gordon. Broadway and Hollywood have always had a strange love/hate relationship when it comes to putting stage plays on film. *A Thousand Clowns* is a good example wherein Sandy Dennis, who won a Tony award for her performance as the likable, but confused, social worker Sandra Markowitz, was passed over for the film version in favor of Barbara Harris. The flip side of the equation is Martin Balsam, who did not appear in the original Broadway production but did win an Oscar for Best Supporting Actor as Murray's older brother Arnold Burns. *(J. D.)*

Resources: Ronald Bergan, Graham Fuller, and David Malcolm, *Academy Award Winners* (London: Multimedia Books, 1992); Herb Gardner, *A Thousand Clowns* (New York: Samuel French, 1962); Isabelle Stevenson, *The Tony Award* (New York: Crown, 1984).

THE THREEPENNY OPERA (1928)
Bertolt Brecht

The Threepenny Opera (1931)

Directed by G. W. Pabst

Adapted by Leo Lania, Bela Balasz, and Ladislas Vajda

Cast: Rudolph Forster (Mackie Messer), Carola Neher (Polly Peachum), Lotte Lenya (Jenny)

Length: 113 minutes

The Threepenny Opera, which in 1928 opened onstage in Berlin as *Die Dreigroschenoper*, was adapted from John Gay's eighteenth-century play *The Beggar's Opera*, itself a parody of sixteenth-century Italian music dramas. Transposed by dramatist Bertolt Brecht and composer Kurt Weill to the mean streets of late nineteenth-century London, the parodistic tale of urban lowlife was intended to prod German playgoers to reflect on the economic and political upheavals of 1928 and, with them, the fate of the Weimar Republic. Although Brecht and Weill were included at the onset of the adaptation process, artistic differences with film director G. W. Pabst arose almost immediately. While preserving the play's social satire with its assumption that criminals and politicians have more in common than not, Pabst softened the play's political critique by shifting greater weight to the story's romance. Many of Brecht's famed "alienation" devices, designed to provoke audiences to progressive political action, were either marginalized or eliminated altogether. Stylistically, the play's hard-edged and self-consciously theatrical decor was made more realistic by Pabst's naturalistic mise-en-scène, which made effective atmospheric use of billowing clouds of tobacco smoke and swirling banks of London fog. Weill's trenchant pop-inflected songs, so crucial to Brecht's strategy of dialectical estrangement, were reduced in the film to the status of adornment; Pabst, in fact, discarded three of Weill's most pivotal plaints, "Ballad of Sexual Dependency," "The Tango Ballad," and "The Ballad for the Hangman." Given the extent of Pabst's alternations, it's not surprising that Brecht and Weill, in separate cases, sued the director and his American coproducer, Nero Films and Warner Brothers/First National. The suits came to naught, and Pabst continued filming. When released in 1931, it was clear that the film bore the realistic mark of Pabst as well as the expressionist signatures of Brecht and Weill. That it crackled with Brecht's sharp sarcasm was, in part, due to the dynamic presence of Carola Neher (Polly Peachum) and Lotte Lenya (Weill's wife, who plays Jenny), holdovers from the 1928 theatrical cast. Despite artistic differences, the film ultimately bears witness to Pabst's basic agreement with Brecht's and Weill's leftist politics. Indeed, as a work in Pabst's oeuvre, it should be thematically grouped with the director's similarly anticapitalist, pro-everyman *Westfront 1918* (1930) and *Kameradschaft* (1931). *The Threepenny Opera* was shot simultaneously in German and French with different casts. In Paris, it became a critical and box office success. In Berlin, with the ascent of the Third Reich, all German prints were seized and destroyed, a testament to the power of Pabst's portrayal of the zeitgeist making Hitler possible. *(C. M. B.)*

Resources: Lotte H. Eisner, *The Haunted Screen: Expressionism in the German Cinema and the Influence of Max Reinhardt* (Berkeley: University of California Press, 1969); Roger Manvell and Heinrich Fraenkel, *The German Cinema* (New York: Praeger, 1971).

See also THE BEGGAR'S OPERA

THE THRONE OF BLOOD (THE CASTLE OF THE SPIDER'S WEB/KUMONOSU-JO)

See MACBETH

THE TIME OF THE CUCKOO (1952)
Arther Laurents

Summertime (1955)

Directed by David Lean

Adaptedby David Lean and H. E. Bates

Cast: Katharine Hepburn (Jane Hudson), Rossano Brazzi (Renato Di Rossi), Isa Miranda (Signora Fiorina), Darren McGavin (Eddie Jaeger), Mari Aldon (Phyl Jaeger), MacDonald Parks (Mr. McIlhenny), Jane Rose (Mrs. McIlhenny), Gaitano Audiero (Mauro), Virginia Simeon (Giovanna)

Length: 100 minutes

Laurents' *The Time of the Cuckoo* opened in New York in 1952 and was adapted to film three years later. Since the cuckoo is a summer visitant to Europe, and Laurents' original title did not suggest the bittersweet love story the film became, the title was changed to the more upbeat *Summertime*. In the play, Leona Samish travels to Venice to find a "wonderful, mystical, magical miracle," which becomes a love affair with Renato Di Rossi, a shop owner who she discovers is married. When she confronts him, he replies that "you want steak; eat ravioli." Because she suspects Rossi has overcharged her for some goblets, and she finds out that the Italian money he got for her at a favorable exchange rate is counterfeit, Leona declares she's "swallowed all the ravioli talk I'm going to." In anger, she also tells Phyl Jaeger that her husband has had a sexual relationship with Signora Fiorina, who owns the pension where the play takes place. At the end of the play, she returns, disillusioned, to America. The film adaptation takes advantage of Venice's beauty and at times has a "travelogue" quality, but taking the action outside is consistent with the upbeat film about a love that cannot last. In the film, Jane Hudson (Katharine Hepburn) travels to Venice for adventure and love, meets Renato Di Rossi (Rossano Brazzi), and is shocked by the erotic postcards and the pickups she witnesses; but instead of rejecting Rossi when she learns he is married, she continues the affair, which she describes as the "happiest time in my life," even though she knows it will "end in nothing." The film contains a wonderfully symbolic scene in which a white flower, which Rossi gives her, drifts slowly out of her reach, just as their love affair does. When she leaves at the end of the film, Brazzi gives her another white flower, a reminder of their affair. The film omits her suspicion about being overcharged for the goblet (she actually learns that the McIlhennys, American tourists at the pension, paid more for the mass-produced ones they purchased), the counterfeit money problem, and her spiteful story about Eddie Jaeger (Darren McGavin) and Signora Fiorina (Isa Miranda). The expression on the face of the departing Jane is not bitter disillusionment but happiness. The story of unrequited love, *Summertime* resembles *Brief Encounter* (1945), which Lean also directed. He and Hepburn were both nominated for Oscars. (*T. L. E.*)

Resources: Michael A. Anderegg, *David Lean* (Boston: Twayne, 1984); Gerald Pratley, *The Cinema of David Lean* (South Brunswick, NJ: A. S. Barnes, 1973).

TORCH SONG TRILOGY (1981)
Harvey Fierstein

Torch Song Trilogy (1988)

Directed by Paul Bogart

Adapted by Harvey Fierstein

Cast: Harvey Fierstein (Arnold), Matthew Broderick (Alan), Anne Bancroft (Ma), Brian Kerwin (Ed), Karen Young (Laurel), Eddie Castrodad (David)

Length: 122 minutes

Rated: R

Harvey Fierstein's trio of related one-act plays gained notice as one of the first works of homosexual drama to have widespread crossover appeal to heterosexuals. According to critic Frances Gray, the popularity of Fierstein's work (especially *Torch Song Trilogy*) is partially due to "his use of forms already familiar from heterosexual romance. . . . Fierstein uses situations that would, but for the sexuality of the protagonists, be the most bewhiskered of clichés" (Gray 320). In *Torch Song Trilogy*, Fierstein manages to exploit these heterosexual romantic clichés by populating them with homosexual (or bisexual) characters. The trilogy's first play, *The International Stud*, takes place in the early 1970s, as Arnold, a drag queen known as Virginia Hamm, strikes up a relationship with the sexually ambivalent

Ed, who he later learns is dating a woman. Play number two, *Fugue in a Nursery*, follows up on Arnold and Ed a year after the first play, as Ed continues to flirt with homosexuality but marries his girlfriend Laurel, and Arnold starts a serious relationship with another man named Alan. The final play, *Widows and Children First!*, is another five years into the future (now the late 1970s); Alan has been brutally murdered, and Arnold is trying to deal with his visiting mother while at the same time forming a parental relationship with a gay teen named David. Although each of the three shorter plays had been previously produced separately, the off-Broadway premiere of the full *Torch Song Trilogy* was in the fall of 1981. The initial production was well received and considered to be at the forefront of the new gay pride era (Parish 392), but it was not filmed until several years later. The delay resulted in differing responses in the reception of the film version. In the period since the play's initial run (largely because of it), Fierstein had become a better-known, mainstream figure in cinema and drama; more importantly, "AIDS had made such a devastating impact that the movie was forced to confine its action to a specific period (1971–1981) so its characters could function as Fierstein had conceived them originally and not have to deal with the disease's impact on the gay lifestyle" (Parish 392). As a result of the differences of time period as well as changes in casting (Bancroft assumed the role of Ma from Estelle Getty, Broderick shifted from playing David to playing Alan), the film of *Torch Song Trilogy* was not received with nearly the same enthusiasm as the play had been seven years earlier. Additionally, the film made the seemingly requisite changes involved in adapting plays to film by opening up the action: whereas in the original stage production *The International Stud* had consisted mainly of soliloquies, the action of *Fugue in a Nursery* was confined to a huge stylized and symbolic bed, and *Windows and Children First!* was staged as if it were a sitcom; in the film Fierstein and director Paul Bogart made all of the settings and character interactions more realistic in nature. *(C. M.)*

Resources: Frances Gray, "Harvey Fierstein," in *International Dictionary of Theatre*, vol. 2: *Playwrights*, ed. Mark Hawkins-Dady (London: St. James Press, 1994); Frances Gray, "Torch Song Trilogy," in *International Dictionary of Theatre*, vol. 1: *Plays*, ed. Mark Hawkins-Dady (London: St. James Press, 1992); James Parish, *Gays and Lesbians in Mainstream Cinema* (Jefferson, NC: McFarland, 1993).

THE TRAGEDY OF OTHELLO: THE MOOR OF VENICE

See OTHELLO

TRIAL AND ERROR

See THE DOCK BRIEF

THE TRIP TO BOUNTIFUL (1953)
Horton Foote

The Trip to Bountiful (1985)

Directed by Peter Masterson

Adapted by Horton Foote

Cast: Geraldine Page (Carrie Watts), John Heard (Ludie Watts), Carlin Glynn (Jessie Mae), Rebecca DeMornay (Thelma), Richard Bradford (Sheriff)

Length: 103 minutes

Rated: PG

Originally written for the Goodyear Television Playhouse and aired 1 March 1953, Foote's teleplay *The Trip to Bountiful* appeared as a play in New York in November 1953. In the play Carrie Watts lives in a cramped, three-bedroom apartment in Houston with her son, Ludie, and his wife, Jessie Mae. Carrie and Jessie Mae feud over Carrie's hymn singing and recurrent efforts to return to Bountiful, her Texas home, which is now uninhabited; and Ludie, recently recovered from an illness and newly employed, is unable to resolve their differences. In order to recover her past and flee her present, Carrie takes her government check and some change and boards a bus that stops at Harrison, twelve miles from her destination. En route, she befriends Thelma, whose husband is in the armed services and who is returning to her parents' home. Soon after she gets off the bus, Carrie remembers that she has left her purse on the bus. Lacking the funds for a hotel, she sleeps on a bench until she is awakened by the sheriff, whom Ludie has called. Because she fears that Ludie will thwart her plans and take her back to Houston, she convinces the sheriff to take her to the farmhouse where she was raised. Ludie finds her there, and after he and Carrie discuss the past, both decide to move on. There is even a reconciliation between Carrie and Jessie Mae. When Foote adapted his play to film, he retained almost all the dialogue, and the basic sets (Houston apartment, bus stations, farm at Bountiful) remain the same. The opening slow-motion shot in the film, a boy and mother running through a field, does provide a welcome addition, for the lyrical shot suggests the close nature of the Carrie-Ludie relationship and helps explain Carrie's quest to return to a past rich in memories. Unlike the evocative outside shots of Bountiful, the outside Houston shots, Ludie and a coworker driving to work and Jessie Mae walking to the drugstore to indulge her passion for movie magazines and Cokes, contribute little to the film except to juxtapose their outside freedom with Carrie's claustrophobic existence. *(T. L. E.)*

Resources: Barbara Moore and David G. Yellin, eds., *Horton Foote's Three Trips to Bountiful* (Dallas: Southern Methodist University Press, 1993); Gerald C. Wood, ed., *Horton Foote: A Casebook* (New York: Garland, 1998).

TRUE WEST (1980)
Sam Shepard

True West (1983)

Directed by Allan Goldstein

Adapted by Sam Shepard

Cast: John Malkovich (Lee), Gary Sinese (Austin), Sam Schacht (Saul), Margaret Thomson (Mom)

Length: 110 minutes

Not rated

Sam Shepard's *True West* (1980) had a difficult journey from its premiere at San Francisco's Magic Theatre, the playwright's West Coast home base, to New York. A 1981 production at the New York Public Theatre, starring Peter Boyle and Tommy Lee Jones, proved a disaster with its original director, Robert Woodruff, being fired by producer Joe Papp and Shepard repudiating his own play, declaring he would never again give another work of his to the Public Theatre. Then out of Chicago came the Steppenwolf Theatre Company's production, directed by Gary Sinese with himself as Austin and the breakout performance of John Malkovich as Lee, which was transferred to the Cherry Lane Theatre in New York, where it enjoyed great success with a succession of stars following this original cast in a long run.

The play is about role reversal. Austin, a reasonably successful screenwriter, spars with his drifter, desert-rat brother, Lee, while he tends their mother's house during her visit to Alaska. The brothers duel over a mythical terrain, involving their father, individualism, and the "West" of the American imagination. In the course of their encounter, Lee forces Austin to face the problematic side of his own nature with the latter brother finally questioning his vocation, values, and identity. While the exchange of character between the brothers is not always plausible and motivated in Shepard's script, the comedy of menace contained therein plays well. Mother (Margaret Thomson) returns to find her sons in epic battle, Cain and Abel at it once again; as Shepard describes the effect, "lights go slowly to black as the after-image of the brothers' pulses in the dark." Tucker Orbison sees this moment as "the dark of the theatre and the dark of our minds."

The Public Broadcasting series *American Playhouse* filmed the Cherry Lane production, aired in January 1984. Allan Goldstein, the director, follows the vitality of Sinese's theatre staging with effective television complements such as skillful use of the moving camera and telling close-ups. Austin's ritual with the stolen toasters as he competes with his larcenous brother in procuring small household appliances is hilarious. As Lee tries to find an old girlfriend's phone number in Bakersfield, we hear the perplexed operator in the video version; this voice was absent from the stage production. Apart from the incisively moving camera, the video version is also notable for some fixed setups where the tension between the brothers is shown in depth through long takes to good effect. The very symmetry of Shepard's script sometimes undermines its suspense and effectiveness. The two men may well stand for the playwright/actor himself and the bipolarity of his own career. Hank Williams' "Ramblin Man," which ends the video version, evokes the distinctive tone of Shepard's art; we are grateful to have an archival documentation of one of his most accessible texts in a notable production. *(E. T. J.)*

Resources: Tucker Orbison, "Mythic Levels in Shepard's *True West*," *Modern Drama* 27 (1984): 506–519; Don Shewey, *Sam Shepard: The Life, the Loves, behind the Legend of a True American Original* (New York: Dell, 1985).

TWELFTH NIGHT (1601)
William Shakespeare

Twelfth Night (1996)

Directed and adapted by Trevor Nunn

Cast: Helena Bonham Carter (Olivia), Imogen Stubbs (Viola), Stephen Mackintosh (Sebastian), Toby Stephens (Orsino), Nicholas Farrell (Antonio), Nigel

Hawthorne (Malvolio), Mel Smith (Sir Toby Belch), Ben Kingsley (Feste), Richard E. Grant (Sir Andrew Aguecheek), Imelda Staunton (Maria)

Length: 105 minutes

Rated: PG

The play begins with a shipwreck off the coast of fictional Illyria that separates identical twins, Viola and Sebastian. Neither twin knows the other has survived, and both are at risk because Illyria is at war with their native country. Viola disguises herself as a boy and goes into the service of young Duke Orsino, who dotes upon the Countess Olivia. Olivia is grieving over the recent death of her father and brother and has therefore abjured the company of men for seven years. Orsino sends Viola, now disguised as "Cesario," to plead his case with Olivia, who finds herself attracted to Cesario. Viola, meanwhile, is falling in love with Orsino in this comedy of confused identities. The plot is resolved when Sebastian appears to replace Cesario, and Viola's true identity is revealed to Orsino. A comic subplot involves a power struggle between Olivia's repressive and puritanical steward Malvolio and her boisterous drunken uncle Sir Toby, who deludes vain Malvolio into believing that Olivia is romantically interested in him, therefore making a complete fool of himself. From the opening tempest at sea Trevor Nunn films the play in such a way that it seems more believable than one might suppose possible. Sebastian and Viola could pass for identical twins once Viola has shorn her locks and fashioned a mustache from the clippings. The nineteenth-century atmosphere beautifully captured by Clive Tickner's cinematography works perfectly well. The film takes some liberties with the play, beginning with a voice-over narration, but succeeds in capturing the music of Shakespeare as no other film has done. It also evokes the psychological depth of the play while making the absurd artificiality of the dodgy, cross-dressing plot somehow believable. The casting is brilliant. Ben Kingsley's Feste is a remarkably melancholy, dour troubadour and serves as the perfect chorus for the folly observed. Nigel Hawthorne's Malvolio is as close to perfection as one could wish for. This is a wonderful adaptation. *(J. M. W.)*

Resources: Stephen Holden, "There's Something Verboten in Illyria," *New York Times* (25 October 1996): C3; David Sterritt, " 'Twelfth Night' Catches Up with '90s," *Christian Science Monitor* (1 November 1996): 15.

27 WAGONS FULL OF COTTON (1955)

See THE LONG STAY CUT SHORT/OR/THE UNSATISFACTORY SUPPER and 27 WAGONS FULL OF COTTON

UNCLE VANYA (1897)
Anton Chekhov

Vanya on 42nd Street (1994)

Directed by Louis Malle from Andre Gregory's *Vanya*

Adapted by David Mamet

Cast: Wallace Shawn (Vanya), Larry Pine (Dr. Astrov), Julianne Moore (Yelena), Brooke Smith (Sonya), George Gaynes (Serebryakov)

Length: 119 minutes

Rated: PG

While there is some debate about the actual date of Chekhov's Russian masterpiece *Uncle Vanya*, it was published in 1897 and was partly derived from his earlier *The Wood Demon* (1889). The environment of the play centers on the life and activity of a provincial estate where destruction of the land and resources is made parallel to the erosion taking place in the lives of the characters, a frequent correlative in the work of this playwright.

The movie is based on a five-year experimental effort of a group of American actors working with director Andre Gregory on a version of Chekhov's play. The actors are seen in contemporary clothes walking down 42nd Street in midtown Manhattan on the way to a rehearsal in a formerly elegant theatre just off Times Square. The performing space itself somewhat embodies the play's content and atmosphere. Before the audience realizes the transformation, the company seamlessly moves from late twentieth-century New York City to late nineteenth-century Russia on a country estate where Dr. Astrov (Larry Pine) is offered some tea or vodka. In September 1991 Louis Malle, who had filmed Wallace Shawn's *My Dinner with Andre* (the latter being Gregory) some years before, saw a run-through of *Vanya*. Two years later Gregory and Shawn asked Malle to film their production of Chekhov in Mamet's adaptation, which turned out to be the final work of the late famed French director. Malle uses his camera with subtlety to let the actors exhibit their art. Much of Gregory's "blocking" is quite static, with the actors merely sitting near one another reciting Chekhov's dialogue. Malle moves his camera like another actor without calling attention to unnatural kinetics but preserving the ensemble effect of a stage performance.

The simple plot presents Vanya (Wallace Shawn) and Sonya (Brooke Smith) coming to the realization that his ex-brother-in-law and her father, Serebryakov (George Gaynes), is so self-absorbed as an aging renowned professor with a young wife, Yelena (Julianne Moore), that he can put on the market the estate that they have kept going for him at great, unappreciated personal sacrifice. Meanwhile, Sonya experiences her failure in attracting Astrov, who has become infatuated with Yelena, as has Vanya; Yelena elects to remain with her elderly, ailing husband. Vanya's abortive and comic shooting at Serebryakov misses the mark. Chekhov avoids melodrama, and decisive, violent action is not really within Vanya's nature or ability. Vanya and Sonya are left at the end of the film equally unrequited in their affections. They will manage the estate together, since Serebryakov decides not to sell it. The play and film move toward Sonya's final lyrical speech of resigned consolation beyond both despair and hope, yet the other characters hardly notice the exchange.

Malle makes convincing and relevant drama of people trapped between the harsh reality of their frustrated lives and the longings of their hearts. He finds the cinematic means and equivalents for Chekhov's simplicity and strength primarily through judicious close-ups of the actors. The film is a curiously satisfying version of *Uncle Vanya*. (E. T. J.)

Resources: Richard Gilman, *Chekhov's Plays: An Opening into Eternity* (New Haven, CT, and London: Yale University Press, 1995); Stanley Kauffmann, "From Russia with Love," *The New Republic* (7 November 1994): 34–36.

THE VIRGINIAN (1904)
Kirk La Shelle and Owen Wister

The Virginian (1929)

Directed by Victor Fleming

Adapted by Edward E. Paramore and Howard Estabrook

Cast: Gary Cooper (the Virginian), Richard Arlen (Steve), Walter Huston (Trampas), Mary Brian (Molly)

Length: 95 minutes

When *The Virginian* reached the screen in its first talking adaptation in 1929 (it had been filmed twice before in silent versions—in 1914 by Cecil B. DeMille and in 1923 by Tom Forman), it was not Owen Wister's 1902 novel that was its source, but his dramatization, written two years later in collaboration with Kirk La Shelle. The play's four acts and five scenes smelted down the sprawling story into a series of episodes located in a ranch house interior, a patch of ground between Judge Henry's ranch and the cowboys' quarters, the interior of Molly Wood's home, and a street corner intersecting the hotel and the saloon (in only one scene was an actual range locale suggested, the campfire scene wherein the rustlers are apprehended by the Virginian and his men). The cattle roundups, runaway stagecoaches, and mounted pursuits were conveyed by reported action and descriptive dialogue. The basic theme of the clash between the moral codes of eastern culture and western experience—as exemplified in the lynching of the rustler, Steve, and the climactic gunfight between the Virginian and the villainous Trampas—was teased out in extended discussions between the Virginian and the newly arrived schoolteacher, Molly. The Victor Fleming film adaptation for Paramount in 1929 retained the basic content of the debates between the Virginian and Molly (Gary Cooper and Mary Brian), while opening out the reported action and offstage events of the play—including the Virginian's rescue of Molly in the runaway stagecoach, the capture and hanging of Steve, Trampas' ambush of the Virginian, and the final gunfight. The scenes between the graceful, laconic Cooper and the bullying, brash Huston are particularly enjoyable to watch. In sum, the Fleming film was not only one of the more technically advanced and imaginative products of the early talkie era but the best of all the screen adaptations and one of the handful of truly distinguished American western movies. *(J. C. T.)*

Resources: James Robert Parish and Michael R. Pitts, *The Great Western Pictures* (Metuchen, NJ: Scarecrow Press, 1976); John C. Tibbetts, "The Stage Goes West: Routes to *The Virginian*," *Indiana Social Studies Quarterly* 34.2 (Autumn 1981): 26–37; Joseph H. Trimmer, "*The Virginian*: Novel and Films," *Illinois Quarterly* 35.2 (December 1972): 5–18.

WAIT UNTIL DARK (1966)
Frederick Knott

Wait Until Dark (1967)

Directed by Terence Young

Adapted by Robert Carrington and Jane-Howard Carrington

Cast: Audrey Hepburn (Suzy Hendrix), Alan Arkin (Roat), Richard Crenna (Mike Talman), Efrem Zimbalist, Jr. (Sam Hendrix), Jack Weston (Carlino), Samantha Jones (Lisa), Julie Herrod (Gloria)

Length: 107 minutes

In the *New York Times* review of the Broadway premiere of *Wait Until Dark* (3 February 1966), Stanley Kauffmann mused that such a second-rate thriller would be more suitable to film. Kauffmann might not have been right about the play's prospects—the original Arthur Penn production was a hit, and the play has been revived on Broadway as well as surviving in regional theatre—but he was right in suggesting its suitability to film. Even before the play was mounted, Warner Brothers bought the rights to the new work by British playwright Frederick Knott, whose *Dial M for Murder* had furnished the material for the 1954 Hitchcock film. Warners signed on British director Terence Young, who had established his credentials for suspense/action in the early James Bond films. With her husband Mel Ferrer producing, the glamorous star Audrey Hepburn was signed to play the glamourless heroine, a recently blinded woman who must fend off a trio of criminals seeking to retrieve a stash of heroin hidden inside a doll handed to her husband at the airport. That airport scene represents the film's only sustained attempt to open up the play; in the film most of the action remains in the cramped living area of a basement apartment in Greenwich Village. Few significant changes were made in the film, which suffers from the implausibilities of the play (why doesn't Suzy just lock the door?) but also moves toward the same gripping climax in the dark. Hepburn's Suzy Hendrix matches the play's heroine in strength and determination, but the film ratchets up the suspense by emphasizing Suzy's vulnerability, giving her a fire phobia and replacing her careful manipulation of fuses to darken her apartment with a frenzied smashing of light bulbs. With her devotion to her husband, Sam, and her better manners toward a neighbor child, this Suzy is even more admirable than the play's Suzy capable of winning over Mike Talman, the con man who poses as Sam's friend in an attempt to find the doll. If Richard Crenna plays Mike as a somewhat more benign character than his stage counterpart, Alan Arkin as Roat turns in an inconsistent performance that wavers between the comic and the sinister. In spite of criticisms of Arkin's performance, however, the suspenseful film proved a box office success and won Hepburn an Academy Award nomination. *(C. M. D.)*

Resources: Jay Robert Nash and Stanley Ralph Ross, eds., "Wait Until Dark," *The Motion Picture Guide*, vol. 9 (Chicago: Cinebooks, 1987); Alexander Walker, *Audrey: Her Real Story* (New York: St. Martin's, 1994).

THE WALTZ OF THE TOREADORS (1956)
Jean Anouilh

The Waltz of the Toreadors (1962)

Directed by John Guillermin

Adapted by Wolf Mankowitz

Cast: Peter Sellers (Gen. Fitzjohn), Dany Robin (Ghislaine), Margaret Leighton (Emily), Cyril Cusack (doctor), John Fraser (Robert)

Length: 102 minutes

Anouilh's postwar French comedy opened in 1956 on Broadway directed by Harold Clurman and in London directed by Peter Hall. In the Broadway play, which received five 1957 Tony nominations, Ralph Richardson played Gen. Leon St. Pé, whose name was changed in the film to Gen. Leo Fitzjohn (Sellers). The film, which moves the action of this bedroom farce to England, begins with a coach dashing through the streets bringing Ghislaine, who has come from France to reunite with the general with whom she had fallen in love seventeen years before at the Garrison Ball. She has paid a servant to obtain incriminating letters from the bedside table of Emily, the general's wife. Armed with evidence of possible infidelity, Ghislaine arrives at the general's grand castle to rescue him from his wife who imagines herself an invalid, whom he hates. Screenwriter Wolf Mankowitz has freed the story from the confines of its stage origins. Sweeping outdoor scenes are incorporated, as are flashbacks of battle, military parades, and the ball where the general (then lower-ranked) and his love danced the "Waltz of the Toreadors." The general, who has quite an eye for the ladies, has believed his tiresome wife to be faithful. The stolen letters are a red herring, but eventually, Emily declares that she had begun a love affair at the Garrison Ball all those years ago. Much visual material fleshes out the film: Emily, who is suicidal, pedals a bicycle past a foxhunt, with the general in pursuit on horseback and the doctor by car; Ghislaine attempts to drown herself in a lake and is rescued by her soon-to-be-lover Robert, the general's secretary (and secretly his son). One escapade follows the next, with Selleresque antics and an attempted wedding interrupted by the cavalry and a court-martial, neither of which appears in the play. At times Mankowitz incorporates action at the expense of the deliciously clever dialogue of the original play. While the play maintains an ironic, light, witty tone throughout, the film swings from slapstick and light debauchery to dark scenes of despair. In the end, the general contemplates suicide but then encounters the new young maid. Life will go on as usual. *(K. O.)*

Resources: Benedict Nightingale, *Fifth Row Center* (New York: Times Books, 1986); David Thompson, *A Biographical Dictionary of Film* (New York: William Morrow, 1976): 224.

WE'RE NO ANGELS

See MY THREE ANGELS

WEST SIDE STORY (1957)
Arthur Laurents; lyrics by Stephen Sondheim;
music by Leonard Bernstein

West Side Story (1961)

Directed by Robert Wise and Jerome Robbins

Adapted by Ernest Lehman

Cast: Natalie Wood (Maria), Richard Beymer (Tony), Russ Tamblyn (Riff), Rita Moreno (Anita), George Chakiris (Bernardo)

Length: 151 minutes

In January 1949 director-choreographer Jerome Robbins approached Leonard Bernstein to ask if he would collaborate with Arthur Laurents on a contemporary urban musical adaptation of Shakespeare's *Romeo and Juliet*. The proposed musical would involve a religious dispute between Jewish and Italian Catholics over Passover and Easter, but the ethnic center of the musical changed after Laurents and Bernstein noticed a newspaper report about ethnic gang violence in Los Angeles in 1955, which resulted in the musical's dispute between two gangs, the "Jets" and the "Sharks," on New York's West Side (rather than the East Side, as originally intended). Bernstein captured the Puerto Rican atmosphere by infusing jazz rhythms and a Latin percussion section into his symphonic score. The original play was not an immediate success in 1957, but it gained popularity on tour in subsequent runs through 1959. Producer Hal Prince noted that *West Side Story*'s eventual success was due to its film adaptation and record profits, rather than its original Broadway production, which received only lukewarm reviews. Ernest Lehman adapted the screenplay produced and codirected by Robert Wise and Robbins. Wise and Robbins intended to film a relatively faithful adaptation of the play, to the point even of opening the film with an overture. Wise shot the dramatic sequences, while Robbins directed the dance numbers. The film integrated location shooting of dance numbers on Manhattan streets with enclosed studio photography on a Hollywood soundstage, combining stark realism, a dark, film noir style, topical serious thematics, and violence with musical fantasy and romance. Wise insisted that the film had to open in New York to capture that milieu realistically, but the remaining nocturnal settings could be done in the studio. Wise shot the film as a musical set against a real background rather than in an impressionistic never-never land. It proved to be the most successful dark musical ever made and the biggest film of 1961, sweeping ten Academy Awards, including Best Picture. *(S. C. B.)*

Resources: Humphrey Burton, *Leonard Bernstein* (New York: Doubleday/Anchor, 1994); Keith Garebian, *The Making of West Side Story* (Toronto: ECS, 1995); Sergio Leemann, *Robert Wise on His Films* (Los Angeles: Silman-James, 1995); Craig Zadan, *Sondheim and Co.* (New York: DaCapo, 1994).

See also ROMEO AND JULIET

THE WHALES OF AUGUST (1980)
David Berry

The Whales of August (1987)

Directed by Lindsay Anderson

Adapted by David Berry

Cast: Bette Davis (Libby Strong), Lillian Gish (Sarah Webber), Vincent Price (Mr. Maranov), Ann Sothern (Tisha Doughty), Harry Carey, Jr. (Joshua Brackett)

Length: 90 minutes

Rated: PG

After being staged in Baltimore in 1980, *The Whales of August* appeared in New York in 1982. The play focuses on two elderly sisters, both widows, who spend their summers on the Maine coast. Libby, who is blind, is a pessimist who awaits her death, personified as the "escort," in November, the same month her husband died. Sarah, whose confidence and strength enable her to "do" for her sister, confronts old age by waiting in vain for the appearance of the whales and by planning for the future. In response to Libby's remark that they are "too far along to be trying something new for the cottage," Sarah states, "My life is not over." In the course of the play Sarah learns to accept change, represented by the absent whales, and to leave her sister, who has become quite a burden. Other members of the cast also deal with aging: Joshua, the plumber, continues to work into his eighties; Tisha, a friend and Maine native, has recently had her driver's license suspended; and Mr. Maranov, a White Russian émigré, has lost his landlady and is looking for a haven where he can stay "afloat." At the end of the play, despite Libby's objections, Sarah decides to put a new window in her cottage and to leave Libby. Her decision does not destroy their relationship; they exchange "I love you"s and are holding hands as the curtain falls. The film adaptation, scripted by the playwright, retains most of the dialogue and, aside from some shots of the ocean, restricts itself to the stage set. Berry and director Anderson do provide a kind of prologue in which Libby, Sarah, and Tisha appear as young women; and they add a real estate agent, who appears at Tisha's instigation. The major change occurs at the end of the film when Berry has Libby make the decision to add the new window, thereby suggesting that she, too, can cope with change and thus eliminating Sarah's decision to leave her. The film ends with the sisters walking to the ocean and having Libby suggest optimistically that the whales may appear. By altering Libby's character, the film dodges the difficult decision Sarah must make about Libby. *(T. L. E.)*

Resources: Erik Hedling, *Lindsay Anderson: Maverick Film-Maker* (London: Cassell, 1998); James Spada, *More Than a Woman: An Intimate Biography of Bette Davis* (New York: Bantam Books, 1993).

WHAT PRICE GLORY (1924)
Maxwell Anderson and Laurence Stallings

What Price Glory (1926)

Directed by Raoul Walsh

Adapted by J. T. Donahue

Cast: Victor McLaglen (Captain Flagg), Edmund Lowe (Sgt. Quirt), Delores Del Rio (Charmaine), Barry Norton (Private Lewishon)

Length: 120 minutes

What Price Glory first appeared at New York's Plymouth Theatre in 1924 with Louis Wolheim and William ("Stage") Boyd in the roles of Flagg and Quirt. Although John Ford also directed a film version in 1952, Walsh's version is generally acknowledged as superior. *What Price Glory* immediately responded to audience desire to confront the issues of World War I following the unexpected success of King Vidor's *The Big Parade* (1925). This three-act stage play was set in France and focused on the male rivalry between Flagg and Quirt, their conflicts over French "drab" Charmaine, and a more realistic attempt to depict both the fascination and horror of modern warfare. As in the play, the film concludes with Quirt's rushing off to join Flagg in battle with the lines, "Wait for Baby!" Although Arthur Hopkins, original stage director, added a note to the published edition warning audience about the profane language, the silent film version was much more extreme, with McLaglen and Lowe mouthing obscenities that never matched the printed captions! The film version opens out the play in several key ways. It begins in China and the Philippines by showing previous rivalries between Sergeants Flagg and Quirt. But the World War I landscape soon reveals a nightmare world of modern warfare that shocked postwar audiences. Charmaine's profiteering father, Cognac Pete, cynically comments, "Where could one see some of the best roses that bloom in Picardy?" His line not only refers to a popular wartime song but also evokes pastoral imagery influencing poets and writers of that generation, as Paul Fussell notes in *The Great War and Modern Memory*. The film also recreates the carnage and desolation of trench warfare in several scenes. As in the play, shell-shocked Lieutenant Moore attempts to "take my boys out of the muck and blood" and utters the key lines, "What price glory, now!" before Flagg overpowers him. But the film also depicts masculine fascination with combat by frequently inserting the shot of a bugler calling its two heroes to combat. Like a Hawks heroine, Charmaine realizes the true nature of male bonding: "Don't fight. Don't fight. You love each other, yes?" She ends the film watching her lovers eagerly march away toward the battlefield: "They are so strong and beautiful. They are too young to die." But *What Price Glory* is not totally against war and omits Quirt's lines in the play, "What a lot of God damn fools it takes to make a war!" *(T. W.)*

Resources: Paul Fussell, *The Great War and Modern Memory* (New York: Oxford University Press, 1975); Laurence Suid, *Guts and Glory: Great American War Movies* (Reading, MA: Addison-Wesley, 1978); James M. Welsh, "The Great War and the War Film as Genre: *Hearts of the World* and *What Price Glory*," in *Hollywood's World War I: Motion Picture Images*, ed. Peter C. Rollins and John E. O'Connor (Bowling Green, OH: Bowling Green State University Popular Press, 1997): 27–38.

WHOOPEE (1928)
Florenz Ziegfeld

Whoopee (1930)

Directed by Thornton Freeland

Adapted by William Counselman

Cast: Eddie Cantor (Henry Williams), Eleanor Hunt (Sally Morgan), Paul Gregory (Wanenis)

Length: 94 minutes

Whoopee! was the sixth of a series of successful shows produced by the redoubtable Florenz Ziegfeld (preceded by *Show Boat, Rio Rita, Rosalie,* and *The Three Musketeers,* among others) in the second half of the 1920s. It opened at the New Amsterdam Theatre on 4 December 1928, and audiences enthusiastically acclaimed its headliner, Eddie Cantor, the songs by Gus Kahn and Walter Donaldson, the elaborate choreography by Seymour Felix, and brilliant costume design by John Harkrider. Based on Owen Moore's 1923 satire *The Nervous Wreck,* it chronicles the seriocomic misadventures of pretty Sally Morgan (Eleanor Hunt) and hypochondriacal Henry Williams (Cantor) in their respective pursuits of romance and adventure in the great Southwest. Emboldened by its popular success, Ziegfeld contracted in 1929 with film producer Samuel Goldwyn to bring it to the screen. The Ziegfeld-Goldwyn collaboration was stormy, however—Ziegfeld particularly objected to some of the casting choices and the deletion of many of the original songs. Yet, as historian Miles Kreuger has noted, the film version was "as close as you'll ever get to seeing a Broadway show of that period." Indeed, everyone involved seems to have been determined to transfer the show to the screen as faithfully as possible. Eddie Cantor and Paul Gregory repeated their stage roles as Henry and Wanenis, respectively; and most of the production was photographed on soundstages in a manner suggestive of a proscenium-based production, wherein the action was photographed from the proverbial third-row-center vantage point. The famed, climatic "Wedding Scene" is a valuable document of the Ziegfeld-style "fashion show": the girls advance in single file toward the camera, each arrayed in an elaborate bridal gown; and a few of the ladies arrive on horseback, sporting Indian headdresses so enormous and cumbersome they have to be supported by showgirls walking alongside. An important exception to this pronounced theatricality was the wholly "cinematic" work of dance director Busby Berkeley. For the dance sequences, particularly the "Stetson Dance," he employed the camera and staging techniques that quickly became his signature style—photographing the showgirls from overhead, arranging them into geometrical formations, intercutting long shots with successive close-ups of the individuals, and so on. Photographed in wide screen and two-color Technicolor (the handful of exteriors shot in the desert Southwest were particularly gorgeous), *Whoopee!* made a big splash with critics and audiences alike, earning $2.3 million. Historian Richard Barrios writes: "It survives today as the summation of filmed musical comedy, vintage 1930" (241). *(J. C. T.)*

Resources: Richard Barrios, *A Song in the Dark: The Birth of the Musical Film* (New York: Oxford University Press, 1995); Miles Kreuger, *Souvenir Programs of Twelve Classic Movies* (Magnolia, MS: Peter Smith, 1979); John C. Tibbetts, *The American Theatrical Film* (Bowling Green, OH: Popular Press, 1985); Richard and Paulette Ziegfeld, *The Ziegfeld Touch* (New York: Harry N. Abrams, 1993).

WHO'S AFRAID OF VIRGINIA WOOLF?
(1962)
Edward Albee

Who's Afraid of Virginia Woolf? (1966)

Directed by Mike Nichols

Adapted by Ernest Lehman

Cast: Elizabeth Taylor (Martha), Richard Burton (George), George Segal (Nick), Sandy Dennis (Honey)

Length: 129 minutes

Edward Albee's drama, published in 1962, about two academic couples who play mind games through a long drunken night, won the New York Drama Critics Circle and Tony awards, helping to establish Albee as a preeminent American playwright. Mike Nichol's controversial film is a remarkably faithful adaptation, with a few predictable emendations. The film adds action to the verbal swordplay, with Martha cleaning up the house while she and George wait for Nick and Honey to arrive in act 1. Moreover, a noisily violent bar scene in the film's second act climaxes in a drunken car ride. The film places less emphasis on Nick's position as a science professor and George's nervousness about genetic tampering. In the play, Albee contrasts this very current, potentially world-altering research with George's field of history to explore modern anxiety about too-rapid change. In the film, the men's fields are used only to distinguish Nick's ambition from George's professional stasis. The film also deletes all reference to Martha's being older than George, although it does retain a (now) rather dated reference to her being more than 100 years old. Considerably abbreviating Nick and Martha's sexual dance of death, the film places more emphasis on the competition between George and Nick. As a result, Martha's confession of her deep feelings for George is sadder and less ironic than in the play. Both film and play feature Albee's incisive dialogue, peeling away artifice and habit to reveal the psychological dynamics of marriage. As Martha and George's names ironically echo the very founders of the United States, their fantasy child may, in fact, be our ideological construct of the country, revealed as sterile by both male leads: George's empty, angry cynicism and Nick's careerist disgust. Similarly, Martha's role as sexual predator and Honey's doggedly cheerful childishness suggest rot and immaturity as the typological extremes of wife-partners. *(K. R. H.)*

Resources: Richard Amacher, *Edward Albee* (Boston: Twayne, 1982); Gerry Mc-Carthy, *Edward Albee* (New York: St. Martin's, 1987); Matthew Roudane, *Understanding Edward Albee* (Columbia: University of South Carolina Press, 1987).

WHOSE LIFE IS IT ANYWAY? (1979)
Brian Clark

Whose Life Is It Anyway? (1982)

Directed by John Badham

Adapted by Brian Clark and Reginald Rose

Cast: Richard Dreyfuss (Ken Harrison), Janet Eilber (Pat), John Cassavetes (Dr. Michael Emerson), Christine Lahti (Dr. Clare Scott), Bob Balaban (Carter Hill), Kenneth McMillan (Judge Wyler), Kaki Hunter (Mary Jo Sadler), Thomas Carter (Orderly John), Alba Oms (Nurse Rodriguez), Kathryn Grody (Mrs. Boyle)

Length: 119 minutes

Rated: R

Clark's play, which began as a one-hour British teleplay and was expanded to a hit play in England and New York, concerns the "right-to-die" issue. Ken Harrison, a sculptor, is a quadriplegic who, after spending four months in the hospital, wants to be discharged from the hospital so that he can die. Dr. Emerson, however, is equally determined to keep Ken alive and states that Ken "must accept his condition." Ken hires Hill, a solicitor, to represent him; and Hill files for a writ of habeas corpus. Emerson's allies include a well-meaning, but insensitive, social worker, Mrs. Boyle, and Dr. Travers, whom Emerson urges to find a staunch Catholic psychiatrist to examine Ken. Dr. Scott, Ken's primary physician, eventually sides with Ken after she decides that Dr. Emerson is behaving like a judge, not a lawyer. The strength of the play lies not in the legal machinations or the ethical questions but in Ken's black comedy as he challenges his adversaries and jokes about his condition. At the end of the play, after Ken wins his case, Dr. Emerson tells him that he can stay at the hospital until he dies. The film takes the play outside the hospital. In the opening sequence, we see an energetic Ken (Richard Dreyfuss) working on his sculpture in Boston (the play took place in England), interacting with his girlfriend, Pat (Janet Eilber), and almost dying in a car crash. Pat assumes a larger role in the film because she is associated with the sculpted hand (derived from Michelangelo's Sistine Chapel) that Dr. Scott (Christine Lahti) admires; when Ken sees the hand, he dreams of a dancing, naked Pat. He sends Pat away for the same reason he wants to die: he is no longer a man or a sculptor. When Dr. Scott visits Ken's apartment and sees his work, much of it related to Pat (who has accepted Ken's decision and moved on sexually), she understands Ken's motives and sides with him. Other changes do not relate to motivation but to making a serious theme more palatable or entertaining: instead of taking Ken to dialysis, John, the orderly (Thomas Carter), takes him to the basement, where John and his band play for him and give him some marijuana. There are also changes in the hearing scene, which is expanded to create more suspense. Many of the lines from the play are retained, but in the film the judge (Kenneth McMillan) adjourns to research legal precedents. The decision is the same; Dr. Emerson (John Cassavetes) offers to let Ken stay "in case he changes his mind"; and Dr. Scott comes to Ken's room, starts to kiss him, and is told, "No." Because the film, unlike the play, suggests that Dr. Scott is falling in love with Ken, the scene is especially moving. The film concludes with the "bipping" of Ken's machine and a shot of the sculpted hand, which enigmatically suggests the hand of God. *(T. L. E.)*

Resources: John Coleman, "Films," *New Statesman* 103 (12 March 1982): 27; Tom Milne, "Whose Life Is It Anyway?" *Monthly Film Bulletin* 49 (3 February 1982): 32–33.

THE WILD DUCK (1884)
Henrick Ibsen

The Wild Duck (1983)

Directed by Henri Safran

Adapted by Tutte Lemkov, Dido Merwin, and Henri Safran

Cast: Liv Ullmann (Gina), Jeremy Irons (Harold/Hjalmar), Arthur Dignam (Gregory/Gregers), Lucinda Jones (Henrietta/Hedvig), John Meillon (Ackland/Ekdal), Michael Pate (Wardle/Werle), Colin Croft (Molrick/Mollison)

Length: 96 minutes

Rated: PG

Filmed in Australia, Anglicized, and updated to the early twentieth century, Henri Safran's adaptation of *The Wild Duck* follows the plot and characterizations of Ibsen's play fairly closely but opens up the dramatic text by fragmenting scenes and adding some dialogue and new locations. There are also some omissions, as Safran focuses on the play's pathos at the expense of its comedy. Jeremy Irons' Harold in particular is less comically contradictory and consequently less charming than Ibsen's Hjalmar. The opening scene of the film establishes the significant metaphors and themes of Ibsen's play. In this scene Wardle/Werle shoots the wild duck, symbolizing the financial and moral harm he caused years earlier to the Ackland/Ekdal family. The wounded duck dives to the bottom of the lake but is rescued by Wardle's dog, much as Gregory/Gregers, Wardle's idealistic and neurotic son, takes it upon himself to "rescue" his friend Harold from the falseness of his marriage with Gina, formerly Wardle's mistress. Instead of establishing Harold and Gina's marriage on a basis of honesty by forcing them to face the truth, Gregory succeeds only in driving the weak-natured Harold to reject both Gina and Hedvig. Safran shows both the walk during which Gregory tells Harold the "truth" about his marriage and Harold's subsequent drunken spree with the cynical doctor Relling/Roland (Rhys McConnochie) and the "demonic" Molvick/Mollison (Colin Croft). During this grotesque escapade Harold ineffectually attempts to commit suicide by falling into the river while Mollison drunkenly sings a hymn. But Roland pulls Harold back, and he loses only his hat. In this added scene Safran is particularly effective in capturing Ibsen's tragicomic tone. Gregory meanwhile has persuaded Hedvig to kill her most treasured possession, the wild duck, in order to demonstrate her love for Harold. In Ibsen's final act, as Hjalmar, persuaded by Gina not to leave home, talks with Gregers, a shot is heard; Gregers assumes that Hedvig has killed the duck. When he discovers that Hedvig has shot herself, Hjalmar rants about the death of his child in his characteristic rhetorical manner, and Relling acidly tells the incredulous Gregers that Hjalmar will find comfort eventually in his new role of bereaved father. In the film Safran cuts back and forth between Harold's breakfast conversation with Gregory and Henrietta's preparations for death in the attic. When the child shoots herself, Harold pauses before taking a bite of toast, and then Henrietta falls in slow motion as the wild duck flies free from her arms. Cutting immediately to Henrietta's funeral, Safran omits Hjalmar's seriocomic rhetoric and minimizes the final bitter exchange between Roland and Gregory. The film ends bleakly with Harold's silent suffering and Gina's abortive attempt to reach out to him. Safran's adaptation is intelligent and moving, especially in Liv Ullmann's sensitive portrayal of Gina, but the final sequence lacks Ibsen's tragicomic irony. *(V. F.)*

Resource: Verna A. Foster, "Ibsen's Tragicomedy: The Wild Duck," *Modern Drama* 38 (1995): 287–297.

WITNESS FOR THE PROSECUTION
(1953)
Agatha Christie

Witness for the Prosecution (1958)

Directed by Billy Wilder

Adapted by Billy Wilder and Harry Kurnitz

Cast: Tyrone Power (Leonard Vole), Marlene Dietrich (Christine Vole), Charles Laughton (Sir Wilfred Robarts), Elsa Lanchester (Miss Plimsoll)

Length: 116 minutes

The 1958 film of *Witness for the Prosecution* was based on Agatha Christie's popular stage adaptation of her short story and was directed by Billy Wilder. The screen play retains the basic plot of Christie's whodunit. This mystery, set in London, concerns a clever scoundrel named Leonard Vole (Tyrone Power). Leonard is accused of the fatal stabbing of Mrs. French, a rich widow with whom he had been friendly—so friendly, in fact, that she wrote him into her will shortly before her demise. Sir Wilfred Robarts (Charles Laughton), an eminent barrister, undertakes to defend the accused. Leonard's wife, Christine (Marlene Dietrich), who is German, seems devoted to him; and we can see the reason in a flashback. This flashback sequence, which is based on references in the play's exposition, is Wilder's major contribution to his literary source. The scene shows how Leonard met Christine while he was serving in the British army during World War II, and she was singing in a smoke-filled basement café in Hamburg. Christine seems to be grateful to Leonard for his willingness to bring her to London as a war refugee. Hence, Sir Wilfred is flabbergasted when she appears in court as a witness for the prosecution and gives evidence that undermines Leonard's alibi for the night of the murder. Later that same evening, Sir Wilfred is summoned to a railway station by a Cockney prostitute who sells him some documentation that plainly indicates that Christine had given false testimony against Leonard and that she did so because she wanted to see him convicted so that she could go off with another man. Sir Wilfred accordingly presents this newly acquired evidence in open court. The jury is shocked at Christine's duplicity and votes to acquit Leonard. Once the courtroom is cleared, Christine approaches Sir Wilfred and lapses into the Cockney accent she had employed when she talked with him the night before, while she was disguised as a prostitute. It seems that Christine had herself fabricated the spurious documentation, which she, in the guise of the prostitute, had then sold to Sir Wilfred so that he could use it against her in court and win the acquittal for Leonard. Christine adds that she had concocted the whole masquerade—not because she thought Leonard was innocent, but precisely because she was certain of his guilt. While Sir Wilfred is still reeling from Christine's disclosure, Leonard casually announces that he is now free to leave Christine for a younger woman. Maddened with jealousy by Leonard's betrayal, Christine snatches from the evidence table the knife with which Leonard had murdered Mrs. French and stabs him to death right in the courtroom. Sir Wilfred now agrees to defend Christine, explaining that she did not murder Leonard; she "executed him." *Witness* has rightly been judged one of the all-time great courtroom dramas on film. What's more, Wilder told this writer that, when Agatha Christine looked back on the films derived from her mysteries, she called *Witness* the best of the lot. "That meant a great deal more to me," said Wilder, "than anything a critic has ever said of one of my films." *(G. D. P.)*

Resources: Bernard Dick, *Billy Wilder* (New York: Da Capo, 1996); Kevin Lally, *Wilder Times: The Life of Billy Wilder* (New York: Holt, 1996).

THE WOMEN (1936)
Clare Boothe

The Women (1939)

Directed by George Cukor

Adapted by Anita Loos and Jane Murlin

Cast: Norma Shearer (Mary Haines), Joan Crawford (Crystal Allen), Rosalind Russell (Sylvia Fowler), Mary Boland (Countess DeLage), Joan Fontaine (Peggy Day), Paulette Goddard (Miriam Aarons)

Length: 133 minutes

At a party one evening, Clare Boothe overheard a vicious, gossipy conversation in the women's room. The conversation inspired her play *The Women*, about a group of high-society women obsessed with men and gossip. The play's unique feature is that no men actually appear in the play, despite their central importance. The play appeared briefly in Philadelphia before premiering in New York in 1936. *The Women* played 657 performances, making it the sixteenth longest-running play to that date. Though many felt the catty women were unique to New York, the play was successful worldwide. A group of G.I.s performed the play in drag during World War II. The play centers on Mary Haines, an honest, attractive, caring woman who discovers that her husband is having an affair with Crystal Allen, a Saks salesgirl. After confronting the younger woman, Mary divorces her husband. Her friends gossip about the affair behind Mary's back but soon find themselves in Reno with Mary, divorcing their own husbands. Two years later, Mary discovers Crystal having an affair with another friend's husband. Using the wiles of her friends, Mary exposes Crystal and wins her husband back. MGM brought George Cukor in to direct the picture. His reputation as a "woman's director" made him a natural choice. Cukor, fired a month earlier from *Gone with the Wind*, replaced Ernst Lubitsch, who was originally assigned to direct the film. Censors gutted much of the acerbic humor, so the studio hired Anita Loos to fill in lost laughs. The cast includes a "who's who" of female stars: Norma Shearer, Joan Crawford, Joan Fontaine, Paulette Goddard, and Rosalind Russell, who, as the catty Sylvia Fowler, impressed many, including Cukor, with her comedic abilities. Audiences enjoyed the barbs and pointed humor of the film. However, the central story fell flat. Cukor commented, "For starters, *The Women* had a very weak and foolish central story, a kind of obligatory story. It just didn't fit with the rest." Another out-of-place element is the fashion show: a color sequence inserted by the studio largely as a gimmick. Dennis Miller directed a musical remake in 1956, *The Opposite Sex*, starring June Allyson, Joan Blondell, and Joan Crawford. *(B. D. H.)*

Resources: Gavin Lambert, *On Cukor* (New York: G. P. Putnam's Sons, 1972); Patrick McGilligan, *George Cukor: A Double Life* (New York: St. Martin's Press, 1991); Stephen Shadegg, *Clare Boothe Luce: A Biography* (New York: Simon and Schuster, 1970); Wilfred Sheed, *Clare Boothe Luce* (New York: E. P. Dutton, 1982).

WOYZECK (1836)
Karl Georg Büchner

Woyzeck (1979)

Directed and adapted by Werner Herzog

Cast: Klaus Kinski (Woyzeck), Eva Mattes (Marie), Wolfgang Reichmann (Captain), Willy Semmelrogge (Doctor), Josef Bierbirchier (Drum Major), Paul Burian (Andres)

Length: 89 minutes

The play exists only as a fragment, unpublished when the writer died in 1837. Though it was not published until 1875 and not staged until 1913, in Munich, the play was experimentally well ahead of its time. Although the text seems relatively complete, the order of the scenes has been disputed. It tells the story of Johann Christian Woyzeck, a soldier beheaded in Leipzig in 1821 for murdering his mistress. Woyzeck is totally exploited, going mad because of a subsistence diet of peas he is paid to eat as part of a medical "experiment" conducted by a loony doctor; he is also mad with jealousy because his mistress is having an affair with a dashing drum major. He hears voices and hallucinates. He is bullied and humiliated both by the doctor and by the drum major. He snaps, buys a cheap knife, and murders his mistress one night by the river, which gives the film a totally repulsive spectacle of violence. Since the play was unfinished, the eccentric, visionary German filmmaker Werner Herzog had a relatively free hand in arranging the sequences cinematically. The play was a natural for Herzog, whose films have focused on madness and aberrant behavior. Cast as Woyzeck, Klaus Kinski had worked before with Herzog, also playing the lead as the obsessed Spanish conquistador in *Aguirre: The Wrath of God* (1972), and provides a riveting screen presence, becoming the very emblem of madness. The adaptation is both powerful and disturbing. *(J. M. W.)*

Resources: Donald Barthelme, "The Earth as an Overturned Bowl," *The New Yorker* (10 September 1979): 119–120; Vincent Canby, "Late for Life," *New York Times* (24 August 1979): B12.

YOU CAN'T TAKE IT WITH YOU (1936)
George S. Kaufman and Moss Hart

You Can't Take It with You (1938)

Directed by Frank Capra

Adapted by Robert Riskin from the play by George S. Kaufman and Moss Hart

Cast: Spring Byington (Penelope Sycamore), Lionel Barrymore (Grandpa Vanderhof), Jean Arthur (Alice), James Stewart (Tony Kirby), Edward Arnold (A. P. Kirby, Sr.), Mary Forbes (Mrs. Kirby), Mishca Auer (Boris Kolenkhov), Dub Taylor (Ed), Ann Miller (Essie), Lillian Yarbo (Rheba), Eddie Anderson (Donald), Donald Meek (Mr. Poppins), Harry Davenport (Judge), H. B. Warner (Mr. Ramsey), Halliwell Hobbes (Mr. DePinna), Clarence Wilson (Mr. Blakely)

Length: 127 minutes

The Kaufman and Hart play was rewritten for the screen by Robert Riskin and changed, but the spirit of the original and the charm of the screwball family headed by Grandpa Vanderhof (Lionel Barrymore) are wonderfully captured in typical Capra fashion. The play is opened up and much expanded from the one hour and forty-five-minute stage production. Additional Capraesque characters are added: a Judge (Harry Davenport), Mr.

Ramsey (H. B. Warner), the nervous real estate agent Mr. Blakely (Clarence Wilson), and the wonderful Mr. Poppins (Donald Meek). Capra stresses the distance between the Sycamores and the stuffed shirt Mr. Kirby, a real-estate developer who is more interested in making money than in preserving family values and neighborhoods. Capra's film opens with Kirby, Sr. (Edward Arnold), not with Grandpa Vanderhof, and Capra spends more time developing the character of the munitions manufacturer. Likewise, more time is spent on the developing relationship between Kirby's son, Tony (Stewart), and Vanderhof's granddaughter Alice (Jean Arthur). The camera follows them to the Monte Carlo ballet. They get sidetracked in the park, where Tony remembers his college idealism. They are diverted by singing, dancing street urchins doing the "Big Apple." They end up at a supper club, where Mr. and Mrs. Kirby are dining with Lord Melville and the Governor and his wife. When Alice is asked, "And you, Miss Sycamore, do you have a family tree?," Tony responds, "My dear sir, don't you know a sycamore *is* a tree?" This is typical of the newly invented dialogue for Tony and Alice, which falls short of Kaufman and Hart's snappier lines. The screenplay devised a confrontation between Vanderhof and Kirby in jail. "It's pretty funny, isn't it?" Vanderhof remarks. "What's funny about it?" Kirby, Sr., wants to know. "The idea of your engineering this whole thing and then getting caught in your own trap," Grandpa explains, just after Vanderhof has said, "You can't take it with you, Mr. Kirby," and just before Vanderhof tells A. P. Kirby off because Kirby has referred to the rest of the men in the drunk tank as "scum." In general, however, the play is not seriously damaged by these Capra touches, and in fact the film is quite endearing. *(J. M. W.)*

Resources: Frank Capra, *The Name above the Title: An Autobiography* (New York: Macmillan, 1971); Malcolm Goldstein, *George S. Kaufman: His Life, His Theatre* (New York: Oxford, 1979); Charles J. Maland, *Frank Capra* (Boston: Twayne, 1980); Joseph McBride, *Frank Capra: The Catastrophe of Success* (New York: Simon and Schuster, 1992).

YOU'VE GOT MAIL

See PARFUMERIE

INDEX

Page numbers in *italics* refer to main entries in the text.

ABOUT THE CONTRIBUTORS

B. D. H. Bruce D. Hutchinson is a Ph.D. candidate in the Department of Theatre and Film at the University of Kansas, Lawrence.

C. M. Chris Meissner is a Ph.D. candidate in Theatre and Film at the University of Kansas.

C. M. B. Charles M. Berg is Professor of Theatre and Film at the University of Kansas and a long-standing member of the Society for Cinema Studies. He is the author of *An Investigation of the Motives for and Realization of Music to Accompany the American Silent Film* (1976).

C. M. D. Carol M. Dole has served as Chair of the English Department at Ursinus College in Collegeville, Pennsylvania. Her essay "Austen, Class, and the American Market" was recently published in *Jane Austen in Hollywood* (1998).

D. S. David Sanjek, an expert in American popular music and popular culture, is the Archive Director for Broadcast Music, Incorporated, in New York. He is coauthor with his father, the late Russell Sanjek, of *American Popular Music in the 20th Century* (1991).

E. T. J. Edward T. Jones is Professor of English and Chair of the English and Humanities Department of York University of Pennsylvania. He contributed to both *The Encyclopedia of Novels into Film* (1998) and *The Cinema of Tony Richardson: Essays and Interviews* (1999). A frequent contributor to *Literature/Film Quarterly*, he has published books on L. P. Hartley and Peter Brook.

G. D. P.   Gene D. Phillips is Professor of English at Loyola University of Chicago and the author of several books on film directors—*Ken Russell* (1979), *John Schlesinger* (1981), *George Cukor* (1982), and *Alfred Hitchcock* (1984)—and other books treating Graham Greene, Joseph Conrad, F. Scott Fitzgerald, William Faulkner, and other writers, including *The Films of Tennessee Williams* (1980). He also contributed to *The Encyclopedia of Novels into Film* (1998).

G. H.   Gary M. Harrington is Professor of English at Salisbury State University in Maryland and teaches drama and Shakespeare. He is the author of *Faulkner's Fables of Creativity* (1990).

H. H. D.   Hugh H. Davis is a Ph.D. candidate at the University of Tennessee, Knoxville. He won the Ray and Pat Brown Award given by the Popular Culture Association in the South at the 1998 convention held in Augusta, Georgia, for his paper entitled "Shogun in the Saddle: Akira Kurosawa and the Western."

J. A.   John Ahearn is a Ph.D. candidate in the Department of Theatre and Film at the University of Kansas, Lawrence.

J. C. T.   John C. Tibbetts teaches cinema studies in the Department of Theatre and Film at the University of Kansas and is coeditor with Jim Welsh of *The Encyclopedia of Novels into Film* (1998) and *The Cinema of Tony Richardson: Essays and Interviews* (1999). Other books include *The American Theatrical Film* (1985) and *Dvořák in America* (1993).

J. D.   Jim Danek is a playwright who teaches in the Department of Drama at Washington University in St. Louis, Missouri. His most recently published plays are *Break Time* and *Kitchy Kitchy Koo* (1988).

J. M. W.   James M. Welsh is Professor of English at Salisbury State University and Editor in Chief of *Literature/Film Quarterly* and the founding President of the Literature/Film Association. Current books include *The Encyclopedia of Novels into Film* (1998) and *The Cinema of Tony Richardson: Essays and Interviews* (1999).

J. S.   John Staniunas teaches directing as an Assistant Professor of Theatre and Film at the University of Kansas.

K. O.   Kathryn Osenlund teaches English at Holy Family College in Philadelphia and contributed to *The Encyclopedia of Novels into Film* (1998).

K. R. H. Karen R. Hamer currently teaches at the University of Maine, Presque Isle. She was a contributor to *The Encyclopedia of Novels into Film* (1998) and has been active with the Literature/Film Association organizing film conferences.

K. Z. Kit Zak teaches English and drama at Salisbury State University in Maryland.

L. C. C. Linda Costanzo Cahir teaches at Centenary College in New Jersey and is a contributor both to *The Encyclopedia of Novels into Film* (1998) and to *The Cinema of Tony Richardson: Essays and Interviews* (1999). She is the author of *Solitude and Society in the Works of Herman Melville and Edith Wharton* (Greenwood Press, 1999).

M. G. Michael Gunter teaches in the Department of Theatre and Film at the University of Kansas and helps to coordinate the film program in Oldfather Studios.

N. I. Nancy Ingle is a Ph.D. candidate in the Department of Theatre and Film at the University of Kansas.

P. A. L. Peter A. Lev teaches cinema studies in the Department of Mass Communications at Towson University, Towson, Maryland. He has organized several conferences for the Literature/Film Association and has served both as President of that organization and as Contributing Editor of *Literature/Film Quarterly*. He is the author of *The Euro-American Cinema* (1993).

R. C. K. Richard C. Keenan is the Acting Chair of the English Department at the University of Maryland, Eastern Shore, Princess Anne, Maryland. He has served as Contributing Editor of *Literature/Film Quarterly* and was one of the contributors to *The Encyclopedia of Novels into Film* (1998).

R. R. Ray Rice teaches in the Department of Communication and Literature at the University of Maine, Presque Isle.

S. C. B. Sheri Chinen Biesen is an independent film scholar trained at the University of Texas, now living and teaching in California.

S. C. C. Stephen C. Cahir is a civil litigation attorney in New Jersey and a perennial student of drama and film. He contributed to *The Cinema of Tony Richardson: Essays and Interviews* (1999).

T. L. E.   Thomas L. Erskine, Professor of English at Salisbury State University, Salisbury, Maryland, is the founding editor of *Literature/Film Quarterly*. His most recent book was the casebook *Charlotte Perkins Gilman: "The Yellow Wallpaper"* (1993).

T. M./I. M.   Terri MacLellan teaches English at the Beaver Campus of Pennsylvania State University in Monaca, Pennsylvania. Her son, Ian MacLellan, is a student of English literature.

T. W.   Tony Williams, Professor of Cinema Studies at Southern Illinois University at Carbondale, is the author of several books, including *Jack London: The Movies* (1992), *Hearths of Darkness: The Family in the American Horror Film* (1996), and *Larry Cohen: The Radical Allegories of an Independent Filmmaker* (1997). He recently coedited *Jack London's The Sea Wolf: A Screenplay* (1998).

V. F.   Verna A. Foster, Associate Professor of English at Loyola University of Chicago, has published numerous essays in *Modern Drama, American Drama, Modern Language Quarterly, Studies in English Literature*, and other journals and is currently working on a book, tentatively titled *Tragicomic Dramaturgy: Renaissance and Modern*.

W. G. C.   W. Gardner Campbell is an Associate Professor of English at Mary Washington College in Fredericksburg, Virginia. He has published and presented essays on film, English Renaissance literature, and instructional technology and is a contributing editor of *A Variorum Edition of the Poetry of John Milton*.

W. K.   William Kemp is Professor of English at Mary Washington College, where he teaches Shakespeare, Jane Austen, and writing. He has published (separately) on John Marston and animal communication.

W. L. H.   William L. Horne teaches in the Department of Mass Communication at Towson University and has been active in organizing the annual conferences of the Literature/Film Association. He recently contributed a chapter on *A Taste of Honey* and *The Loneliness of the Long Distance Runner* to *The Cinema of Tony Richardson: Essays and Interviews* (1999). He is writing a book entitled *"See Shooting Script": The Role of the Screenplay in Film Theory and Criticism*.